History, Society and the Churches

OWEN CHADWICK

History, Society and the Churches

Essays in honour of
OWEN CHADWICK

Edited by

DEREK BEALES

and

GEOFFREY BEST

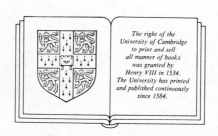

The right of the
University of Cambridge
to print and sell
all manner of books
was granted by
Henry VIII in 1534.
The University has printed
and published continuously
since 1584.

CAMBRIDGE UNIVERSITY PRESS

Cambridge
London   New York   New Rochelle
Melbourne   Sydney

Published by the Press Syndicate of the University of Cambridge
The Pitt Building, Trumpington Street, Cambridge CB2 1RP
32 East 57th Street, New York, NY 10022, USA
10 Stamford Road, Oakleigh, Melbourne 3166, Australia

First published 1985

Printed in Great Britain by the University Press, Cambridge

Library of Congress catalogue card number: 84–21375

British Library Cataloguing in Publication Data

History, society and the churches: essays in honour of Owen Chadwick
1. Church and the world.   2. Europe – Church History
1. Beales, Derek   11. Best, Geoffrey
261.1′094   BR375

ISBN 0 521 25486 8

Contents

Contents

Contributors

Professor Derek Beales is *Professor of Modern History, University of Cambridge, and a Fellow of Sidney Sussex College.*

Professor Geoffrey Best is *Honorary Professor of History and Sometime Dean of the School of European Studies, University of Sussex.*

Dr T. C. W. Blanning is *Lecturer in History, University of Cambridge, and a Fellow of Sidney Sussex College.*

Professor C. N. L. Brooke is *Dixie Professor of Ecclesiastical History, University of Cambridge, and a Fellow of Gonville and Caius College.*

The Rev. Professor Henry Chadwick is *Regius Professor Emeritus of Divinity, University of Cambridge, and a Fellow of Magdalene College.*

Professor Giles Constable is *Professor of History, Harvard University, and Sometime Director of Dumbarton Oaks.*

Dr Eamon Duffy is *Lecturer in Divinity, University of Cambridge, and Fellow and Tutor of Magdalene College.*

Professor G. R. Elton is *Regius Professor of Modern History, University of Cambridge, and a Fellow of Clare College.*

Dr Boyd Hilton is *Fellow, Tutor and Lecturer in History, Trinity College, Cambridge.*

The Rev. Professor John McManners is *Regius Professor Emeritus of Ecclesiastical History, University of Oxford, and a Fellow of All Souls College.*

Dr John Morrill is *Lecturer in History, University of Cambridge, and a Fellow of Selwyn College.*

The Rev. Dr E. R. Norman is *Lecturer in History, University of Cambridge, and Dean of Peterhouse.*

Professor Keith Robbins is *Professor of Modern History, University of Glasgow.*

Contributors

The Rev. Professor Gordon Rupp *is Dixie Professor Emeritus of Ecclesiastical History, University of Cambridge, and an Honorary Fellow of Emmanuel College.*

Dr Jonathan Steinberg *is Lecturer in History, University of Cambridge, and Fellow and Tutor of Trinity Hall.*

Dr Blair Worden *is Lecturer in Modern History, University of Oxford, and Fellow and Tutor of St Edmund Hall.*

Preface

The production of this volume was demanded by the fame and stature of the historian to whom it is presented; its character was determined by the nature of his unique contribution to British historical studies. Holder successively of Cambridge's chairs of ecclesiastical and (by implication) general modern history – author, lecturer and teacher equally of what could certainly be called religious history and what could not be called anything but history *tout court* – a clergyman-professor of a kind once common in Cambridge but now very rare – he has become distinguished for the ease with which he crosses compartmental boundaries and confounds conventional distinctions.

The range of his writings is unusually wide, their diversity extraordinary. Yet unity is there too in the characteristic which has given its theme to this collection. Here is a historian who has vindicated more than any other in Britain today the principle that the history of religion and the churches is a normal and proper part of history in general, and is indeed indispensable to much of it. Here, therefore, are essays by a group of professional colleagues which in varying degrees and from a variety of points of view (not all, for example, would call themselves Christian or religious) exemplify that principle and give the whole, we believe, a coherence not often found in studies ranging, as do those of Owen Chadwick himself, from the first Christian centuries to the years of his own lifetime.

The editors in conclusion gladly admit debts of gratitude to the many colleagues who have in one way or another assisted this enterprise; among them, inevitably, some who would have liked to contribute to it themselves but for whom, in a work of limited size and definite character, no room could be found. Thanks are equally due to the Cambridge University Press and its staff, and in particular to William Davies.

Owen Chadwick and his work

GEOFFREY BEST

Owen Chadwick took up the first of his two Cambridge chairs in 1958. He gave his inaugural lecture on 3 November of that year. In its opening passages about 'the continuity of Christian history' he remarked that he would depart from 'the pleasant custom' on such occasions of referring to the work of his predecessor and even perhaps some assessment of it; for, he said, 'Norman Sykes is at the height of his powers, and it would be unfitting to pay tribute to him as if his work were over.'

A young Cambridge don myself when I heard that lecture, I am somewhat in the same position now as he was then. Along with all other friends and admirers I see with joy, gratitude and pride a historian still at the height of his powers, retired from high office and so freer than ever before for scholarship. It would be as unfitting as it is, fortunately, impossible to pay tribute to him as if his work were over. But some tribute must be paid, something however inadequate and provisional must be said by way of introduction to a volume of essays written in honour of him, or else there will be disappointment among the non-Cambridge thousands who will open the book with desire and expectation of learning something about the man behind the 'Chadwick' they meet so often on book-shelf and reading-list. He has himself affirmed, after all, that 'a partial understanding of the man [may well be] necessary to a right judgement of his historical work'; and that presumably may still be the case even when the 'partial' has to be understood in more senses than one.

Owen Chadwick (strictly speaking, William Owen) has lived in Cambridge for virtually the whole of his working life. Much travelled, indeed, in pursuit of archives and as coveted visiting lecturer, but homing always to the city, university and colleges so unmistakably dear to him. His Cambridge beginning was when he went up to St John's to read classics in 1935. By universal account (including his own) he went up no less to play rugby football, at which he was extremely good. He had been captain of rugger, as well as school captain, at Tonbridge; he played for Cambridge against Oxford three years running, and in 1938 captained the team. It was, I am told, not easy in those boisterous early years to foresee a future as priest and scholar. But in the course of 1938 two things happened. What became for most of us the year of Munich was already for Owen Chadwick the year of Niemöller; the distinguished Pastor Martin Niemöller, 'picked up (on his release from prison) and taken to...Sachsenhausen. In that moment', he has recently told us, in some reconstruction of the thoughts of himself when young, 'Niemöller looked from England like the European conscience standing on moral principle against tyranny; the freest man in Germany despite his confinement.' Some fire was lit in his mind, his heart, his soul – how can or dare one measure which? – which has burned ever since.

The year of Niemöller was also, and in its impact upon him in fact somewhat earlier, the year of Charlesworth: Martin Charlesworth, fellow of St John's; historian, Christian, friend and, without setting out to be so, guide and inspiration to very many younger members of the college. Owen Chadwick was among these. Other serious occupations now joined that of rugby football, and other high skills began to prove themselves. In the summer of 1938 he was placed in the First Class of the Historical Tripos (part 2). He stayed on for a fourth year to take theology (part 2): a First again. Then he went to Cuddesdon theological college, and was ordained.

How deep has been his love for Cuddesdon and of what texture his debt to it, those who read his history of the college and his 1966 sermon may judge for themselves. The historian notes that even if it did not wholly make, it must certainly have cemented, the bond between him and, so far as England alone is concerned, his one great source of inspiration most clearly external to Cambridge: that church-shaking group of scholars, mystics and divines emphatically called the Oxford Movement, alias the Tractarians. Cuddesdon was founded by them and, no doubt developing what they began as any continuing organism must develop through time and changes of circumstance, it has remained the most 'Tractarian' of the Church of England colleges. Much of Owen Chadwick's finest work, deep and concentrated, has been about those men of Oxford and their place not just in English but in world Christendom; see especially that unusually readable piece of European intellectual history, *From Bossuet to Newman*, that thrilling tale of religious adventure in Africa, *Mackenzie's Grave* and, what some good judges have considered the best single thing ever written about it, his long introduction to *The Mind of the Oxford Movement*.

The Cuddesdon year was the first of those few he has spent *not* in Cambridge. The year of the Battle of Britain and 'the blitz' was not well-suited for the launching of academic talent. From Cuddesdon he went as curate for two years to Huddersfield (St John's); until the war was over he served as chaplain at Wellington College, in Berkshire; then he returned to Cambridge in 1947 as fellow and dean of Trinity Hall, to begin in real earnest, and, as it turned out, for good, the life which has included the highest distinctions, the most responsible offices, that Cambridge can propose.

For convenience's sake I will do what Owen Chadwick has not often been able to do – separate his so to speak official and administrative existence from his life as scholar, teacher and writer. The astonishing thing is that his great activity in the latter modes has coexisted through most of his life with great activity in the former, to an extent which is simply beyond the understanding of the less gifted, less industrious and less self-disciplined of us. To name only those offices (by no means only university ones) which must have occupied much of his mind and time, he was from 1965 to 1977 chairman of the trustees of Wolfson College; from 1973 president of the university's rugby football club; from 1966 to 1970 chairman of the Archbishops' Commission on Church and State; since 1978 he has been a Trustee of the National Portrait Gallery, and, since 1981, president of the British Academy. Through the two academic years 1969–71 he was Cambridge's Vice-Chancellor; years when the tide of radical, even by British standards mildly revolutionary, student and faculty activism was at its height. The 'Garden House riot' was only the most notorious of many troubles that had to be dealt with on top of all the University's ordinary business, which at the same time he was observed to conduct with unusual grace and dignity.

The honour of knighthood was conferred upon him in 1982; the extraordinary distinction of membership of the Order of Merit in 1983. These and other posts and honours on which it would be otiose here to linger constitute a roll weighty by far beyond whatever came the way of most famous scholars; and yet the weightiest of all and the most persistent is still to be mentioned. In 1956 he was appointed Master of Selwyn College, and Master he remained until his retirement from Mastership and Regius Professorship alike in 1983.

Being Master of a college can be made much or little of, according to taste; and in some cases a college may be the better off for its Master's inattention. This Master has given hugely of himself to Selwyn, to the college's great advantage. So long and signal a service to a college and its university demands particular notice.

Selwyn was not quite a college in the fullest Cambridge sense when he went there, although for all practical purposes people accepted it as one. Strictly speaking it was only an 'approved foundation', prevented from becoming a college proper (as defined by act of parliament) by its requirements that its fellows and scholars must be members, and its Master a clergyman, of the established church. The movement to 'normalize' its statutes and charter, begun before Owen Chadwick's arrival, came to fruition in 1958. The way was cleared for rapid developments. More people wanted to go there and consequently more dons were needed to teach them, more rooms and services to look after them. Selwyn has undergone something of a transformation under his Mastership. The handsome Cripps building is only the most conspicuous of many material developments. In 1956 there were 282 undergraduates, 29 post-graduates and only 18 fellows; all of course were male. In 1982 the numbers were respectively 337, 71 and 47; with women among them since 1976. At the same time, both scholarly and sporting performances improved, to the extent that the college rose from the bottom to better positions in the university's unofficial 'league table' of tripos results and – a distinction that must have peculiarly gratified him – won the rugger cup twice in the seventies.

The Master's Lodge has been memorable to its visitors through these 27 years because beside the Master there has always been his wife Ruth, welcoming and generous, gentle and serene; of an importance to him whose vast extent one could estimate if one's respect for the most private and personal things of life were to permit one to do so. An academic commemoration like this, after all, makes no call for extended family particulars. Yet one other family matter does merit notice, being entirely public and of unusual interest to the community of scholars. Owen Chadwick's younger brother Henry was also, until his (early) retirement in 1982, a Regius Professor at Cambridge (of divinity) after a career of similar distinction and accomplishments (part of it in Oxford). Both brothers, for example, have given the Hulsean, the Birkbeck and the Gifford Lectures. Both have been 'heads of houses' (Henry of Christ Church). Both are fellows of the British Academy and members of the American Academy of Arts and Sciences. And each, by the 1983 *Who's Who*'s account anyway, has been awarded six honorary doctorates, in Britain and abroad. Has Oxbridge, one wonders, ever before been graced by such a pair of brothers?

Almost all of Owen Chadwick's major scholarly works have been accomplished alongside such public and official activity, and I must conclude with a glance at them, for many readers of this book will be familiar with only one side of his *oeuvre*, and some will not even know that. I attempt this, however, with much diffidence. His modesty will make him dislike it, my own modesty makes me shy about doing it, and in any case readers who are seriously interested in assessing his stature and quality as a historian can best and easily do so with the aid of Dr Duffy's bibliography (below, pp. 301 ff).

It will very quickly strike the inquirer that the works are so readable because they are quite conversational, and that they are attractive because they are confiding. Those who have heard him preach or lecture know all about this. He addresses his reader as directly as he addresses an interlocutor, an audience. He is an exceedingly elegant and accomplished lecturer – in the best sense of the word a stylish performer – and the best qualities of writer and lecturer are more closely allied in him than is common. He likes to tell a story, to explore a situation, to try to unravel a mystery. For those Gallophiles and *Annalistes* who consider the writing of what they call *histoire événementielle* a sin, he is one of the greatest sinners going. For those, however, who do not understand how to do justice to the movement of history and the force of circumstance without some story-telling, he appears as a master of the craft, and never better than in the tautest, tightest-woven tales – of which his *Victorian Miniature* (considered by some to be his masterpiece) is an outstanding example.

His first book, dedicated to M. P. Charlesworth, was on St John Cassian, 'our earliest western monastic theorist'. That early interest in the early church has not been sustained. The Cambridge lecture list's sporadic trickle of offerings on it peters out in 1966–7; the bibliography reveals but few returns to it, and those mostly apropos of St Benedict. Nor did he linger long around the Reformation, on which he has written a well-known, workmanlike Pelican book and which prompted him to undertake what he is delightfully good at: character assessments, notably of Martin Luther and John Knox. The continuing spread of his general knowledge of church history is clear enough in the bibliography of it which he compiled, and more than once revised, for the Historical Association. But the greater part of his *oeuvre* lies in post-Reformation history. In history, though not, one gathers, in theology, he is a modernist.

Much of his writing and lecturing has been about English church, State and society since the industrial and French revolutions. The two-volume study of *The Victorian Church* is his biggest single publication. Well-qualified reviewers tended to remark that with all its gusto, learning, charm and penetration it fell a bit short on balance and proportion. To the extent that their complaint was not just that he had not written the book *they* would have written, and setting aside the obvious but important fact that no one else could have written the book he actually wrote, their complaint had some justification. It *is* rather a personal interpretation, written by a scholar who writes as he pleases. He shows less interest in Dissent than in the Establishment, less liking for the Evangelicals than for the Oxford Movement, and less love for town than country. What he writes about most warmly is the country clergy and their, generally speaking, quiet continuance in well-doing in those parts of England not yet sophisticated by machinery and macadam; what, in another place, he calls their 'reasonable, quiet, unpretentious, sober faith in God and way of worship'. On the politics of established churchmanship and its manifold complications, above all the legal and constitutional ones, he is unmatched; as might be expected of an Anglican well-known for his conviction as to the continuing value of establishment.

His other largest work, *The Popes and European Revolution*, is part-product of that growing interest in the modern histories of Italy and Germany which has been visibly unfolding in his university lectures since the later sixties: 'Church and State under Hitler' in 1964–5, 'The Papacy and the European Powers in the 19th Century' in 1972–3, and so on up to 'Italy and the Papacy 1814–1945' in 1980–1 and (what indeed was only in part about Germany) 'The Ethics of War 1914–45' in 1981–2. For the sources of the German interest, it is perhaps needless to go further than the year, already mentioned, when he was pondering upon the persecution of Niemöller, profoundly impressed by Waldemar Gurian's book on *Hitler and the Christians*, and beginning to place this contemporary assault on Christianity in its longest-term historical context with the inspiring aid of James Bryce's *Holy Roman Empire*. The history of the Papacy, which has exercised an independent fascination over him (springing no doubt partly from his beloved Victorians' preoccupations with it, and his Victorian professorial predecessor Lord Acton's love–hate attitude towards it), here appears as a bridge between his German and Italian concerns. To no historico-ethical problem does he seem to have devoted more anxious labour than that of the Papacy's conduct of its relations with the Italian Fascist and German National Socialist regimes. His 1980–1 Ford Lectures at Oxford were precisely on the German aspect, and at the time of writing are being extensively revised for publication.

In tackling these particular episodes Owen Chadwick is confronting the most difficult of all tests to which a historian can put himself: the most difficult and, as he has expressly acknowledged, the most intractable. In his address at the service in Great St Mary's in memorial of his immediate predecessor in the Regius chair, he spoke of Sir Herbert Butterfield's awareness of 'the war within himself over the nature of the historian's task', the problem of bringing 'historical understanding and moral conviction...into harmony, when moral judgement corrupts the *historian* and yet moral judgement is the essence of the *man*'. In acknowledging this difficulty and in not admitting, to the best of my knowledge, that there is any mortal means of resolving it, he places himself philosophically very close to Butterfield, whom he loved and admired, and with him at some distance from Lord Acton, by whom both men have been fascinated. Their dislike of judging appears to have both theological and psychological bases. Only God is in a position to understanding everything that goes on in the human soul and everything that in

6

the process presses upon it. We are not to judge lest we be judged. Personality in any case is unique. His writings often insist on 'the mystery that is in every human being': 'all men are unique, but some men are more unique than others', 'human beings are often rather odd'. Of the Quietist Molinos he remarked that he was 'as mysterious a personality as most personalities, and no historian will presume to probe too far within'.

Some of us who have ventured to probe presumably too far, feeling justly rebuked, can find no line of defence but that of wondering whether ultimate mysteriousness really is so universal a characteristic as he affirms and whether some people in some times and places are not actually rather simple and straightforward – but that is no argument to pursue here... Certainly no eminent British historian alive today more consistently displays the lovely virtue of charity in his writings; and those privileged to know (so far as the mysterious in him allows one to know!) the writer, believe they know that it comes from the heart. His works are strikingly innocent of hostile judgments. Preferring simply to ignore the merely ignorant and incompetent, about the worst quality he will attribute to another scholar is that of being 'doctrinaire'. An ultra-protestant clerical pamphleteer who sought to kill his beloved Cuddesdon, and who did, in fact, cause it damage, he merely calls 'quaint', and hints at senility. In my reading of him I have come across no severer put-down of another historian than his slow-fused comment on the prolific medievalist Coulton's *Art and the Reformation*: 'Despite its title this is about medieval art and architecture, and is probably Coulton's best book.'

Unmistakable throughout all is his affectionate respect for history and historians, his conviction that the historian's work is worthwhile and within its limits valuable. Many of his smaller writings, many passages in his larger ones, are about historians and archivists and the libraries and archives in which they work. His conviction as to the value of what they consequently do is the old, straightforward, unanswerable one that nothing with any historical existence – from nation and church down to village and person – can be understood without reference to its history. But the claim is made in modest terms and nothing much is said of the use that man and men might make of such understanding. At the last, this noble Christian scholar's religious convictions merge with his scholarly commitment to confide our destiny into the hands of God – where it has been all the time anyway. The confidence, even optimism, that is (by modern positivist standards) missing from the surface of his works is to be found in their religious substructure. Commenting in his 1966 Cuddesdon sermon on the alien quality which reflective and experienced Christians must detect in the society and world around them, he yet affirms that this world is God's world, that his purpose for the world is to be trusted, that change, even a change that looks menacing, may be brought within the scope of providence... This land, though strange, is not the land of Baal, nor of Moloch, nor of Dagon, nor of Thor, nor of Stalin. It is still the land of the Lord...

Owen Chadwick gave his second Cambridge inaugural lecture, when he succeeded Butterfield, on 27 November 1968. Its closing paragraphs will suitably bring our introduction to a close, for they nicely epitomize the idea of history by which he is guided and by which posterity will in due course place him.

There is (or was) a view that though the historian is a man he ought not to be. Of course he ought to seek impartiality in the sense of understanding and fairly representing both sides. But he can only become totally detached by ceasing to be a man and therefore by ceasing to be a historian. The man who knows that his personality enters historical study and yet seeks to keep it in control and to broaden his vision will make more contribution to our understanding than the man who believes total detachment possible; though the totally detached may still contribute to the materials of history...

St Augustine had a saying, Nemo nisi per amicitiam cognoscitur, you need to be a friend of a man before you understand him. So by analogy is our relation to men of the past, societies of the past, even documents in the archives. You may suspect, you ought to suspect them all as sure to mislead you vilely unless your critical sense is ever alert; but they do it (for the most part) by their inadvertence or their partial vision. You need no white paint, you need to try to see things as they were. But you need to be inside their minds and to forget the future which they could not know, and to come towards them with the openness of mind, the readiness to listen, which a man gives to a friend. Trevelyan had this among his strengths. He was the kind of man, as well as the kind of historian, who understood what St Augustine meant, that the human race is known in friendship.

Augustine on pagans and Christians: reflections on religious and social change

HENRY CHADWICK

Although the modern world has tried hard to persuade itself that religion and morality are an individual's entirely private affair, the evidence of its social character is writ rather too large in history for this thesis to look very plausible to historians. Among the greatest and most momentous features of the later Roman empire, the factor that obviously marks the transition from what we think of as 'ancient' to what we think of as 'medieval' is the change from paganism to Christianity. How that change came about is something we are better able to describe than to explain. The ultimate springs of human behaviour and motivation in so sensitive a matter are not often readily accessible to us, even when the people we wish to understand are alive before our eyes. *A fortiori* we shall know a lot less about people who have been dead over 1500 years. Few of them could read or write, and of those who could only a small minority tell us about their feelings. When they do tell us about the process of their conversion from paganism to Christianity (as in the case of Justin in the mid-second century, or most fully Augustine in his *Confessions* and philosophical dialogues), the instinct of the learned is to suggest that such accounts are primarily literary. That is not to say that the underlying fact of conversion is to be doubted, but only that the way in which Justin and Augustine relate the story of their conversion is so pervaded with literary reminiscences (in Justin from Plato, in Augustine's case with a rich mosaic of allusions to Persius, Plotinus, the book of Genesis) that one can hardly treat their narrative as unvarnished reporting.

The pagans did not know they were pagans until the Christians told them they were. The very concept of 'paganism' is a Jewish–Christian construct. 'Paganism' is a term used by Latin-speaking Christians from about 300 onwards to describe the cults of the gods whether of Roman or Greek or Punic ancestral tradition. It is a lump word, a Christian category imposed on all non-monotheists to describe the unbaptised 'civilian' or 'non-combatant' whom they hoped to enlist in Christ's army, but who remained held by

9

social tradition or prejudice or the blinding influence of diabolical counter-feit. Augustine is aware that the term is Christian argot. His normal noun is *paganitas*, but once at least (*DQ 83, 83*) we have the half Greek form *paganismus*, which suggests that this form of the word was used by the considerable Greek-speaking element in the Christian population of the seaport of Hippo Regius.

The Christians who grouped all non-monotheists together as 'pagans' created an invisible social wall between themselves and their non-Christian neighbours. Convinced that idolatry was a pollution to the conscience, they withdrew from participation in social activities where the veneration of the gods played a part, and the extent of that withdrawal was necessarily con-siderable. There was a strong Christian self-consciousness of standing over against the *saeculum*, the world alienated from God, oblivious of him, and essentially concerned with the four secular loves – power, honour, wealth, and sex. Towards the cult of the old gods the Christian attitude was one of deep moral disapproval, and this helped to generate powerful social tension. One has only to browse in the pages of Tertullian or Clement of Alexandria or the *contra Celsum* of Origen to be aware of a prickly defensiveness.

In North Africa, as Christians became more numerous, they became more self-confident – enough for some of the more zealous to emerge into the public squares and to make themselves prominent by demonstrations or even by insulting pagan shrines with a hiss or physical attack. A pagan complaint recorded early in the third century by the African writer Minucius Felix (*Octavius* 8, 4) declared that the Christians 'spit at the gods'. A generation earlier the pagan Platonist Celsus says that he knew of defiant Christians showing their contempt for statues of Apollo and Zeus by reviling and striking them, and calmly waiting for the god to take revenge (Origen, *contra Celsum* VIII, 38). In Africa zeal could go a long way. Well before the tensions and polarities introduced by the great persecution of Diocletian in 303, there were occasions when raiding parties of Christian militants would assault a pagan shrine and carry off any easily movable cultic objects. In the *Gesta apud Zenophilum* of 320 (an inquiry before the *consularis* into the records of the church at Cirta) we learn that Purpurius, the bishop of Liniata, had once removed from the temple of Serapis some casks of vinegar, pre-sumably intended for ceremonial ablutions of the statue at an annual festival, to remove the carbon deposit left by pious candles. Purpurius was a man known for his strong-arm methods. At a council held at Cirta, perhaps in 305, the old primate of Numidia, Secundus of Tigisi, directly taxed Purpurius with the report that in the prison at Mileu he had killed his sister's two sons (perhaps to prevent them from compromising their faith by apostasy, on the principle that it would be better to lose one's life than one's eternal bliss).

Purpurius replied that the story was true, and that he would perform the same service then and there for anyone who challenged his action.

In Augustine's time in North Africa the Catholic population normally tended to confine its attacks on pagan cult to words, and not to resort to blows. Violence they left to the schismatic Donatists, at least for the most part. Nevertheless, reports certainly reached Carthage and Hippo of the scenes in the Greek East, both during Julian's revival of paganism when defiant Christians earned their martyr's crown by attacks on temples, and also when the advent of Theodosius I led to a series of onslaughts on great pagan citadels like the Serapeum at Alexandria, dismantled in 391. For the African Christians to sit back quietly and do nothing beyond holding an all-night dance at St Cyprian's shrine was to invite accusations that one was compromising with evil spirits by tolerating the sorcery and mumbo-jumbo of pagan cults.

In a sermon preached at Carthage probably on 14 September 399 (*Sermo* 62, 7–8) Augustine exhorted the Carthaginian Christians not to smash pagan idols and shrines on estates which were in pagan hands and were not Christian property. Only a few weeks previously the emperor Honorius had posted an edict to Africa directing the suppression of idols (*C. Theod.* xvi 10, 18). At Carthage the plebs were only too keen to get on with the job, and Augustine thought they should be restrained. Lately they had acquired the title to the 'Mappalia', land close to the harbour on which St Cyprian's tomb was located (*S. Denis* 11) and where his mid-September feast was marked by high junketings on the part of the Christians who sang and danced through the night of the vigil (Augustine, *Sermo* 311, 5, 5). Once they had acquired the property, they destroyed all pagan altars, groves, and heathen inscriptions. As they had paid good money for the land, Augustine thought them entitled to do so. But he pleaded with the Carthaginians not to invade estates owned by pagan landowners to smash their shrines. First one must smash the pagan beliefs in their hearts. One must pray for them and not infuriate them. The destruction of religious property should be left to criminal bandits (*pravi homines*) and to Circumcellions – the IRA branch of the Donatist movement, notorious for their audacious atrocities, maiming and blinding their victims. Circumcellions must be no model for Catholics.

The year 399 was one of high tension between pagans and Christians at Carthage. In March the counts Gaudentius and Jovius closed the temples and overthrew the statues of the gods (Aug. *de civitate Dei* xviii 54). A sermon on Psalm 149 speaks (*En. Ps.* 149, 13) of the 'extinction of pagans'; but then assures the congregation that 'killing' the heathen is the Bible's way of talking about their conversion to Christianity, a matter of inner conviction rather than outward coercion. It seems a fair deduction that Augustine was anxious to dissuade any of his hearers from understanding 'extinction' rather more literally. Physical intimidation of pagan neighbours had awkward consequences.

Another sermon preached at Carthage on 16 June 401 (S. 24, 5) tells of a noisy demonstration in the streets when the Christian plebs had shouted slogans against the pagans of the city. The excited plebs was inclined to regard the bishops as weak, hanging back in the move against pagan cultus. Not only the pagans were scared; it seems that the bishops were also. Meeting in formal synod at Carthage on 16 June 401 the bishops were reminded that the emperors required the 'amputation' of the remains of idolatry through-out Africa, such remnants being found 'in many places along the sea-coast and in various inland estates'. When a council met at Carthage in September of the same year, the bishops had evidently met legal opposition from pagans, pleading that the emperor's edicts had specified only cult statues, not sacred groves or trees, or other pagan monuments. The council decided to petition the emperors to decree the destruction of all forms of pagan shrine. (See the excerpts from the chancery register of the church of Carthage, printed in C. Munier, *Concilia Africae a. 345–a. 525*, Corpus Christianorum 259, 1974, pp. 196 and 205.) The point underlines the bishops' hesitations: they might easily be held responsible in court and the church chest fined if their people in-dulged in 'spontaneous' demonstrations of a violent kind. They wanted to be sure of their legal ground. At Carthage in 401 the plebs had already heard that pagan cult had ended in Rome. So the people destroyed a Carthaginian statue of Hercules, to show that the zeal of the African churches did not lag behind Italy. In *Sermo* 24 Augustine does not dare suggest that the plebs had been overdoing it. He can hardly go further than a quotation of Matthew 11.28: 'Learn of me, for I am meek and lowly of heart', but without ex-plicitly pointing the moral that gentleness may persuade, while violence leaves sullen resentment and smouldering anger. It was not good for the church when heretics, schismatics, Jews, and pagans found it necessary to club together to oppose Catholic intolerance (S. 62, 18). And what a large Christian population could do in Carthage without fear of reprisal could not be done everywhere in North Africa. At Sufes in Byzacena, the Christians overturned a statue of Hercules, and the pagans of the town rose up in fury to kill sixty of them (Aug. *Ep.* 50).

Augustine's second sermon on Psalm 32 (*En. Ps.* 32.ii.10) notices how enraged pagans become at Christian feasts with their public processions, but rejoices that the church can safely proceed on the road, 'for our street is defended by the emperor'. Evidently it needed to be so defended.

Following Augustine's indications, historians associate the Donatist Cir-cumcellions of Numidia with violence directed against Catholic people and buildings. Optatus of Mileu, writing about 370, and then Augustine provide dreadful catalogues of apparently mindless atrocities – flinging a blinding mixture of lime and vinegar into the eyes of Catholic clergy as they moved about their parishes; assaulting Catholic basilicas, where they liked to wash the floors with a mixture of salt and water as if they were disinfecting a public lavatory. They also used to whitewash the walls, probably to censure the gradually growing Catholic custom of decorating church walls with pictures of Christ and the Apostles, Daniel in the lions' den, Moses striking the rock, or other Biblical themes. The Circumcellions seldom left a basilica without smashing the altar, sometimes (if he happened to be available) over the head of the poor Catholic bishop. Intimidation was general, and the Numidian population sympathised with their hostility to Catholicism and to the government even when the violence seemed to go too far. Public statements issued by Donatist bishops deploring the resort to violence were ineffective. In towns where the Donatists were a large majority (which was in most places in Numidia) the Catholic bishop might be warned by his Donatist opposite number that he would be wise to abstain from any public declaration in criticism of the Donatist party, and that if he were not silent by choice, he soon would be by necessity.

When in the 340s the imperial government put coercive pressure on the extremist Donatist zealots of Numidia, they committed suicide. They threw themselves over cliffs, and the Catholic community then experienced the baffling situation that their Donatist neighbours directed passionate resentment against them, as if the Catholics had pushed them over.

The Circumcellions knew that power grew out of the end of a thick stick. Armed at first with wooden cudgels called by them Israels, later with knives, swords, axes, lances, and an altogether more metallic arsenal, peasant gangs in Numidia used to ambush Catholic bishops on their pastoral travels in the countryside attached to their city. Terror was struck into the heart by their warcry 'Deo Laudes'. They had a Punic name Cutzupitae (Aug. *Ep.* 53, 2) or Cotopitae, which is explicable as a word meaning 'harvesters' cognate with the Hebrew *gatap*. Perhaps many of them were migrant farm workers seasonally employed on the olive harvest.

Much modern scholarship has tended to see in the Circumcellions a movement originally independent of the religious struggles between Catholic and Donatist, and especially to see in them proto-Marxists or Levellers with an egalitarian ideology. Some of them wanted to liquidate the landlords. Optatus (iii, 3) tells us of socially disruptive bands in upper Numidia in the mid-fourth century, led by Axido and Fasir who called themselves 'duces sanctorum'. The title implies a potent religious content to their ideology. According to Optatus their intimidation made it impossible for creditors to sue for recovery of debts or for landlords to move safely about their estates without being rudely pushed out of the driving seats of their gigs and made to run before their own serfs. It is therefore certain that about 340 the Circumcellions were identified with a peasants' revolt, a jacquerie requiring suppression by Taurinus the count of Africa (*Prosopography of the Later Roman Empire* I 878 gives his career). Circumcellion reaction to Taurinus' move led to the sending of further officials, Paul and Macarius, and a bloody suppression by the count Silvester about 345–7 (*PLRE* I 842). Optatus' evidence makes it impossible to deny that, perhaps sparked off by the news of Constantine II's death in 340 and consequent tension between the two brothers, Constans and Constantius II, there was dramatic social disorder in Numidia during the next decade in which the Circumcellions figured prominently. Augustine tells us that the farmers dreaded the soldiers sent to suppress the peasants quite as much as the disorder (*En. Ps.* 136, 3).

We may not safely or wisely assume that almost all North African Catholics were Latin-speaking, respectable, bourgeois, and urban, and that almost all Donatists were alienated, Punic-speaking rustics who struck first and asked questions afterwards. In Augustine's sermons (113, 2 and 178, 4) we find two clear references to Christian social dissidents who do not appear to be Donatist at all. So among the population up country there were Catholic Christians who also regarded themselves as entitled to take direct action against landlords of whom, for religious or social reasons, they disapproved. What ideology may have moved them we can only guess. But history has many hero outlaws popularly admired for their daring and dash in robbing the idle rich, like Robin Hood in medieval England, and Jesse James or Billy the Kid in American folklore, who distributed their gains to the poor and thereby won support for yet further raids on the property of the rich.

> Jesse was a man, a friend of the poor;
> He would never see a man suffer pain.
> And with his brother Frank he robbed the Chicago bank
> And stopped the Glendale train.

There was a good deal of this kind of action in the fourth century.

If, as Optatus' evidence suggests, religion was a motivating force for the aggressions of Numidian peasants, it is important to ask what possible objectives they had in mind. There has been so much excitement concentrated on their role in the Donatist schism and on the levelling, jacquerie element that perhaps we have paid insufficient attention to evidence that the Circumcellions were particularly prominent, and probably originally known, in the holy war against pagan cult.

In a famous passage of his *Enarrationes in Psalmos* (132, 2) Augustine informs us that while catholic people called them 'Circumcelliones' because they wandered 'circum cellas', that is round the martyrs' shrines, they called themselves 'Agonistici'; which we may translate 'the militant tendency'. They were bands dedicated to celibacy and evangelical homelessness, like the Son of Man who had nowhere to lay his head. They included members of both sexes. They did not call themselves *monachi*, were like itinerant communes, and were among the numerous critics of the immobile *monasteria* which Augustine was busily trying to found in North Africa.

In more than one passage, Augustine specifies that the Agonistici specialised in causing the maximum of disruption at pagan festivals, where they used to mount an unstoppable charge upon the band of musicians, the *symphoniaci*, who were a normal feature of pagan religious occasions. The Agonistici made a concerted rush, and smashed the instruments of the orchestra. They would also assault *iuvenes*, the *collegium* of young men who used to parade in full armour at religious festivals. The young pagans made use of their swords and despatched their assailants. Augustine says, no doubt with more than a touch of rhetoric, that they offered them up to their gods as human sacrifices (*Ep.* 185, 12; the other main texts are *Sermo* 62, 17; *contra Gaudentium* i, 28, 32; 38, 51).

The militants greatly prized their martyrs and built shrines to their memory – *cellae* – to which on the anniversary they would return (Aug. *c.ep. Parmeniani* III 6, 29) to sing hymns in honour of their heroes and to celebrate, *more africano*, in plentiful potations of wine. Since the time and place presumably coincided with the pagan festivals at which the martyrdoms first occurred, the confrontations must have tended to be annual and so a recurrent cycle. Hence their cry 'Deo Laudes'. They were echoing the dying words of Christian martyrs like Cyprian.

If this is something like a true reading of the evidence, the Circumcellions are likely to originate neither as an anti-catholic force of violent schismatics, born of the response of resentment at the tough coercion imposed under Macarius in the 340s, nor as social revolutionaries whose hostility to the authority of government could naturally have led them into association with the religious cause of the alienated Donatists. In the first instance their *raison d'être* was the conflict with pagan cult, and other features of the Circumcellion movement were secondary to that.

On this hypothesis I venture, with proper diffidence, to suggest the probability that the Agonistici antedate the rise of the Donatist schism in 311. For the Donatist schism itself originated in an already existing tension between hawks and doves. The militant African Christians thought it their duty to reject not only paganism but even the least manifestation of compromise or cooperation with a pagan government. Other Christians, among whom were Mensurius the bishop of Carthage and his archdeacon Caecilian, wanted to live a quiet life of modest virtue and saw no reason to erect a wall of hostility between themselves and their pagan neighbours. So the militant tendency in the North African church was a state of mind widely diffused before Diocletian's edict of persecution was posted at Carthage in 303. Tertullian's writings richly illustrate the internal tensions within the Christian community at Carthage a century earlier. He himself so often sides with the defiant puritan spirit and so abrasively criticises the Christians who thought, for instance, that following the example of Joseph and Daniel one could accept office as a magistrate, that it is a surprise to find him rejecting any suggestion that a true Christian could physically attack idols (*Apol.* 44; *Scap.* 2). The dissidence of nonconformist dissent is so strong in Tertullian that one might have expected him to sympathise with the attackers of whom pagan critics complained. In reply to Celsus' charges, Origen also replies that Christians obedient to scripture would never revile or assault a pagan shrine. Nevertheless, it is certain that hawks existed. Early in the fourth century the Council of Elvira in southern Spain (by Granada) declared that those Christians who die in consequence of assaults on pagan shrines may not be reckoned among the martyrs (canon 41); in other words, they rank as suicides (a view taken a century earlier by Clement of Alexandria). In the *Martyrs of Palestine* Eusebius of Caesarea records acts of provocative and defiant sacrilege (*MP* 4, 8, 9); and in the time of Julian's pagan revival we hear of a lot of this kind of thing, especially in Syria. Towards the end of the reign of Constantius II (337–61) Christians had felt sufficient support at the top to risk the rage of pagans by smashing polytheistic shrines. At Baalbek (Heliopolis) a deacon named Cyril destroyed statues, and as soon as Julian became emperor the pagan worshippers murdered him in revenge. At Arethusa in Syria the bishop Mark had taken over a pagan temple and turned it into a church, an act for which, on Julian's accession, he paid dearly with death after prolonged and exquisite torture. In Egypt the military commander Artemius cooperated with the Arian bishop George of Alexandria in overthrowing idols; under Julian, George was lynched and Artemius executed. At Antioch there was a series of confrontations between the numerous Christian population and the advocates of polytheism. Vivid pictures of these and similar episodes are painted in the *Church History* of Theodoret (esp. books 3 and 4). Theodoret was writing in 450 at a time when the emperor Theodosius II was supporting the Monophysite doctrines of the bishops of Alexandria, and had imposed silence on Theodoret as the most formidable theological critic of the Alexandrian theology. Theodoret was therefore very interested personally in the length to which it was either useful or a conscientious duty to take opposition to a government advocating

error. His stories not only reflect Syria's pride in its heroes but also speak, to those with ears to hear, of his own dilemmas.

The evidence for muscular Christianity in the fourth and fifth centuries is on the whole well known. Less frequently noticed is the evidence for drastic militant activities before the age of Constantine the Great. If we are to believe the *Elenchos* of Hippolytus, Callistus at Rome earned such credit with the Christian community for having vandalised a synagogue that it set him on the path to the papacy in 222. The *Elenchos* is a work inspired by such hatred for Callistus that the story has to be treated with reserve; but the fact that Hippolytus thought it all perfectly possible still makes it relevant to this inquiry.

There is rather more evidence than the books tell us that the Christians were not always very respectful of private property. In the pages of Ambrose one can find a portrayal of his social ideal; it has not much room for private property-rights. Augustine himself was normally a defender of private property, and admonishes the poor that, whatever their degree of destitution, their duty not to steal is absolute. Thieves are outraged if they themselves are robbed. Respect for the property of others is, like respect for their life or their spouse, a basic command inherent in the Golden Rule, and recognition of its force requires no special revelation. (See *Confessions* ii, 4, 9; *En. Ps.* 57, 1; 61, 16.) Yet Augustine also accepts the utopian and potentially revolutionary principle that the right to private property is limited by the justice with which it is used: 'Quod iuste non tractat, iure non tenet' (*Sermo* 50, 2–4), a sentence that would surely have delighted John Wycliffe. For Augustine all positive law is subject to the test of a higher tribunal in the moral law of God; 'Ubi iustitia vera non est, nec ius potest esse' (*City of God* XIX, 21; similarly *En. Ps.* 145, 15). Augustine had trouble with fellow-Christians who thought moral obligations to those outside the Christian society were less stringent than those they owed to members of the household of faith. A prickly and egocentric correspondent in Minorca, Consentius, outraged him by the doctrine that a Catholic Christian is under no obligation to keep faith with heretics like the Priscillianists, and was duly admonished in the treatise *contra Mendacium* of 420. Augustine's seventieth tractate on St John's Gospel (70, 18) has to deplore Christian traders who felt morally entitled to do down a pagan customer, who might then come and complain bitterly to Augustine that he had not expected a Christian merchant to fleece him.

So to his people at Hippo he gives the exhortation: 'Love unbelievers in such a way that they wish to become brothers in your faith' (*in Ep. Joh.* 10, 7). 'Do not insult them, pray for them' (*En. Ps.* 65, 5; *Sermo* 90, 10). The fact that this exhortation was necessary discloses how tense social relations could become. One recalls the revealing sentence in the *Confessions* (ix, 3, 6) where Augustine is speaking of the consequences of his conversion for his relationship with Verecundus, the well-to-do Milanese grammarian (i.e. teacher of literature) with a Christian wife who lent Augustine and his friends the villa at Cassiciacum: 'I did not allow my conversion to end my friendship with him...'. In some cases it was evidently otherwise. Indeed, in the *Confessions* (iv, 4, 7f) Augustine himself expresses the conviction that true friendship is the gift of God alone, and is never merely natural sympathy. But Augustine held a very high doctrine of friendship. The confidence and love of friends, he remarked (*City of God* xix, 8), is the only thing that makes bearable the misery and misunderstandings of life. To love a friend is 'to love God in him', either because God is in him, or in order that he may be so (*Sermo* 336, 2). For where friends disagree about fundamental religious questions, they will also disagree about human values. One who scorns divine things will adopt a different estimate of human things (*Ep.* 258, 2 to Martianus, a contemporary in Augustine's student days at Carthage). The Christian bond of brotherhood imparts an 'eternal' dimension to a natural delight in a friend's company and trust (*c. ii epp. Pelag.* i, 1; *Ep.* 155, 1). In short, Augustine well understood the social intensity which could encourage a polarisation of the Christian community over against the surrounding pagan society. In the Donatist community that sense of polarisation seems to have been even stronger than in the Catholic community of North Africa, which for the most part (not invariably) enjoyed the support of government officials.

Social tension was in part allayed (though there could be circumstances where the effect was the reverse) by the ancient patronage system. In most cases the coloni and the serfs on the estates of a pagan landowner would be pagans. Catholic landowners were expected to build churches on their estates for the benefit of their farm workers. A well-known sermon of John Chrysostom on Acts (18, 4f) tells Syrian landowners they have a responsibility to erect not only agora and bathhouse but also churches on their farms where the workers may pray before going out to the fields, and where at the Sunday liturgy the priest will name the name of the founder and benefactor at the intercessions. On 29 May 397 three zealous Christians protested against a pagan procession by a river in the vicinity of Trent in North Italy. They were killed by the outraged peasants. Maximus of Turin preached in commemoration of the three martyrs, and used the occasion to impress on Christian landowners their duty to convert their dependants, and not to say 'the religion of the peasants is none of my business' ('Nescio, non jussi; causa mea non est, non me tangit': *Sermo* 106, Corpus Christianorum 23 p. 417, ed. A. Mutzenbecher, 1962; Augustine mentions these martyrs in a letter of 412: *Ep.* 139).

An element in Augustine's role as a defender of the faith was always to constitute a walking refutation of the scorn of educated nobles for the simplicities of the church. But he himself lacked the high social standing by birth that could enable him to address them on equal terms. The conversion of a senator had vast consequences for his dependants. 'If only *that* senator became a Christian, none would remain pagan...but the ark is going round Jericho's walls, and they will soon fall' (*En. Ps.* 54, 13).

Where the *possessor* of the land was Donatist, his farm workers were Donatist too.

Crispinus, the militant Donatist bishop of Calama (the next town adjacent to the territory of Hippo, to the west-south-west), succeeded in putting in the best bid for the lease of a large imperial estate near Hippo, and immediately subjected the eighty Punic-speaking but Catholic peasants to compulsory immersion in a Donatist font. To Augustine's complaints he replied that this was only doing exactly what the Catholics did when they acquired an estate (*c. litt. Petiliani* ii, 83, 184). Crispinus was fiercely anti-Catholic, and tried to liquidate his Catholic opposite number Possidius by an ambush (Aug. *c. Cresconium* iii, 46, 50f). Augustine's vehement objections to his baptism of the eighty peasants seem in part to be based on objection to a breach in the convention *cuius regio eius religio*, the operation of which had been hitherto to the advantage of the Catholics in Numidia where the Donatists constituted a large majority until 411–12. Crispinus evidently succeeded in special efforts to raise the resources to gain control of the estate.

At the beginning of the fourth century in Spain the Council of Elvira had to enact that Christian landowners might not accept rent, no doubt paid in kind, which had been offered in sacrifice to idols (canon 40). Gradually, as the fourth century proceeded, more and more land passed into Christian hands. The number of pagan temples that underwent building repairs and restoration after 305 is small (as Claude Lepelley has pointed out, *Cités de l'Afrique rom.* i, 297). After the edicts of Theodosius some African temples were destroyed, while others were quickly converted for church use (Aug. *Sermo* 163, 2; *Ep.* 232, 3). Naturally the pagans were thrown on to the defensive. A letter of 412 mentions an opulent pagan landowner near Hippo whose praise of Augustine was laced with irony (Aug. *Ep.* 136). The imperial edicts forbidding pagan sacrifices on pain of death caused much sullen resentment (*En. Ps.* 103, ii, 4), not least because they virtually equated ancestral cults with sorcery and the cult of evil spirits.

By the ancient tradition throughout the Mediterranean world, religious observances were a normal part of a citizen's life. To the pagans, the rites were the primary thing. Probably the myths came in to explain the rites more often than the rites were enacted in consequence of the myths. The rites linked the tribe, the people of the locality, with friendly spirit-powers who would guard their interests, grant rain (*En. Ps.* 98, 14) such as North African farmers badly needed, who would also give oracles to guide both society and the individual towards right decisions in obscure matters like success in love affairs or in medical treatment or in a delicate property-deal with high risks (*City of God* x, 11, 2). Some people expected the clergy at their local church to provide a similar service, offering mass to further worldly ambitions, or even a requiem to bring about their enemy's death (*Sermo* 90, 9). One recalls how the critics of Augustine's ordination to be bishop at Hippo complained that some blessed bread which he sent to a lady was not spiritual consolation but a love-token to assist a would-be adulteress in achieving her ends (*c. litt. Petil.* iii, 16, 19; that such requests were made to clergy is evident from Aug. *de continentia* 27).

The explanations which pagan priests offered for their traditional rites and ceremonies did not need to be consistent or coherent; pagan myth did not have the status of Christian dogma. The two principal Christian concerns, right conduct and correct belief as a ground of social unity within the community, have hardly any analogy in ancient polytheistic practice. Augustine once contrasts the cohesion given by mutually tolerant pagan cults with their incompatible myths and the fierce divisiveness of church rivalries in North Africa (*de util. ieiunii* 9). The stories of the gods might sometimes stimulate the imagination; but one could attend pagan temple ceremonies without the least implication that one believed the stories of the gods being propitiated. No one thought that the gods might be better pleased if one tried harder to believe in the old myths, like believing six impossible things before breakfast. So the social tensions arising out of religion were not immediately easy for philosophic intellectuals to take seriously. People did not riot for Artemis unless monotheists had insulted her.

For some eight centuries before Augustine's time, philosophical criticism, especially from the Academy and the Epicureans, made the defenders of traditional cults inclined to reinterpret the gods as symbols of natural forces – Hera (or Juno in her Latin dress) is air, Poseidon (or Neptune) water, Zeus (or Jupiter) the world-soul. The pagans, remarked Augustine (*c. Faustum* 20, 9), know their myths are either poetic fancies or allegories of nature and life. Augustine was unsympathetic to the syncretisers who wanted to identify all the gods as different ways of speaking about an ultimate mystery that we cannot hope to grasp in words, even though he himself in more than one place declares that the mystery of God cannot be compassed by human intelligence, and that any statement we make about God which we are able to comprehend must for that reason be inadequate to its subject (e.g. *Sermo* 117, 5). In the Greek East in the 360s Themistius had pleaded that the very diversity of cults and beliefs is a testimony to the transcendent mystery of God beyond knowledge, who alone is a fitting object of worship if we have first recognised how unknowable he is. Themistius made this argument a ground for a policy of religious toleration, which was imperial policy in the time of Valens and Valentinian (Theodoret, *HE* iv, 24 on Valens' toleration of Jews, pagans, and heretics; Ammianus Marcellinus xxx, 9, 5 on Valentinian's refusal to issue edicts requiring his subjects to follow his own form of worship). At Rome the pagan prefect Symmachus in 384 pleaded for the restoration to the senate house of the Altar of Victory and the continued toleration, without confiscation of endowments, of the old religion: 'for by one road only one cannot attain to so great a mystery'. The relativistic epistemology underlying these pagan pleas for toleration was not the unanimous late pagan view, but Augustine found it in the influential writings of Porphyry (*City of God* x, 32).

Augustine was himself very ready to say that there are many ways to the knowledge of God (not only in his early dialogues cf. *Ep.* 103, 2). A phrase in the *Soliloquies* that 'Wisdom is not attainable by only one way' (*Solil.* i, 13, 23) later received a qualification when he came to write his 'Revisions' (*Retract.* i, 4, 3), where he feared it might be taken to mean that 'there is another way apart from Christ'. He did not naturally want to concede that pagan cult is a true way to God. His youthful correspondence with Maximus of Madaura about 390 (*Epp.* 16–17) and about eighteen years later with another pagan, Nectarius of Calama (*Ep.* 104, 11) shows him rejecting the very possibility that veneration of demonic counterfeits might be a path leading to the truth. Yet he can acknowledge that the intention of the worshippers (and in Augustine's ethic intention is all-important) is to aspire towards the one true God (*c. Gaudentium* i, 23, 38), even when they offer sacrifices to Caelestis (Tanit) or the old Punic Baalsamen, 'lord of heaven', or Baal shamayim (*Q. Hept.* vii, 16). A priest of Attis, on the other hand, who blandly assured Augustine that the gentle self-castrated god with a Phrygian cap and a lamb on his lap is really a Christian too was abruptly met by a vehement negative (*Tr. in Joh.* 7.6; cf. Jerome, *Ep.* 107, 2).

It is not to be forgotten that pagan writers of the third century like Cornelius Labeo (*City of God* ii, 11) and Porphyry (both in his vegetarian tract *De Abstinentia* and in fragments cited by John Philoponus, *de Opificio Mundi*) allow that some of the gods of polytheistic cult are malevolent powers, not at all good, just, friendly tribal spirits akin to their worshippers.

The pagan intellectuals of Augustine's generation found in their historical and antiquarian interests a welcome refuge from the unpleasantness of the contemporary world. Varro, Livy, Cicero, Sallust, and Vergil fed their souls. Augustine's mind was well furnished with the books of these great authors.

In the *City of God* the principal source for his description of pagan religion is Varro's 'Antiquities of the Divine Things' (*Antiquitates rerum divinarum*), a work whose reconstruction depends largely on Augustine's quotations. In this work Varro tried to schematise and classify the different cults, but without professing, still less imposing, any fixed structure of belief. Varro let himself go in the minute listing of every possible deity, and carefully explained just which department of life or nature each god or goddess presided over. The resulting impression, probably not the consequence of unkind select quotation by Augustine, is one of the amazing triviality of the old Italic cults. It stands in contrast to Varro's own belief as a learned man, that the highest god is the world-soul, which is also fire. Like many of his time, Varro thought the supreme god venerated in many places under different names. (*City of God* iv, 12; vii, 6. The surviving remnants of Varro's work are gathered by B. Cardauns, Wiesbaden 1976; thereon H. D. Jocelyn in *Rivista di filologia e di istruzione classica* 108, 1980, 100–22.)

The veneration of kings as divine heroes Varro justified by the argument that, although nonsense, it is useful nonsense, since a belief in one's infallibility has a beneficial effect on the king concerned, who is at least then moved to behave in a much more responsible way than would otherwise be the case.

In the last analysis Varro's position approximates to that of the sceptical Cotta in Cicero's *Nature of the gods* or indeed to Montaigne: as one cannot be certain of anything, one has a duty to maintain the old traditions.

Astonishment is sometimes expressed that Augustine's anti-pagan polemic in the *City of God* is so literary in manner and substance. He uses as his main source for paganism not the still living cults of North Africa but an antiquarian writer of the first century BC, who was already consciously archaising at the time of writing. From the *City of God* one would hardly guess the existence of the sharp social tensions I tried to describe earlier in this paper. Did Augustine fear to make a frontal attack on paganism as a contemporary issue lest he create a moral vacuum? He was sensitive to the fact that in parts of Numidia the fearful conflicts between Catholic and Donatist had been driving some of the peasants to apostatise in disillusion and to revert to the well-tried ceremonies of an immemorial rural past (see the newly found *Ep.* 20* p. 105 ed. Divjak). It might be one thing to undermine belief in pagan religion, quite another to convince them that the more strenuous Christian life and faith was a categorical imperative. The old pagan cults had no strong moral content, and hence their relative weakness before the tough-minded missionary monotheism of the Christians. But the higher forms of pagan religion in the fourth century were far from devoid of moral sensitivity. The gods were understood by pagans from time immemorial as providing sanctions for the essential duties of the family and tribe and to be closely linked with survival. By belonging to a certain family or tribe, one acquired social obligations and rights within a group; and that group included the gods of the family and 'state'.

The Christians had, of course, a lot going for them in the fourth century, above all the support of the emperors other than Julian. But at the time of Constantine's conversion they were surely a relatively small minority in the empire, especially in the West, and it is anything but an easy matter to explain why paganism failed in the great conflict with the church that looms so large on the stage in the lifetime of Augustine. Was it that the chaos of the third century, the disintegration of the central government, the drastic inflation attested in the food prices shown in Egyptian papyri, the deserted farms and villages attested in the *Vita Prima* of Pachomius and elsewhere, had a cumulative effect in undermining old social and religious ties? The change of religion was felt to mark a profound alteration in the social structure. And this change is too superficially considered if the question is put simply in terms of the social role of a Christian bishop as the *persona* of his city, representing a divine presence by his sacramental functions, a benediction on the city's virtues and a curse on its vices, interceding for his fellow-citizens whether with heaven or with emperors, taxmen, and invading Huns and Vandals. Although there are fourth-century anticipations foreshadowing this last development (the first attested case of a bishop serving as imperial ambassador is as early as 324), it cannot be seen to be in full operation until the fifth century, when the advent of the barbarian rulers pushed aside the old Roman administration, except in Theoderic's Italy, while leaving the churches intact as vehicles for the transmission of the old order.

In any event the change was very gradual. In part the failure of paganism may be explained on the basic proposition that anything the pagan gods could do, the *Deus christianorum* could do better, and how much more besides. But time was required to persuade everyone of this. Hence the emotional crisis of 410 when Alaric's Goths took Rome: what, people asked, were St Peter and St Paul, St Laurence, and other patron-martyrs doing to allow that? Parents long continued to arrange for a sacrifice to the old gods to gain health for their sick baptised child (*Ep.* 98, 1). A considerable proportion of Augustine's congregation at Hippo remained observant of old superstitions; they avoided the day following the Kalends for starting a journey, and made decisions only after consulting astrologers' almanacs with a note of unlucky 'Egyptian' days (*Expos. in Ep. ad Galat.* 35). To discover what the future might hold some of them visited professional diviners and astrologers (*Tr. in Joh.* vi, 17). When an astrologer was converted, Augustine drew emphatic attention to his presence in the church congregation and to the intention to have a solemn bonfire of his books of horoscopes (*En. Ps.* 61, 23; cf. *Tr. in Joh.* viii, 8). He unsuccessfully tried to dissuade his flock from using the planetary names for the days of the week (*En. Ps.* 93, 3). They insisted on having tokens and talismans; so little copies of the four gospels would be used as amulets (*Tr. in Joh.* vii, 12). Infants were brought to baptism in quest of physical health (*Ep.* 98, 5) rather than spiritual regeneration (at least as a priority). The catalogue of local African wonders in *City of God* (xxii, 8) includes two instances of adults, one a physician, the other a retired actor, whose baptism brought them cures – of gout and of malformation or malfunction of the genital organs respectively. The eucharistic host was successfully applied to the eyelids of an infant whose eyelids were stuck (*Op. impf. c. Julianum* iii, 162). These stories are recorded by Augustine as astonishing rarities, not as typical cases. It was an everyday matter, however, for Christians celebrating African martyrs to be as intoxicated or indeed as unchaste as their pagan neighbours had long been at festivals of the pagan gods (*in Ep. Joh.* iv, 4). They were tenacious in celebrating 1 January and Mid-summer in traditional ways which Augustine thought unedifying at least in association (*Sermo* 196, 4; *S. Morin* i, 4 p. 592; *S. Frangip.* viii, 5 p. 231, for bonfires on 24 June). Faustus the Manichee nettled Augustine by accusing the Catholic Church of simply continuing pagan customs under other names by their veneration of the martyrs and their observance of solstices, with the Nativity on 25 December and St John Baptist on 24 June (*c. Faust.* 20, 4).

Although the African churches took special pride in their martyrs and set great store by their celebration on anniversaries, Augustine sought to wean his people from dependence on physical manifestations of divine presence associated with the intercessions of the saints. 'The Christian *populus* celebrates martyrs with religious solemnity to be stirred to imitation and to be associated with their merits and to be assisted by their prayers' (*c. Faust.* 20, 21). The altar at St Cyprian's shrine is not dedicated to Cyprian as if he were a god; we see in the saint himself an altar to God (*S. Denis* xiv, 5 p. 70). To honour the martyrs without imitating their dedication and holiness is to flatter them with lies (*Sermo* 325, 1). One might take a relic of St Stephen on a journey as protection from danger (*Ep.* 212, CSEL 57/4, p. 372, 7–10). But Augustine dislikes very much those who speak of miracles as events 'contrary to nature'; they are for him events that trigger faith and are out of line with what little we know about nature, a knowledge which is gravely incomplete (*City of God* xxi, 8). 'When events happen in a stream of flowing successiveness in a regular track, they are called natural; when they are unusual and for the admonition of mankind, they are called miracles' (*De Trinitate* iii, 6, 11). God does nothing contrary to nature, but sometimes surprises us with what we do not expect (*c. Faust.* 26, 3). The only miracles of ultimate importance are located in the spiritual citadel of the soul, the moral transformation of man by grace (*Sermo* 89, 1–3; 98, 1–3). The catechist should turn the convert seeking instruction in preparation for baptism away from miracles and dreams towards God's word in holy scripture (*Cat. Rud.* vi, 10).

Augustine's interest in the psychology of the will led him frequently to note the mysteriousness of spiritual decisions: 'How many enemies of Christ are in our day being suddenly drawn to Christ by a secret grace' (*c. ii epp. Pelag.* i, 37). Suddenly converted actors and harlots much surpass tepid Christians in patience, self-control, faith, hope, and charity (*DQ Simpl.* i, 22). 'You hear men expressing amazement: I used to know him, what a drunkard he was, what a ruffian, what a lover of circus and amphitheatre, what a man for fraud; and now he serves God, how innocent he has become' (*En. Ps.* 88, 6). Augustine never suggests that either cures through saintly intercession or the pressures of social coercion explain the large majority of conversions.

Polytheists expected the gods to whom they offered sacrifices not only to manifest a general care for the empire of the local community, but also to intervene with special providences on behalf of individuals in special need: to give protection against raiding barbarians, or to avert plague from their crops or infertility from their spouse, or most particularly to grant restoration to physical health. In situations of religious rivalry miracles assumed special importance as vindicating the group to which they were granted. Both pagans and Christians had therefore to offer cures or other signs in order to compete effectively. The rivalry greatly sharpened the promotion of the several causes.

Augustine expresses himself in sceptical terms about pagan miracles such as the never-quenched lamp ever burning at the Temple of Venus (*City of God* xxi, 6), but at other times he grants that portents occur, which are explained as demonic rivalry, morally inferior because of the polytheistic cause they support (x, 16). Unbelievers were sceptical of the gospel miracles, especially the Virgin Birth and the Resurrection (*Ep.* 102; *De agone christiano* 12, etc.), pointing to the divergent genealogies of Jesus in Matthew and Luke (*Sermo* 51, 16) or the variations between the evangelists in the resurrection narratives (*Sermo* 240, 1; cf. *De consensu evangelistarum*). The young Augustine defended the biblical miracles, but long regarded special providences in the physical order as ambivalent. The Donatists were claiming that prayers were answered at the shrines of their special heroes, Donatus and Pontius (*Unit. eccl.* xix, 49–50). So it was well to remember the miracles of Pharaoh's magicians in opposition to Moses (*Sermo* 90, 5; *De Trinitate* iii, 7, 12). The old Augustine became increasingly convinced of the truth of occasional cures at the shrines of Catholic martyrs in North Africa. Though relatively infrequent and only locally known, miracles (he came to believe) had not wholly ceased. Relics of martyrs healed a blind man at Milan in 386 (*City of God* xxii, 8, 2); holy oil from the lamp at St Stephen's shrine (8, 19) or earth from the Holy Land (8, 7) appeared the occasion of remarkable events for which people had prayed. Augustine himself may not have experienced a miracle directly, but in the *Confessions* (x, 35, 56) he acknowledged how welcome a sign from God would have been to him at certain moments. It is very unusual in his work for a miracle to be the instrument of conversion as in *Ep.* 227, of AD 428–9, such cures as do occur being normally granted to already practising believers. He did not want his flock to look for such special providences. The sacraments were enough (*De. bapt.* iii, 16, 21).

The church had to provide alternative and Christian forms of celebration on the days long associated with pagan rites. People did not cease to hope and pray for health and success in love, commerce, or a career, once they had become Christians. Conversion did not mean for everyone the renunciation of a secular career and marriage which it meant for Augustine at Milan in 386; and Augustine himself, ascetic though he became, did not wish everyone else to think that way. Lay Christians doing the things of the *saeculum* 'keep the wheel of the world's business turning', in ways that can be applied to the service of God (*QEvang.* ii, 44, 1). Unlike Tertullian, Augustine thought a Christian who had opportunity to become a magistrate had a duty to do so (*City of God* xix, 6). He was defensively aware of those who thought that Christian salvation was good for the world to come, and that to be safe and successful in this life one needed to turn to the inferior spirits who seemed to have most of it in their control (*En. Ps.* 34, i, 6). Moreover, there remained many pagans among the wealthy and senatorial classes who exercised great influence on their dependent clients (*Confessions* viii, 4, 9). The educated pagans resented the church and the social influence of effective bishops. More than once Augustine speaks of the 'hatred' felt towards the church by pagan aristocrats (*En. Ps.* 103, iv, 4), and of their anger when they found the government protective of the Christian interest (*City of God*, vi preface and chap. 1). Augustine was alarmed to discover the hypocrisy of high officials who found it to their advantage to profess benevolence to the church while their private thoughts and domestic conversation were bitterly hostile. They would hardly have been tranquillised by Augustine's stern remark that contemporary pagans used a flood of words but had as much to say as the mute (*Confessions* i, 4, 4 end).

The conflict between Greco-Roman polytheism and Christian monotheism ended by changing the structure of ancient society, and the shift of religious allegiance is the main single constituent marking the transition from what we call 'ancient' to what we call 'medieval'. There is a possible trap here. We need to beware of a tautology when we ask if the change in religion was a cause of the end of the western Roman empire, when what we principally mean by 'the end of the western empire', or the end of the ancient world, is a change in religion. A change in religion bringing about a change in religion is not to the historian very illuminating language. And there were of course other changes in the fifth and sixth centuries: the fainéant line of western Roman emperors may not have been much missed, and no one in 476 really noticed that the western empire was coming to an end. But domination of the western provinces by Germanic tribes was bad for the old landowners and for old Roman culture, though it was not always adverse to the social influence of Christian bishops, especially of the papacy. As Augustine himself noted, the conversion of the Roman world brought a diminution of tolerance. The unspeakable rancour between Donatist and Catholic in Africa, or between Monophysite and Chalcedonian in Syria and Egypt, brought catastrophic political troubles to both Greek East and Latin West, and facilitated the Islamic conquests of these alienated regions.

Augustine mentions with pain the way in which pagans pointed an accusing finger at Christian divisions (*Sermo* 47, 28), at the Christian propensity to argue about ever more refined points of doctrine like the mysteries of the Trinity (*Expos. Ep. Rom. inchoata* 15), and to take disputes to the point of suspending eucharistic communion and treating separated brethren as heathen outsiders. The consequences of this feature of Christian history have not yet been exorcised, and their legacy is writ large in the annals of Europe. It is among Augustine's more attractive characteristics that he sought reconciliation. His mastery of Latin literature and his profound impregnation with Neoplatonism enabled him to build bridges to the cultured despisers (who thought it 'ostentatious' of God to have chosen fishermen for the witnesses of his revelation, *Sermo* 197) and, with infinite patience, to try to restore social and ecclesiastical harmony to a Romanised African society ravaged by division in a way perhaps only Ulstermen can understand.

The diversity of religious life and acceptance of social pluralism in the twelfth century*

GILES CONSTABLE

When the prelates at the Fourth Lateran Council forbade the foundation of new religious orders and required anyone who wanted to enter religious life to choose a house of an approved order and any new religious house to follow the rule of an approved order, they gave as the reason 'lest the excessive diversity of religions should introduce grave confusion into the church of God'.[1] This decree reflected a widespread concern in the late twelfth and early thirteenth centuries, but it tried to close the stable door after the horse was out. The creation of new religious houses and orders had already for over a century presented an unprecedented challenge to the values and order of the medieval church. The reformers of the eleventh and twelfth centuries, as Knowles put it,

split the single traditional version of the monastic life into twenty different divisions, as it were the colours of the spectrum, each realizing a potentiality implicit in the monastic life but neglected by most contemporary manifestations, and thus meeting a need in the more complex and articulated society of the later Middle Ages.[2]

* This essay is a revised version of a paper presented at the conference on 'Consciousness and Group Identification in High Medieval Religion' at York University, Toronto, on 7–9 April 1978. It benefited from the comments of several participants, especially Professor Caroline Bynum and the Rev. Leonard Boyle. The abbreviations *PL* and *MGH* will be used in the notes for, respectively, the *Patrologia latina* and *Monumenta Germaniae historica*.

[1] IV Lateran (1215) can. 13, in Giuseppe Alberigo (ed.), *Conciliorum oecumenicorum decreta*, 3rd edn (Bologna, 1973), p. 242. See Raymonde Foreville, *Latran I, II, III et Latran IV* (Histoire des conciles oecuméniques, VI; Paris, 1965), pp. 296–7: 'Il concerne seulement l'organisation élémentaire de toute maison religieuse, et la Règle fondamentale susceptible d'orienter toute nouvelle fondation soit vers l'*ordo monasticus*, soit vers l'*ordo canonicus*.'

[2] David Knowles, *From Pachomius to Ignatius: A Study in the Constitutional History of the Religious Orders* (Sarum Lectures, 1964–5; Oxford, 1966), p. 16. The shift is reflected in the titles of the successive parts of Knowles's history of monasticism in England, of which the first volume, which goes to 1215, was entitled *The Monastic Order in England* and the following volumes, *The Religious Orders in England*.

The unity of the monastic order and pre-eminence of the religious way of life were so widely accepted in the early Middle Ages that it was hard for people to accept this diversity in the forms of religious life, each claiming to embody the highest ideal of Christian life on earth and to be the surest way to salvation. Out of this confusion, which the Council sought to avert by prohibiting new orders, there developed a tolerance and, later, approval of religious diversity, which was an important aspect of the pluralism of modern European society and of the ever-accelerating movement, as Henry Adams saw it, from unity to multiplicity.[3]

Differences in ideas and customs were recognized in the early Middle Ages but were commonly fitted into a framework of underlying unity. The lapidary formula *diversi sed non adversi*, which at least one scholar has called magical, was first used by Anselm of Laon in 1117, but the idea behind it is found in the Church Fathers and in writers of classical antiquity.[4] Quintilian's view of the difficulty of choosing between the differing opinions of earlier writers may have inspired Ambrosiaster, when he said that the apparently contradictory words of the Evangelists did not disagree in meaning, and Ambrose, who wrote, 'Although the Evangelists do not seem to have said contrary things, they said diverse things.'[5] Cassiodorus applied this principle to the writings of the Church Fathers, who 'said not contrary but diverse things';[6] and Gregory the Great used it to accommodate the differences in ecclesiastical customs and liturgical usages of the early medieval

---

[3] See the last paragraph of chapter 34, entitled 'A Law of Acceleration (1904)', of Henry Adams, *The Education of Henry Adams*: 'The movement from unity into multiplicity, between 1200 and 1900, was unbroken in sequence, and rapid in acceleration. Prolonged one generation longer, it would require a new social mind.' I am indebted for this reference to Professor Charles Connell of West Virginia University.

[4] There is a considerable scholarly literature, and some disagreement, on this subject: see especially J. de Ghellinck, *Le Mouvement théologique du XIIe siècle*, 2nd edn (Museum Lessianum: Section historique, X; Brussels – Paris, 1948), pp. 517–23; Henri de Lubac, 'A Propos de la formule: *Diversi, sed non adversi*', *Recherches de science religieuse*, XL (1952), pp. 27–40; Paul Meyvaert, 'Diversity within Unity, a Gregorian Theme', *Heythrop Journal*, IV (1963), pp. 141–62, reprinted in his *Benedict, Gregory, and Others* (Variorum Reprint CS61; London, 1977); and Hubert Silvestre, 'Diversi sed non adversi', *Recherches de théologie ancienne et médiévale*, XXXI (1964), pp. 124–32, and *Revue d'histoire ecclésiastique*, LX (1965), pp. 987–8. Carolly Erickson, *The Medieval Vision* (New York, 1976), pp. 53–4, commented on its use by Hugo Metellus and by Abelard, saying that 'Clearly the motto meant different things to them.'

[5] Silvestre, 'Diversi', pp. 130–1, who also suggested that Martianus Capella's definition of *differentia* 'quae res inter se diversas, non adversas ostendit' (which derives from Cicero) may have inspired the formula of Anselm of Laon.

[6] Cassiodorus, *De institutione divinarum litterarum*, XIV, ed. R. A. B. Mynors (Oxford, 1937), p. 40, cited by Silvestre, 'Diversi', p. 131. Cassiodorus mentioned Hilary of Poitiers, Rufinus, Epiphanius, and the councils of Nicaea and Chalcedon.

church. Among the questions addressed in Gregory's *Libellus responsionum* was: 'Are there varying customs in the churches, even though the faith is one, and is there one form of mass in the Holy Roman Church and another in the Gallic churches?'[7] In his reply, and also in the *Regula pastoralis* and *Moralia* on Job, Gregory stressed the theme of diversity within unity, basing it on Christ's description of the many mansions in His Father's house and on the principle of the diversity of individual gifts. For Gregory the universal church itself, Meyvaert said, 'consisted of a plurality or diversity of churches'.[8]

Isidore of Seville expressed the same view, in a negative way, when he commented, referring to how monks wore their hair, that 'It is wrong to have a different style, where there is not a different way of life.'[9] He thereby implied that people who lived differently might wear their hair differently. Hair-style was in fact an important mark of social, ethnic, and regional diversity in the early Middle Ages. In the ninth century the question of whether or not priests should shave became a major point of controversy between the Greek and Latin churches. Ratramnus of Corbie in his *Contra Graecorum opposita Romanam ecclesiam infamantium* said: 'This usage of clerics [cutting the hair and beard] is not uniform in all churches and varies and diverges according to the custom of the greater ones', and his contemporary Bishop Eneas of Paris argued that different peoples might follow different customs 'so long as it does not depart from the catholic faith'.[10] Two centuries later Pope Leo IX made the same point in a letter to the patriarch of Constantinople: 'For it should be known that differing customs according to time and place are no obstacle to the salvation of believers, provided one faith...commends all people to one God.'[11] Regino of Prüm in the preface to his *De synodalibus causis*, written about 900, said:

Just as different nations of peoples differ from each other in descent, customs, language, [and] laws, so the holy universal church diffused over the whole world of lands, though joined in the unity of faith, differs within itself in ecclesiastical customs. Various customs in ecclesiastical offices are found in the kingdoms of the Gauls and of Germany, others in the eastern kingdoms, [and] in the lands across the sea.[12]

[7] Bede, *Historia ecclesiastica gentis Anglorum*, I, 27, ed. Bertram Colgrave and R. A. B. Mynors (Oxford Medieval Texts; Oxford, 1969), p. 80. Colgrave translated this as two separate questions; Meyvaert, 'Diversity', p. 144, made it into a single statement.

[8] Meyvaert, 'Diversity', p. 155, who said later (p. 162) that 'the era of unity on the basis of uniformity' began in the eighth century, when there was 'a deliberate policy of unification in the domain of the liturgy'.

[9] Isidore of Seville, *Regula monachorum*, XII, 4, in *PL*, LXXXIII, 883A.

[10] Ratramnus of Corbie, *Contra Graecorum opposita*, IV, 5, in *PL*, CXXI, 322C; Eneas of Paris, *Liber adversus Graecos*, CLXXXVI, *ibid.*, 747C.

[11] *PL*, CXLIII, 764B.

[12] Regino of Prüm, *De synodalibus causis*, pref., ed. F. G. A. Wasserschleben (Leipzig, 1840), p. 2.

This acceptance of diversity with regard to ideas and customs did not extend to religious beliefs and standards of perfection, concerning which there was a wide measure of agreement in the early Middle Ages.[13] A life of prayer, withdrawal from secular life, and dedication to God was almost universally regarded as the highest ideal of life on earth, and monks and nuns were seen as a distinct order of society, superior to both the clergy and the laity. This professional division of society into monks, clerics, and laymen, as well as the later occupational division into those who prayed, fought, and worked, regarded monks as primarily responsible for the spiritual welfare of society. Most monks at that time were not in holy orders and were forbidden to perform clerical duties without special permission. Their function was to do the work of God, and above all to pray. The concern of the Carolingian rulers for monastic regularity was largely owing to their desire to win the favour of God for themselves and for their realm.[14] William of Aquitaine founded the abbey of Cluny, according to his foundation charter, out of love for God and concern for the souls of the king, himself, his family and followers, 'and for the state and integrity of the catholic religion'.[15] The caritative activities of monks, though mentioned in the charter, were secondary in William's mind.

This unity in theory and purpose was compatible with a high degree of variety in practice. Especially in the so-called period of the mixed rule, from the sixth to the eighth centuries, every house had in effect its own rule and was held together by loyalty to the memory of the founder, adherence to its own traditions, and dependence on its own special spiritual and secular patrons. Even after the general acceptance of the Rule of Benedict in the ninth century, there was probably less uniformity between individual houses than many contemporary reformers, and some later scholars, have claimed. During this period, however, the first signs of a stress on uniformity of

---

[13] See Silvestre, in *Rev. d'hist. ecc.*, LX, p. 987: 'Celle-ci connut un grand succès au moyen âge et déjà, sous des formes approchantes, à la période patristique, soit qu'on l'appliquât aux divergences constatées dans la Bible, soit qu'elle visât les désaccords entre les Pères eux-mêmes, soit qu'on y eût recours à propos d'une différence d'opinions plus apparente que réelle sur un sujet quelconque.'

[14] Charlemagne's famous capitulary *De literis colendis* is concerned not with the general level of education among his subjects, as is often said, or even of teachers and preachers, but specifically with the education of monks – 'our faithful orators' – upon the correctness of whose prayers the welfare of the empire depended: *MGH, Leges: Capitularia regum Francorum*, 2 vols. (1883–97), I, p. 79, no. 29. See F. L. Ganshof, *Recherches sur les capitulaires* (Paris, 1958), pp. 45–6, and Luitpold Wallach, *Alcuin and Charlemagne: Studies in Carolingian History and Literature* (Cornell Studies in Classical Philology, XXXII; Ithaca, NY, 1959), p. 214.

[15] *Recueil des chartes de l'abbaye de Cluny*, ed. A. Bernard and A. Bruel, 6 vols. (Collection de documents inédits sur l'histoire de France; Paris, 1876–1903), I, p. 125, no. 112.

practice among special groups of monasteries, often to the exclusion of other houses, can be seen in the emergence of systematized collections of customs.[16] Cluny in the late tenth and eleventh centuries produced four distinct customaries, which established the type of monasticism known as Cluniac and defined the order of Cluny and later orders which were influenced by it.[17]

The interdependence of the three orders of society is emphasized in two speeches attributed respectively to Bishops Burchard of Worms and Gerard of Cambrai in the early eleventh century. When Burchard saw the number of clerics entering monasteries in his diocese, he allegedly brought together monks from several houses and told them

> that everyone who fears God and acts justly is acceptable to Him, not only the monk but also the canon and likewise the layman. It is not good for all who work on a ship to insist on the same occupation, as if there were either all pilots and no sailor or all sailors and no pilot... We should likewise recognize, brothers, that we cannot all do everything. For if everyone were monks and canons, where would be the laymen? ... For the family in the church of God is diverse, [including] not only monks but also canons and faithful laymen... A canon may not therefore leave his monastery for the monastic life without permission; but he should labour in common with his brothers; and if he desires to lead a stricter life, let him attend to works pleasing to God within his own monastery.[18]

Burchard here had in mind the professional orders of monks, clerics (whom he called canons), and laymen. Gerard of Cambrai referred to the occupational orders of prayers, fighters, and tillers in a speech delivered in 1036, following a decree of the Frankish bishops concerning the truce of God. The tillers were 'raised to God by the prayers of the orators and defended by the army of the fighters', he said. The fighters in turn collected revenues from agriculture and tolls and were supported by the prayers of holy men. As was proper in a speech concerning the truce of God, Gerard emphasized that the office of fighting was not blame-worthy 'if there is no sin in the

---

[16] See the *Corpus consuetudinum monasticarum*, ed. Kassius Hallinger, 9 vols. to date (Siegburg, 1963–), esp. the general introduction to vol. I. The increasing use of common bodies of written customs, which was an aspect of the transfer from oral and mimetic tradition to reliance on texts, is discussed by Brian Stock, *The Implications of Literacy: Written Language and Models of Interpretation in the Eleventh and Twelfth Centuries* (Princeton, 1983).

[17] On the issue of clothing, see Kassius Hallinger, *Gorze-Kluny. Studien zu den monastischen Lebensformen und Gegensätzen im Hochmittelalter*, 2 vols. (Studia Anselmiana, XXII–XXV; Rome, 1950–1), II, pp. 696–701, and, on the emphasis on uniformity within individual orders, Gerd Zimmermann, *Ordensleben und Lebensstandard. Die Cura corporis in den Ordensvorschriften des abendländischen Hochmittelalters* (Beiträge zur Geschichte des alten Mönchtums und des Benediktinerordens, XXXII; Münster West., 1973), pp. 115–16, 207–8.

[18] *Vita Burchardi episcopi*, XVII, in MGH, *Scriptores: Scriptores* in fol., 34 vols. (1826–1980), IV, p. 840. Burchard used the term *monasterium* here to refer to a house of canons.

consciousness', and he justified the variety of occupations in society by referring to the many mansions in God's house.[19]

These texts also show that by the early eleventh century the lines between the clerical and monastic orders were becoming blurred. The distinction broke down further in the eleventh and twelfth centuries, when an increasing number of monks entered holy orders and when ecclesiastical reformers applied to clerics the rules of celibacy and community life that had previously characterized monks and nuns. Many groups of canons adopted rules resembling those of monks, and sometimes derived from them. Their houses were called monasteries, and they themselves were called regular canons in order to distinguish them from secular canons, who like other clerics owned property and lived in separate households.

The distinction between the monastic and lay orders was similarly blurred by the two new institutions of lay brothers and military orders. Scholars are still uncertain precisely when and where the old type of monastic *conversi* – illiterate and unordained monks who had entered a monastery as adults but who could, and often did, learn to read and write and take holy orders – were replaced by the new type of *conversi*, who constituted a closed category in a monastery, from which no graduation was possible, and who performed special, and usually menial, duties.[20] The new type is found especially in Italy and south Germany in the last quarter of the eleventh and first quarter of the twelfth centuries, and it spread rapidly among the new religious orders, which were thus freed from dependence on lay servitors. They were referred to as *conversi laici*, *fratres*, and frequently *barbati*, from their beards which distinguished them from the unbearded clerical monks.[21] Contemporaries disagreed over whether they were monks or laymen, and in practice they constituted a group whose way of life resembled in many respects that of laymen.

The new military orders also formed a bridge between the monastic and lay orders, since their members were both soldiers and monks. Bernard of Clairvaux stressed the novelty of this combination in his *De laude novae militiae*, written between 1128 and 1136 for the Knights of the Temple.

A new type of fighting force may be said to have arisen upon earth... A new type of fighting force, I say, unknown to earlier ages, which fights equally and unceasingly in the twofold war both against flesh and blood and against 'the spirits of wickedness in the high places'.

[19] *Gesta episcopum Cameracensium*, III, 52, in *MGH, Scriptores* in fol., VII, p. 485.
[20] See the references in my article on '"Famuli" and "Conversi" at Cluny: A Note on Statute 24 of Peter the Venerable', *Revue bénédictine*, LXXXIII (1973), pp. 326–50, reprinted in *Cluniac Studies* (Variorum Reprint CS109; London, 1980).
[21] See my introduction to the forthcoming edition by R. B. C. Huygens of Burchard of Bellevaux, *Apologia de barbis*.

There was nothing remarkable, Bernard continued, in waging either physical war against enemies or spiritual war against sins, but for the same person to engage in both wars was new and noteworthy. The Templars, he said, 'seem milder than lambs and fiercer than lions, so that I should be in doubt whether to call them monks or soldiers were it not suitable to call by both those names those in whom neither the mildness of the monk nor the fortitude of the soldier is lacking'.[22]

The idea that monks could be soldiers or laymen would have been unthinkable in the early Middle Ages, when the special status of the monastic order was universally recognized, in spite of the loose usage of referring to monks as lay because they were not in holy orders. Hermits also to some extent cut across the established typology of forms of religious life.[23] Many twelfth-century religious leaders, such as Norbert of Xanten, Robert of Arbrissel, and Bernard of Tiron, spent parts of their lives as hermits, pilgrims, and wandering preachers. When Stephen of Muret, the founder of the Grandmontines, was asked by two visiting cardinals whether he was a monk, hermit, or canon, he replied that his glory was nothing, thus showing not only his humility but also his desire to avoid the established categories of religious life.[24] Unlike a canon, he said, he could not rule a church; he was not called a monk, which was a term of sanctity and singularity, 'although all Christians can be called monks'; and he did not avoid worldly affairs and stay in his cell like a hermit.

New and anomalous types of religious life sprang up all over Europe. Bands of laymen were attached to religious houses, like those described by Bernold of Constance in his chronicle under the year 1091,[25] and independent groups of lay penitents lived together in north Italy in the second half of the twelfth century.[26] The lost (or perhaps unwritten) second book of the *Libellus de diversis ordinibus et professionibus qui sunt in aecclesia*, which was written in the fourth or fifth decade of the twelfth century, probably in the

---

[22] Bernard of Clairvaux, *Opera*, ed. Jean Leclercq a.o., 8 vols. in 9 (Rome, 1957–77), III, pp. 216, 221, tr. Conrad Greenia (Cistercian Fathers Series, XIX; Kalamazoo, Mich., 1977), pp. 129–30, 140.

[23] The three sections of the first book of the *Libellus de diversis ordinibus et professionibus qui sunt in aecclesia*, ed. G. Constable and B. Smith (Oxford Medieval Texts; Oxford, 1972), are devoted to hermits, monks, and canons.

[24] *Vita venerabilis viri Stephani Muretensis*, XXII, and *Vita ampliata*, XXXIV, in *Scriptores ordinis Grandimontensis*, ed. Jean Becquet (Corpus Christianorum: Continuatio Mediaevalis, VIII; Turnhout, 1968), pp. 121–3, 141.

[25] Bernold of Constance, *Chronicon*, *sub anno* 1091, in *MGH, Scriptores* in fol., V, pp. 452–3; see also *sub anno* 1083, *ibid.*, p. 439.

[26] See in particular the articles of G. G. Meersseman collected in vol. I of his *Ordo Fraternitatis. Confraternite e pietà dei laici nel Medioevo*, ed. G. P. Pacini, 3 vols. (Italia sacra, XXIV–XXVI; Rome, 1977).

diocese of Liège, was devoted to the 'worshippers of God', as the author called them, both men and women, who were neither canons, monks, hermits, nor recluses.[27] Much work remains to be done on lay religious confraternities and corporations, on lay *familiares* who were associated with religious houses where prayers were offered for their salvation, and on the men who became monks *ad succurrendum*, at the end of their lives, in order to enter the next world clothed in the monastic habit. Crusaders, pilgrims, and penitents all had a recognized legal status, if only for a limited time, and added to the complexity of the typology of forms of consecrated life.

Some of the new religious houses and orders of the twelfth century like-wise defy any easy classification. Most of them claimed to follow the Rule of Benedict, but usually interpreted in the light of various customs, which formed the real basis of new orders. Scholars are not agreed over whether or not the Carthusians followed the Rule of Benedict or whether they should be called hermits or monks, since they lived alone in cells gathered around a common cloister.[28] At the same time, the uniformity of observance within each order tended to be tightened, so that the sense of belonging to a reli-gious order, in any house of which a similar way of life was followed, increasingly replaced the sense of belonging either exclusively to an indivi-dual community or to the monastic order in general. Some houses of regular canons were indistinguishable from those of monks and had abbots as superiors. Even more confusing for contemporaries were the so-called double houses of men and women, like those founded by Gilbert of Sempringham, who gathered together nuns, canons, lay sisters, and lay brothers into single communities.

The sense of competition fostered by this diversity of forms of religious life showed itself not only in polemical writings but also in outright conflicts between religious houses. Rivalry for property, patronage, and recruits had always to some extent existed, but it was sharpened by the emergence of rival standards and ideals of religious life. Writing to Bernard of Clairvaux in 1144, Peter the Venerable deplored 'the hidden and execrable variety of minds' which alone, he said, divided men who were joined in the Christian name and unified in the monastic profession and which kept them 'from the sincere unity of hearts in which they seem to be congregated'.[29]

---

[27] *Libellus*, pref., ed. Constable, p. 5. See introduction, pp. xix–xx.

[28] See Bernard Bligny, *L'Église et les ordres religieux dans le royaume de Bourgogne aux XIe et XIIe siècles* (Collection des cahiers d'histoire publiée par les Universités de Clermont, Lyon, Grenoble, IV; Paris, 1960), pp. 268–9, and Jacques Dubois, 'Quel-ques problèmes de l'histoire de l'ordre des chartreux à propos de livres récents', *Revue d'histoire ecclésiastique*, LXIII (1968), pp. 34–7.

[29] Peter the Venerable, Ep. 111, *The Letters of Peter the Venerable*, ed. Giles Constable, 2 vols. (Harvard Historical Studies, LXXVIII; Cambridge, Mass., 1967), I, p. 277:

Religious houses in the twelfth century, like those in earlier times, fought for the favour of supernatural and secular patrons, and for the privileges and economic favours which came from both. The Virgin was expected to defend the new Cistercian houses dedicated to her just as much as Sts Peter and Paul were expected to look after their rights and property at Cluny. Perhaps the principal rivalry, however, was for recruits, without whom no religious house can survive. Some of the sharpest controversies arose over the transfer, or *transitus*, as it was called, of members from one religious community to another. Such moves were technically forbidden without the permission of the superior, but they became increasingly common. Some houses were populated primarily by fugitives from other houses, and many prominent figures moved from one house to another. The practice in canon law of allowing moves to stricter but not to less strict houses did little to help the situation, since there was no accepted hierarchy of strictness. It led in particular to some acerbic exchanges between monks and regular canons, who often asserted the superiority of their ideal of a life both in and out of the world to the monastic ideal of withdrawal and prayer. The regular canon Anselm of Havelberg said in his *Epistola apologetica pro ordine canonicorum regularium*, written about 1150, that 'The order of canons is higher (*sublimior*) in the church than [that] of monks' and argued that clerics, like Christ, combined the active and contemplative lives into a true *vita apostolica*. 'Just as a good and perfect monk should be loved and imitated more than an inept cleric,' he wrote, 'so a cleric living well and regularly is without doubt always to be preferred even to the best monk.'[30]

Contemporary observers of the religious scene were aware of these developments. The author of the *Libellus de diversis ordinibus* worked out what

'Et cum eos ut dixi Christianum nomen coniungat, cum monastica professio uniat, sola eos mentium nescio quae occulta et nefanda varietas separat, et ab illa sincera cordium unitate in quam videntur congregati disgregat.'

[30] Anselm of Havelberg, *Epistola apologetica pro ordine canonicorum regularium*, in *PL*, CLXXXVIII, 1125C, 1136C; see Georg Schreiber, 'Studien über Anselm von Havelberg zur Geistesgeschichte des Hochmittelalters', *Analecta Praemonstratensia*, XVIII (1942), p. 38; Kurt Fina, 'Anselm von Havelberg [I]', *ibid.*, XXXII (1956), p. 85; Gabriella Severino, 'La discussione degli "Ordines" di Anselmo di Havelberg', *Bullettino dell'Istituto Storico Italiano per il Medio Evo*, LXXVIII (1967), pp. 86–7, 107, stressing that canons, unlike monks, have a role in the world. See also the *Coutumier du XI siècle de l'ordre de Saint-Ruf*, ed. A. Carrier [de Belleuse] (Etudes et documents sur l'ordre de St-Ruf, VIII; Sherbrooke, Que., 1950), p. 97, no. 69: 'Et scorum Patrum inexpugnabili sentencia sancitur, canonicum ordinem omnibus ecclesie ordinibus preponendum merito. Nec mirum, cum Xpo et apostolis eius succedat, in predicacionis, baptismatis ac reliquorum ecclie sacramentorum officium subrogatus.' This customary in fact dates from the second half of the twelfth century: see Charles Dereine, in *Revue d'histoire ecclésiastique*, XLVI (1951), p. 356, and *Scriptorium*, V (1951), p. 109, and XIII (1959), p. 244.

was perhaps the first typology of forms of religious life, showing the parallels between the various types of monks and canons who lived, respectively, close to, far from, and among other men and finding biblical prototypes for each. Otto of Freising in the seventh book of his *Chronica*, which goes to 1146, stressed the variety of types of religious life and praised them all for leading pure and holy lives and for living together in monasteries and churches with one heart and one soul. They glowed internally, he said, with the varied splendours of the virtues and wore externally clothes of diverse colours, fulfilling the words of the Psalmist: 'All the glory of the king's daughter is within in golden borders, clothed round about with varieties.'[31] In the description of various types of religious life in the chronicle of Petershausen, which ends in 1156, the monks, canons, bishops, and priests are followed by virgins, solitaries, recluses, wandering preachers, pilgrims, and beggars, who will also be carried by the angels 'with Lazarus into the bosom of Abraham'.[32]

These writers all turned to the Bible to justify the various forms of religious life they saw around them. The author of the *Libellus* found a prototype in both the Old and New Testaments for every type of life except that of the so-called secular monks, who did not observe the monastic profession. The life of hermits, for instance, was exemplified by Abel in the first age, by the patriarchs in the second age, and by Christ when He withdrew 'Himself alone' into the mountain in John 6. 15.[33] Otto of Freising cited both the variegated robe of the princess in Psalm 44 and the description of the primitive church in Acts 4. 32 – 'The multitude of believers had but one heart and one soul' – which was a key text for twelfth-century religious reformers and had far-reaching implications for the organization of religious institutions and of society as a whole. The Petershausen chronicler used the account in Luke 16. 22 of how the dead beggar 'was carried by the angels into Abraham's bosom', an image also used by contemporary artists to depict the salvation of various types of people. The many mansions of John 14. 2, which were cited in support of diversity by Gregory the Great and Gerard of Cambrai, were also often used to show the legitimacy of varying types of religious life.

The themes of celestial harmony and social unity were likewise cited as evidence that God intended people to be saved in different ways. Otloh of

---

[31] *MGH, Scriptores rerum Germanicarum in usum scholarum separatim editi*: Otto of Freising, *Chronica*, ed. A. Hofmeister (1912), pp. 370–1, tr. Charles C. Mierow (Records of Civilization; New York, 1928), pp. 446–7.

[32] *Die Chronik des Klosters Petershausen*, ed. Otto Feger (Schwäbische Chroniken der Stauferzeit, III; Lindau – Constance, 1956), pp. 30–6.

[33] See *Libellus*, intro., p. xxiv.

St Emmeram in the eleventh century said: 'Almighty God has in His hand all men predestined to the harmony of the celestial life, like a lute arranged with suitable strings, and He destines some indeed to the sharp sound of the contemplative life and assigns others by regulating to the depth of the active life.'[34] The author of the *Libellus*, after stressing the differences among hermits, said: 'If it displeases you that all men in this calling do not live in the same way, look at the Creation fashioned by the good Creator in various ways, and how a harmony has been achieved from different chords.'[35] Goscelin of St Bertin wrote in his *Liber confortatorius*:

The palm of Christ is denied to no sex, no age, no condition. Every earthly being and child of man, one and the same rich and poor, kings and princes, young men and virgins, old and young, boys, girls, sucking and crying babes, are crowned either with martyrdom, virginity, or continence... In that unanimity of peace, the distinctions of differing qualities will not exist for division or dissonance, but for a most beautiful harmony of varied ornaments, just as a field is decorated with various flowers, a picture with various colours, and a basin with various stones.[36]

These themes of harmony and unity, derived from the sphere of aural and visual aesthetics, were rhetorical topoi, but they reflected a serious concern for the relation of differing groups and individuals in the church and helped to lay the basis for an acceptance of religious diversity. It was also a commonplace to stress the universality of God's love. 'In everyone He duly regards not grade or sex but sanctity of life', said Sigiboto in his *Vita* of St Paulina, the founder of Paulinzelle.[37] Ivo of Chartres in his letter to the monks of Coulombs in effect denied the traditional hierarchy of forms of religious life by stressing the universality of the church and criticizing those who claimed that it belonged to just a few wandering ascetics, forgetting that 'Each person has their own gift from God and that in the house of God one person walks this path and another that and that all branches do not behave in the same way.'[38] The author of the *Libellus*, after mentioning the differences in monastic customs concerning food, clothing, and manual

---

[34] Otloh of St Emmeram, *In Psalmum LII commentarius*, in *PL*, xciii, 1110A.
[35] *Libellus*, I, ed. Constable, p. 17. On the freedom of hermits to live as they pleased, see my paper on 'Liberty and Free Choice in Monastic Life and Thought', to appear in the proceedings of the fourth Pennsylvania – Paris – Dumbarton Oaks Colloquium.
[36] Charles Talbot, 'The Liber confortatorius of Goscelin of Saint Bertin', *Analecta monastica*, iii (Studia Anselmiana, xxxvii; Rome, 1955), pp. 55, 113.
[37] Sigiboto, *Vita Paulinae*, pref., in *MGH, Scriptores* in fol., xxx, 2, p. 911: 'Amat Christus doctores, amat coniugatos, amat continentes: in his fructum sapientiae, in illis de sobole matris ecclesiae fedus coniugale, in illis gratiam continentiae, virginale meritum, coniugale consortium, viduale votum et meritum sic remunerans, ut in omnibus non gradum vel sexum sed vitae sanctitatem mercede compenset.'
[38] Ivo of Chartres, Ep. 192, in *PL*, clxii, 201C.

labour, said: 'I desire to show that although they live differently they aspire from the one beginning to the one end that is Christ.'[39]

The phrase *diversi sed non adversi*, first formulated by Anselm of Laon, was often used in twelfth-century theological and legal writings. In similar and analogous forms it was also applied to the differences in religious life. In the *Altercatio monachi et clerici utrum monacho liceat praedicare* of Rupert of Deutz, the monk said: 'For you [are] only a cleric; I am both a monk and a cleric. These are diverse...but not contrary.'[40] Idungus of Regensburg in his *Argumentum super quatuor questionibus*, written about 1142/5, also said: 'The clericate and the monachate go together very well in the same person, since they are not opposed although diverse (*non sint opposita, licet diversa*).'[41] Peter the Venerable ended a letter written to Bernard in 1149, stressing the need for unity of faith: 'May the divided hearts be slowly united by this remedy, and when they shall see nothing separated between them, let them learn at the inspiration of Him who "breatheth where He will" to be one concerning things that are different but not opposed (*de diversis ne dicam adversis*).'[42]

Arguments of this sort were particularly used by defenders of the old black Benedictine houses, who stressed the traditional unity of the monastic order against the divisive tendencies of the reformers. Guibert of Nogent discounted differences in fasting and singing in his *De pignoribus sanctorum* because, 'Although they differ in act they do not disagree from the sense of faith.'[43] Rupert of Deutz compared the church to Noah's ark, with differing dimensions, in his discussion of the issue of *transitus* in the commentary he wrote on the Rule of Benedict in 1124/5. Although he distinguished the professions of monks and clerics, and regarded the former as stricter and higher than the latter, he attached no moral value to this difference, saying that 'Each person is blessed in his own order.'[44] The author of the so-called

---

39 *Libellus*, II, ed. Constable, p. 28.

40 *PL*, CLXX, 540B; see Silvestre, 'Diversi', p. 126n., and John H. Van Engen, *Rupert of Deutz* (Publications of the UCLA Center for Medieval and Renaissance Studies, XVIII; Berkeley – Los Angeles – London, 1983), pp. 310–12, dating it 'ca. 1120–1122'.

41 R. B. C. Huygens, *Le Moine Idung et ses deux ouvrages: 'Argumentum super quatuor questionibus' et 'Dialogus duorum monachorum'* (Biblioteca degli 'Studi Medievali', XI; Spoleto, 1980), p. 59. Idungus used 'diversa quamvis non adversa' in his *Dialogus*, II, *ibid.*, p. 139.

42 Peter the Venerable, Ep. 150, *Letters*, ed. Constable, I, p. 371. Silvestre, 'Diversi', p. 126n., cited this and another use, in the *Vita* of Norbert of Xanten, in *MGH*, *Scriptores* in fol., XII, p. 683.

43 Guibert of Nogent, *De pignoribus sanctorum*, I, I, in *PL*, CLVI, 612D.

44 Rupert of Deutz, *Commentarium in regulam Benedicti*, IV, 13, in *Opera omnia*, 4 vols. (Venice, 1748–51), IV, p. 319. See Van Engen, *Rupert*, pp. 237 n. 55, and 313, on the date.

Riposte to Bernard's criticisms of the old monasticism (who may have been the Cluniac abbot and archbishop, Hugh of Rouen) vigorously defended variety. 'The holy fathers established many ways of living in the church, so that ordinary men of the world, living according to them, might offer to God the multiple proofs of the virtues... Religion is not in the clothing but in the heart.'[45] The variety of vocations in the church was also stressed by the author of the *Nouvelle réponse*, written about the middle of the twelfth century, who said that 'Everyone has his own gift from God.'[46]

Peter the Venerable returned repeatedly to these issues in his letters to Bernard of Clairvaux, especially the long letter written in 1144, defending the diversity of observances and customs within the monastic order. According to Peter, communities that change their customs, or follow different customs, do not thereby lose their love or cease to be Christians. He defended diversity even within a single order, which should be united by a single purpose. It is a matter of no concern, he said, 'if one comes to the same place by a different path, to the same life by different roads, to the same Jerusalem, which is above, that is our mother, by various journeys'. Both here and in his letter of 1149 he stressed the need for unity of faith among monks who differed in their ways of life.[47]

This point of view was shared by many clerics and canons, including some regular canons. Master Hilary of Orléans, writing in 1117/25 to a monk of the abbey of St Albinus at Angers, said that the Lord's command for men to deny themselves, carry His cross, and follow Him could be obeyed in various ways, each of which was good so long as it was sincerely followed. 'Take on the life as well as the habit of your order,' he urged.[48] After the

---

[45] André Wilmart, 'Une riposte de l'ancien monachisme au manifeste de saint Bernard', *Revue bénédictine*, XLVI (1934), pp. 324, 343. Between these quotations he said, among other things, that monks resembled the various types of soldiers mentioned in the Bible. On the author and date, see Charles Talbot, 'The Date and Author of the "Riposte"', in *Petrus Venerabilis, 1156–1956*, ed. Giles Constable and James Kritzeck (Studia Anselmiana, XL; Rome, 1956), pp. 72–80. In his *Dialogi*, VII, 6, Hugh wrote that monks and clerics were joined by the same faith and grace in Christ, 'quorum diversus est habitus, sed unus in eis est Christus. Diversa membra in uno corpore non eumdem habent actum, sed eumdem habent spiritum; pro quo uno diversa illa dicimus corpus unum': E. Martène and U. Durand, *Thesaurus novus anecdotorum*, 5 vols. (Paris, 1717), V, col. 973E.

[46] Jean Leclercq, 'Nouvelle réponse de l'ancien monachisme aux critiques des Cisterciens', *Revue bénédictine*, LXVII (1957), p. 90; see *ibid.*, intro., pp. 80–1.

[47] Peter the Venerable, Epp. 111 and 150, *Letters*, ed. Constable, I, pp. 277–80, 294, 368–9. See Raphael Molitor, *Aus der Rechtsgeschichte benediktinischer Verbände*, 3 vols. (Münster West., 1928–33), I, pp. 47–8, on Peter's stress on love, and Zimmermann, *Ordensleben*, pp. 223–4.

[48] Nikolaus M. Häring, 'Hilary of Orléans and his Letter Collection', *Studi Medievali*, 3rd ser., XIV (1973), p. 1097, no. 10.

prior of La Charité had admitted a canon on the grounds that monastic was superior to canonical life, he received a letter from an anonymous canon saying that neither order was better than the other. Black was the colour of humility and abjection; white, of purity and exaltation. 'We are all evil,' the letter concluded, 'and where all are evil, none are better.'[49] When the prior of St Barbe resigned in order to become a Premonstratensian canon, thus leaving a moderate monastery for a strict canonical house, he stressed that his change of place and colour was worthless without a change of life. Although he had departed in order to serve God in a particular place and way, he said, God is served in all parts of the world, and men fight for the same king.[50] The image of an army united in leadership and purpose but differing in appearance and usages was also used by Hugh of St Victor and Peter the Venerable.[51]

The ideals of harmony and diversity within unity were accepted even by reformers who promoted new and, in their view, superior ways of religious life and who encouraged *transitus* from less strict houses to their own. Bernard of Clairvaux, in spite of his belief in the superiority of the Cistercian to all other forms of monastic life,[52] none the less defended the legitimacy of diversity. In his *Apologia*, where he strongly criticized the Cluniacs, he deplored the quarrels between various groups of monks and canons and said that the church was made up of different orders united in a single love and faith, like the princess 'clothed round about with varieties', Joseph's seamless coat of many colours, and the many mansions in the house of God. 'Diverse men receive diverse gifts, one this and the other that, whether they be Cluniacs, or Cistercians, or regular clerics, or even faithful laymen, in fact every order, every language, every sex, every age, every condition, in every place, for every time, from the first man to the last.' 'Let each man observe by which way he walks,' Bernard continued, referring to the many

---

49 *Cujusdam canonici regularis epistola ad priorem Charitatis*, in PL, CCXIII, 718D–719A. See also the discussion of the ways of unity in the letter by Hugh Farsit (d. after 1143) to the Premonstratensians translated in the *Histoire littéraire de la France*, XII (Paris, 1763), p. 296, and published in G. van Elsen, *Beknopte Levengeschiedenis van den H. Norbertus* (Averbode, 1890), pp. 390–5, which I have not seen.

50 E. Martène and U. Durand, *Amplissima collectio*, 9 vols. (Paris, 1724–33), I, col. 784B.

51 Peter the Venerable, Ep. 4, *Letters*, ed. Constable, I, p. 145; Hugh of St Victor, *On the Sacraments of the Christian Faith* (*De Sacramentis*), tr. Roy J. Deferrari (Mediaeval Academy of America Publication LVIII; Cambridge, Mass., 1951), p. 4. See also n. 45 above.

52 Bernard of Clairvaux, *De praecepto et dispensatione*, XLVI, in *Opera*, ed. Leclercq, III, p. 285; *Sermo de diversis*, XXII, 2 and 5, *ibid.*, VI, 1, pp. 171, 173, etc. According to M. Anselme Dimier, 'Saint Bernard et le droit en matière de *Transitus*', *Revue Mabillon*, XLIII (1953), p. 80, Bernard suggested more than once that Cîteaux was the only true way to heaven.

mansions, 'so that a diversity of ways may not lead him from a single just way, for whatever mansion he reaches he will not be excluded from his Father's house.'[53] In *De praecepto et dispensatione* he specifically defended the diversity of observance within the monastic order, saying that although all monks make a single profession according to the Rule, 'since not everyone has a single intention in his heart, a non-single [i.e. diverse] observance can undoubtedly be celebrated in different places without losing salvation and without damaging one's profession'.[54] Bernard was therefore ready to accept that motives as well as behaviour varied and that different types of religious life were suited to different people, all of whom would be saved.[55]

This attitude also showed itself in the widespread concern in the twelfth century for the religious life of women. Gaucherius of Aureil, according to his biographer, knew 'that neither sex is excluded from the kingdom of God. Wherefore he tried to build the heavenly Jerusalem out of the double wall, that is, of men and of women, and he constructed the habitation for women a stone's throw from his cell, distributing what little he had to both men and women.'[56] The biographer of Gilbert of Sempringham compared his order, with its double houses, to the chariot of God, 'which has two sides, that is, one of men and the other of women; four wheels, two of men, clerics and laymen, and two of women, literate and illiterate; two beasts dragging the chariot, the clerical and monastic disciplines'. He went on to praise 'this marvellous unity of persons and churches and this unheard-of community of all things, which made all things one and one thing all in the diversities of so many hearts and such great monasteries'. The ideal here was paradisiacal harmony in which men and women lived side by side united in spiritual love.[57]

---

[53] Bernard of Clairvaux, *Apologia*, VI and IX, in *Opera*, ed. Leclercq, III, pp. 86–7, 89.

[54] Bernard of Clairvaux, *De praecepto et dispensatione*, XLVIII, in *Opera*, ed. Leclercq, III, p. 286.

[55] On Bernard's attitude toward diversity, see Jean Leclercq, 'Saint Bernard of Clairvaux and the Contemplative Community', in *Contemplative Community*, ed. M. Basil Pennington (Cistercian Studies Series, XXI; Washington, D.C., 1972), pp. 88–97, and, in intellectual matters, the introduction by Bernard McGinn to *On Grace and Free Choice*, tr. Daniel O'Donovan (Cistercian Fathers Series, XIX; Kalamazoo, Mich., 1977), pp. 32–3, citing Bernard's Sermon 81 on the Song of Songs. Some of these points are discussed, and the same sources cited, in my article, 'Cluny – Cîteaux – La Chartreuse. San Bernardo e la diversità delle forme di vita religiosa nel XII secolo', *Studi su S. Bernardo di Chiaravalle. Convegno internazionale, Certosa di Firenze, 6–9 novembre 1974* (Rome, 1975), pp. 93–114, reprinted in *Cluniac Studies*.

[56] *Vita beati Gaucherii*, in P. Labbe, *Nova bibliotheca manuscriptorum librorum*, 2 vols. (Paris, 1657), II, p. 562.

[57] *Vita s. Gileberti confessoris*, in William Dugdale, *Monasticon anglicanum*, eds. John Caley, Henry Ellis, and Bulkeley Bandinel, 6 vols. in 8 (London, 1846), VI, 2, pp. *ix–x (after p. 945).

By the middle of the twelfth century the variety and multiplicity of forms of religious life were accepted facts, and there were signs of a change in attitude from tolerance to approval. Anselm of Havelberg gave a famous defence of diversity and innovation in the first book of his *Dialogi*, where he said that in the six ages between the coming of Christ and the Day of Judgment, 'in which one and the same church is innovated, the Son of God being present, not a single and uniform [status] but many and multiform statuses are found'. He described this variety, which included the new monastic and canonical orders, the military orders, and the Greek religious orders.

Let no one be astonished or dispute that the church of God is divided by an unchanging God into various laws and observances before the law, and under the law, and under grace, for it is fitting that as the ages proceed the signs of the spiritual graces should grow, making the truth itself increasingly clear, and thus the knowledge of truth with its effect of salvation grows from age to age; and so at first good things, then better things, and finally the best things were proposed. This variety was created not on account of the mutability of an unchanging God, Who is 'always the selfsame' and Whose 'years shall not fail', but on account of the changing infirmity of the human race and the mutation in time from generation to generation.

In the title to the last chapter Anselm again asserted that 'The church of God, which is one in faith, one in hope, one in charity, is multiform in the variety of its diverse statuses.'[58]

The differences between the various ways of life open to Christians were seen as of relatively little importance. The one and only rule for Stephen of Muret was the Gospel of Christ, according to the *Liber de doctrina* or *Liber sententiarum* compiled by his disciples before 1157.

All Christians who live in unity can be called monks, especially those who according to the apostle are more removed from secular affairs and think only about God (2 Tim. 2. 4)... There would be an infinite number of rules if they were made by men, for each of the doctors in his time taught either by speaking or by writing how a person should go to God. If they made a rule, therefore, it could be said: '[There are] as many rules as prophets; as many rules as apostles; as many rules as doctors.'... Whoever holds to the rule of God can be saved, with or without a wife, which cannot be done under the rule of St Benedict; for it is of great perfection, but the rule of

---

[58] Anselm of Havelberg, *Dialogi*, I, 6 and 13, ed. Gaston Salet (Sources chrétiennes, CXVIII; Paris, 1966), pp. 64, 114, 116 (= *PL*, CLXXXVIII, 1148BC, 1159AB, 1160AB). Various scholars have studied Anselm's views on the diversity of religious orders: Schreiber, 'Studien', pp. 55–6; Ernest W. McDonnell, 'The *Vita Apostolica*: Diversity or Dissent', *Church History*, XXIV (1955), pp. 21–2; Kurt Fina, 'Anselm von Havelberg [V]', *Analecta Praemonstratensia*, XXXIV (1958), pp. 13–41; Amos Funkenstein, *Heilsplan und natürliche Entwicklung. Formen der Gegenwartsbestimmung im Geschichtsdenken des hohen Mittelalters* (Munich, 1965), pp. 60–7; Severino, 'Discussione degli "Ordines"', pp. 100–1.

St Basil is of greater perfection. It is all taken from the common rule, however, that is, from the Gospel.[59]

Peter of Celle spoke with approval of the *seminaria* of every type of religious order that were planted by Archbishop Eskil of Lund in his diocese, and he stressed that the differences between monks and canons were *accidentalia*.[60] The Carthusian Adam of Dryburgh condemned the quarrels between religious houses, saying that 'The entire ordained custom of any church is religious and good.'[61] In the early thirteenth century Peter of Blois wrote to the abbot of Evesham: 'All works, devotions, and counsels come down to one thing... The order of the Cluniacs is holy, so is the order of the Cistercians, and the Lord entrusted to both the ministry of reconciliation and the business of salvation. No one should be disturbed', he concluded, in terms resembling those used in the *Libellus* about the diversity of hermits, 'by the diversity of orders among men, for there is order also in the stars.'[62]

James of Vitry gave a classic picture of the pluralistic nature of Christian society in his *Historia occidentalis*, which was completed a few years after the Fourth Lateran Council. 'We consider to be religious', he wrote, using the term in the sense of members of religious houses, 'not only those who renounce the world and go over to a religious life, but we can also call regulars all the faithful of Christ who serve the Lord under the evangelical rule and live in an orderly way under the one highest and supreme Abbot.' He went on to list clerics, priests, married people, widows, virgins, soldiers, merchants, peasants, craftsmen, 'and other multiform types of men', each having its own distinct rules and institutions 'according to the diverse types of talents' and making up collectively the single body of the church.[63] For James the entire body of the faithful was, as it were, a gigantic religious community under the Abbot God. Those dedicated to a formal religious life were no longer at the top of the scale of perfection for James, who said that no religious order or type of life, however strict, was more pleasing to God than the order of priests who cared for the spiritual needs of the faithful.

The author of the thirteenth-century customary of the Augustinian canons of Barnwell shared this view, without going as far as James of Vitry. There

---

[59] *Scriptores ord. Grand.*, pp. 5–6. See also the references in n. 24 above.
[60] Peter of Celle, Ep. I, 20, in *PL*, CCII, 423AB, and *De disciplina claustrali*, II, *ibid.*, 1103D–1104B.
[61] Adam of Dryburgh, Sermon 3, in *PL*, CXCVIII, 464D–465A.
[62] Peter of Blois, Ep. 97, in *Opera omnia*, ed. J. A. Giles, 4 vols. (Oxford, 1847), I, p. 306.
[63] James of Vitry, *Historia occidentalis*, XXXIV, ed. John F. Hinnebusch (Fribourg, 1972), pp. 165–6. See Joseph Greven, *Die Anfänge der Beginen* (Vorreformationsgeschichtliche Forschungen, VIII; Münster West., 1912), pp. 201–2, and McDonnell, '*Vita Apostolica*', pp. 21–2.

were many paths to the celestial Jerusalem, he said, of which some were stricter and some less strict. The important thing was for men to persevere in the calling to which God summoned them. 'Let those who lead a religious life learn, not only these and those but also all and each, of whatever habit or profession, province or region, dignity or order; let them learn, I say, and keep to the straight way that leads to the city, not to vanity but the way of his calling to which the Holy Spirit calls him.' The author went on to describe, among these ways, the one by which the regular canons walked to the city.[64]

In the course of the twelfth century there was thus a dramatic change in social and religious values. The monastic life came to be regarded as only one, and not necessarily the best, way to salvation. The acceptance of the legitimacy of various callings opened the way for the emergence of new ideals of religious life. Some of these developed within and to some extent at the expense of the older institutions but did not replace them, and eventually, like the Cistercians, conformed to their standards. Others, like the regular canons and later the mendicant orders, challenged the older scale of values and prepared the way for an age of pluralism which accepted not only various forms of religious life but also diversity of belief, which was seen as essential for the instruction and purification of true believers and, later, as a social ideal in itself.[65]

This development can be traced in the successive versions of the story of the three rings, which first appeared in a sermon of the thirteenth-century Dominican preacher Stephen of Bourbon, where the true ring won the legitimate daughter her rightful inheritance.[66] In the *Gesta Romanorum* the ring belonging to the third son represented Christianity and proved its authenticity by performing various miracles, but the similar rings belonging to the two older brothers, and representing Judaism and Islam, were not without value, since God the Father gave land to the Jews and power to the Saracens.[67] The rings in *The Decameron*, a century after their first appearance, were indistinguishable, like the three religions they represented. 'Each of them considers itself the legitimate heir to His [the Father's] estate', said Boccaccio;

[64] John Willis Clark, *The Observances in Use at the Augustinian Priory of S. Giles and S. Andrew at Barnwell, Cambridgeshire* (Cambridge, 1897), pp. 32–5.

[65] See Herbert Grundmann, 'Oportet et haereses esse', *Archiv für Kulturgeschichte*, XLV (1963), pp. 129–64, and C. N. L. Brooke, 'Heresy and Religious Sentiment: 1000–1250', *Bulletin of the Institute of Historical Research*, XLI (1968), pp. 115–31, esp. 121–3.

[66] A. Lecoy de la Marche, *Anecdotes historiques, légendes et apologues tirés du recueil inédit d'Etienne de Bourbon* (Société de l'histoire de France; Paris, 1877), pp. 281–2, no. 331. See Stith Thompson, *Motif-Index of Folk-Literature*, 2nd edn, 6 vols. (Bloomington, Ind. – London, 1975), IV, pp. 40–1, nos. J462.3.1f.

[67] *Gesta Romanorum*, ed. Hermann Oesterley (Berlin, 1872), pp. 416–17, no. 89.

'each believes it possesses His one true law and observes His commandments. But as with the rings, the question of which is right remains in abeyance.'[68]

The acceptance of a variety of forms of religious life in the twelfth century did not mean that all types of life were regarded as equally valuable. Many of the writers cited in this article had firm views about the respective merits of the religious houses and orders about which they were writing. Peter the Venerable defended the Cluniacs and old black Benedictine monasticism; Bernard of Clairvaux was the champion of the Cistercians; and Anselm of Havelberg, of the regular canons. Yet each in his own way was ready to accept, and even to praise, the others. By the early thirteenth century the old monastic order had lost its consciousness of unity as well as its position of superiority and had been replaced by a multiplicity of religious orders representing different ideals of Christian life on earth. The confusion which the Fourth Lateran Council hoped to avert by prohibiting new religious orders already existed, and it had already changed the view of monasticism and of its role in the church and in society generally.

[68] Giovanni Boccaccio, *The Decameron*, I, 3, tr. G. H. McWilliam (Harmondsworth, 1972), pp. 86–7. See A. C. Lee, *The Decameron, Its Sources and Analogues* (London, 1909), pp. 6–13, citing other versions in vernacular literature and earlier secondary works on this tale.

The churches of medieval Cambridge[1]

C. N. L. BROOKE

There can be few cities and universities at once so parochial and so cosmopolitan as Cambridge. That is my excuse for taking a piece of local history both to illustrate the entanglement of city and church in the middle ages – the intimate links between urban and ecclesiastical history – and to do homage to a citizen of Cambridge, Master, Professor, priest, Doctor of

The following abbreviations are used in this chapter:

Brooke and Keir	C. N. L. Brooke and G. Keir, *London 800–1216: The Shaping of a City* (London, 1975).
KH	David Knowles and R. N. Hadcock, *Medieval Religious Houses, England and Wales* (London, edn. of 1971).
Lobel	(*Atlas of*) *Historic Towns*, II, ed. M. D. Lobel and W. H. Johns (London, 1975), Fascicule on Cambridge.
OMT	*Oxford Medieval Texts.*
PCAS	*Proceedings of the Cambridge Antiquarian Society.*
RCHM, Cambridge	*An Inventory of the Historical Monuments in the City of Cambridge*, 2 parts, Royal Commission on Historical Monuments (England) (London, 1959).
VCH Cambs	*The Victoria Histories of the Counties of England: A History of the County of Cambridge and the Isle of Ely*, esp. III, *Cambridge*, ed. J. P. C. Roach (London, 1959).
Venn	J. Venn, *Biographical History of Gonville and Caius College*, III (Cambridge, 1901).
Willis and Clark	R. Willis and J. W. Clark, *The Architectural History of the University of Cambridge and of the Colleges of Cambridge and Eton*, 4 vols. (Cambridge, 1886).

[1] I have been much helped in the preparation of this paper by Mrs Alison Bennett, Professor R. B. Dobson, Mrs Catherine Hall, Dr Roger Highfield, Dr Damian Leader, Dr Roger Lovatt, Mrs Dorothy Owen, Dr Miri Rubin-Ungar and Dr Patrick Zutshi; and I am deeply grateful to the editors for their help and encouragement, and for the opportunity to join in this act of grateful and affectionate homage. A version of this essay was given as a lecture in the Lilley–Pennsylvania Programme at the University of Philadelphia, and I owe warm thanks also to Professor Edward Peters and Dr Thomas Waldman.

Divinity and historian, whose scholarly fame has spread throughout the known world.

Any attempt to make sense of the history of Cambridge in the middle ages must keep the churches constantly in view. The city stands where the Roman Road from Colchester was joined by the medieval road from Trumpington, as it headed for the river, across it and on towards Huntingdon. The true main street of Cambridge in the middle ages ran from the Trumpington Road along the old High Street of Cambridge, which now has many names from Trumpington Street to St John's Street, along Bridge Street, across the bridge, 'the one bridge that gives name to a County', in Maitland's phrase,[2] and up Castle Hill past the castle. On this relatively short stretch of road (about one mile in length) there were twelve parish churches in the thirteenth century, and elsewhere in Cambridge two or three more.[3] Most of these churches were founded between the tenth and the twelfth centuries, and they illustrate better than any other surviving evidence the areas of growth, the prosperity and something of the sentiment of the town in this period. For the twelfth and thirteenth centuries the religious houses perform the same function – the nuns of St Radegund, whose ample enclosure still keeps their successors, Jesus College, surrounded by some 10 acres of garden and grass almost in the heart of the city; the canons of Barnwell further out; the short-lived canons of the Holy Sepulchre in the centre, whose church survives as a monument to the crusading era; the Hospital, now college of St John's, in the Jewry, founded about 1200 to be the centre of social welfare in the town. To these were soon added the houses of friars; for all the four main orders, and one or two others, were established in Cambridge in the thirteenth century, and three of them set a mark on its topography which can still be discerned. Finally, from the late thirteenth century on came the colleges. It has often been disputed whether they were in origin educational or religious institutions; but in truth we understand nothing of the inwardness of the early colleges if we do not try to grasp that they were both combined – this has given them the name of college, and the inextricable union of learning and devotion enabled them to survive. Cambridge was never a large town in the middle ages; but it was unusually rich in the variety of its churches, and these in their turn are exceptionally important to the understanding of its history.

One of the notable changes in the study of medieval urban history in recent decades has been a much closer interest in the churches of medieval cities. I take as symbol of this the career of one of the most eminent European historians of the society and economy of the medieval town, Cinzio Violante,

2 F. W. Maitland, *Township and Borough* (Cambridge, 1898), p. 37.
3 For details of parish churches and religious houses, see Appendix.

whose early work comprises above all the social and political history of Milan and other Italian cities, and who has been led by the nature of the evidence and the nature of the task from the secular structure of the cities to their churches – and so to become one of the foremost ecclesiastical historians of our day.[4] My own interests have moved in the other direction: it was the contrast between the immense cathedral of St Paul's and the almost innumerable parish churches which flocked about it in medieval London which first revealed to me the intimate link between parish churches, parish boundaries and settlement patterns in the growing towns of eleventh- and twelfth-century Europe – which Gillian Keir and I studied in our book on *London 800–1216*.[5] In London there were 99 parishes within the city walls; their average size was less than $3\frac{1}{2}$ acres. This is an extreme example of an English phenomenon now well known. The studies of Martin Biddle, Derek Keene and their colleagues at Winchester have transformed our knowledge of medieval towns and shown above all how archaeological and documentary evidence can combine to reveal the pattern and shape of a medieval city and its growth.[6] Winchester was larger than Cambridge, a royal city of some prestige; but never a place which we should recognise as large. Yet it had about 50 parish churches at the height, in the thirteenth century. Similar figures have been calculated for York, Lincoln, Norwich and a number of other towns;[7] and what is especially remarkable is that these were parish churches. In the same period the Italian cities large and small revived and grew on a scale which far outshone the English; and in many of them the citizens, however anti-clerical they pretended to be, lavished their resources on church-building. But the great baptisteries which were often rebuilt in this epoch remind us that virtually all the babies of Pisa or Florence were baptised in the baptistery, not in a font in a small parish church;[8] and in many

---

4 See esp. C. Violante, *Studi sulla Cristianità medioevale* (Milan, 1972), pp. xxiii–xxxii – appreciation by J.-F. Lemarignier and A. Vauchez.

5 Brooke and Keir, esp. chap. 6; cf. Brooke in *A History of St Paul's Cathedral*, ed. W. R. Matthews and W. M. Atkins (London, 1957), pp. 1–99, 361–5.

6 See esp. *Winchester Studies*, II, ed. D. J. Keene, *Survey of Medieval Winchester* (Oxford, 1984); *Winchester Studies*, I, ed. F. Barlow, M. Biddle, D. J. Keene *et al.*, *Winchester in the Early Middle Ages* (Oxford, 1976), chap. IV; M. Biddle and D. Hill, 'Late Saxon planned towns', in *Antiquaries Journal*, LI (1971), pp. 70–85.

7 See C. N. L. Brooke, 'The missionary at home: the church in the towns, 1000–1250', in *Studies in Church History*, VI (1970), pp. 59–83, esp. pp. 66–79 and references; cf. J. Campbell, 'The church in Anglo-Saxon towns', in *Studies in Church History*, XVI (1979), pp. 119–35, esp. pp. 126–30.

8 See C. N. L. Brooke, 'The medieval town as an ecclesiastical centre', in *Medieval Towns, Their Archaeology and Early History*, ed. M. W. Barley (London, 1977), pp. 459–74, esp. pp. 461, 465; E. Cattaneo, 'Il battistero in Italia dopo il Mille', in *Miscellanea G. G. Meersseman*, I = *Italia Sacra*, XV (Padua, 1970), pp. 171–95.

of these towns there was to all intents and purposes only a single parish down to the twelfth century.[9] Large churches, monastic churches and tiny oratories proliferated in Italy as elsewhere, but there was nothing parallel to the proliferation of tiny parishes in England, nor on any comparable scale in other parts of northern Europe either. This makes the English parish churches of special value. We may not be able to analyse all the reasons why they multiplied.[10] Scandinavian influence has been conjectured; but towns with many churches spread far outside the Danelaw. Parishes seem to have multiplied in towns at a time when ecclesiastical authority was weak, but this does not readily explain why York and Canterbury and London and Winchester should all bear witness to the phenomenon. However it be explained, the fact seems clear: in many English cities, including Cambridge, groups of citizens, or a landowner in league with his tenants and neighbours, built little proprietary churches, and the parishes represented the community which supported and built the churches – which were in their turn the social centre, the status symbol, of their communities, as well as the centre of cult and devotion. From St Peter without Trumpington Gate (now Little St Mary's) to All Saints by the Castle, long since departed, we can trace a pattern of churches and dedications which shows Cambridge to be character-istic of such towns. In Cambridge, All Saints, St Mary, St Peter and St Andrew claimed two churches each; St John the Baptist, Holy Trinity, St Michael, St Benedict, St Clement, St Edward King and Martyr and St Botolph, one. In London, including the suburbs, there were fourteen dedi-cated to St Mary alone, ten to All Saints or All Hallows, seven to St Michael, five to St Peter, four each to St Benet and St Botolph, three to St Andrew.[11] Of the saints most popular in London, only Olaf is missing from Cambridge. With St Bride he represents the Viking element there; and in Cambridge we have another favourite Viking dedication in St Clement, who, though an early Pope, spread his churches all over Scandinavia.[12] Some of these saints were universally popular, some were not. If we cast our eyes, as did many twelfth-century Englishmen, to St James of Compostela in the north of Spain, we should find churches to Mary, Michael, Peter, Benedict and the Holy Trinity; we should find churches to St Martin and above all the

9 This simplifies a complex story still only partially unravelled.
10 For first attempts see Brooke (n. 7); Campbell (n. 7); Brooke and Keir, chap. 6.
11 See list in Brooke and Keir, p. 123, cf. p. 138n. on dedications; F. Arnold-Foster, *Studies in Church Dedications*, 3 vols. (London, 1899) remains the basic tool.
12 For St Bride and St Olaf, see Brooke and Keir, pp. 139–42; for St Clement, E. Cinthio, 'The churches of St Clemens in Scandinavia' in *Särtryck ur Res Mediaevales Ragnar Blomqvist...oblatae = Archaeologia Lundensia*, III (Karlshamn, 1968), pp. 103–16 (cf. *idem* in *Acta Visbyensia*, III (Visby, 1969), pp. 161–9), correcting Brooke and Keir, p. 141n.

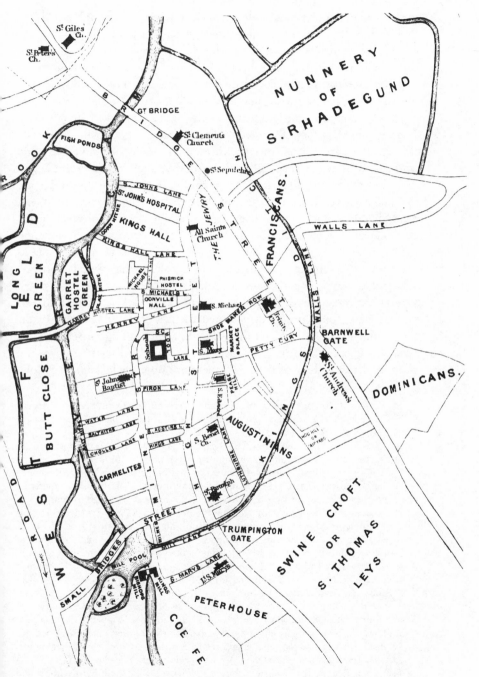

Cambridge before the colleges, from Willis and Clark, IV, Plan I

great cathedral of St James, both of which were represented in London; we should find three more not represented (so far as I know) in any English city.[13] The churches of Cambridge thus have highly conventional dedications; but they take us the more surely back into that strange world in which tiny communities, sometimes sustained by a rich citizen or a lord from outside the town, built a parish church every hundred yards or so.

We can rarely date the foundation of any of these churches with precision. But we know that they all existed by the thirteenth century, and the formation of their parishes, and the pattern they formed in later times, strongly confirm the view that they reflect above all the pattern of settlement before the cold hand of canon law froze the parish maps of most of England in the mid and late twelfth century.[14] Much change could have taken place in later times; but under the palimpsest revealed to us by the earliest surviving parochial map of c. 1800 we can discern a pattern which shows its medieval origin clearly enough.[15] Most of the churches lay by or near the High Street and its northern extension, and the parishes spread about this central highway, taking streets and junctions, not as boundaries but as centres – they form natural communities not created by the artificial hand of the map-maker, such as were, for example, the planned parishes of New Salisbury of the thirteenth century.[16] Away to the west, between the High Street and the river, lay a grid of streets now partly obliterated by King's College, and close by the west door of King's Chapel once stood the church of St John

---

[13] Sts Susanna, Felix (presumably the Roman martyr, not the English Felix), Pelagius. For the churches of Santiago de Compostela see *Le Guide du pèlerin de Saint-Jacques de Compostelle*, ed. J. Vielliard (Mâcon, 1938), pp. 84–7.

[14] See Brooke (n. 7); Brooke and Keir, chap. 6. It is clear that in some towns, such as London, and a great number of country villages, the parish boundaries became fixed in the twelfth and thirteenth centuries – and in the country may reflect much earlier boundaries. There are undoubtedly many towns in which parish boundaries changed substantially in later centuries, especially in those in which the number of churches fluctuated substantially; and this is being shown in detail for Mercian towns in the studies of Mrs Alison Bennett. For Cambridge, see next note.

[15] The Cambridge parish boundaries in the map of c. 1800 are conveniently reproduced in Lobel, Cambridge, map 6. Many of the oddities are due to the relation between urban settlement and open field and the later adventures of tithes, much of which has been elucidated in C. P. Hall and J. R. Ravensdale, *The West Fields of Cambridge* (Cambridge Antiquarian Rec. Soc., III, 1976, for 1974–5): see below, pp. 56–8. But there is a nucleus in the pattern within the area of the city settled in the twelfth and thirteenth centuries which seems very likely to represent a pattern of that age: it shows a natural grouping about the church and the main streets and road junctions, similar to that in London, and suggestive of a natural community of neighbours. Detailed research on medieval evidence may well modify this hypothesis.

[16] See K. H. Rogers, *Salisbury*, in (*Atlas of*) *Historic Towns*, I, ed. M. D. Lobel and W. H. Johns (London, 1969), esp. p. 4 and map 7.

the Baptist, St John Zachary.[17] To the east, along the Roman Road, lay and still lie Holy Trinity and St Andrew the Great; and further west the large expanse of Barnwell Priory territory came later to comprise until the nineteenth century the huge parish of St Andrew the Less. Barnwell was founded soon after 1100. The only other church to which we can give any sort of secure date is St Benet's, whose tower is unlikely to be later than about 1000[18] – and a monument it remains to the wealth and devotion of landlords and burgesses in this part of Cambridge, relatively remote from the original centre of the city on Castle Hill. Beyond it, to the south, just within the Trumpington Gate, lies the church of St Botolph, one of the best-loved saints of pre-Conquest East Anglia. But there is some reason to think that Botolph's remarkable interest in town gates belongs to the era of the Norman Conquest, and I am not convinced that our St Botolph's is Anglo-Saxon in origin. In Colchester the Normans built the fine religious house of St Julian and St Botolph just outside one of the gates; and in London four gates boast churches dedicated to him. Of these only one can be securely dated: it is of the early twelfth century, built outside Aldgate by the Canons of Holy Trinity Priory, an offshoot of St Botolph's Colchester, and of it this has been written: 'It cannot be proved, but it seems highly probable, that it was from Colchester priory that the canons took the dedication of their extra-mural church to this East Anglian saint, and from Aldgate that Botolph spread to the other gates of London still untenanted, perhaps also to his very similar situation by the south gate of Cambridge.'[19]

Two of the parish churches have a history of special interest. St Giles in our day is an ugly Victorian church nestling under the Norman castle; but within lie the remains of a small church – moved there from a site a few yards further south – revealing in characteristic form the features of the Saxo-Norman overlap; and documentary evidence dates it to *c.* 1092.[20] It was

[17] St John Zachary was moved by Henry VI to make space for King's. It is clear that a grid of tiny streets and lanes lay about Mill St before the mid-fifteenth century; in the present state of knowledge one cannot know how intensively settled these lanes were, but there was evidently a community to form the parish of St John, and the maps in Willis and Clark suggest a complex history of land settlement and use in the thirteenth and fourteenth centuries.

[18] See the cautious appraisal in H. M. and J. Taylor, *Anglo-Saxon Architecture*, I (Cambridge, 1965), pp. 129–32; a date later in the eleventh century is not impossible. Documentary evidence for the church starts possibly in the late eleventh century (*VCH Cambs*, III, p. 126, citing a thirteenth-century source). It is unfortunate that for Cambridge we have so far had none of the archaeological investigation of churches which has transformed our knowledge of urban churches in many towns, most notably Winchester, London and Lincoln.

[19] Brooke and Keir, p. 146, with discussion of the evidence.

[20] On St Giles, H. M. and J. Taylor (n. 18), pp. 132–4; *Liber memorandorum ecclesie de*

founded by the Lady Hugolina, the pious wife of the Norman sheriff Picot, who features in the records of the local religious houses alternatively as a rapacious persecutor of the monks of Ely and as a devout partner of his wife in founding a small house of canons dedicated to St Giles and St Andrew. Within its modest chancel six canons are said to have worshipped, in somewhat cramped style and uncomfortably close to the soldiers on the hill above. In the early twelfth century St Andrew and the canons moved out of the town to the ample site of Barnwell Priory, which was formed out of the old community of St Giles and rapidly became the largest religious house in Cambridge; from that day on St Giles became a parish church. At some date not long after the First Crusade another group of Augustinian canons regular, belonging to the small and ephemeral order of the Holy Sepulchre, seems to have settled in the churchyard of St George, and to have built about 1130 or so the round church in imitation of the Holy Sepulchre in Jerusalem which still stands where the High Street joined the Roman Road.[21] The canons faded, but their church survived; and has been since the twelfth century, like St Giles, a parish church.

Thus the history of parish churches and religious houses cannot be kept entirely separate, and if we look from the parishes to their tithes, we shall find them even more closely intertwined. Barnwell Priory enjoyed (or at any rate received) the tithes of all the three parishes north and west of the river Cam, St Giles, its own parent and *fons and origo*, St Peter and All Saints by the Castle.[22] The parish of St Giles alone covered most of the west field, most, that is, of what is now west Cambridge. This reflects an intention already implicit in its foundation as a church for canons: its founders reckoned that the canons would have pastoral responsibility for the townsfolk on that side of the river, and also for the castle; and for this they were prepared to pay lavishly by the assignment of tithe. In due course Barnwell Priory also

Bernewelle, ed. J. W. Clark (Cambridge, 1907), pp. 38–42. There are problems about the authenticity of the charters in the Barnwell chronicle which may throw some doubt on the story of its origin; but the history seems to me more plausible than the documents and to fit convincingly both the architectural evidence and the context in eleventh- and twelfth-century fashion and the formation of communities of canons. Cf. *Liber Eliensis*, ed. E. O. Blake (Camden 3rd Series, XCII, 1962), pp. 210–12.

[21] M. Gervers, 'Rotundae Anglicanae' in *Actes du XXIIe Congrès International d'Histoire de l'Art* (Budapest, 1969, publ. Budapest, 1972), pp. 359–76, at p. 363. The identification had occurred to the present writer when contemplating the corrupt list of houses of the canons of the Holy Sepulchre cited by J. C. Dickinson in *Trans. Royal Hist. Soc.*, 5th Series, I (1951), p. 73 and n.

[22] Hall and Ravensdale (n. 15), p. 76; below, p. 72. The normal process by which religious houses received tithes – i.e. the major tithes, one third being reserved for the vicar where one was needed – was appropriation, by which the bishop made the religious house the rector of the parish: for details see Appendix.

absorbed what was left of the little priory of Holy Sepulchre, taking the advowson and apparently the tithes; and they acquired for a time the advowson of St Botolph's, until they were overtaken there by the rising tide of another remarkable civic institution, Corpus Christi College.[23] There has been much dispute as to how effectively monks and canons of the eleventh to the thirteenth centuries performed the pastoral work of the numerous churches which came into their charge.[24] On the one hand, the logic of the movement which brought them so many churches, and the readiness of pope and hierarchy to allow them to receive tithe, make clear that it was widely assumed that they represented a powerful force in the pastoral movements of the age. On the other hand, there was a steady flow of reforming legislation and propaganda which reminded monks – and in due course canons regular too – that their place was in the cloister, that they should be inward looking, given to prayer not to preaching or to serving the outer world. The size and beauty of the naves of numerous monastic churches demonstrate that the church and the world were expected to meet there in the eleventh and twelfth centuries, even more perhaps than later.[25] But there is also abundant evidence that as the twelfth century went on, and passed into the thirteenth, monks became too devout, or too idle, or too superior, to engage in pastoral work themselves. By a curious irony, the canons, whose institutions were formed to give them a destiny clearly different from monks – more outward looking, more closely linked to the world and the parish – rapidly became assimilated to monks. Even in the early twelfth century the canon of Liège who wrote the fascinating comparison between different orders, the *Libellus de diuersis ordinibus*, reckoned there was more difference between communities living in town and country than between communities of monks and canons.[26] The impulses and practices of the Cistercians and the Premonstratensians, two of the most notable orders

[23] Hall and Ravensdale, pp. 78–9; below, p. 71.
[24] See U. Berlière in *Revue Bénédictine*, XXXIX (1927), pp. 227–50, 340–64; G. Constable, *Monastic Tithes* (Cambridge, 1964), esp. pp. 145ff; D. J. A. Matthew, *The Norman Monasteries and Their English Possessions* (Oxford, 1962), esp. pp. 51–65; M. Chibnall in *Journal of Eccl. History*, XVIII (1967), pp. 165–72; Brooke in *Studies in Church History*, VI (1970), p. 82n. Dr Chibnall's cautious warning against reading too much into the evidence was shrewd and salutary; but the implication of Constable's work on tithes and of the design of monastic churches – especially their large naves – is that some form of monastic pastoral work in parishes and the mingling of the laity in monastic churches and services was taken for granted in this period – even though the tide of reforming propaganda against both was also flowing strongly.
[25] Cf. R. and C. Brooke, *Popular Religion in the Middle Ages, Western Europe 1000–1300* (London, 1984), esp. pp. 88–90. But in the later middle ages there were steps taken to exclude the laity even from the naves of some Benedictine houses.
[26] Ed. G. Constable and B. Smith (*OMT*, 1972).

of reformed religious of the age, were very close, far closer than those of many other orders; yet the Cistercians were monks with the literal observance of the Rule of St Benedict as the essence of their call; the Premonstratensians were canons founded by St Norbert the missionary, one of the great pastoral leaders of the twelfth century. If the fashion for the inward-looking religious life brought them close together, in spite of the very real differences between the rules of Benedict and of Augustine which inspired their lives, they were sometimes brought together by more worldly tastes, like Chaucer's 'monk', who seems to have been deliberately sketched with features of both monk and canon, who scorns impartially the precepts of Benet and Austin, and whose hearty love of hunting (we are given to understand) might be appropriate to any religious of his kind.[27] If we ask the question what did the canons of Barnwell actually do in return for the tithes they received, we shall receive no clear answer.[28] In principle they ought to have done both everything and nothing, for the impulses and rules of the age demanded both of them; in practice we may conjecture – and it can be no more than conjecture – that they did much in 1150, little in 1300. Even more obscure must be the role of the nuns of St Radegund, who were founded in the mid-twelfth century and so were able to receive a splendid enclosure close to the heart of the city, which explains the great area of grass and trees which now comprises Jesus College.[29] They also received the tithes of St Clement's and All Saints Jewry; and their precinct enjoyed parochial rights, at least from the mid-thirteenth century, so that the nave of their church, that part of Jesus College Chapel which is now buried in the Master's Lodge, was their parish church.

The Jewry was evidently the business centre of the city, and lay where the two great roads meet; and here about 1200 the citizens and the bishop joined to found the Hospital of St John.[30] Just as St Radegund's was swept aside about 1500 by the bishop of Ely to make way for a college, so a few years later St John Fisher, bishop of Rochester and Chancellor of the University, collaborated with the Lady Margaret Beaufort, mother of King Henry

---

[27] Cf. C. Brooke and W. Swaan, *The Monastic World, 1000–1300* (London, 1974), pp. 133–4.

[28] See in general n. 24; on the canons regular, see J. C. Dickinson, *The Origins of the Austin Canons and Their Introduction into England* (London, 1950), chap. VI, which represents, perhaps, a minimal view, but rightly emphasises the paucity of evidence.

[29] *VCH Cambs*, II (1948), pp. 218–19; A. Gray, *The Priory of St Radegund, Cambridge* (Cambridge Antiquarian Soc., Octavo Series, XXXI, 1898), esp. pp. 20–4; Hall and Ravensdale (n. 15), p. 76. Professor R. B. Dobson has pointed out to me that Clementhorpe priory outside the walls of York had a similar enclosure with parochial rights for a community of nuns (see his forthcoming paper). This is a very interesting parallel.

[30] For current studies, see below; cf. meanwhile, *VCH Cambs*, II, pp. 303–4. On the Jewry, *VCH Cambs*, III, pp. 95–6; Lobel, p. 10.

VII, to convert the Hospital into the College of St John.[31] Thus the site and the institution have had a continuous history, and the Hospital's muniments are, with those of St Radegund's, the best preserved among the religious houses of medieval Cambridge – also, it must be said to the shame of generations of Cambridge historians, the most neglected. In recent years the College muniments have been most carefully sorted and catalogued by Mr Malcolm Underwood, and a study of the Hospital in its context, as the centre of the charitable institutions of medieval Cambridge, undertaken by Dr Miri Rubin-Ungar. The Hospital is a very characteristic emanation of the time. One can see a kind of progressive decline in the status and stature of religious endowments over the twelfth and thirteenth centuries, and a corresponding rise in the number of modest gifts and modest institutions. From the royal foundations of the tenth century one passes down through the Cistercian, Augustinian and Premonstratensian houses, mostly founded by substantial landlords, of the twelfth century, to the hospitals of the late twelfth and early thirteenth centuries and so the houses of Friars.[32] What makes the Hospitals especially characteristic of the turn of the twelfth and thirteenth centuries, however, is their place in the urban history of the period, for most of the Hospitals of any port or significance were in towns.[33] After a century of rapid urban growth and expansion, there was evidently a strongly felt need for institutions to handle the multiplying problems of the urban poor and destitute. Hospitals might serve the orphan, the sick, the aged; special diseases like leprosy demanded special institutions, and the delectable leper chapel outside the further gates of Barnwell Priory, along the Newmarket Road, is one of the finest surviving monuments of the twelfth-century care for lepers.[34] But the large Hospital within the walls, like St John's, was essentially a municipal affair – and it was financed by the growing number of moderately wealthy citizens who wished to save their souls and serve their sick or impoverished neighbours with the same money. I have little doubt that the choice of site in the Jewry was deliberate and significant.[35] The medieval Jewish community only existed in Cambridge

---

[31] E. Miller, *Portrait of a College: A History of the College of St John the Evangelist, Cambridge* (Cambridge, 1961), chap. I. A full study of the Lady Margaret and her work for Cambridge has been undertaken by Mr Malcolm Underwood.

[32] See KH; Brooke and Keir, pp. 325–37; for St John's in its context among medieval Hospitals, M. Rubin-Ungar, 'Charitable Activity in the Middle Ages: The Case of Cambridge' (PhD, Cambridge, 1984), provides a store of information; for Cambridge houses, see Appendix.

[33] Brooke and Keir, pp. 325–37.

[34] *VCH Cambs*, II, pp. 307–8; *RCHM, Cambridge*, II, pp. 298–9.

[35] Mrs Rubin-Ungar has shown that the Hospital engaged in a modest form of money-lending; this is one of the indications that one of its functions was to rival the function of the Jewish community. On the Cambridge Jewry, see *VCH Cambs*, III, pp. 95–6.

from the reign of William the Conqueror to the reign of Edward I – the Jews were expelled from Cambridge in the 1270s, before the general exodus of 1290; yet they have left their mark on its topography, and their name survived in several features of the neighbourhood, especially the churches of All Saints and Holy Sepulchre in Jewry, for centuries after they had departed. To put the matter plainly, the city prospered by their financial expertise and the flow of silver they could command, and resented their presence and their religion as the merchants of Venice resented the much more substantial Jewish commu. ·y of Venice; our own world is too full of tragic cases of the expulsions of prospering ethnic minorities for this to occasion us any surprise, however repugnant it may be. Nor must we underestimate the religious element in the Hospital: it is significant that bishop and city collaborated to set up a pious institution which was also a modest Monte di Pietà – a moneylending institution. We cannot prove whether the Christian moneylender lent for interest; it would be naive to suppose it was all charity. But the intent is clear, to establish a symbol and monument of Christian welfare in the heart of Jewry. Its success was no doubt part of the reason why the civic community was able to dispense with the Jews earlier than in other English cities – though the occasion of their departure was a fiat from Queen Eleanor, widow of Henry III.

After the Hospital came the friars, and they swarmed in Cambridge to such an extent that at their height there were no less than six houses.[36] Those which survived to make their mark on the town were naturally the 'orders four' – the Franciscans and Dominicans whose sites are now represented by the post-Reformation, puritan colleges of Sidney Sussex and Emmanuel, the Austin Friars between the Guildhall and Pembroke Street, and the Carmelites by the river, now part of Queens' College.[37] In recent studies of the siting of houses of friars in medieval cities, three kinds of sites have emerged as especially characteristic. First, there is the slum, right in the heart of the city, where the community most needed their services, and where they in turn could be used to help in a modest measure of slum clearance, bringing plumbing to the city centre. Such may have been the Austin Friars, for theirs is the most central site, though it was the Franciscans who organised

---

[36] Below, Appendix; KH, pp. 214–15, 222, 224, 233–4, 239, 241, 247–8, 249; and a seventh, if the Bethlehemite house in Trumpington St referred to by Matthew Paris, *Chronica Majora* (ed. H. R. Luard, Rolls Series, 1872–83, v, p. 631) ever took shape; but probably it was never established; see KH, p. 250.

[37] Below, Appendix; Lobel, map 4; J. R. H. Moorman, *The Grey Friars in Cambridge* (Cambridge, 1952). For the incorporation of the Carmelites in Queens', see the dramatic story revealed by the documents in W. G. Searle, *The History of the Queens' College, Cambridge* (2 parts, Cambridge Antiquarian Soc., 1867–71), I, pp. 222–33.

the laying of the first known water conduit.[38] A second kind of site lies out in a growing suburb, set where land was plentiful and the new populations, not catered for by the existing parishes, would cluster. Such was the site of the Blackfriars, the Dominican Friars, in Cambridge, set well beyond the Barnwell Gate. The third, not certainly authenticated in England but carefully documented in Switzerland and Austria, was the site adjacent to, or overlapping, the city wall – a site which remained officially the property of the civic community, since the Franciscans could hold no property themselves, and which the community could use for its own purposes – to see that the wall was kept in good order and not obscured by a mushroom growth of tiny houses; and the citizens could also use the conventual church as a town hall.[39] When the chapel of the Blackfriars became the dining hall and lecture room of Emmanuel College it is not certain that this was in all points a new function for it. Of the site beside the walls there appear to be classic examples in England in the Greyfriars and the Blackfriars in London, placed in their commanding situation beside Newgate and the river respectively by city fathers and by the king in the mid- and late-thirteenth century.[40] In Cambridge the Franciscans occupied just such a site, and the precincts of Sidney Sussex College today are witness that the friars commanded both sides of the King's Ditch, which in fenny Cambridge served for town wall or rampart.[41]

After the friars came the colleges. They arrived slowly, for the university was fully established before the first college was founded in Cambridge in the late thirteenth century; and it was not until the fifteenth century that there came to be any inkling that one day they might dominate the university: the conversion of Oxford and Cambridge into collegiate universities in which virtually every student and teacher was a member of a college came between 1450 and 1550.[42] Few major changes in the history of our universities

---

[38] Moorman (n. 37), pp. 52–4. For the original site of the Franciscan house, and its removal, see Appendix.

[39] For the sites of Friars' houses, see Brooke (n. 8), pp. 463–5; A. Murray, in *Studies in Church History*, VIII (1972), pp. 83–106, at pp. 84ff; B. E. J. Stüdeli, *Minoritenniederlassungen und mittelalterliche Stadt, Franziskanische Forschungen*, XXI (Werl/Westf., 1969). Cf. Brooke and Keir, pp. 336–7.

[40] Brooke and Keir, pp. 336–7; Brooke (n. 8), pp. 468–70; A. R. Martin, *Franciscan Architecture in England* (Brit. Soc. of Franciscan Studies, 1937), pp. 176–204; W. A. Hinnebusch, *The Early English Friars Preachers* (Rome, 1951), pp. 20–55.

[41] On the King's Ditch, Lobel, p. 5 and map 4. When Great St Mary's was under reconstruction in the late fifteenth century the Franciscan church was used for university gatherings; D. Leader, 'The Study of Arts in Oxford and Cambridge at the end of the Middle Ages', (Univ. of Toronto PhD thesis, 1981), p. 27.

[42] See below, p. 68; *VCH Cambs*, III, *passim*, esp. p. 189; Leader (n. 41), p. 112; A. B. Emden in *Medieval Learning and Literature: Essays Presented to R. W. Hunt*, ed. J. G. A. Alexander and M. T. Gibson (Oxford, 1976), pp. 353–65.

have been less understood; the history of this great transference of influence and authority has yet to be written; and one reason for this is that the fashion has been to treat the history of colleges as part of the history of education. Lip-service is always paid to the religious intent of college founders; no one denies that most or all of them were chantries as well as centres of study and learning; but the question is often put – were they primarily educational or religious institutions? – and the answer almost invariably implies, educational.[43] There are many reasons for this, of which two stand out. In the past college histories were the work of pious alumni, who looked back from their own day and assumed more continuity of purpose than actually existed. In some respects the Reformation made little difference to most colleges; but it abolished the whole principle and idea of the chantry. Colleges remained monuments to their founders and benefactors, and benefactors' services and memorials of various kinds provided the appearance of continuity even in this regard. To the outward eye, King's Chapel is no less a monument to Henry VI and Henry VIII, no less a plea to God for mercy on the saint and the sinner (to simplify a remarkable contrast in human character), than when it was built.[44] But within, there was a real difference. Prayers for the dead had to cease after the Reformation; in recent times they have returned, and we are the less aware of how great the difference was in the sixteenth century. Many of the fellows of medieval colleges were chantry priests as well as students, and this profoundly affected their outlook and way of life. The difference comes out most clearly if we compare William of Wykeham's two foundations, the colleges of St Mary of Winchester in Winchester itself and in Oxford, New College.[45] In both the Chapel is integral and very large; the chantry element was evidently substantial. The founder was a man of immense ability and generosity, well aware of what he himself lacked in piety and learning; like many great patrons, he had a real sympathy for what he patronised, but little understanding of it. His visits to his foundations were rare.[46] Perhaps he knew as little of prayer as he did of learning. But he was

43 This seems implicit even in the admirable studies of A. B. Cobban of *The King's Hall within the University of Cambridge*... (Cambridge, 1969), esp. p. 18, and of *St Catharine's College, Cambridge, 1473–1973*, ed. E. E. Rich (Cambridge, 1973), pp. 1–32, esp. pp. 7–13, which after paying fair tribute to the founder's desire to have a chantry firmly sets a more academic purpose in the foreground.

44 *VCH Cambs*, III, pp. 376–9, 385–91 (J. Saltmarsh); *RCHM, Cambridge*, I, pp. 98–104 (A. R. Dufty).

45 See esp. J. Harvey in *Winchester College: Centenary Essays*, ed. R. Custance (Oxford, 1982), pp. 77–93; *New College, Oxford, 1379–1979*, ed. J. Buxton and P. Williams (Oxford, 1979), pp. 147–92 (G. Jackson-Stops).

46 There is no evidence that he ever visited Oxford (*New College, Oxford* (n. 45), p. 157). If the itinerary printed by T. F. Kirby in *Wykeham's Register* (Hants Record Soc. 1896–9), II, pp. 621–9, gives a sound guide, he spent a few days only in Wolvesey,

determined that future generations should be taught and trained, that young men without substantial means should find the path to the clerical elite which he had found by less satisfactory means. And he was determined that they should repay him by intensive and constant prayer for his soul, without which he (not unreasonably) supposed that his soul's destiny might be doubtful, and at best its sojourn in purgatory excessive. After the Reformation the fellows of New College remained celibate until the late nineteenth century, as in other colleges: they were young academics for the most part, and the college framework provided a natural function for them in the changing Oxford of the sixteenth, seventeenth and eighteenth centuries. At Winchester, with the departure of the chantry, the function of the fellows departed too. Most of the teaching was done by the headmaster and second master, and others came later to be hired; the fellows did a little teaching, and maintained the services, at least in principle; but what use could a protestant college chapel make of a platoon of chantry priests? Furthermore, by a dispensation whose origin is obscure, they were allowed to marry; and very rapidly the fellowships of Winchester became desirable sinecures, and so remained until the nineteenth century – vestigial indicators in a reformed church of one of the pillars of the unreformed.[47]

In the conception of William of Wykeham's foundations education, learning, liturgy and ceaseless prayer for the dead were wholly indistinguishable; and we shall miss the flavour of the medieval college and its founders if we allow them to slip apart. In some prayer figured larger, in some smaller; in none was it absent. The story indeed has many ironies, and the greatest perhaps is its denouement. When Henry VIII had swallowed most of the religious institutions of England, his advisers pointed out to him the wealth of the Cambridge colleges. It is true that the masters and bursars of the colleges stage-managed a visitation designed to prove that they were very impoverished institutions not worth dissolving – leaving a body of evidence which has grievously misled some modern historians not accustomed to the techniques of college bursars.[48] But it must also be true that in his mind's

his palace in Winchester, most years, which would have allowed occasional unchronicled visits to Winchester College. On Wykeham, see esp. P. Partner, 'William of Wykeham and the historians', in *Winchester College* (n. 45), pp. 1–36.

[47] On the nature of the body of fellows of Winchester after the Reformation, see esp. R. Custance, 'Warden Nicholas and the Mutiny at Winchester College', in *Winchester College* (n. 45), pp. 313–48.

[48] The records of the visitation of 1546 are printed in *Documents Relating to the University and Colleges of Cambridge*, I (London, 1852), pp. 105–294. It was in the capable hands of Matthew Parker, John Redman and William May, three of the dominant figures of Cambridge in this era – May was only prevented by death from becoming archbishop of York soon after Parker became archbishop of Canterbury in 1559. See *VCH Cambs*, III, p. 177.

eye he saw King's Chapel and reckoned that his future destiny – his memory on earth and his hopes of heaven – lay with its preservation. And so he left the colleges and indeed enhanced them, and attached his name as founder to Christ Church at Oxford and Trinity at Cambridge; and while preparing the ground which destroyed the English chantries within less than a generation, deliberately saved the colleges so that his own chantries might survive.

There is, however, quite another way to look at the college chapels. The colleges were miniature religious communities, differing from monasteries in that their inmates were secular clergy – some of them, an increasing number, not clergy at all – and that they took vows only of the most temporary character. But the life of the chapel was a central element in the college. If we inspect the chapels which survive, we rapidly find some diversity of design and function. In the thirteenth and fourteenth centuries it was common for college chapels to be combined with parish churches, or, for the most modest foundations, to be a chantry within a parish church. From the mid-fourteenth century and especially from the time of William of Wykeham, it became increasingly common to build chapels within the college complex, and in the fifteenth century chapels and oratories multiplied, until even so modest a foundation as Gonville Hall seems to have had three chapels by the mid-fifteenth century;[49] and from the Reformation on a single, principal college chapel was an almost invariable element in a college until the days of Henry Sidgwick and the agnostic colleges of the nineteenth century. Even today, in the lavishly planned chapel of Robinson College, the most recent in Cambridge, with its magnificent windows by John Piper, we can see some remarkable elements of continuity.

It has usually been supposed that the union of college chapel and parish church was a marriage of convenience, and that it came to an end when the convenience declined. Thus Merton Chapel became entirely satisfactory to the fellows of Merton as the parishioners of the ancient parish of St John declined, and the nave was never built;[50] whereas in its counterpart in Cambridge, St Peter without Trumpington Gate, the church and chapel of

---

[49] See Appendix: an aisle in St Michael's (probably: see n. 57), its own chapel, and the Master's oratory over the ante-chapel: Venn, III, pp. 155–8; Willis and Clark, I, pp. 190–1; C. Hall and D. A. H. Richmond, in *PCAS*, LXXI (1981), pp. 95–100. The multiplicity of chapels and altars was partly to meet the practical needs of a number of priests; but for a fuller analysis, see below pp. 66–8 .One should recall also the presence of the religious houses, with their many altars, and one monastic college – see Appendix, Buckingham College.

[50] On the conversion of St John's Church into Merton Chapel, see J. R. L. Highfield, *The Early Rolls of Merton College, Oxford* (Oxford Hist. Soc., New Series 18, 1964 for 1963), pp. 63–4, 404–6; for the early chaplains, pp. 74–5. For Little St Mary's see Appendix.

Peterhouse, parishioners and a notable civic guild of St Mary flourished and multiplied, until the church became Little St Mary's. In the end St Peter accepted the wish of his Fellows for greater privacy and, in the seventeenth century, migrated to the new-built chapel within the college court. One has to admit that this account gains some colour from the absence of reference in college statutes to the parochial function.[51] Yet it is well known that college historians cannot live by statute alone; and the buildings themselves cry out against such an interpretation. Merton College Chapel was built in the late thirteenth century to be college chapel and parish church combined, and in the mid-fourteenth the chapel of Peterhouse was rebuilt in close imitation of it; meanwhile Hervey de Stanton, the great royal servant who founded Michaelhouse in Cambridge (now absorbed in Trinity College) performed a similar function with St Michael's Church – save only that he completed the task whereas the other two churches have never been finished. These three churches are prime evidence for the early conception of a college chapel. At Merton a chancel was built so large that it looks on its own much like a later, hall-shaped college chapel – and indeed its strange shape, comprising large chancel, substantial crossing and no nave, appeared entirely satisfactory to William of Wykeham and his architect when they were designing New College Chapel to be part of a large quadrangle, so that New College has a T-shape and an ante-chapel making it not unlike Merton.[52] It is evident from a glance at Merton Chapel and at Little St Mary's that a nave was intended in both cases. At Merton, it is said, the matter was only finally decided when a canny Warden of the sixteenth century sold the land on which the nave should have been built for the foundation of Corpus Christi College next door;[53] and at Peterhouse it was solved by dividing the large chancel into two so that fellows and parishioners could be accommodated in the existing structure. Their history may show some modification of the original interest in combining two functions; but they serve also to emphasise the original intention. The relations of town and gown in Oxford and Cambridge somewhat resemble those of clergy and laity in the Italian cities of the twelfth and thirteenth centuries, where the laity, when

---

[51] For what follows see Appendix. For references to parochial clergy in statutes, see God's House statutes of *c.* 1452 in *Early Statutes of Christ's College, Cambridge*, ed. H. Rackham (Cambridge, 1927), pp. 24–5, owing something perhaps to the reference to chaplains celebrating in the parish church (St John Zachary) in the Clare statutes of 1359 (*Documents Relating to the University and Colleges of Cambridge*, II (London, 1852), pp. 141–3). There are no such references e.g. in early Merton statutes.

[52] A comparison dismissed as superficial by W. Hayter, *William of Wykeham* (London, 1970), p. 49; but an accidental plan like that of Merton Chapel can none the less stimulate an architect's imagination.

[53] Cf. *VCH Oxfordshire*, III, p. 225 and refs. cited.

not engaged in dethroning the bishop, depriving the clergy of all secular authority and murderous anti-clerical riots, were pouring their resources with a lavish hand into building churches and endowing religious institutions of every kind.[54] By the same token, the citizens of Cambridge, who combined in two of their most powerful guilds to found the unique civic college of Corpus Christi in the 1350s, yet turned against their own college and tried to destroy it when the banners of riot and rebellion were raised in the city in 1381 under cover of the Peasants' Revolt.[55] I believe this to be a very significant coincidence.

Thus Merton and Peterhouse made a show of providing for fellows and parishioners alike which did not quite come to fruition. In St Michael's Church in Cambridge we have a more elaborate complex, historically the most interesting parish church in either town. It is almost perfectly square, a shape no doubt partly dictated (as often in urban churches) by the land available for rebuilding a smaller church. Basically, it is a three-aisled church in which the division between nave and choir is only marked by a token chancel arch and a screen; but in this case the screen was uniquely placed so that the chancel is twice the length of the nave. Thus the parishioners had a very small nave and two aisles attached to it; the fellows of Michaelhouse had a large chancel in which their stalls could be placed[56] – and on either side substantial chantry chapels. The chapel in the north aisle apparently became in due course, soon after the middle of the century, a chapel for the fellows of Gonville Hall over the road, and so it remained until a much later date – perhaps, in some measure, until the Reformation.[57] Gonville Hall only slowly acquired its first complete court. The first step was to add to the old houses in which it was first established on its present site a brick-built chapel in the late fourteenth century. The final completion of the court came in the 1430s, when the west end of the chapel was linked to the nearby Master's lodge by a building in two storeys, the lower an ante-chapel, the upper a private oratory for the Master of the College (invariably at this time in practice, though not in law, a priest).[58]

[54] Cf. Brooke and Keir, pp. 5–7, 13.   [55] *VCH Cambs*, III, pp. 8–12, 371.

[56] The present stalls are evidently not original: tradition has it that they came from Trinity, i.e. from the chapel of the other college which preceded Trinity, the King's Hall (*RCHM, Cambridge*, I, p. 286). F. Blomefield, *Collectanea Cantabrigiensia* (Norwich, 1750), p. 43, enshrines a tradition that the scholars of Michaelhouse used the south aisle; but the codicil to Hervey de Stanton's will, quoted by Willis and Clark (III, p. 490 and n.) leaves no doubt that the chancel itself was their choir.

[57] Venn, III, p. 158, who rightly observes that William Somersham's will suggests a close link between Gonville Hall and the chapel of the Annunciation in St Michael's – and this implies that the tradition noted by Blomefield (*loc. cit.*) that the north aisle was used by Gonville Hall may well be correct.

[58] See n. 49.

We enter here into a strange, half-explored world of late medieval devotion. The mass, the eucharist, which in the early church had been in its essence the meeting place of clergy and laity, had become divided into two quite different kinds of ceremony: the large, public, festive mass attended by the laity, and the private mass, the personal meeting of the celebrant and his maker, with at most one or two witnesses present.[59] The practice of daily mass for priests became normal in the tenth and eleventh centuries; by the fifteenth it had entered so deeply into the religious sentiment of the age that many devout priests evidently coveted their own private place in which to celebrate it, just as in yet more recent times, taking advantage often of necessity, it has been regarded by some holy priests as a special privilege to be allowed to celebrate mass in their own houses. We are on the edge here of something very deep in the nature of late medieval devotion; my statement is superficial, but in some sense the search for privacy in worship is a crucial explanation of the proliferating private oratories and chapels and pews – of which the transept pews in Christ's Chapel in Cambridge are outstanding examples not yet clearly explained.[60]

These two phases can be most clearly seen in Corpus Christi College, Cambridge. Here survives in structure, and in many details, the earliest complete, enclosed college court. It is a modest version of the New College court of thirty years later, comprising dining hall, library and staircases of student chambers. For the historian of medieval building it is of exceptional interest since it represents the canonisation of the chamber principle first recorded in surviving structures in the first wing of Mob Quad at Merton, Oxford (early fourteenth century). The substantial private rooms for two or three fellows and scholars were to provide the basic living quarters in Oxford and Cambridge from the fourteenth to the seventeenth centuries, when the Legge and Perse Buildings of Gonville and Caius College were built, in whose attics the young Robert Willis – one of the greatest of nineteenth-century architectural historians – explored and measured them in the description he made of his own college before the attics and the buildings

---

[59] On the theological background to these changes see G. Macy, *The Theologies of the Eucharist in the early Scholastic period* (Oxford, 1984); for the wider context, cf. C. W. Dugmore, *The Mass and the English Reformers* (London, 1958), part I; C. Brooke, *Medieval Church and Society* (London, 1971), pp. 179–82.

[60] See *RCHM, Cambridge*, I, pp. 28–9; I owe this point to Mr D. A. H. Richmond. Since the upper chambers adjacent to the chapel were, according to the Foundress' statutes, built for her own use and that of the Visitor, the Chancellor and bishop of Rochester, John Fisher, it is conceivable that these 'pews' were built for the use of Foundress and Visitor on formal occasions – to supplement the informal viewing point which can be reached from the Foundress' chambers themselves.

were destroyed by Alfred Waterhouse.[61] But we are exploring Corpus for a chapel and not for its chambers, and in the fourteenth-century court we shall not find one. For the founders intended their college to be a limb and foster child of the city; they intended its fellows and scholars to worship for ever in St Benet's parish church and to foster its life in their turn;[62] and so we have come full cycle, and the youngest and the oldest of our specimens are linked in St Benet's tower presiding benignly over the old court at Corpus.

Thus we have traversed my three stages in the history of a medieval city – the period of creative growth, from the tenth to the twelfth centuries, when the spread of churches and parishes punctuated and in the end remained almost the sole visible evidence of the town's growth to maturity; then the era of religious houses and Hospitals, when a mature community looked to its welfare, spiritual, physical and material; third the age of the colleges, when the spiritual welfare of the citizens and of many external benefactors became entangled in the endowment of academic chantries, which is the best definition of the pre-Reformation Oxbridge college I can muster. This third stage has many parallels abroad, especially in Paris, from which the idea of an academic college sprang;[63] in the precise form and destiny of the academic colleges, it is of course peculiar to Oxford and Cambridge. In this regard they have fossilised a curious feature of the late medieval academic scene – though it would be superficial to suggest that that is the whole truth about them. But there is an epilogue to my story which is really peculiar to Cambridge alone. In both the English universities a strange movement led to the conquest of the universities by the colleges in the period between 1450 and 1550.[64] By the mid-sixteenth century virtually every student and every don was a member of a college. In Cambridge this coincided with the formation of the academic quarter by the river – later completed beyond the river by the great landscape gardening schemes of the sixteenth to eighteenth centuries which we call the Backs. There are few parts of Britain less naturally attractive than Cambridgeshire, few cities more beautiful than Cambridge; and here lies the secret of its beauty. In profane terms, it must be that Cambridge like so many towns declined in population after the Black Death, and the space between the High Street and the river, the complex of lanes about Mill Street, always the least populous of the central areas, sharply

61 Willis and Clark, I, pp. 186–7 (Caius), 250–88 (Corpus); III, pp. 297–327, esp. 305–11 (Caius); cf. RCHM, Cambridge, I, pp. 48–9, 53–7.

62 VCH Cambs, III, pp. 371–3; Willis and Clark, I, pp. 271–3.

63 On the Paris colleges, see esp. A. L. Gabriel, Student Life in Ave Maria College (Notre Dame, 1955) and The College System in the 14th-Century Universities (Baltimore, 1962).

64 See above, p. 61 and n. 42.

declined in population and value. This is the economic explanation – land was cheap.[65] The political explanation is that King Henry VI, by a great act of power, disrupted the whole structure of this part of Cambridge in the mid-fifteenth century to found King's College, shifting a parish church and a grammar school and destroying numerous houses – yet never having the resources to build more than the torso of a college; leaving a great building plot which is now a large expanse of grass.[66]

But that is not the whole story: the economic and political explanations do not explain either in gross or in detail how this remarkable academic quarter was formed. There is a complex history here in which numerous impulses, religious and secular, economic and aesthetic, have made their creative contribution. But we have been concerned with those elements in the history of Cambridge which illustrate widespread phenomena of the European middle ages. What is unique to Cambridge is not my theme.

APPENDIX

This is a list of churches with basic references to standard accounts of their early history and architectural history. The date is in each case the earliest known for the church, doubtless often very much later than the actual foundation. The most substantial early lists of parishes are in the Valuation of Norwich of 1254 and the Hundred Roll of 1279; the latter includes surveys – with all the qualifications modern scholarship has added to them – which are invaluable: *Valuation of Norwich*, ed. W. E. Lunt (Oxford, 1926), pp. 218–19; *Rotuli Hundredorum*, II (Record Commission, 1818), pp. 356–93; for the advowsons of parish churches, pp. 392–3 (1279).

Parish Churches

Chiefly based on H. M. Cam's articles in *VCH Cambs*, III.

All Saints by the Castle: 1219, but gravestones found in nineteenth century of ? c. 975 × 1050. *VCH Cambs*, III, p. 123. Its parish was united with St Giles in 1365, and the church subsequently fell into ruins, which survived at least into the seventeenth century. Tithes to Barnwell Priory after appropriation, 1257 × 64.

---

[65] On Cambridge and other parallel late medieval towns, see Lobel; J. Cooper in *VCH Oxfordshire*, IV, pp. 35–48; Keene, *Winchester Studies*, II (n. 6).
[66] Cf. *VCH Cambs*, III, pp. 376–9, 385–8; and Willis and Clark, I, pp. 317–50, 368–80, 465ff, for details of the process.

69

All Saints by the Hospital or *All Saints Jewry:* 1077 × 93 (*VCH*, ultimately from Matthew Paris, *Gesta abbatum S. Albani*). Appropriated to St Radegund's late twelfth century (prob. 1180, if date correct in A. Gray, *Priory of St Radegund* (Camb. Antiqu. Soc. 1898), p. 91). Demolished 1865. *VCH Cambs*, III, p. 124; *RCHM, Cambridge*, II, p. 254.

Holy Sepulchre Jewry and *St George:* the original grant of the site for Holy Sepulchre in the graveyard of St George (an earlier church of which nothing else is known) and adjacent land is of 1113 × 31. *VCH Cambs*, III, p. 124, citing *Cartularium monasterii de Rameseia*, ed. W. H. Hart and P. A. Lyons (Rolls Series, 1884–93), I, pp. 145–6; M. Gervers in *Actes du XXIIe Congrès International d'Histoire de l'Art* (Budapest, 1969, publ. Budapest, 1972), p. 363; *RCHM, Cambridge*, II, pp. 255–7. Appropriated to Barnwell Priory by mid-thirteenth century.

Holy Trinity: ?1174, cited by *VCH Cambs*, III, pp. 124–5, without reference; occurs 1198 × 1215 (see below). *RCHM, Cambridge*, II, pp. 257–60. The advowson was given to West Dereham Abbey (Premonstratensian) 1198 × 1215 and licence to appropriate 1225 × 8 (H. M. Colvin, *The White Canons in England* (Oxford, 1951), p. 134).

St Andrew the Great: 1200. Appropriated (see n. 22) to Ely Cathedral Priory, 1174 × 89. *VCH Cambs*, III, pp. 125–6; *RCHM, Cambridge*, II, pp. 260–1; Cambridge University Library, Ely Diocesan Records, EDC Bi.1.68 (I owe this reference to Mrs Owen).

St Andrew the Less: a parish covering much of east Cambridge from a date uncertain down to the mid-nineteenth century. The chapel *ad portas* still surviving seems to have served as a parochial chapel. The parish comprised the precinct of Barnwell Priory (see below), and the whole east field of Cambridge which paid tithe to Barnwell. It seems likely that it originally formed simply the Barnwell precinct; when it became a fully fledged parish is not clear. The chapel *ad portas* is thirteenth century; like the priory it seems always to have been dedicated to St Andrew. *VCH Cambs*, III, p. 126; *RCHM, Cambridge*, II, p. 263. (The parish does not appear in 1254 in the *Valuation of Norwich*; it is reckoned a vill separate from Cambridge in 1279, *Rotuli Hundredorum*, II, 393ff; and there was a 'capella de Bernewelle' in 1291, *Liber memorandorum ecclesie de Bernewelle*, ed. J. W. Clark (Cambridge, 1907), p. 201).

St Benet: 1077 × 93, but the tower and tower arch may well be of *c.* 1000, and are certainly eleventh century. Linked to Corpus Christi College from 1352, and appropriated in 1578; also sometimes used by the University. H. M. and J. Taylor, *Anglo-Saxon Architecture*, I (Cambridge, 1965), pp. 129–32; *VCH Cambs*, III, pp. 126–7; *RCHM, Cambridge*, II, pp. 263–6.

St Botolph: c. 1200 (1197 × 1215), when it was appropriated to Barnwell
Priory; the advowson was acquired first by Corpus, then by Andrew
Dockett, the rector of St Botolph's and founder of Queens', to whom the
advowson passed. *VCH Cambs*, III, p. 127; *RCHM, Cambridge*, II,
pp. 266–9 (and Cambridge Univ. Lib. MS. QC 33).

St Clement: c. 1218, though the dedication suggests a Viking origin (see p.
52, n. 12); appropriated to St Radegund's 1220 × 5. *VCH Cambs*, III, pp.
127–8; *RCHM, Cambridge*, II, pp. 269–71.

St Edward King and Martyr: before 1254; but the dedication may suggest an
eleventh-century date; a pre-Conquest coffin is said to have been found
nearby, and the structure goes back to the early thirteenth century (not
twelfth); the advowson was granted to Barnwell in the period 1229 × 54;
in 1446 the parish was amalgamated with St John Zachary (see below) and
appropriated to Trinity Hall. *VCH Cambs*, III, pp. 128–9; *RCHM,
Cambridge*, II, pp. 271–4. The east end was rebuilt in the time of Henry VI
to accommodate chapels for Trinity Hall and Clare lost with St John's.

St Giles by the Castle: built *c.* 1092 (pp. 55–6 and n. 20); the canons transferred to Barnwell 1112, and the church remained a parish church – it was
restored to Barnwell and appropriated 1189 × 97. Taylor, *Anglo-Saxon
Architecture*, I, pp. 132–4; *VCH Cambs*, III, p. 129; *RCHM, Cambridge*, II,
pp. 274–5.

St John Zachary (the Baptist)*:* 1217. It stood on the west side of Milne St,
either under or to the west of the west front of King's Chapel (see
J. Saltmarsh in *VCH Cambs*, III, p. 386 and n. 19). In drought conditions
signs of foundations have been seen west of the chapel, but these have not
been excavated. It was demolished by Henry VI in 1446 and the parish
amalgamated with St Edward's (see above: *VCH Cambs*, III, p. 129). The
college chapels were moved to St Edward's, but St John's was rebuilt by
Henry VI on the site of the present Squire Law Library – perhaps as a
modest chapel of St Edward's. It had disappeared by the mid-sixteenth
century (Saltmarsh *loc. cit.*; Willis and Clark, I, pp. 548–51).

St Mary the Great: 1205 (some twelfth-century ornament *could* come from
another building); appropriated after 1342 to the King's Hall, hence to
Trinity College in the sixteenth century. Its use by the University doubtless goes back to the thirteenth century, and the University organised its
rebuilding in the late fifteenth (from 1478) and sixteenth centuries. *VCH
Cambs*, III, pp. 129–31; *RCHM, Cambridge*, II, pp. 275–80.

St Mary the Less, formerly *St Peter outside Trumpington Gate:* 1207, but it
first occurs in a lawsuit describing the tenure of the church over a period
of well over 100 years, perhaps much longer. It contains fragments of
pre-Conquest masonry. Appropriated to St John's Hospital (1197 × 1215),

transferred to Peterhouse in 1284. It was rebuilt 1340–52 to be college chapel and parish church combined, and the parish church re-dedicated to St Mary in 1352. *VCH Cambs*, III, p. 131; *RCHM, Cambridge*, II, pp. 280–3.

St Michael: 1231; but the plea of that year referring to it, and the Hundred Roll entry of 1279, take the history of its advowson back into the twelfth century. In 1323–5 it was acquired by Hervey de Stanton, rebuilt and appropriated to his new college, Michaelhouse; and the new church was designed, like St Mary the Less, though on quite a different model, to be college chapel and parish church combined; the north choir aisle seems later to have been used as a college chapel by Gonville Hall (see p. 75). *VCH Cambs*, III, pp. 131–2; *RCHM, Cambridge*, II, pp. 284–6.

St Peter by the Castle or *ultra pontem*: ?1217 (see W. E. Lunt, *Valuation of Norwich* (Oxford, 1927), pp. 534–5, 538); it has a door of the twelfth century, another of the early thirteenth, and a twelfth-century font – which could perhaps come from another church. But we have no reason to suppose that it did. It was appropriated to Barnwell, evidently, at an early date, but this is obscure: it 'would appear to have lost its identity as a separate tithe-receiver at an early date' – and in effect to have been linked with St Giles and All Saints by the Castle (see *The West Fields of Cambridge*, ed. C. P. Hall and J. R. Ravensdale (Cambridge, 1976), p. 76). *VCH Cambs*, III, pp. 132–3; *RCHM, Cambridge*, II, pp. 287–8.

Religious houses

Articles in *VCH* are by D. M. B. Ellis and L. F. Salzman.

Barnwell Priory (Augustinian canons): originally at St Giles (see above); founded 1091, for (?) secular canons; became regular and moved to Barnwell early in the twelfth century; the move took place in 1112; dissolved 1538. *VCH Cambs*, II, pp. 234–49; KH, pp. 138, 146; *Liber memorandorum ecclesie de Bernewelle*, ed. J. W. Clark (Cambridge, 1907); *RCHM, Cambridge*, II, pp. 299–300.

Cambridge, St Edmund (Gilbertine canons): absorbing earlier chapel of St Edmund, in site of what is now old Addenbrooke's Hospital; founded 1291, dissolved 1539. *VCH Cambs*, II, pp. 254–6; III, p. 133; KH, p. 197.

Cambridge, St Radegund (Benedictine nuns): founded mid-twelfth century, before 1154; dissolved 1496 for foundation of Jesus College. KH, pp. 253, 257 (dated too early); *VCH Cambs*, II, pp. 218–19; III, p. 421 (J. G. Sikes and Freda Jones); *RCHM, Cambridge*, I, pp. 81–98; A. Gray, *The Priory of St Radegund, Cambridge* (Cambridge Antiquarian Soc., 1898). I am much indebted to Mrs Sally Thompson for advice on St Radegund's.

Friars, Franciscan: founded *c.* 1226 in the synagogue beside 'the house of Benjamin the Jew'. The documents quoted by C. P. Hall and J. R. Ravensdale, in *The West Fields of Cambridge* (Cambridge Antiquarian Rec. Soc., III, 1976 for 1974–5), pp. 65, 144, seem to prove that the long-lasting £4 rent of the Mortimer estate was attached in the early-thirteenth century to the messuage of Benjamin, and in the fifteenth to the Tolbooth, and so strongly confirm the view of H. P. Stokes, *Studies in Anglo-Jewish History* (Edinburgh, 1913), pp. 113–14, that the house of Benjamin lay in Butter's Row by the Guildhall where the Tolbooth was later built; and this in turn confirms the view long held that the Friars began in that area and moved later to the site of Sidney Sussex College, which was undoubtedly their final destiny. Without this evidence one would have supposed from the documents showing them expanding on their original site in 1238 that they had stayed there, and there is no specific evidence of a move, nor any other secure evidence of Jews by the Guildhall – their ultimate site did indeed lie in or near the Jewry (for the documents of 1238 etc. see A. G. Little, *Franciscan Papers*... (Manchester, 1943), pp. 128–31, and in his first, 1909, edn of *Tractatus Fr. Thomae...de Eccleston De Adventu Fratrum Minorum in Angliam*, pp. 167–8). Presumably the attempts to improve the original site failed and the Friars moved to the site of Sidney Sussex *c.* 1240 or soon after. Their house was dissolved in 1538. See further J. R. H. Moorman, *The Grey Friars in Cambridge* (Cambridge, 1952), chaps. I, III; KH, pp. 222, 224; *VCH Cambs*, II, pp. 276–82.

Friars, Dominican: founded before 1238, dissolved 1538, the site was later used for Emmanuel College. KH, pp. 214–15; *VCH Cambs*, II, pp. 269–76; W. A. Hinnebusch, *The Early English Friars Preachers* (Rome, 1951), p. 89.

Friars, Carmelite: founded in Chesterton, 1247; moved to Newnham, 1249; to Milne St *c.* 1292; dissolved and the site incorporated in Queens' College, 1538–44. KH, pp. 233–4; *VCH Cambs*, II, pp. 282–6; W. G. Searle, *The History of the Queens' College, Cambridge* (2 parts, Cambridge Antiquarian Soc., 1867–71), I, pp. 220–33; Willis and Clark, II, pp. 3–6.

Friars, Austin: founded before 1289; dissolved 1538 (it was on the north side of Pembroke St). KH, pp. 239, 241; *VCH Cambs*, II, pp. 287–90; *RCHM, Cambridge*, II, p. 299; F. Roth, *The English Austin Friars*, I (New York, 1966), pp. 250–3.

Friars of the Sack: founded 1258; dissolved 1307, and the site granted to Peterhouse. KH, pp. 247–8; *VCH Cambs*, II, pp. 290–1.

Friars of the Blessed Mary or Pied Friars: founded 1273 (possibly after a modest start in 1256); dissolved after 1319. KH, p. 249; *VCH Cambs*, II, pp. 286–7.

There is reference to a house of Bethlehemite Friars in 1257, but it is doubtful if it was ever established. KH, p. 250; see above, n. 36.

For Buckingham College, see below. I have not included monastic hostels.

Hospitals

These are now being studied by Miri Rubin-Ungar, to whom I am much indebted: see p. 59 n. 32).

St John the Evangelist: founded *c.* 1200; dissolved 1509–11 and incorporated in St John's College. KH, pp. 316, 349; *VCH Cambs*, II, pp. 303–7. A substantial part of the original hospital buildings was incorporated in the college and survived until the building of the new chapel in 1868–9 (Willis and Clark, II, pp. 296–308).

St Anthony and St Eloy: founded before *c.* 1361 for lepers; apparently an almshouse after 1526. KH, pp. 316, 349; *VCH Cambs*, II, p. 307.

Stourbridge, St Mary Magdalene: founded as a leper hospital chapel, mid-twelfth century; a chapel under a warden by 1279. KH, pp. 333, 395; *VCH Cambs*, II, pp. 307–8; III, pp. 132–3; *RCHM, Cambridge*, II, pp. 298–9.

For vestiges of other hospitals, see KH, p. 349; for other chapels, *VCH Cambs*, III, p. 133.

Colleges (in chronological order) and their chapels, to 1500

Peterhouse: founded 1284, see above, Little St Mary's. The chapel within the precinct is seventeenth century.

King's Hall: founded in (or shortly before) 1317, more effectively 1337. From 1342 Great St Mary's provided a college chapel, and there was some link with the parish church, All Saints Jewry, but an oratory within the college was built at an uncertain date; a new chapel was built *c.* 1464–85, and replaced by Trinity Chapel in the sixteenth century. Willis and Clark, II, pp. 435, 449n., 449–51, 455–8. Cf. A. B. Cobban, *The King's Hall* (Cambridge, 1969), p. 224.

Michaelhouse: founded 1324. See above, St Michael's.

Clare: founded 1326, see above, St John Zachary and St Edward's; but Clare evidently also had a chapel in its own precinct well before 1401: Willis and Clark, I, p. 81.

Pembroke: founded 1347. The first chapel was probably begun *c.* 1355–6, but the earliest firm evidence of its use is in 1398. C. Hall and H. Richmond in *PCAS*, LXXI (1981), p. 96; Willis and Clark, I, p. 135. For the papal licence of 23 March 1355, and the subsequent licence 'to found a chapel with bell and bell-tower' of 6 Aug. 1366, see P. Zutshi, 'Original Papal Letters in England, 1305–1417: A Study and a Calendar' (Cambridge University PhD Thesis, 1981), pp. 401–2, 437, nos. 242, 298).

Gonville and Caius, as *Gonville Hall:* founded 1348, moved to its present site 1353. The chapel was built between *c.* 1354 and 1394; meanwhile a tradition very likely to be correct asserts that the north choir aisle of St Michael's was used by the college. In 1431–41, as part of extensive building work, an oratory for the Master was built over the ante-chapel. C. Hall and H. Richmond in *PCAS,* LXXI (1981), pp. 95–100; Venn, III, pp. 1–17, 155–8; Willis and Clark, I, pp. 157–61, 165–170, 190–7. *RCHM, Cambridge,* I, pp. 74–6. The earliest known evidence relating to the use of St Michael's is in F. Blomefield, *Collectanea Cantabrigiensia* (Norwich, 1750), p. 43 – but for confirmation, see n. 57.

Trinity Hall: founded 1350; the chapel seems to have been built between 1352 and 1366; an aisle in St John Zachary was also used as a college chapel, and this was transferred to St Edward's in the mid-fifteenth century (see above). *RCHM, Cambridge,* II, p. 245; C. W. Crawley, *Trinity Hall* (Cambridge, 1976), pp. 21, 32–3; Willis and Clark, I, pp. 220–2.

Corpus Christi College: founded in 1352 by the Gilds of Corpus Christi and St Mary; from the first St Benet's was used as the college chapel (and some services held in St Botolph's), and the college was later often known as Benet College. When Thomas Cosyn was Master (1487–1515), two oratories were built on the south side of the church, one above the other, and these, and so St Benet's itself, linked to the college by a 'gallery approach.' *RCHM, Cambridge,* I, p. 48; Willis and Clark, I, pp. 271–88; *VCH Cambs,* III, pp. 126–7.

Buckingham College: founded 1428 as a house of studies by Crowland Abbey, in which other monasteries seem to have joined; refounded 1542 as Magdalene College; the original chapel of the late fifteenth century partly survives. The early history was similar to that of Gloucester College, Oxford, whose buildings survive in Worcester College; but the much greater uniformity of Magdalene (even allowing for later changes) suggests that the completion of the first court was planned under the patronage of a notable benefactor, presumably the second Duke of Buckingham, Henry (1460–83), who evidently worked in collaboration with the abbot of Crowland, John of Wisbech. Cf. *VCH Cambs,* III, p. 450 (F. R. Salter); *RCHM, Cambridge,* II, pp. 137–41.

God's House: founded in 1439 primarily for training grammar school masters, moved to make way for King's in 1446 to the present site of Christ's, and refounded by the Lady Margaret Beaufort in 1505 as Christ's College.

On the chapel, see above, p. 67: it is commonly supposed to incorporate God's House Chapel, but there seems little visible indication of any structure earlier than *c.* 1500. Ex inf. H. Richmond; but cf. *RCHM, Cambridge*, I, pp. 25–32, esp. 25–6 and plan facing p. 28; Willis and Clark, II, pp. 192, 205ff; A. H. Lloyd, *The Early History of Christ's College, Cambridge* (Cambridge, 1934), pp. 319–29; cf. also *VCH Cambs*, III, pp. 429–30 (H. Rackham).

King's College: founded 1441, and a first chapel built in the 1440s, collapsed *c.* 1536; the present chapel was built in various campaigns between 1446 and 1515, finally completed in 1538. *RCHM, Cambridge*, I, pp. 98–103, 105–31 (A. R. Dufty); Willis and Clark, I, pp. 317ff, 368–80, 465–534.

Queens' College: founded 1446–8; the original founder and first President, Andrew Dockett, was rector of St Botolph's, and the college acquired the advowson in 1460; but a chapel (1448) was incorporated in the original design for the old court, and is now part of the library. *RCHM, Cambridge*, II, pp. 167–70; *VCH Cambs*, III, pp. 408–10 (R. G. D. Laffan); Willis and Clark, II, pp. 1–13, 36ff.

St Catharine's: founded 1473 by Robert Wodelarke, Provost of King's; his tiny group of buildings fronting Milne Street (Queens' Lane) contained a chapel built in the 1470s, but little is known of it; it was preserved until the new chapel was built (consecrated 1704). Willis and Clark, II, pp. 87–91, 96–7.

Jesus: founded 1496 by Bishop John Alcock, by conversion of the dissolved house of St Radegund (see above); and from the first the nuns' church was used as the college chapel, shorn of its aisles and with part of its nave cut off to form domestic quarters, now all part of the Master's lodge. *RCHM, Cambridge*, I, pp. 81–91; Willis and Clark, II, pp. 115–41.

'True History': Martin Luther and Thomas Müntzer

GORDON RUPP

The year 1984 marks the centenary of the founding in Cambridge of the Dixie Chair in Ecclesiastical History. It is timely to recall that on the memorial in Peterborough Cathedral of Mandell Creighton, the first holder of that office, are inscribed the words 'He tried to write true history.' The tomb, a few yards away, of Katherine of Aragon is a reminder of the problems involved, not least in regard to the history of the Reformation. Creighton's successors, one way or another, have all had to face the daunting business of seeking truth, and may take comfort in a sentence in one of those astonishing sermons of Samuel Johnson 'We cannot make truth: it is only our business to find it.'

If there were good fairies present at the founding of the Dixie Chair, they brought no gifts to the ecclesiastical historian which other historians do not possess, either in qualities of mind – integrity, fairness, balanced judgment – or in the choice of tools or methodology. It is true that from the Acts of the Apostles onward, church history has mostly been written 'from faith to faith', certainly from the time of Bede to Gibbon, though thereafter it seems to have been written more and more by unbelievers. And it might be urged that the church historian is as moved by vested interests of his mind at least as much as the Marxist. But at least he recognizes the church as the ultimate 'Volk' and takes seriously the priorities of belief and action of those who lived in the Christian centuries. Their faith and devotion are not simply a chapter in the history of ideas, and cannot be dismissed as mythology as though there were neither rhyme nor reason in history, no divine purpose undergirding the whole.

The development of Müntzer studies in recent years illuminates the impact of conflicting ideologies on historical writing. After the collapse of the Peasant War, and the execution before Mühlhausen in June 1525 of Thomas Müntzer, he became for Protestants a great bogy man, a Man of Blood, a super Guy Fawkes the mention of whose name caused a shudder to men as different as John Knox and John Wesley. At the root of this was Luther's reading of the story of the man he regarded as an 'arch-Devil' as it was recorded in narratives by Melanchthon and Bullinger. But in this century not only the Lutherans, but the Mennonite historians have been against him, their own non-violent tradition making them regard him as an alien in the early Anabaptist, radical tradition. At the other extreme are the Marxist historians. Their long standing interest in the Peasant Wars in Germany became centred on Müntzer afresh when the heartland of Müntzer and Luther, Thuringia and the Harz mountains became a Communist state. This has certainly not made the task easier for historians in that land. I remember breakfasting in a drab hotel just inside the Berlin wall with Franz Lau, a fine historian and an authority on both Luther and Müntzer, not long before his death and how gloomily he spoke of his difficulties in such a context. Not that Marxist historians themselves think of their historical studies as being in any sense inhibited. For them, what they write is 'true history', and a scientific explanation of the forces operative in history. It is true that the Marxist interpretation has its own complexities and developments. Although the nineteenth-century views of Engels and Zimmerman are treated with reverence[1] there have been changes in their interpretation of the Peasant War and Müntzer's role in it. In 1960 Max Steinmetz could still conceive of Müntzer as the true spiritual ancestor of the much discussed 'frühbürgerliche Revolution' – the 'konsequentesten Ausdruck der Volksreformation in Deutschland'.[2]

More recently, as the quincentenary Luther celebrations have made plain, Müntzer has been relegated as the great failure, while Luther becomes once more the man who set free the forces which ultimately led to the socialist revolution. (The spirit of Müntzer might wryly comment that once again he had been betrayed by the comrades in the interest of their own 'Eigennutz'.) Although there have been some Marxist historians who have tried to reckon with Müntzer's theology (Zschäbitz, Smirin, Bensing) there has been no real admission of its importance and it has generally been half-hearted, while it is seen at best as an operative mythology irrelevant to the primary consideration of his social and political teaching. None the less, there has been real discussion, and a flow of learned articles about Müntzer in Eastern Germany continues.[3]

[1] Abraham Friesen, *Reformation and Utopia: The Marxist Interpretation of the Reformation and its Antecedents* (Wiesbaden, 1974).
[2] *Die frühbürgerliche Revolution in Deutschland*, ed. Gerhard Brendler (Berlin, 1961), ch. 1, p. 15.
[3] A useful introduction to recent studies is the anthology of essays: *Thomas Müntzer*, eds. Abraham Friesen and Hans-Jürgen Goertz (Darmstadt, 1978). See also articles and reviews by S. Bräuer in the *Luther-Jahrbuch*, 1978, 1979, 1981.

Between such contrary winds of doctrine as those of Lutherans, Mennonites and Marxists the English student may find it difficult to stand upright, and rather like the Irishman who meeting a street brawl asked 'Is this a private fight, or can anybody join in?' But at least he has no confessional axe to grind if, in comparison, his curiosity seems but feeble motivation.

But it has not been by any means all polemically conditioned. Two church historians of eminence, Karl Holl and Heinrich Böhmer, gave a new depth to the enquiry by recognizing the originality and depth of Müntzer's thought and directing attention to Müntzer's writings. In recent decades Günther Franz has provided a much handier tool than was previously available in an up-to-date and critical edition of Müntzer's writings and letters.[4] Walther Elliger's massive biography and his not to be neglected shorter essay may have its limitations (his running battle in the footnotes with the Marxists has provoked an opposite irritation) but it is a careful, blow by blow account and surely demonstrates that it is quite impossible to understand Müntzer apart from his religion, his theology and, indeed, his liturgies.

In this essay I wish only to comment on two questions which arise from recent discussions: in what sense was Müntzer ever a follower of Luther, a 'Martinian'?; and when did he cease to be one?

The young scholar Thomas Müntzer like many other contemporaries who later differed from Luther (Ulrich Zwingli, Oecolampadius, Bucer) began by hailing him as a champion at the beginning of the great church struggle. We know that Müntzer followed developing events closely (he was present at the Leipzig disputation of 1519) and he seems to have read most of the pamphlets in the debate between Luther, Karlstadt and John Eck. He welcomed Luther's onslaught on the Roman church, and on the tyranny of the church in Germany, and in association with other 'Martinians' like Günther, he took part in confrontation with the Franciscans. He fully shared Luther's antagonism to Popery. In his last terrible invective against Luther he unexpectedly conceded that Luther, like Saul, had made a good beginning. In all this he shared the common cause of the Reformation. It is noticeable that his intimate family friend, Hans Pelt of Halberstadt, in 1521, in the letters he wrote when Müntzer was in Prague, brought Thomas the latest news about Luther, and gave some account of his most recent writings.[5]

It is true that until the spring of 1523 Müntzer tried to keep up some kind of friendly relationship with Wittenberg, but before that date it was already clear that his gospel had a different shape from that of Luther. For if on his

---

[4] Gunther Franz, *Thomas Müntzer, Schriften und Briefe* (= *Quellen und Forschungen zur Reformationsgeschichte*, XXXIII) (Gütersloh, 1968). W. Elliger, *Thomas Müntzer, Leben und Werk* (Göttingen, 1975).

[5] Franz, *op. cit.*, letters nos. 26 and 28 on pp. 373, 377.

way to Prague he seems to have debated Melanchthon's own B.D. Theses, one must agree with Gottfried Maron that the whole of Müntzer's theology underlies his appeal to the Bohemians in his apocalyptic Prague Manifesto. Martin Schmidt saw a deep affinity with Luther in that both men had a 'Word of God' theology. This was, of course, a Biblical concept, and the Fourth Gospel in which it is prominent meant much to both men. But although Müntzer speaks of the Eternal and the Created Word, it is the Living Word which addresses men and creation directly and which is the primary reference. But Luther will have nothing to do with such an un-mediated religion. For him, sinful men cannot have a direct encounter with the holy God. It is God who has come to men in the incarnation of His son, and the good news about Him is mediated through the outward preaching of the gospel, through the study of the inspired Scriptures and by means of the Sacraments. Through them faith comes, and the Spirit is given.

In these years, and under the stress of conflict, the categories of Word and Spirit were forced apart, with the radicals appealing more and more to the Spirit, and the Lutherans stressing the objectivity of Word and Sacraments. To Müntzer it seemed that the Lutherans had unbalanced the relation between the spirit and the letter, and had turned the Bible into a disastrous deception – 'Bible, Bibble- Babble!' – hiding the gospel from common men by telling them to read the Bible, or accept their authority in its inter-pretation. Missing the inwardness of true religion, they merited his dismissal of them as modern Scribes (Schriftgelehrte). There is an interesting parallel with William Law who in his later writings has a similar strong invective against Biblical scholars – he too was a mystic involved in radical action – as a Non-Juror and Jacobite. It seemed to Müntzer that the preaching of Justification 'sola fide' was disastrously facile. 'All you have to do is believe!', whereas his 'theology of the Cross' stressed the necessity of renunciation and suffering. It is sad that he never knew how close he came to Luther in making 'Anfechtung', temptation, the corollary of faith as Luther described it in letters to his friends and would do publicly in later writings like his sermons on the Book of Jonah (1526).

Luther on his side had become more and more alienated by what he heard of Müntzer's agitation at Zwickau and the vehemence of his attack on the humanist Egranus. The advent of Müntzer's associates, the 'Zwickau pro-phets', at Christmas time 1521, provoked a minor crisis in Wittenberg in which Luther had to intervene to help a bewildered Melanchthon; and this led to private interviews with some of these men in the following year, though Müntzer himself kept out of it. But by now Luther lumped Müntzer with all these radicals who now included Karlstadt. The uproar consequent on Müntzer's liturgical experiments in Allstedt in 1523, and above all the violent attack by Müntzer and his friends on a shrine at Mallerbach, confirmed Luther's worst fears, and thereafter they became public enemies. Müntzer blamed his final expulsion from Allstedt on Luther's letter to the Saxon Princes (1524)[6] and thereafter thought of him as his arch-enemy. Thus Müntzer's letter to Luther (9 July 1523) marks the end of any kind of friendly relationship from Müntzer's side.

The second, more complex, question is the relation between Müntzer's theology and his active role in what is misleadingly called his 'Volksreformation'. The core of his gospel he clothed in vocabulary drawn from late mediaeval spirituality and it is not yet possible to make many affirmations about the extent to which it represents his own original synthesis, and how much it derives from a wider radical movement with perhaps obscure connections with sectarian anti-clerical and mystical movements, Waldensian, Hussite, Taborite and the still mysterious 'Friends of God'. Certainly there seems to have been a background of ideas and a radical jargon common to Müntzer and to Karlstadt, Hans Denck and Sebastian Franck.

Müntzer was a man of learning for whom books counted. We know that he bought and read many learned works; that he had read and re-read the works of Augustine and perhaps of Jerome; that he had read Basil and Tertullian among the fathers; was interested in contemporary pamphleteering (Reuchlin, Erasmus). I think he had read Plato, including the *Parmenides*[7] and probably Nicholas of Cusa, and Raimond of Sabunde. His early ministry was among nuns, and these were the devout congregations to whom John Tauler had expounded his mystical doctrines. There can be little doubt that Müntzer was steeped in Tauler and in the pseudo-Taulerian 'Book of the Poor in Spirit'. We know that he also had read Henry Suso[8] and if we had not an explicit evidence for this would have concluded it from his dialectic between the 'bitter' and the 'sweet' Christ.

He had read the *Theologia Germanica*, though I suspect it had not the importance for him that it had for Andrew Karlstadt (who quotes whole passages from it). It is known that Müntzer carried round with him a great double volume. In it were the works of John Tauler, and also the remarkable anthology of mystical writings edited by Le Fèvre in 1513 as *Liber trium virorum et spiritualium virginum* – it included the visions of S. Hildegard of Bingen and the apocalyptic writing from the sub-apostolic church, the Shepherd of Hermas.

---

[6] 'Letter to the Princes of Saxony concerning the Rebellious Spirit', in *Luther's Works*, the American edition, XL, pp. 49–59. S. Bräuer, 'Die Vorgeschichte von Luthers 'Ein Brief an die Fürsten...', *Luther-Jahrbuch*, 1979, pp. 40ff.

[7] Franz, *op. cit.*, pp. 16–17.

[8] *Ibid.*, p. 356.

Using an orthodox Christology Müntzer inseparably associated Christ's work 'for us' with his work 'in us'. The goal of the Christian life is 'conformity with Christ', and this is no legalistic and outward imitation, but the deep inner sanctification of the soul, through the tribulation which brings faith, and through sharing in the sufferings of Christ. He loves the images of Tauler and Suso, of the soul as a wheat field, of the Spirit as the plough, and of the difference between a 'honey sweet' and 'bitter' Christ. Obsessive with him is the image of water, as signifying the divine instrument of tribulation.

But it must be emphasized that this description of the sanctification of the individual soul is entirely different from the atomistic and individualist view of salvation in later Pietism and Moravianism. It is here that his liturgies fall into place and give the corporate reference. Nobody better understood the great Augustinian conception of 'Totus Christus' as 'the whole Christ, Head and Members'; and indeed for him not only the whole People of God but the whole of creation are bound together; 'The whole of Holy Scripture is about nothing else – as are all the creatures – than the crucified Son of God.'[9] It is this corporate reference which may underlie Müntzer's references to the 'Part' and the 'Whole' – where a doctrine which may have been noted in *Parmenides* is joined with the teaching of the Epistles to the Colossians and the Ephesians.[10]

When we ask how these doctrines are related by Müntzer to his active fight against the ungodly and to a so-called 'Volksreformation' we must recognize that for him 'Volk' is not the German nation, but the People of God, 'the Elect Friends of God'. His only gesture towards the idea of an Elect Nation is his appeal to the Bohemians. But it is his apocalyptic which bridges his view of salvation, and the 'inward religion' of individuals and his denunciations of the ungodly which led to his participation in violent acts and eventually in the Peasant War.

One of the most luminous of recent discussions of Müntzer's apocalyptic is an article by Gottfried Maron, 'Thomas Müntzer als Theologe des Gerichts'.[11] He draws attention to the importance of the radical usage, and especially Müntzer's use, of the word *Urteil* – judgment – and shows that it has always eschatological and indeed apocalyptic undertones. He suggests that it illuminates the importance for Müntzer of the Bible. He suggests that for Müntzer the Bible is rather like the English Common Law, a volume of cases and precedents, that it is indeed the Common Law of the People of

---

[9] Franz, *op. cit.*, p. 324; G. Rupp, *Patterns of Reformation* (London, 1969), p. 287.

[10] Franz, *op. cit.*, p. 418.

[11] *Zeitschrift für Kirchengeschichte*, LXXXIII (1972), reprinted in Friesen and Goertz, *op. cit.*, pp. 339–82.

God, full of divinely wise saws and instances, so that the stories of Moses and God's Elect, of Gideon, of David, of Elijah and the Prophets of Baal, and the figures of Elijah and John the Baptist are examples of divine judgment which have a univocal relation to the divinely authenticated judgments (John 7 and 8) of Müntzer and his comrades as they await the inauguration of the New Age.

In this connection we may draw attention to the fact that Müntzer's vade-mecum included the Shepherd of Hermas, that sub-apostolic apocalyptic in which a central figure is the church. It is the story of a revelation to a common man (Hermas is a Roman slave) but the central image is that of the church, and the building of a great tower of stones, which are of two kinds – the sound, good stones which are the 'elect', and the rejected stones which are the reprobate and the ungodly. And though when Müntzer wrote to Hans Zeiss 'He who wants to be a stone of the new church must risk his neck otherwise he will be rejected by the builders'[12] the primary reference must be to Ps. 118, verse 12, I do not think we can ignore Hermas.

A further study by Reinhard Schwarz, *Die apokalyptische Theologie Thomas Müntzers und der Taboriten*,[13] seeks to relate Müntzer's apocalyptic to the radical Taborite notions which he may have encountered in Zwickau and Saaz, and which plausibly underlies his appeal to the Bohemians. And though the Taborite sources and the striking parallels are of early date, there may be something of a relationship similar to that between the militant Lollardy in England of the mid-fifteenth century and the ideas of Wycliffe half a century before. But two qualifications must be borne in mind when talking about Müntzer's apocalyptic. While there is an evident debt to the Joachitic tradition of consecutive ages of Revelation (and also in Daniel and Revelation) Müntzer has no doctrine of a thousand year millennial kingdom or of such a rule of Christ and his saints as have been explicated from Revelation 21.6. It is therefore improper to discuss Müntzer's views as 'Chiliast'. And in the second place his vision does not centre in the Second Coming of Christ, nor is it Christocentric as is his concept of sanctification of the individual. That pseudo-Joachitic treatise 'Super Jeremiam' which Müntzer had read[14] is an attempt to pin-point prophecy, by up-dating Joachim's eleventh century 'concordances' in terms of the thirteenth century. But Müntzer never goes in for such pin-pointing beyond his assertion that the people of Prague are on the edge of the New Age. And apart from his 'a new church' vision he does not seem to have had any kind of detailed programme of what

[12] Franz, *op. cit.*, p. 418.
[13] Tubingen, 1977 (= *Beiträge zur historischen Theologie*, herausgegeben von Gerhard Ebeling, LV).
[14] Franz, *op. cit.*, p. 398.

is to come. He believes the church underwent a Fall in the sub-apostolic age and there is a new church about to be formed, so that he comes close to what Marjorie Reeves says about the '*viri spirituales*' of the later Middle Ages, 'it was not so much the recapturing of the life of the Apostles that they expected as the creating the life of the new apostles'.

But the overall, over-arching doctrine which makes his thought and action coherent, and unites the mystic, biblical and apocalyptic elements, is the doctrine of Predestination. At the centre of his thought and action is his conception of 'the Elect' or 'the Elect Friends of God'.[15] And here there is a suggestive parallel with the *De Operibus Dei* of Martin Cellarius (1527). He was one of Müntzer's radical associates and had taken part in the interview with Luther at Wittenberg in 1522. It is a rare work, while even rarer is the English translation, in a fine Italianate hand, which Dr Robert Williams discovered in a parish vestry in Reigate.[16]

Without minimizing differences between the two men one may suggest that it is this doctrine of Predestination (fully worked out in the later Middle Ages, and well before John Calvin) which underlies Müntzer's dualist chiaroscuro, his division of men between the Elect and the ungodly. It underlies his doctrine of assurance and his frequent references to the irrevocable judgments and will of God. More important, in Cellarius' tract it is shown how Predestination is linked on the one hand with the doctrine of Providence (and so with the created order) and on the other with apocalyptic. Dr Williams notices similarities between the language and images of Cellarius and Müntzer while others beside himself have noted the debt of Cellarius to the apocalyptic notions stemming from Joachim de Fiore.[17]

The fact that Müntzer believed that by a divinely inspired 'Urteil' the Elect can discriminate among the Elect and the ungodly had important and drastic implications for him as it had for some Lollards and would have for some Puritans and Covenanters in the next century. The Elect are not simply individuals interspersed invisibly within a mixed church but they can associate together. And for Müntzer the children of Israel were the 'Elect' People of God and their doings examples and precedents for the behaviour of the 'Elect' 'in these last dangerous days'.

This is the root of Müntzer's chiaroscuro, and of his obsession with the

---

15 In an analysis of Müntzer's vocabulary, H. O. Spillman, *Untersuchungen zum Wortschatz in Thomas Müntzer's Deutschen Schriften* (Berlin, 1971), shows that Müntzer uses the phrase 118 times and this includes 35 references in his liturgy.

16 Translated by the English reformer and Marian exile, T. H. Parry. See R. L. Williams, 'Martin Cellarius and the Reformation in Strasbourg', *Journal of Ecclesiastical History*, XXXII, no. 4 (October, 1981), pp. 471ff.

17 Williams, *op. cit.*, Friesen, in Friesen and Goertz, *op. cit.*, p. 394.

conflict with the ungodly which seems to underlie all his ministry. In one of the early letters (1517) his friend Claus refers to him as 'the chastiser of the unrighteous'. If by a use of his capacity for judgment – 'Urteil' – Müntzer believed he could recognize the godly, by that same charisma he could pick out the ungodly, and this was made easier by the simple fact that the reprobate are known when they persecute the Elect. This is how Müntzer came to write off Duke Ernest of Mansfeld by his very act of forbidding his subjects to attend Müntzer's liturgy. And while for conscientious or pragmatic reasons Müntzer was prepared to suspend judgment about the evangelical Saxon Princes, it is the division between the Elect and the ungodly which underlies his whole programme of action.

This dualism is the indispensable background to discussion of the meaning of Müntzer's covenanted bands and associations. To translate his use of 'Bund' and 'Verbündnisse' as 'leagues' seems to miss the Biblical and theological concepts which underlie them.[18] Although we cannot quite write off Thomas Müntzer from among the founders of an imminent 'Covenant Theology' we can be sure he did not miss the hundreds of references to God's Covenants with his Elect in the Old Testament (and a score or so in the New). And whether we think of his small dedicated company in Allstedt or the later peasant army with its white banner and Rainbow (the Noachic covenant being one of the primary Biblical covenants) it seems important that it was not in the first place a covenant or association between men, but a solemn oath 'Coram Deo'. We have to remember that feudal society was shot through with oaths and fealties, and Müntzer repeatedly makes plain that his form of covenant is a higher loyalty since it is made to God. Its members swore with uplifted hands to defend the gospel (the implications of this were to develop from the attack on Mallerbach to the Peasant War). Müntzer's great preachment in 1524 on the Covenant between Israel and God in the time of Josiah has not survived but it is not to be isolated as though it alone was responsible for the growth of covenanted associations which followed. And Müntzer did no doubt believe that he and his group of associates in Allstedt were among the Elect and we might think of them as paralleled by the way in which the troopers of Cromwell's army, in Colonel Whalley's regiment, turned themselves into a 'gathered church' with Richard Baxter as their chaplain. But Müntzer had a firm doctrine of the relativities of divine and natural law and what he has to say at this point is of critical importance.

There were those like Karlstadt who deprecated such associations as a reliance on the arms of men rather than on God. There were others who had

---

[18] M. Bensing gets into difficulties in his discussion 'Idee und Praxis des "Christlichen Verbündnisses" bei Thomas Müntzer', in Friesen and Goertz, *op. cit.*, pp. 299–338.

objected, in his liturgy when he made the whole congregation join in the consecration, which, they said, meant that the ungodly could share the divine mystery. It is important to note his comments on these arguments: 'The members (Bundesgenossen) must not think they will find freedom through this...for he is cursed who puts his trust in man...when the godly make a covenanted association there may be bad people among them but they will not accomplish their will.' And in a critical sentence he concludes: 'The Covenanted Band is nothing but an Emergency Device (Notwehr) which is to be denied to nobody according to the judgment of all rational men.'[19]

In Schweitzerian language it belongs to Müntzer's *Interimsethik* in this critical period between the revolutionary action of the godly and the New Age. But if it is centred on an oath to God it has obvious implications for men's relations with one another. Whether we take seriously Müntzer's admission under torture that his Allstedt band were to have 'all things in common' (Acts 2.42) or think that there was simply to be a kind of Three Muskateers loyalty, 'All for one and one for all' in terms of Müntzer's important distinction between 'Eigennutz' and 'Gemeinnutz', this is a dimension not to be ignored. It has been suggested that in fact Müntzer's apocalyptic did not result in a detailed programme and in coming months he would have little to add to the very practical 'liberties' claimed by the South German and Mühlhausen peasants in their articles, beyond a not very practical application of sumptuary laws and a gesture to the civic imperialism of Mühlhausen over its surrounding villages and lands.

The events concerning Müntzer's involvement in the Peasant War and some of the reasons for its failure have been skilfully outlined in a recent article by Dr Scott.[20] There would have been a Peasant War had there never been a Müntzer, and even in Thuringia its course would not have been greatly changed. In fact his own leadership was halting and often ambivalent though he kept up his agitation for violence to the end, using his Deuteronomic theology to justify the execution of the envoys of Duke Ernest while almost his last words on earth were to direct the Princes to the Book of Kings (and so to Jehu, Elijah and the Prophets of Baal). Unlike Zwingli he does not seem to have been an avid student of military campaigns, had probably no military capacity and must have stood beside his captains like a Krushchov at Stalingrad.

Martin Luther, despite the polemic, had shrewdly seen the differences between his Reformation and that of Müntzer and in his Wittenberg sermons in 1522 and in a series of tracts expounded the futility of violence.

---

[19] Franz, *op. cit.*, p. 423 lines 5–7; Rupp, *Patterns*, pp. 299–300.
[20] 'The "Volksreformation" of Thomas Müntzer in Allstedt and Mühlhausen', *Journal of Ecclesiastical History*, xxxiv, no. 2 (April 1983).

More important than his doctrine of the Two Kingdoms was his corollary that it was fatal to mix those kingdoms together and, with the weapons of the Earthly Magistrate, to try to bring about a Christian society on earth. 'They believed Christ would erect a new kingdom and empire and they would sit and reign in it as masters and break to pieces their enemies and the evil world.'[21] Perhaps it is not fair to Müntzer simply to confront his thought and action with the Lutheran pattern: he has something in common with Zwingli. Martin Bucer like him made the doctrine of Predestination the framework of his view of Reformation, and made use of Platonic notions in directing the notion of *Eigennutz* (which was important for him, too) towards a vision of a Christian society. Of the major reformers perhaps it is John Knox who comes nearest to him in the violence of his invective against the ungodly and who like Müntzer disdained 'all that crap about mercy'. It is Lord Eustace Percy's comment on John Knox which explains the Müntzer story as a cautionary tale.

When once a man sets out to establish the Kingdom of God as an earthly polity, it matters little whether he defies the state or invokes its aid, whether the sword he plans to take is the rebel's or the king's. In either case however much he may flatter himself that he has drawn the sword only as an emergency measure he can never sheathe it again. Those who appeal to force for the limited means of mere social order can limit their use of it – not so the man who appeals to it as an instrument of perfection. The man who takes that sword is happy if he can perish by it: if he lives he will be bound slave to it all his days.[22]

[21] Luther WA 32 388: Friesen, in Friesen and Goertz, *op. cit.*, p. 384.
[22] E. Percy, *John Knox* (London, 1937), p. 289.

Europe and the Reformation[1]

G. R. ELTON

It did not need the modern dream of European unity to stimulate thought about the concept of Europe, but an endeavour devoid of much historical understanding has helped to draw attention to the question. The new, current and so far distinctly uncertain Europe has little in common with what went before. Down to 1945, Europe was a continent containing a collection of political entities; it knew so little of unity that its quarrels guided the quarrels and futures of the rest of the world; it invented, embodied and exported the ideas and aspirations which it thought were common to humanity; and its civilization everywhere set the standard of civilized existence. Since 1945, Europe has tried to transform itself into one of the very large units which, some think, will in future characterize the global structure; its civilization is so much under attack that the ideas of other large entities are treated not only as valid in themselves but as more acceptable than those traditionally associated with the European civilization. It has ceased to be a continent and has once more become a peninsula attached to the largest landmass in the world. It is the old Europe that shall be considered here, a historical fact however much it may by now have receded into history. That old Europe did not, as endurance goes in the world's history, last very long – perhaps half a millennium, perhaps less – but before it tore itself to pieces and allowed the brute facts of size to overwhelm it, it had dominated all history in a way that no other region has ever done. More than China, more than Rome, more than Christendom or Islam, it governed the largest surface area ever so put together under a visible aegis, and it was only the second world war with its aftermath that revealed how little its dominance had

[1] This is an essay, not an article – that is to say, very few footnotes. It embodies speculation rather than the product of research. Though it must seem a poor thing to offer to so careful a scholar as the recipient of this volume, it may perhaps be excused as a tribute to the range and fertility of his own speculative thought.

altered the regions it dominated (though none escaped some fairly weighty influence). What were the roots of that Europe?

The emergence of the concept, the notion, of Europe has been sufficiently studied;[2] here I am concerned with the fact, the historical operating reality. As Denys Hay shows conclusively, it was only in the eighteenth century that the vision of Europe gained general acceptance and replaced earlier forms of self-identification by the peoples who inhabited the continent. By then the word had lived through a long history, from the provincial term employed by Greeks and Romans to the barely convincing equation with Christendom which gave it some identity in the years after the end of Rome. What it had not ever been until some two or three hundred years ago was the name of a separate, cohesive and distinguishable continent: and no wonder. There, after all, it sat, stuck on huge and populous Asia by the longest continuous line that could be found anywhere around its limits. Africa is also linked to Asia, but by an isthmus; it took only a few years of digging a ditch to mark a separation which had always been visible. Where, indeed, does Europe meet Asia? Along the Don, as the geographers of the sixteenth century liked to think? At the Urals, as the Enlightenment proposed and the nineteenth century (mistakenly) accepted?[3] A river line that a punt can cross, a mountain range lying far from any notable manifestation of European influence and readily crossed or by-passed by nomads going west or railways going east – these are poor definitions for a continental frontier. Geographically, therefore, Europe has never had much meaning, the more so because even oceans could not hold it in: the British Isles, with all their peculiar differences, are, and during the era of ascendancy unquestionably were, an essential part of Europe. The *fact* of Europe must therefore be defined by non-geographical criteria – by structures and practices, and by a self-consciousness which extended over an area enclosed by well-defined but easily breached lines.

I am, of course, well aware that the communities within this Europe show much variety and some differences that are hard to reconcile to one another. In what follows I shall not so much ignore those particularities as try to identify common and shared properties. By comparison with the differences found between European and non-European peoples those that divide the inhabitants of Europe cease to matter. Let us therefore look at Europe by pinpointing those structures and practices, those grounds of self-consciousness.

As Mandell Creighton noted nearly a century ago, when the Europe we are after stood at an apogee and when European historians identified the

---

[2] Denys Hay, *Europe: The Emergence of an Idea* (2nd edn, Edinburgh, 1968).

[3] *Ibid.*, pp. 123–5.

things among which they lived with the whole world, the most obvious difference between the medieval structure and that found later lay in the establishment of independent political entities called states, which based themselves on a concept of mutually exclusive and markedly differing nationalities. The earlier period, he reckoned, had witnessed the promulgation of a 'European commonwealth'; the later was 'mainly concerned with the rise and fall of nations'. For him, modernity implied 'the frank recognition ...of nationality, and all that it involves'.[4] Now no one would wish to draw a precise date line between the earlier and the later concepts, but that does not rob Creighton's definition of an essential truth. Medieval Europe knew effective supra-national institutions, especially, of course, the Latin Church whose organization and influence covered the whole region; indeed, they provide the best description of what 'Europe' might have meant at the time. Whatever independence localized Churches and monasteries enjoyed, they remained provinces within a single empire. Similarly, social strata linked across the often uncertain boundaries between the political entities that coexisted within the 'universal' realm: dividing lines ran at least as much horizontally – between, for instance, nobility and commonalty – as they ran vertically between Englishmen and Frenchmen, Burgundians and Italians, Bavarians and Saxons. Movement across those approximate frontiers was easy and common, for the wandering students drifting from university to university as much as for crusading knights or travelling merchants. As the successive invasions of England, and the English invasions of France, demonstrated well enough, the sea formed more of a highway than a moat. It was, in fact, at a level lower than nation or state that better defined sub-entities existed – for instance in the towns with their often self-regarding attitudes to strangers, or the regions (Anjou, or Swabia, or Herefordshire) which could attract more consistent loyalties than the supposed kingdoms of which they were part. The availability of a common language assisted the sense of a commonwealth: Latin united all the heirs of Rome. But in reality this commonwealth hardly merited the name of Europe. Its real centres remained Mediterranean – Rome and Jerusalem, two places lying on the fringe of the physical mass called Europe and inexorably tied to ancient Asia. Indeed, ancient Asia kept reminding Europe of its lack of self-command by repeated and usually lasting invasions, and Asia retained its sway over the supposed eastern marches of this alleged Europe. Russia, the Ukraine, even the Balkans (whether in Byzantine or Turkish hands) received everything they needed, from government and politics to religion, from oriental sources.

None of all this had survived by the time the nineteenth century revealed

[4] Mandell Creighton in *The Cambridge Modern History*, 13 vols. (Cambridge, 1904–11), vol. I, p. 2.

the image of Europe Triumphant which has dominated Europe's own vision of itself for some 200 years. Now it consisted of nation states – separate and totally independent structures claiming allegiance from their inhabitants on the grounds of a national identity. That identity existed independently of any language-defined nationality which, though quite common, was in no way indispensable: neither Welshmen nor Czechs, even when in due course they became conscious of a new kind of nationality based on language, felt out of place in the realms of Great Britain or Austria–Hungary. (In both cases a separatist nationalism had to be whipped up by romantic intellectuals, a process which took a long time.) What gave such firm shape to collections of sometimes multi-fashioned peoples – what constituted the essence of their nationality – was rather allegiance to a particular monarchic dynasty. These nation states, to be truly European, had apparently to be monarchies (even down to mini-monarchies in places like Luxemburg and Liechtenstein); genuine old republics surrendered to the monarchic principle in post-Napoleonic Netherlands and Belgium, or in Venice, absorbed into the kingdom of Italy. Only Switzerland preserved a contrary principle, for which reason it tended to be regarded as an interesting fossil. These monarchies varied in many respects but shared the one quality that mattered – the monopoly of rulership; moreover, ties of common interest and intermarriages made the royal families of the day into a curious kind of supra-national estate. Most important of all, whatever the terms of rulership, they all presided over states ordered by the law. Despite talk of absolutism during the seventeenth and eighteenth centuries, no European monarch could ever identify the law of his realm with his own mere will; the state that Louis XIV liked to think was himself in fact had a life of its own settled in the law, and genuine despotisms of the kind familiar in the history of Asia, Africa or pre-Columbian America are unknown in the history of Europe. Though the law differed from realm to realm, and though the limitations on kingly power also varied in extent and effectiveness, both law and limitation defined those monarchies in ways which clearly distanced them from such rulers as Hellenistic kings, Roman emperors, or late-medieval popes, not to mention grand moguls of India, emperors of China, Sultans of Ottoman Turkey.

The role of the law sprang from another peculiarity of these states. They contained only free and property-owning men, those too poor to own property being nevertheless treated as potential possessors. This Europe knew neither slaves nor serfs, though the latter had been set fully free in several kingdoms only in the course of the eighteenth century; it accommodated no man whose condition differed absolutely from that of any fellow-subject. That the same principle did not equally apply to women was another structural element held in common, but at least women shared the personal freedom conceded to men. The absence of proper female emancipation did not distinguish these states either from the past or from contemporary structures elsewhere: it distinguished them from their successor structures of the twentieth century. Certainly there were hierarchies of wealth, esteem and rights, but these did not include the bodily subjection of one inhabitant to another. A moment's reflection upon the history of mankind reveals how very unusual such a principle was. The hierarchies of wealth differentiated styles of life, but the fact remained that what a man owned, however little it might be, was his own – not held from another but vested in himself. The law that ruled these states defined what a man possessed, aimed to defend his rights and enforce his duty to respect the rights of others, and thus anchored his personal individuality in his claim to individual possession. Certainly, it will not do to be too starry-eyed about this. No one would deny the continuing limitations to a freedom which varied from practical totality in Great Britain to touches of class-bound despotism in Hungary, nor would anyone wish to deny the unreality of much of this law-based independence in the face of economic exploitation and personal chicanery. What is here at issue are not the facts of individual experience but the framing facts of the polity – its separate existence and its command over a body of free men held together by a system of law which did not either embody the ruler's mere will or yield to its vagaries.

This determined belief in the existence and supremacy of law – any legal system relevant to a given situation – came out rather interestingly in the endeavour to provide a law which would control and perhaps mollify the contacts between the political entities that made up Europe. If war between them was to be the inescapable consequence of their possessing total and self-contained independence, it came to be thought the more desirable to provide rules for the conduct of war and perhaps legal principles and institutions which might offer opportunities for resolving conflict short of war. It cannot be said that these endeavours accomplished the elevated purposes to which they aspired: power remained far more untrammelled by law between the states than within them. Nevertheless, the respect paid to the theorists of international law, the rules developed for war at sea and blockade, the International Court at the Hague and the Geneva Convention governing the treatment of prisoners of war, all underline a quite impressive desire to regulate inter-state relations within the European system in a fashion which gave a touch of coherence even to the most obviously disruptive aspects of that system. In these moves to limit the disasters of war the European continent testified to a consciousness of its own existence and to a willingness to allow this consciousness to be embodied in those legal forms which rather more effectively ordered relations within each component part.

All these states also acquired identity from ideological beliefs effectively common to their respective inhabitants. National sentiments of a comprehensive sort were essential both to the emergence of the state and to its separation from similar neighbouring states. What particularly characterized this stage of European statehood was the fact that the ideologies in question could be either religious or secular – or more precisely, that a religion-based ideology differed in no significant way from one that was not religious. Furthermore, apparent samenesses in religious adherence did not diminish the differences between the states in ideological content and effect: sharing a religion did not create friendship. All the states claimed to be Christian but the truth of the claim did not reduce the effect of inter-state boundaries. They defined their Christianity in various, mutually opposed, denominations, but these too did not provide means for coming together or reasons for hostility. Catholic France and Catholic Spain were France and Spain first, Catholic after, even though in both countries the Catholic Church and faith lay at the heart of their nationality. Adherence to different denominations played no part in the relations of states with one another: addicted to war, they no longer knew wars of religion. Nor did the coexistence of different denominations diminish the internal cohesion of states, however much hostility individual believers still felt towards other Churches. Thus, as the war of 1870 showed clearly enough, the components of a Germany about to become politically united all allowed a passion for German nationalism to overrule any remaining differences between Protestants and Catholics. The secular ideology of Germanism triumphed readily over religious ideologies which still retained full reality – and this was the general experience in Europe. The clearest proof of a fact itself well enough known lies in the appearance, in country after country, of national symbols, immediately recognizable and acting as instinctive rallying points. The symbols might be flags (Union Jack, Tricolour, Schwarz-Weiss-Rot), or heraldic devices (somnolent lions, imperial eagles, double-headed eagles, crowing cocks), or cartoonists' shorthand (Marianne, the German Michel, John Bull). All shared the important quality of immediate recognizability, a quality which both stimulated and reflected the shared national ideology they symbolized. One possible test for membership of the European continent may be found in the existence of symbols adopted not in the country itself but by outsiders, usually with hostile intentions: in Russia, which lay outside Europe, the Russian bear carried no nation-wide recognition, in this way resembling the dusky maiden which automatically meant India to the English but not to the Indians.

Separateness and individuality are most notably demonstrated by two sides to one coin – the refusal to allow any outside entity to intervene internally, and the consequent readiness to go to war with other members of this continental group. Europe was no community but a collection of mutually suspicious polities frequently fighting one another; efforts at restraining belligerence confined themselves to the meeting of separate and equal representatives at diplomatic congresses – a device, as experience proved, usually successful only after the exhaustion of war.

A collection of identifiable structures, even if they shared so many characteristics (including mutual exclusiveness) hardly, however, makes a collective. To what extent did this Europe of independent entities hang together over and against other independent structures in other parts of the world? There were things that made for a true and shared European feeling, things which to some extent subdued and overrode the political splintering that dictated the behaviour of states. Two facts of existence deserve special attention, both of them quite real though the terms used for them do not sound like it: the mode of production, and the intellectual climate. There is no need to go at length into the fact that the European community was in the main capitalist: the system everywhere operated on the assumption that the market should be allowed free play. (Political considerations, especially apprehension of popular unrest, ensured that the play should nowhere be absolutely free.) The factory, the railway and the steamship, the three revolutionary devices upon which the world-wide expansion of wealth depended, invented in England, rapidly spread over all of Europe. In due course they were to travel much further afield, but in the nineteenth century only Europeanized territories (like the United States) adopted these European artefacts wholeheartedly and effectively. It can fairly be said that the limits of Europe may be defined by the spread of the capitalist economy, dominant in the gravitational centre (west and middle) of the continent, thinning out towards the edges in Spain, southern Italy, the eastern marches and Scandinavia, and barely visible in what, solely for geographical reasons, is called European Russia and Turkey in Europe.

No sensible historian likes playing with concepts like 'intellectual climate', but the thing exists. European culture emerges as an entity from the interesting fact that even violent nationalism did not prevent the adoption of literary hero-figures from other nations. Shakespeare, Cervantes, Dante, Goethe, Balzac were read throughout the continent and formed identical standards of taste everywhere; the translator, first flitting about the stage in the sixteenth century, by the nineteenth had become a characteristically European type, unknown elsewhere. In retrospect, it is arguable that the gradual penetration into the west of the great Russian novelists with their very different view of the world produced the disintegration of a common European tradition. However, imaginative literature and poetry are not themselves peculiar to that tradition; distinguishing characteristics arise more from underlying attitudes and assumptions than from the mere fact of a shared literary production. Three of these attitudes call for consideration: science, history and religion.

The medieval queen of the sciences, theology, and her prince-consort, philosophy, survived, of course, into modern times but only by retreating from the throne to the purlieus. It was a combination of natural science – the investigation of nature – and human history – the study of the past as a road towards an understanding of human society – that came to determine intellectual and spiritual attitudes in nineteenth-century Europe. These concerns not only stole the show by the manifest successes they scored in answering the questions they professed to be addressing, but clearly also governed common reactions to questions not within their domains. Most problems received a treatment which combined the rational method of the sciences with the relativist and 'organic' notions promoted by the study of history; and all disciplines acquired the professionalizing characteristics aspired to by the dominant enterprises. The point emerges most clearly when one looks at what happened to religion in that age, for religion ought by its nature to have managed best to resist both rationalization and relativism. It did not, although, of course, surrender was never complete. Two features most plainly distinguish European Christianity of the sixteenth to nineteenth centuries. One was the conscious effort to cleanse it from all elements of magic (magic, not mystery). The second was the increasingly general admission that there need not be only one valid Christian faith and that other religions too merited respect as partaking of the truth. The elimination of magic – that rational acceptance of visible occurrences contrary to the laws of nature which formed a major component in all religious practices and interpretations even among the supposedly rational Greeks – began with the attack on the mass, progressed through the eighteenth-century's endeavour to reduce faith to ethics, and culminated in the next century's desire to remove all contradictions between faith and human experience. It exemplified the triumph of science. The surrender of total exclusiveness began with the explosion which wrecked the medieval Church, continued through the enforced acceptance of several Christian Churches as legitimate, and culminated in the nineteenth century's recognition that the form taken by the worship of God was decided not by inspiration but by past conditioning. It exemplified the triumph of history.

We are so used to the shape of the things handed down by the nineteenth century that most of what has been said here will appear obvious and is widely regarded as normal. We have grown up in a continental Europe typical of the nineteenth century and its aftermath; many of us still think in the terms then defined and cannot recognize how unusual these terms are in the long history of mankind. These convictions are reinforced by the undoubted fact that that continental Europe, even if it came to full fruition in that last century, was certainly not invented then. Its deep roots reach back into history, and especially for those who do not see a dividing line between medieval and modern times it is far from clear that those roots do not represent some sort of eternal reality. In that case, even shattering events like the Turkish conquest of the middle east, or the Reformation, or the Thirty Years War, or even the French Revolution (whose real impact in any case awaited the twentieth century) need not necessarily have done more than accentuate and mildly redirect longstanding and manifestly 'continental' features of this European scene. But I do not find I can agree with this: to me it seems clear that there was no such thing as a true European continent for most of the time that history is found in what was to become Europe. Can we then establish when a definable Europe emerged from its non-continental prehistory – when the potential possession of a continental identity turned into actuality?

To restate the definition: Europe's identity as a continent derived from external events, from the reaction to such events, and from the development of practices and ideas original to the region. It involved a transfer of the centre of gravity away from the Mediterranean and especially from the near east to the triangle Germany–France–England; the setting up of fully separated nation states, internally secure and related to one another by conflict rather than by cooperation or subjection (though a conflict slightly modified by efforts to substitute law for force); the capitalist economy; and a world of ideas dominated by the natural sciences and the study of history. None of these elements was absolutely new and unprecedented. The medieval aggregate of peoples living in what became Europe did not always look to the south and sorted itself into mutually hostile units resembling modern states, though the practice of permitting a dispersed exercise of power and the absence of internal peace help to distinguish these pseudo-states from what came after. The preoccupation of German emperors with Italy, the practice of the crusade, the role of the papal Church, the transnational precepts of chivalry, even the English king's ambition to win the crown of France backed by his longstanding rule of territories in which he was a vassal of that crown – all these make it very plain that antecedents do not equal sameness. Capitalism has rightly been discerned in medieval Italy and can be found elsewhere, but it neither freed itself from conceptual limitations upon its operation (theories of a just price and the condemnation of usury) nor promoted industrialization, the only mature embodiment of its principles. Pre-modern science and history, even where pursued for their own sakes, stood in the service of religion – offering an explanation and justification for a God-created and God-ruled universe; by the nineteenth century the roles were reversed. In all conceivable respects, the European area of, say, the twelfth or the fourteenth century differed from what is found in the same region in the eighteenth or nineteenth; and the difference may fairly be summed up by saying that a new, separately self-conscious, continent had in the meantime arisen.

Traditionally, and familiarly, this 'rise of Europe' has been linked to the supposedly cooperative effects of the Renaissance and the Reformation, supported by the voyages of discovery; of late, however, all these once cataclysmic events have been depreciated to mere episodes in a continuum. We now find strong humanist convictions centuries before Petrarch (not to mention Erasmus); the medieval Church, we now know, ceased to be monolithic long before Luther; Vikings (even Welshmen) are paraded as explorers of eminence well before the age of explorations. Much of this writing-down is fully justified, but some is not. Leaving aside the seafarers, since neither Leif Erikson nor Christopher Columbus in any way transformed Europe whatever else they may have achieved, we should not altogether overlook the Renaissance. However it may be defined, it contributed heavily to the renovation of ideas, of education, indeed of science and history which went to the shaping of the 'modern' European mind, especially once it freed itself of the magic element which some scholars (notably the late Frances Yates) have tried to make its chief characteristic. But it is true that the Renaissance will not answer the call for a root of modern Europe, for two reasons. In the first place, Europeans returned to the ancients on several occasions after the fall of Rome and the collapse of its civilization, without thereby making a continent of their habitat; in the second, insofar as the Italian Renaissance abetted by its northern successor concentrated attention upon the classical past, it reinforced the attraction of the Mediterranean and hampered – or at least failed to promote – the specifically continental emergence of Europe.

The claims of the Reformation, on the other hand, still look strong. By freeing Europe from the dominance of Rome and the lodestar of Jerusalem – by making it possible to be a Christian without dreaming of reconquering the holy places – it greatly encouraged that turning away from the Mediterranean which constituted the first condition for an independent and continental Europe. Because it failed in its ambition to conquer the whole Church it terminated the notion of a single Christian Church, a notion that had always (in the west) so far triumphed over every threat of disruption; it was this that led to the diversity within Christianity plus the possibility of uncensored thinking about religion that are among the hallmarks of the 'real'

Europe. The Reformation, together with the Counter-Reformation's step-by-step reaction to it, transformed Italian and Erasmian humanism into that classical curriculum of schools and universities which for centuries distinguished the European educational system from any other system designed by man. The Reformation's attack on a sacerdotal priesthood and the miracle of the mass led the way towards the elimination of the magical element in religion, an elimination which post-Tridentine Catholicism, although it kept the mass as a sacrifice, also sought to achieve; it was in the aftermath of the Reformation that the powerful strains of pre-Christian magic prevalent in the popular religion of the middle ages came under attack everywhere.[5] This is not to forget that reformers both Catholic and Protestant emphasized the mysteries of religion and resisted all attempts to allow reason to rule faith. However, such resistance is itself hostile to magic, for magic is the means by which reason comes to terms with incomprehensible reality. When Luther, Calvin and Loyola strictly separated the realms of faith and reason they removed the bridge between them which magic had constituted. Lastly, it was the Reformation that enabled the characteristic nation states of modern Europe to free themselves from external political constraints.

On the other hand, it may be thought extravagant to allot to the Reformation any claim to have promoted the study of natural science and history: did it not revive the primacy of religion and theology in the intellectual preoccupations of Europe? It did so, but only for a short time. Once the denominational divisions became accepted the heated debate on points of the faith waned rapidly, to be replaced by the true prime concern of modern European intellectual life, a philosophical world view derived from science and history. However, the Reformation did not only work, as it were, negatively in this matter, making theology distasteful and irrelevant, but by its insistence on the Bible as a historical document which required strict historical analysis and contained a guide to past and present (and often also future) history, Reformation theology pointed the way to history as the study of man quite as much as the collapse of the theological explanation of the creation led to the victory of natural science. With regard to the interrelation of Reformation and capitalism, those who have seen a necessary link between them have proved misleading guides, but it remains true that post-Reformation religion soon abandoned all attempts at controlling economic enterprises or their justification. It also remains true that by the nineteenth

[5] For a Protestant country the story is familiar from Keith Thomas's *Religion and the Decline of Magic* (London, 1970), but it may not be so well known that the effort to recover the lands lost to the Reformation led the Church of Rome along similar rationalizing lines in the recasting of its faith which ensued in the wake of Trent.

century most Christian and just about all Protestant preaching accepted the facts of the capitalist economy.

Perhaps I need not emphasize that the emergence of what I have called the real Europe cannot be explained by any single cause. All sorts of things contributed to it, from the invention of printing and gunpowder to the idiosyncrasies of Louis XIV. The Europe with which we have been familiar sprang from many origins reaching back to Greece and Rome and Judaea, reaching outwards to India and China and Peru, reaching downwards into the greedy souls of men and upwards into their often touching spiritual aspirations. If, however, we wish to identify one event which more than any other enabled this multitude of circumstances and influences to produce the continent of Europe, that event, it would seem, must be the Reformation at work on both the minds and the lives of the European nations. One way, therefore, of defining the territorial extent of the continent involves analysing the reach of lands where the Reformation and the papal reaction to it took effect: and this test, too, while it admits Poland and Transylvania, eliminates Russia.

By chance, it seems to me, it is possible to test this thesis touching the Reformation's role in the making of Europe by a species of counterfactual device or falsification, methods I do not usually regard as advisable in checking historical reconstructions. For the Europe of which I have spoken is dead and gone. We no longer live in an identifiable continent composed of separate and independent national states. Instead those states have become to a notable extent integrated into two supra-national agglomerations, facing each other along a line which runs right through the middle of the old Europe. Thus Europe has once again become an appendage to the true Asiatic continent, though the western half, thanks to the power of the United States, retains a precarious hold on anti-Asian independence and a mild illusion that it constitutes a separate continent. The unifying culture has vanished together with the separating politics, and this is true not only of the drastic cultural contrast between east and west but of the west alone as well. Witness the decline of Latin and the fact that very few people now read other nations' literature for pleasure: the activity is confined to professional teachers. (A future unifying culture may perhaps emerge from what are at present the preferences of the young since these have a trans-national appeal; but if it does it will owe more to America than Europe and lack civilization.) The ascendancy of law over power has gone – gone far more definitely than ever it weakened in the more authoritative states of the old Europe. Fascism and Communism have produced genuine despotic regimes within the boundaries of Europe – despotisms of the kind perfectly familiar in Asiatic history but not indigenous to that of Europe. The truth of this fact was signalled most resoundingly when the ancient Asian practice of mass extermination (genocide) became accepted policy right in the heartland of what had been the European continent. The essentially liberal complex of ideas, including such things as uncensored thought and writing, regard for the individual, and most characteristically a legal view of personal and social relationships (not to be confused with abstract justice), has totally vanished from the eastern half and unmistakably retreated from the western remnant too. Though many will still do it, it gets harder by the hour to maintain a conviction of Europe's existence.[6]

This offers the opportunity for the counterfactual test: if the Reformation was instrumental in producing the continental Europe visible from the mid-sixteenth to the early twentieth century, what would have happened to that region without the Reformation? This is a question which permits of no historically valid answer, but it can now be rephrased to read: was the disappearance of that continent in any way associated with the removal of the Reformation and its effects? While we cannot take the Reformation away from the sixteenth century and from the consequences that ensued, we can ask whether the Reformation was taken out of the subsequent agglomerate (continental Europe) before that was seen to disintegrate. If this happened, the case for treating the Reformation as essential for the existence of the kind of Europe here discussed becomes even stronger. And the answer is, yes: the Reformation vanished before the Europe mainly created by it vanished in its turn.

The point comes out in various ways. One essential message which the Reformation handed to the Europe it helped create taught that institutionalized Christianity is the true religion but that it could properly be embodied in a variety of such institutions; it also taught that an advanced religion does without that element of magic which had formed an indispensable component of all faiths since before time began. In the course of the nineteenth century, this message began to pall as the reformed religions began to deteriorate into an ethical liberalism in which faith in God to all appearance played no essential part. There is no need to labour the waning of institutionalized religion; except in the Church of Rome, the state of the pews each Sunday tells its

---

[6] By a curious coincidence I received the day after I wrote this passage a circular from the Institute for Modern and Contemporary History at Rome which offered to cure the alleged 'identity crisis facing Europe' by a cooperative rewriting of history without the 'remaining nationalistic prejudices'. No doubt a proper ambition (or it would be if UNESCO had not already shown what kind of harvest that notion brings), but removing one of the solid foundations underlying the true (vanished) Europe will hardly cure the crisis. All it will do is assist in the death of Europe. Not that that death, of course, is necessarily a bad thing: it all depends on what may follow the funeral.

own story. And that Catholicism which revived from about 1870 onwards really marked a return to pre-Reformation times (where the Church has now again arrived), with its renewed emphasis on the pope's absolute rule, the reassertion of universalist claims, and the restoration of a fair bit of magic. What else were Döllinger and Acton defending than the Church of Rome as fashioned by the response to the Reformation against a Church which meant to forget the Reformation? This return to the middle ages also lay behind the ambitions of the English Tractarians with their Anglo-Catholic offspring: Pusey, Hurrell Froude and Newman explicitly attacked the Reformation as a disaster. As the rational forms of Christianity thus lost their hold, magic reentered by both the front and back doors – the front door of ritualism and the back door of esoteric faiths like theosophy. This latter manifestation of dissatisfaction with reason has now reached notable proportions in the religious smörgasbord of California which has also adopted the device of the old magic religions for attaining a 'higher spiritual' state – the use of hallucinogens. Quite predictably, the seekers after magic have in the main turned to Asia. The decline of the Reformation benefited Roman Catholicism and it benefited the decline of all religious faith as well; but more spectacularly it led to the collapse of Christian self-confidence which has made so many turn towards Buddhism, Shintoism, or indeed any available guru imported or native. The only positive counterattack seems to be coming not from organized Protestantism but from the sort of fundamentalist religion shot through with revivalist practices whose sixteenth-century manifestations both Luther and Calvin denounced with furious vigour. No doubt of it: the Reformation has been retreating for so long that it has dropped over the horizon. Whether ecumenical dreams of reunification constitute cause or effect of this collapse I must leave to better instructed observers to decide; and I ought probably also to add that I am myself merely reporting, having no stake in any of these religions.

Social criticism has played its part in this undermining of self-confidence. Once it was adjudged that a capitalism which appeared to exploit the many to the advantage of the few, and which could be charged with possessing no social conscience, marched hand in hand with the reformed religion, the fate of twentieth-century Protestantism was effectively sealed. (Not, perhaps, for ever: there are signs of doubt. As it is coming to be realized that before wealth is redistributed it had better first be created, and as it is becoming plain that no system has ever been so successful in creating wealth as capitalism was and is, the socialist commonplaces of yesterday are heard ever more rarely.) I have before this caused some annoyance, to put it no more strongly, by drawing attention to the part played by Tawney's *Religion and the Rise of Capitalism* in creating especially among the speakers of English (and in the last century English-speaking people formed the frontline of Protestant-ism) an entrenched hostility to the Reformation as the champion of false and materialist gods.[7] Despite my critics I still think it did precisely that. Speaking indeed with the tongues of Hugh Latimer and Thomas Lever, who saw in the reform the only hope of social improvement, Tawney denied to the adherents of Latimer's and Lever's religion the right to regard themselves as capable of producing social betterment. Joining hands with the battle against Fascism, this apparently authoritative demonstration turned what were really aspirant young Protestants in the rather vital generation between the wars towards Communism. Unable to do without a faith they found it unsurprisingly – since they shared the lack of a genuine historical under-standing that marked so much of the inter-wars revisionism – in the religion of Marx. Christopher Hill's is a good case in point: one of nature's Calvinists, he instead espoused the Asiatic version of historical materialism whose actuality sits so very ill with his warmhearted and generous personality. Many of that generation were really seeking the assurance given by a doc-trine of predestination, but in their search they found that the Lutheran–Calvinist tradition had been removed from the spectrum of religious beliefs available to young men much troubled by the state of the world and deter-mined to help improve it. Once the Reformation had become irrelevant to the young of that age it had in effect abdicated its hold altogether. Once again, I emphasize that I am not judging but describing.

Similarly, the intellectual message of the Reformation had started to weaken long before wars and the rise of global powers finally put an end to the European continent. The Reformation played an important part in giving to Europe a concept of individual rights anchored in law; the twen-tieth century has replaced this by a concept of individual claims anchored in economics. Except insofar as the latter leads much too readily to that over-riding of other individual claims (unrestrained selfishness) which the rule of law was designed to discipline, there is no cause to despise a transformation in mental processes which (leaving aside much pointless wailing and some very false purposes) has eliminated defects in society once regarded as God-given and inescapable. However, this transformation in thinking about the law – one of the chief pillars of European self-consciousness – cannot be re-conciled to the Protestant religion which, since it sets its face against any principle of sensual satisfaction, had to be in decline before such a change could come about. It was also, as has been said, the Reformation which opened the door to humanist principles in education and learning that from the later sixteenth century became generally accepted in Europe, Protestant or Catholic, and gave it one of its most manifestly identifying marks:

[7] See especially *Reformation Europe* (London, 1963), pp. 314–15.

humanist principles in education and learning have been under attack since the later nineteenth century and are now fighting a rearguard action which the makers of educational policy tend to regard with hostility or amusement or contempt.

It does, therefore, look as though the suppression of the continent of Europe, achieved by the new advance of Asia into its western peninsula in the wake of two great wars, was preceded by the accelerating collapse of all the major movements derived from the Reformation of the sixteenth century. The Reformation more than any other thing gave rise to that temporary phenomenon, Europe as a separate area of the world's land masses, and the decline of the Reformation prepared the ground for that phenomenon's disappearance. Presumably this is not the whole truth, and to some – especially to those who persist in believing that Europe still exists – it will be no sort of truth at all. The signs are against them.

The attack on the Church of England in the Long Parliament, 1640–1642

JOHN MORRILL

The problems of England in the 1630s stemmed from having a strong monarchy and a weak king. With a secure title, an effective and ubiquitous legal system, declining levels of public violence, a balanced (peacetime) budget and strong and pervasive ideologies of order and obedience, Charles I had many advantages over his predecessors. But he was a wholly incompetent king, mishandling patronage in such a way as unnecessarily to alienate powerful figures amongst the peerage and gentry, interfering in due process of law, breaking his solemn word when it suited him, blundering away his political initiatives in a self-imposed war with the Scots. But his greatest folly was to put himself at the head of a faction in the Church whose aims jarred significantly with the preferences and beliefs of the greater part of his subjects. By 1640, Charles' government was profoundly unpopular, and above all for its religious policies. Innovation in religion was even more compulsively listed in the petitions and addresses to the Long Parliament than was ship money. Yet England was psychologically far from civil war in 1640. The absence of a pretender made the simple remedy to his misgovernment (a *coup* on the precedents of 1399, 1461, 1485 or as a foreshadowing of 1688) impossible. It made civil war less likely; but it meant that if it did come, it would be a far more radical experience. It would involve a questioning of far deeper values, beliefs, certainties.

It is my contention that what made civil war possible in 1642 was a crisis of religion. Elsewhere I have argued that there were three linked but separable 'perceptions of misgovernment' in the 1630s and 1640s,[1] each playing a different role in the shaping of the civil war: the 'localist', the 'legal-constitutionalist' and the 'religious'; and that while the first two created political stalemate, the third proved to have the ideological dynamism to drive minorities to arms. The momentum of 'constitutionalist' argument in 1642

[1] J. S. Morrill, 'The Religious Context of the English Civil War', *Trans. Roy. Hist. Soc.*, 5th ser., XXXIV (1984).

was not sufficient. In this essay, I want to look more closely at how religious issues presented themselves to the Long Parliament.

In its first session (November 1640 to September 1641) the constitutional debates were conducted within a rhetorical and intellectual framework little different from that of the 1620s. No one who had attended the debates on the Petition of Right could be shocked by the arguments used against ship money, the prerogative courts, the evil counsellors.[2] Yet there was already a significant shift in the whole framework of reference within which the religious issues were discussed and this was causing an irrevocable division within the House of Commons.

Jacobean Parliaments had been little troubled by religious disputes.[3] The regular bills against pluralism, and for stricter observance of the sabbath, were in no sense 'puritan' bills, and the bishops would have said Amen to their pious intentions.[4] There was some anxiety about the legislative status (rather than the content) of the canons of 1604 and about the powers of High Commission, but this stemmed as much from the common law mind as from puritanism, and we no longer make easy connections between those two influences.[5]

But in the very last parliamentary session of the reign, and in the sessions from 1625 to 1629, religion returned as a major and increasingly bitter issue.[6] The cause was not a reawakening of puritan militancy but Court sponsorship of a group of divines whose writings appeared to depart sharply from the evolving spectrum of liberal protestant beliefs which had formed the agenda of the Jacobean debates. Some of these writings were sharply critical of pre-destinarian beliefs; others challenged the status of the *ecclesia anglicana* as on the protestant side of the unbridgeable gulf between the Christian reformed and antichristian Roman churches; or they sought to exalt the power of the king and to decry the power of parliaments, so that 'the subjects' goods must be arbitrarily disposed'.[7] Yet those who denounced these 'Arminians' did

---

2 See, for example, the case made for the 'normality' of the Long Parliament by Sheila Lambert, 'The Opening of the Long Parliament', *Hist. Jnl*, forthcoming. Lambert concentrates on constitutional and financial questions and not on religious ones.

3 E.g. C. Russell, *Parliaments and English Politics 1621–1629* (Oxford, 1979), pp. 26–32 and *passim*.

4 K. Parker, 'English Sabbatarianism, 1558–1642' (Univ. of Cambridge Ph.D. thesis, 1984), chap. 5 and 6.

5 J. P. Kenyon, *The Stuart Constitution* (Cambridge, 1962), pp. 126–9, 176–8. James in 1611 adjusted the membership and powers of the Court to take account of parliamentary criticisms.

6 Russell, *Parliaments and Politics*, pp. 29–32, 167–8, 230–3, 404–14, and *passim*; N. R. N. Tyacke, 'Arminianism in England in Religion and Politics, 1603–1640' (Univ. of Oxford D.Phil. thesis, 1968), *passim*.

7 *Complete Collection of State Trials*, eds. W. Cobbett and T. B. Howells, 33 vols. (London, 1809–26), IV, p. 26.

so for impeccably conservative reasons; to protect the Church of England from innovation and subversion.[8] None of the debates led to calls for change in a more protestant direction: for restrictions on episcopal power, for the reform of the prayer book or the abolition of 'superstitious' furnishings and fixtures in the church, all matters pursued by the Long Parliament in its first eighteen months. It cannot be doubted that the religious temper was raised by aggressive Court sponsorship of new opinions.[9] The reactions in the Commons and, to a lesser extent, in the Lords were not the reactions of M.P.s speaking to briefs or mandates from their constituents so much as reactions to what they found while present at the political centre. Only twenty petitions relating to religious issues were presented to the House in all the parliamentary sessions of the 1620s.[10] From the outset, the Long Parliament was inundated by petitions from individual parishes, from counties, from groups of ministers. Probably 800 parishes petitioned in the first two years of the Parliament denouncing their ministries as scandalous in life, doctrine or liturgical fashion.[11] All counties sent in addresses for and/or against episcopacy, the book of common prayer, and many took other religious issues.[12] The pressure on M.P.s was thus now largely from without. While the pressure grew out of the perceived threat to the established church, that threat was no longer seen as emanating from a handful of clerics puffed up by the patronage of Buckingham. It stemmed from an 'army of priests which doth many ways advance the design and plot of popery', an army commanded by the archbishop of Canterbury himself.[13] As Harbottle Grimston put it: Laud

is the only man, the only man that hath raised and advanced all those that, together with himself, have been the authors and causes of all our ruins, miseries, and calamities

[8] M. Finlayson, *Historians, Puritanism and the English Revolution* (Toronto, 1983), pp. 79–104. For reasons which will become clear I do not share Finlayson's account of the religious dynamics of 1640–1.

[9] As in the promotion of Montagu and Mainwaring shortly after they had been attacked in Parliament: and in the imposition of Buckingham as Chancellor of Cambridge, a move closely linked to the theological disputes there and to Buckingham's espousal of the Arminian position at the York House Conference; V. Morgan, 'Court, Country and Cambridge University: The Making of a Political Culture 1558–1642' (Univ. of East Anglia Ph.D. thesis, 1984), chap. 1.

[10] An approximate figure reached by browsing the *Commons Journal* but confirmed in a private communication from Dr W. Abbott.

[11] W. A. Shaw, *A History of the Church During the Civil Wars and Under the Commonwealth*, 2 vols. (London, 1900), II, p. 177. For the 100 + reported back to the House by September 1642, *ibid.*, II, pp. 295–304.

[12] A. Fletcher, *The Outbreak of the English Civil War* (London, 1981), pp. 91–124, 191–227, etc.

[13] From Francis Rous' speech carrying up the impeachment articles against John Cosin to the House of Lords, *State Trials*, IV, p. 26.

we now groan under that hath sat at the helm, to steer and manage all the projects that have been set on foot in this kindgom this ten years last past.[14]

It soon became clear to an increasing number of M.P.s that the threat to the protestant foundations of the Church of England was so great, and the penetration so deep, that remedial action was insufficient. Only the total demolition of the existing edifice, only the sterilization of the site and the erection of a new Temple could protect the nation from Antichrist.[15] This is the all important point: the fact that there was much hazy talk of 'primitive' episcopacy,[16] much imprecision about the future form of the church, that there is little evidence of committed presbyterianism has led historians to speak of the 'moderation' of 1641–2. Two things in particular are often stressed: that no bill against episcopacy was approved until the summer of 1642 and that the managers of the Long Parliament played down potentially divisive religious issues in the first session in order to allow less divisive constitutional reforms to be effected. It is hoped to demonstrate that this latter point is simply incorrect, and that there were very straightforward reasons why no bill could be approved. But principally the essay seeks to argue that ecclesiological indecision is not the same thing as religious moderation. In 1641 religious issues polarized the House of Commons into those who stood by the pre-Laudian church and those who were acting *de facto* to replace it; in 1642 religious issues divided those who remained at Westminster into those committed to seek fresh guarantees of the settlement of 1641 and those committed to fight for those guarantees.[17]

Between November 1640 and the spring of 1642 little legislative progress was made despite the best intentions of the managers of the Commons, but this did not prevent them from crippling the old religious order and adumbrating a new one by virtue of an assumption of unwonted judicial and administrative powers.[18] Laud and his henchmen were incarcerated, suspended,

---

[14] *Ibid.*, IV, p. 318. It is not being asserted here that the allegations were true. Nor that there is a coherent 'Arminianism' to which all 'Laudians' subscribed. Our concern is with what was said and believed at the time. For wise words on how the actions of the Laudians did constitute an affront to mainstream protestant opinion, see W. Lamont, *Godly Rule* (London, 1969), pp. 56–68.

[15] See below, pp. 118–19.

[16] Historians commonly conflate two distinct forms of 'primitive' episcopacy – the 'reduction' of the powers of bishops within the existing structure; and the establishment of preaching superintendants within an entirely new ecclesiastical order established in the wake of the abolition of the old order.

[17] Morrill, 'Religious Context', pp. 164–78.

[18] The standard accounts are Shaw, *English Church*, I, pp. 1–122, II, pp. 175–85, and the splendid recent study by Fletcher, *Outbreak*, pp. 91–124, and *passim*. A recent thesis by W. Abbott, 'The Issue of Episcopacy in the Long Parliament' (Univ. of Oxford D.Phil. thesis, 1982), is valuable on one aspect of the question. I am grateful

silenced; the church courts stilled; the parish clergy made accountable to committees of the House; religious literature licensed by another committee; liturgical laissez-faire encouraged; iconoclasm permitted. The House of Commons was depriving ministers of their freehold; restoring those silenced by Star Chamber or High Commission; endorsing arrangements for lectureships; claiming the jurisdiction of the ordinary over church furnishings, etc. Note the emphasis on the House of Commons. A principal reason for the failure to proceed by legislation, for acting on what has been termed 'the dictatorial assertion of a semi-political, semi-judicial court exercising an authority which can only be described and justified as revolutionary',[19] was that there was no majority for radical reform within the Lords. A majority in the Upper House remained stubbornly committed to the programme of 1628 – the defence of the Elizabethan settlement from 'Arminian' innovation.

A good example of the contrast between the sentiment of the two Houses can be found in their attitude to iconoclasm. On 23 January 1641 the Commons determined to act summarily to select commissioners in each county to deface, demolish or otherwise get rid of *all* 'images, altars or tables turned altarwise, crucifixes, superstitious pictures, ornaments and relics of idolatry' from all churches.[20] This was to go far beyond the reversal of recent innovations; it was to 'throw to the moals and the bats every rag that hath not God's stamp and name upon it',[21] to complete that left incomplete in the first Reformation. Yet only days earlier, the Lords ordered that 'the parsons, vicars, and curates in the several parishes shall forbear to introduce any rites or ceremonies that may give offence otherwise than those which are established by the law of the land'.[22] Their concern, as throughout the next twelve months, was that 'divine service should be performed as appointed by the Acts of Parliament of the Realm, and all disturbers of the same severely punished'.[23] In individual cases where innovations by ministers were uncovered, as with east-end railed-in altars, the Lords ordered a restoration so that the tables stood in 'the ancient place where they ought to do by the law, and as it hath done for the greater part of these three score years last past'.[24] There was no point in trying to press a bill for a wider iconoclasm

---

to Dr Abbott for showing me a draft of his thesis some time before it was submitted. I have not seen the final version. The theological issues are explored in G. Yule, *The Puritans in Power* (Sutton Courtney, 1981), chap. 5.

[19] Shaw, *English Church*, II, pp. 175–6.
[20] *Commons Journal*, II, p. 72. (hereafter C.J.).
[21] The call of Stephen Marshall in his sermon to the House of Commons at their Fast on 17 November 1640, Brit. Lib., Thomason Tracts (hereafter T.T.), E 204(9), p. 40.
[22] *Lords Journal*, IV, p. 134 (hereafter L.J.).
[23] *L.J.*, IV, pp. 100–1, 107, 113, 133, 225.
[24] *L.J.*, IV, p. 174.

through such a House (as the events of early September 1641, discussed below, also demonstrate). Equally the limited progress of anti-episcopal legislation may owe as much to the certainty that it would fail in the Lords as to lack of zeal in the Commons. The simple bill against the temporal authority of the bishops (and especially against their seats in the Lords) was comfortably defeated in the Upper House in the first session,[25] and ignored by it in the second session after a similar bill had passed all stages in the Commons within a week of the end of the recess.[26] Only the suicidal petition of the twelve bishops on 30 December against decisions taken after they were intimidated from taking their seats by the mass picket around Westminster Hall revived the peers' interest in the bill.[27]

The House of Lords, then, constituted a legislative stymie upon the House of Commons, at least until the expulsion of the bishops and the haemorrhage of royalist peers to York in the spring of 1642 gave the radicals their chance to bring the two Houses into line. Almost immediately the series of bills which had been marking time in the Commons – bills for abolishing superstition and idolatry, for uprooting scandalous ministers, for stricter sabbath observance and against pluralism and non-residence – were sent up and passed in the Upper House,[28] to be included in the Nineteen Propositions sent to the king in early June.[29] This legislative block had not, however, prevented the managers of the Commons from ensuring that such bills were in the pipeline. It was not fear of dividing the Commons but certainty of defeat in the Lords which had slowed down legislative progress. Those actually or potentially divisive ecclesiastical bills had been read before or at the same time as the less controversial remedial constitutional legislation.[30]

The Commons were thus forced into 'arbitrary' action to achieve reform; intense external pressures constantly reinforced the need for that reform.

[25] *C.J.*, II, pp. 114, 127; *L.J.*, IV, p. 256.

[26] *C.J.*, II, pp. 291–3 (21/23 October); 1st reading in the House of Lords, 23 October, but no second reading until 4 February 1642 after which it quickly passed all remaining stages (*L.J.*, IV, pp. 402, 562, 564, 580); Shaw, *English Church*, I, pp. 117–19.

[27] J. Rushworth, *Historical Collections*, 7 vols. (London, 1659–1701), IV, pp. 466–8; S. R. Gardiner, *The History of England from the Accession of James I to the Outbreak of the Civil War*, 10 vols. (London, 1884), X, pp. 120–6; B. S. Manning, *The English People and the English Revolution 1640–1649* (London, 1976), pp. 74–94.

[28] Bill for Abolishing Superstition, *C.J.*, II, pp. 79, 84, 162, 183, 199, 212, 246, 278,; replaced by a different bill in February 1642, *C.J.*, II, pp. 436, 437, 465, 476, 493, *L.J.*, IV, pp. 669, 679, V, pp. 210, 212, 248; Bill against Scandalous Ministers, *C.J.* II, pp. 109, 162, 183–4, 208–11, 491, 516; *L.J.*, V, pp. 19, 35, 156; Bill for Stricter Sabbath Observance, *C.J.*, II, pp. 348, 356.

[29] *L.J.*, V, pp. 97–9; Kenyon, *Stuart Constitution*, pp. 244–7.

[30] Indeed one can say that legislatively there was more activity in terms of ecclesiastical legislation in the first few months than in terms of constitutional legislation, and the two sorts of bill jostle one another in June and July 1641.

That pressure came in part from the waves of petitions, in part from the full discovery of the transgressions of the clergy in recent times, in part from the urgings of the preachers and pamphleteers.

We have already noted the contrast between the paucity of religious petitions to the Parliaments of the 1620s and the wealth of such petitions to the Long Parliament. Several hundred petitions poured in from parishioners alleging ceremonialism, unsound preaching (or no preaching at all) and moral laxity in their ministers.[31] Francis Rous, carrying up the impeachment articles against Cosin to the Lords, said that 'when a great man is coming, his sumpters, his furniture, his provisions, go before him: the pope's furniture, altars, copes, pictures and images are come before him; and if we believe Mr Cosin the very substance of the Mass; a certain sign that the pope is not far off'.[32] The House of Commons cannot but have been rattled by the evidence of enthusiastic espousal of popish ceremonialism by hundreds of the clergy. These were not the lone fanatics pursuing some private religious vision who had troubled Parliaments in the past. Here were men taking their cue from the bishops and not merely railing off the altar on a raised dais at the east end, or bowing to it and refusing communion to those who would not kneel before it, but who preached, as the rector of All Hallows, Barking, did: 'that they are black toads, spotted toads and venomous toads, like Jack Straw and Watt Tyler, that speak against the ceremonies of the Church; and that they were in the state of damnation'.[33] By no means a majority of the petitions were ever read in the House or reported from the committees to the House. But many members were well aware of the magnitude of the outcry: Sir Edward Dering had more than seventy such petitions against Kentish ministers in his papers.[34] W. A. Shaw suggests that the total number of parish petitions may have been around 800.[35] Something of the pressure they must have exerted can be seen from the business at just one meeting of the committee of religion, held on 16 November 1640.[36] The committee received a petition from Lincolnshire clergymen against the increase in popery, 'idle and frivolous ceremonies', the canons and for fresh laws against fornication, adultery and sabbath-breaking; several petitions against the imposition of altars and organs, against ministers who would not communicate those who

[31] For some examples, see *C.J.*, II, pp. 35, 139, 149; *The Journal of Sir Simonds D'Ewes from the Beginning of the Long Parliament to the Opening of the Trial of the Earl of Strafford*, ed. W. Notestein (New Haven, 1927), pp. 65, 77, 270, 276, 281, 419.

[32] *State Trials*, IV, p. 27.

[33] *C.J.*, II, p. 35.

[34] 'Proceedings Principally in the County of Kent in Connection with the Parliaments Called in 1640', ed. L. B. Larking, *Camden Society* (1862), pp. 101–240.

[35] Shaw, *English Church*, II, p. 38.

[36] *D'Ewes*, ed. Notestein, p. 38.

refused to kneel; against the pulling down of an ancient parish church in the shadow of St Paul's to provide building materials for the cathedral; and a report of the excommunication of a man who had proceeded against his minister for 'false doctrine'. Day in day out M.P.s were inundated with stories of a spreading cancer in the church, promoted and nourished by its leaders.

There is some evidence that the petitioning was orchestrated. One of Sir Edward Hyde's correspondents told how John Lilburne had come down with warrants to get signatures for a petition against him as a persecuting or innovating minister. Archdeacon Marler, in another letter to Hyde, reported how

> your House hath sent forth encouradgements and derections for busy men to traduce at such as be not of the faction...wherein such as ar zealous in the cause both of the clergy and layty...have mett together and consulted how to informe against such as we orthodox and obedient clergymen and to furnish your house with arguments for the overthrow of the hierarchy of the church.[37]

In January 1641, indeed, the Commons called for a survey of scandalous clergy from each county: the draft reply of five Herefordshire clergy survives, giving the great majority of the 193 ministers surveyed as scandalous, and pinning responsibility on the bishops, 'the main atlases which upholds the babel of confusion in church and commonwealth'.[38] Mrs Pearl finds evidence that the timing and content of London petitions was organized within the House.[39] One consequence of all this, according to a friend of Sir Edward Dering's, was 'the Monstrous Easye receipt of Petitions att the Standing Committees makes Authoritye declyne'.[40]

The flood of petitions was, then, both sustained by radical M.P.s wishing to reinforce the threat, as they saw it, of 'the army of priests' to the integrity of English protestantism, and was intended to soften up the concerned middle ground by constantly reinforcing the scale of that threat. This in turn was further strengthened by wider petitions on the urgent need for radical reform.

The most important of these were the London petition for root-and-branch reform (presented with 15,000 signatures on 11 December 1640),[41] a digest of county petitions subscribed by 750 clergy in all and presented to the House of Commons in late January 1641;[42] and the wave of county root-and-branch petitions (nineteen in all) which were launched with those from Kent and

37 Bodl. Lib., MS Clarendon 19, fo. 281, MS Clarendon 20, fo. 13.
38 Bodl. Lib., MS 206 Corpus Christi. I am grateful to Paul Gladwish for lending me his microfilm copy of this manuscript and for his comments on it.
39 V. Pearl, *London and the Outbreak of the Puritan Revolution* (Oxford, 1964), pp. 212–16.
40 Quoted in P. Zagorin, *The Court and the Country* (London, 1969), pp. 229–30.
41 Rushworth, *Historical Collections*, IV, pp. 93–7.
42 No copy of this petition survives. See Shaw, *English Church*, I, pp. 23–7.

Essex in mid-January.[43] Cumulatively, these were an even more stunning indictment of the state to which the Laudians had reduced the Church. Despite the reluctance of some historians to accept it, the aim of the petitions was unambiguously to be rid not only of the Laudians but of a church order so easily subverted by them. Certainly, as Mr Fletcher has suggested, there was only a limited comprehension of what the radical rhetoric would lead to. Sir Edward Dering, in a telling rewriting of the Ministers' Remonstrance, recorded that 'this hierarchical power may be totally abrogated, if the wisdom of this honourable House shall find it cannot be maintained by God's Word and to his glory'.[44] It must remain an open question just how soon a majority in the Commons wished to uproot episcopacy: it is clear that from early on in the Parliament a growing number accepted the need to uproot the Eliza-bethan settlement. Primitive episcopacy could either be a 'reduction' of the existing system, or part of a new system. Since the overwhelming concern of M.P.s was *religious* renewal, not *ecclesiastical* renewal, their flexibility and lack of precision on this point is not the problem which has worried historians. Lack of zeal for an articulated presbyterianism is not evidence of religious 'moderation'. Some have argued that the adoption of a more radical language was intended to placate the Scots, and disguised continuing religious con-servatism; it is more likely that it revealed a growing commitment to *a* fresh start but not *a particular* fresh start.[45] Thus, when the Commons voted in early February to refer the substance of the Ministers' Remonstrance to a committee, it reserved to itself debate on the future of episcopacy. This has usually been taken as evidence of caution, a refusal to commit so sensitive an issue to a committee of the kind so readily packed. But the fact that the question was already accepted as an open one, and to be aired where it could create greatest heat, is just as significant. On 25 January 1641, John Pyne, the Somerset radical, wrote to Thomas Smyth of Ashton Court that 'the heat in the lower House increases... [the Remonstrance] will require great consideration and time, especially episcopacy which hath so many advocates and so strong a party in our House'. In such circumstances, the managers were grasping nettles, not avoiding them.[46]

Petitions formed the first source of pressure on M.P.s, reinforcing the need for radical reform. The revelations of committees of enquiry into ecclesiastical misgovernment constituted a second, allied source. The most obvious of

---

[43] Fletcher, *Outbreak*, pp. 92–6.
[44] *Ibid.*, Lamont, *Godly Rule*, pp. 83–8.
[45] E.g. P. Crawford, *Denzil Holles, First Lord Holles* (London, 1979), pp. 43–52; C. L. Hamilton, 'The Basis of Scottish Efforts to Create a Reformed Church in England, 1640–1', *Church History*, xxx (1961), pp. 171–88; Yule, *Puritans in Power*, pp. 118–20.
[46] Fletcher, *Outbreak*, p. 97; Bristol Rec. Off., MS 36074, fo. 139.

these was the Committee for Scandalous Ministers, which looked into the petitions alleging 'vitiousness of life, errors in doctrine, contrary to the Articles of our Religion, and for the Practising and Pressing superstitious innovations contrary to Law'.[47] The reports of the committee merely reinforced the message of the petitions themselves, but they also made a pattern out of them. When John White, chairman of the committee, celebrated the expulsion of the one hundredth delinquent minister in a tract, he called it *The First Century of Scandalous Ministers, Malignant Priests, Made and Admitted unto Benefices By the Prelates, in whose hands the Ordination of Ministers and government of the Church hath been.*[48] It was not episcopal neglect but episcopal design which had created the pollution in the church.

Very few committee papers survive from the Commons.[49] But one important report from the committee set up to establish 'abuses of the universities in matters of religion' does survive to reveal an alarming picture, at least at Cambridge. The principal concern of the report was to investigate six preachers whose sermons reveal a startling range of theological speculation and also suggest deep divisions within the *Caput*, or committee of college Heads. None of the errant preachers had been punished and some had been aided by the intervention of the archbishop's chaplain. Some of the sermons were palpably in breach of the articles of religion, notably the eleventh on Justification. As late as August 1640, the Commons committee were told, William Norwich, Fellow of Peterhouse, preached in the University Church defending the need for works of satisfaction, recommending private confession, declaring that works had to accompany faith in the process of justification and urging the use of ceremonies. The Vice-Chancellor (John Cosin), with the support of a bare majority of the Heads, dismissed charges against him. While the University Church resounded to such preaching, the committee found that godly preachers had been silenced and that the Heads had encouraged not only popish teaching but also popish ceremonies: there were decorated altars, bowing and turning to the east in twelve of the sixteen colleges.[50] Dr Morgan has recently pointed out that after 1600 the Crown had taken an increasing interest in the elections to Cambridge Fellowships,

---

[47] Shaw, *English Church*, II, pp. 177–85.
[48] Brit. Lib., T.T., E 76(21).
[49] Except in brief summaries in some of the parliamentary diaries (e.g. *D'Ewes*, ed. Notestein, pp. 38–9, 150) and extracts from the Committee of Religion, of which Dering was chairman, 'Proceedings in Kent', ed. Larking, pp. 80–100.
[50] Brit. Lib., Harl. MS 7019, pp. 52–93, especially pp. 53, 61, 71, 73, 76–85. I owe my knowledge of this manuscript to David Hoyle who also kindly showed me a copy of his unpublished paper based upon it. See also J. D. Twigg, 'The University of Cambridge and the English Revolution' (Univ. of Cambridge Ph.D. thesis, 1983), chap. 2.

and specifically to Headships, viewing the colleges more as cathedral chapters than as independent corporations. The subversion of Cambridge followed the extended use of royal *congés d'élire*.[51]

Amongst the very earliest acts of the Long Parliament was the release from prison of the principal victims of the Laudian regime: Burton, Bastwicke and Prynne; Leighton; Lilburne; Smart; and Thomas Wilson.[52] Committees were set up to investigate the circumstances of their trial and punishment, the reports of their committees coming in at intervals. These reports consistently emphasized not only that they had suffered for upholding orthodoxy, but that proceedings against them had been arbitrary or in breach of the rule of law.[53] This was a much more prominent theme in the investigations of the Lords' committees which in the 1640s reviewed several hundred cases from the lower courts. Mr Hart, who has investigated this process, is in no doubt that many of the worst instances of the abuse of due process lay in the church courts. Several ministers had been ejected on flimsy or trumped-up simony charges to make way for Laudians like Dr William Beale; ministers were ejected or suspended on the evidence of a single witness; the Court of Arches refused to hear appeals from a number of churchwardens or others in cases relating to altar rails, apparently because Laud 'had given order that no inhibitions should go into Northamptonshire, Bedfordshire or Buckinghamshire without his special knowledge'.[54]

There can be little doubt that it was the intention of the parliamentary managers to exploit this flow of information that linked together the ills of the church into a grand conspiracy. Far from playing down religious issues, they amplified and focussed them. While it is possible to exaggerate the importance of 'king' Pym in the early months of the Long Parliament,[55] his role was an important one. Nowhere is this more evident than in his

[51] Morgan 'Court, Country and Cambridge University', *passim*.
[52] *C.J.*, II, pp. 22, 24, 25, 40.
[53] E.g. *C.J.*, II, pp. 90, 102, 123, 124, 134; *D'Ewes*, ed. Notestein, pp. 83, 240–1; Rushworth, *Historical Collections*, IV, p. 253.
[54] J. Hart, 'The House of Lords and the Reformation of Justice' (Univ. of Cambridge Ph.D. thesis, forthcoming), chap. 4; see Farren vs. Clarke, H.L.R.O., Main Papers for 6 February 1641; Garfield vs. Clarke, H.L.R.O., Main Papers for 22 December 1640; Bloxam vs. Sandiland, H.L.R.O., Main Papers for 5 January 1641 and 10 March 1641; *L.J.*, pp. 155, 181; also H.L.R.O., Main Papers, 8 February 1641, *L.J.*, IV, p. 181.
[55] Lambert, 'Opening of the Long Parliament', argues that Pym's role has been greatly exaggerated. Many of her points are of substance, but it seems to me that it reduces Pym from the most important manager of the Commons into being one of the most important, especially with regard to religion which the article ignores. The article also rightly stresses the important role of the peerage in the events of 1640–2. It is vital however, to distinguish the role of individual peers from the role of the House of Lords.

promotion of religious issues in the early weeks. On the 7th of November it was Pym who presented the petitions of the wives of Burton and Bastwicke to the Lower House; on the 9th he sought a committee 'to see that papists depart from town'; on the 10th, when Peter Smart revived his petition from the Short Parliament about Cosin's innovations at Durham Cathedral, 'Mr Pym desired to consider who promoted Dr Cusons to be dean', a clear escalation. In the following days and weeks, he brought in three petitions against unjust proceedings in the Court of High Commission; he was one of those who spoke against the canons; and he was the first M.P. to suggest that Laud should be impeached for treason. He was appointed to most committees on religion, including both the Grand Committee and the more specific enquiries into the cases of Leighton and Lilburne.[56] This is not compatible with the common view of him as putting religious issues on a back burner until the less controversial measures to remedy the secular ills of the commonwealth had been approved.[57]

It is, perhaps, worth stressing the virulence of the attack on the leading churchmen, more violent in tone than the attacks on counsellors and judges. Laud was impeached in December 1640, Wren bailed pending the drawing up of articles, committees set to work to draw up charges against Piers of Bath and Wells and that majority of the bishops who had supported the canons of 1640. Cosin, Master of Peterhouse, and a number of officials of the church courts were also investigated. This was a wider trawl than amongst the lay authors of misgovernment. Once again, however, the Commons ran into a stone wall in the Lords who simply failed to take action on any of the impeachments.[58]

It is true that there is no reference to 'Arminianism' in any of the impeachment articles (in comparison with the debates of the late 1620s).[59] But the articles against Laud speak of his espousal of 'divers doctrines and opinions contrary to the articles of religion'.[60] Furthermore, the innovating ceremonialism of which all were accused was intended to exalt the altar and subdue the pulpit, to emphasize the sacramental grace of the communion promiscuously offered to all who would kneel to receive it. One obsessive theme, however, runs through all the Commons investigations: the usurpation of the royal supremacy: Laud 'traiterously assumed to himself a papal

56 *C.J.*, II, p. 24; *D'Ewes*, ed. Notestein, pp. 4, 17, 21, 136, 149, 162, 163, 169.
57 See also the dominant position accorded to religious issues in his major address to the Commons on 7 November, Rushworth, *Historical Collections*, IV, pp. 21–4.
58 *State Trials*, IV, pp. 22–41, 63–82, 315ff. For the Commons' appeals to the Lords to take up the cases, see, e.g., *C.J.*, II, pp. 292, 333–4.
59 Russell, *Parliaments and Politics*, pp. 404–14, and *passim*; H. Schwartz, 'Arminianism and the English Parliament 1624–1629', *Jnl Brit. Studs.*, XII (1973).
60 *State Trials*, IV, p. 327.

and tyrannical power, both in ecclesiastical and temporal matters...to the disinheron of the Crown, dishonour of his Majesty and derogation of his supreme authority in matters ecclesiastical'[61] (as Pym glossed it, 'he hath made the king's throne a footstool for his own and their pride');[62] Wren 'assumed to himself an arbitrary power;[63] Cosin was alleged to have said that 'the king hath no more power over the church than the boy who rubs my horse's heels';[64] Montagu is supposed to have written to Laud that 'the bishoprick of Norwich, since the total desolation and dissolution of the former bishoprick by King Henry the eighth, who stole the sheep and gave not so much as the trotters for God's sake, is a meane thing';[65] and Sergeant Wilde, moving the impeachment of the thirteen bishops for their role in the making of the canons, described the latter as containing 'in them divers matters contrary to the king's prerogative'.[66]

The attack on the clergy was intended to demonstrate the existence of a popish conspiracy against the commonwealth. The king had been seduced by the papists at Court and the spawn of the papists in the Church into surrendering his power into their hands. Much of the rhetoric of 1640–2 was apocalyptic: Sir John Wray's speech on 25 November 1640 is often quoted but infrequently glossed:

> What must we do then to preserve our Religion safe and sound to us and our posterity, that our golden candlestick be not removed? Why, the only way is to fall to our work in earnest and lay the Axe to the Root, to unloose the long and deep Fangs of Superstition and Popery, which being done the Bark will soon fall down.[67]

The Church of England is here identified with one of the seven golden candlesticks described in the Book of Revelation. The struggle against popery was matched by the struggle for a New Jerusalem. The deeper the perception of a Popish Plot – as it unravelled itself in 1641 through the machinations of army plots, the Irish Rebellion, the Attempt on the Five Members – the greater the need to push forward to complete the Reformation, to fall in with God's Will that His work be done.[68] Here the conviction, the rhetoric,

---

[61] *Ibid.*, p. 326.   [62] *Ibid.*, p. 322.   [63] *Ibid.*, p. 35.   [64] *Ibid.*, p. 25.

[65] W. Prynne, *A Breviate of the Late William, Archbishop of Canterbury* (London, 1645), p. 555.

[66] *C.J.*, II, p. 233.

[67] J. Nalson, *An Impartial Collection of the Great Affairs of State From the Beginning of the Scotch Rebellion in the Year 1639 to the Murder of King Charles I*, 2 vols. (London, 1682–3), I, p. 513. For a fuller discussion of the theme of 'protestant apocalyptic imperialism', see P. Christianson, *Reformers and Babylon* (Toronto, 1978), and Lamont, *Godly Rule*, both *passim*.

[68] For the widespread belief that there *was* a Popish Plot and for evidence that, in a sense, there was, see the excellent recent book of C. Hibbard, *Charles I and the Popish Plot* (Chapel Hill, 1983), chaps. 8 and 9, taken up and developed throughout Fletcher, *Outbreak*.

the authority of the preachers was all-important. We know that those who delivered Fast Sermons to the Long Parliament were carefully chosen and that they preached to encourage the godly. Their sermons were emphatic on the need for Reformation, but less clear on the means. They reinforced the split between the political conservatism of emergent parliamentarianism and the religious commitment – 'Consider what some say of Solomon', said Edmund Calamy, 'that it was his great fault, that he bestowed more time in building of his owne house, than he did in building the house of God.'[69]

In his study of the Fast Sermons, John Wilson distinguishes the 'prophetic' from the 'apocalyptic' tradition of preaching. In the former – espoused by the preachers of 1640–2 – the minister 'delivered' the 'word' from the Lord, a 'word' embodying judgment and mercy contingent upon the people turning or returning to Him. It emphasized 'human ability to exercise agency'. (The 'apocalyptic' tradition emphasized not an offer from God requiring human acquiescence, but God's irresistible action quite independently of human agency. This style of preaching was taken up by other preachers later in the 1640s.)[70] This is a crucial distinction. Preachers like Cornelius Burges, Stephen Marshall, Edmund Calamy and Thomas Goodwin all took Old Testament stories of God's offers to Israel and the consequences of human acceptance or rejection of those offers.[71] The history of Israel was precisely and literally matched to the history of Britain. The terrible choices were hammered home:

If a Nation doth evil in God's sight, God will repent of the good he intended...when God begins to draw back his mercies from a Nation, that Nation is in a wofull plight ... But on the contrary, if we turn from our evil ways, God will perfect his building, and finish his plantation, he will make us a glorious Paradise, an habitation fit for Himself to dwell in.[72]

Thomas Goodwin reminded the Commons how the Israelites were freed to 'build the Temple and restore God's worship' after 'the Babilonian Monarchy [Rome's type] had trod downe the holy city, and laid waste the

[69] Brit. Lib., T.T., E 133(18), p. 50 (E. Calamy, *God's Free Mercy to England*).

[70] J. F. Wilson, *Pulpit in Parliament* (Princeton, 1969), pp. 198–200, and *passim*. More generally, see H. R. Trevor-Roper, 'The Fast Sermons of the Long Parliament', in *Religion, the Reformation and Social Change*, ed. H. R. Trevor-Roper (London, 1867), pp. 294–314. These sermons were only the most immediate and pressing of the advices offered to Parliament. Both Christianson, *Reformers and Babylon*, and the introduction to *Milton Prose Works*, ed. D. M. Wolfe, 8 vols. (New Haven, 1956–83), I (1956), discuss the wider literature.

[71] E.g. Brit. Lib., T.T., E 204(8), C. Burges, *The First Sermon Preached to the Honourable House of Commons*; T.T., E 133(9), S. Marshall, *Meroz Cursed*; T.T., E 131(29), E. Calamy, *England's Looking Glass*; T.T., E 147(13), T. Goodwin, *Zerubbabel's Encouragement to Finish the Temple*.

[72] Brit. Lib., T.T., E 131(29), Calamy, *Looking Glass*, p. 58.

Temple and worship of God'. But after laying the foundations and establishing the principal ceremonies of the faith, they found themselves hampered by 'a company of Samaritans that were adversaries of the Jewes...a generation of men who were not heathens in their profession for that they professed the same religion with the Jewes...and yet were not true Jewes either, nor perfectly of the same religion, but a mungrell and mixt kind...intermingling heathenish idolatries with Jewish worship'. These Samaritans were initially 'but underhand adversaries, for they friendly offer to build with them but so as with an intent to have defiled and spoiled the work', but later they openly opposed it: 'they troubled them (all they could) in building. And they ceased not here, but further, they incensed and made the Court against them...both by hiring counsellors...and also by insinuating to those mighty Persian kings...'. Only with the appearance of the prophet Zachariah many years after the release from Babylon was Zerubbabel encouraged to drive out the Samaritans and bring the people back to their task. The application to English history since the Reformation is self-evident.[73]

The spiritual imperatives were clear. As the managers of the Commons ducked and weaved in the constitutional debate, responding to royal escalations of the conflict, making the minimum claims to a share in power compatible with self-preservation and the protection of the reforms achieved by due legislative process, they thrust forward with ecclesiastical revolution. We have seen how, until the spring of 1642, legislative remedy was denied to them. We have seen how the revelations in petitions, in the investigations of the Houses and their committees, opened the eyes of members to the apparent magnitude and central coordination of a plot against the protestant foundation of the church. The preachers warned them, with terrible historical examples, of the consequences of deferring or withholding action. For those with a dualistic view of the world, as the battleground of immanent forces of Good and Evil, the years 1640–2 saw the mists clear, the future certain.[74] It became less and less a question of tinkering with the Elizabethan settlement in order to render it safe from another William Laud: there was a necessity to build such a church as would make all men obedient to God's word and turn them into His loving servants. Then indeed would the fruits of peace and prosperity flourish. The political struggles over the church in these years were not in essence sterile debates over ecclesiology: they were an attempt to realize a transformation in Man. For the next twenty years, those driven on to lead the Revolution were caught up with that elusive task, to hold onto their glimpse of Zion's glory.

[73] Brit. Lib., T.T., E 147(13), Goodwin, *Zerubbabel's Encouragement*, pp. 3–6.
[74] The powerful hold of apocalyptic anti-catholicism is explored by Hibbard, *Charles I and the Popish Plot*, *passim*.

Yet such language and such rhetoric repelled as many as it attracted.[75] While it was possible, all too possible, to see Charles I in 1641 as mendacious, or as the tool of a papist conspiracy, it was also possible to see him as a chastened and wiser king: as a man who had accepted constitutional reform, remodelled his Council, abandoned the Laudians, appointed moderate bishops. It was also possible to lay alongside the threat of popish risings the reality of popular disturbances in London and elsewhere, a perceived collapse of social order which the parliamentary leadership at the least condoned. A great many of those who denounced most bitterly the innovations of the Laudians did so out of concern for and love of the evolving practice and piety of the Elizabethan and Jacobean church. They were not unmoved by the revelations of 1641, but they put them into a different context. Less obsessive in their anxieties about Catholicism, they looked harder and less indulgently at the fissures within radical protestantism, at the spread of separatism and at doctrines of social levelling preached by some of the separatists.

These were the circumstances in which the attack on the Church of England took place: from an apparent unity in 1640 against the Laudian experiment with a general rhetorical appeal for reform to the confrontation of 1642 between 'the true reformed protestant religion by law established without any connivance of popery or innovation' and 'the godly reformation'. It was this which made civil war necessary.

Between the summoning of the Long Parliament and the outbreak of the civil war, then, notwithstanding the failure of its attempts at legislation, the two Houses had toppled the Church of England and had equipped themselves to turn it into a department of state under gentry control. Few bishops by the summer of 1642 retained any authority in their dioceses; most church courts had ceased to function; there was no mechanism to enforce, and parliamentary encouragement to modify, the liturgy and formal worship of the church; the outward and visible sign of Laudian innovation – the altar rail – had vanished in most parishes far more speedily than it had gone up. A vacuum had been created which the Houses were proceeding to fill.

From early in 1641 ministers were deprived of their livings and freehold by order of one or other of the Houses: the assumption of this quasi-judicial, quasi-executive power was wholly without precedent and went undefended. No comparable assertion in the civil sphere is to be found before 1643.[76] Early examples included Edward Finch of Christchurch, London, too drunk

75 Morrill, 'Religious Context', pp. 172–4.
76 D. H. Pennington, 'The Making of the War, 1640–2', in *Puritans and Revolutionaries*, eds. D. Pennington and K. Thomas (Oxford, 1978), pp. 161–85 examines the growth of parliamentary executive control of finance which is much more hesitant and circumspect in questions of legality; see also Morrill, 'Religious Context', pp. 169–70.

to take communion to the sick, a whoremonger and an innovator (and, perhaps most to the point, brother of the disgraced Lord Keeper);[77] Immanuel Uty, for popery in teaching and ceremony, for haunting alehouses and saying that the bishops not the king headed the church;[78] and George Preston of Rotherthorpe, Northamptonshire, who thought that 'Parliaments in England never did any good nor never would, but that his hogs were fit to make Parliament men of, and their sty a place fit for them to sit in', and that those who gadded to sermons were 'like jackdaws that hopped from twig to twig; and that they did go to several churches to commit whoredom'.[79] By 1642 the number was escalating: over seventy were dispossessed between February and July 1642.[80]

At the same time the House of Commons was setting aside judgments in Star Chamber and High Commission against puritan martyrs of the 1630s. A special committee was set up to consider abuses of ecclesiastical jurisdiction in Lincolnshire;[81] in the case of Peter Smart, the prebend of Durham who had tangled with John Cosin, the proceedings in High Commission were adjudged 'illegal and unjust and ought not to bind'. His degradation from the ministry was reversed and his livings (in plurality) restored, and Cosin and his judges ordered to pay damages and costs. While the Commons proceeded in many such cases by committee fiat, the Lords proceeded in another fashion, building on but greatly expanding their formal procedures of judicial review.[82]

On 14 June 1641, the Commons ordered that there be sermons every Sunday afternoon in every cathedral church;[83] on 8 September, they went further: 'It shall be lawful for the parishioners of any parish...to set up a lecture and to maintain an orthodox minister at their own charge, to preach every Lord's day where there is no preaching, and to preach one day in every week when there is no weekly lecture.'[84] From the end of the summer onwards, the Commons spent much time ratifying appointments in particular parishes, creating lectureships by combination and imposing sanctions on vicars and rectors resisting 'men thrusting their sickles into another man's harvest'.[85]

By the summer of 1641 the Commons had assumed power to license

[77] *C.J.*, II, p. 139; Brit. Lib., Harl. MS 163 (D'Ewes' Journal), fo. 537.

[78] *C.J.*, II, pp. 65, 148; Brit. Lib., Harl. MS 163, fo. 190; *D'Ewes*, ed. Notestein, pp. 232–3.

[79] *D'Ewes*, ed. Notestein, p. 270.   [80] Shaw, *English Church*, II, pp. 295–300.

[81] *C.J.*, II, p. 56.

[82] *Ibid.*, p. 71, and cf. *ibid.*, p. 90 (Bastwicke), p. 102 (Burton), p. 123 (Prynne), p. 124 (Leighton), p. 134 (Lilburne).

[83] *Ibid.*, p. 174.   [84] *Ibid.*, pp. 281–3, and cf. p. 206.

[85] *Ibid.*, pp. 381, 484, 485, 488, 491, 492, etc. (over fifty between March and June 1642 alone). See also *Private Journals of the Long Parliament*, eds. W. H. Coates, A. S. Young, V. F. Snow (New Haven, 1982), p. 355.

sermons and other books, and the fact that this activity grew out of powers granted to a sub-committee of the Grand Committee of Religion displays the importance of the licensing of religious works. The committee, initially chaired by Sir Edward Dering, also investigated the publication of 'unsound' works.[86]

These developments helped to polarize the House of Commons; the assumption of such powers and the pursuit of ends so hostile to the sustaining of the established religion were bitterly resented. The greatest disputes, however, on the eve of the summer recess, in Houses thinned by departures for the country after a ten-month session, concerned the orders against innovations. By a resolution on 1 September, altar rails were to be removed, chancels levelled, communion tables settled in the nave, crucifixes, candles and images taken away, bowing banned and sabbatarianism strictly enforced. Churchwardens had full authority to put this into practice, justices of the peace and mayors the duty to report those who disobeyed to Parliament after the recess. The device was a controversial addition to the growing stock of assumed executive powers; but it met a double (and related) challenge. In the Commons, Culpepper successfully moved that 'we would likewise provide a remedy against such as did villifie and contemne the common prayer book established by act of parliament' and it was referred to a committee how this might be phrased. The resultant draft was then rejected after a long and acrimonious debate on 6 September. The issue was then taken up by the Lords who also sought to protect the prayer book and to reiterate their commitment to the 'religion as by law established'. In issuing its declaration on its own, the Commons made the astonishing claim about the Lords' statement:

which being presented to the House of Commons, it was thought unseasonable at this time, to urge the severe execution of the said Laws: whereupon it was voted that they do not consent to those orders... [and] that it may be understood that the last order of the Lords was made with the consent of 11 Lords... We expect that the Commons... quietly attend the Reformation intended without any tumultuous disturbance of the worship of God.[87]

Not surprisingly, the House found itself with many problems arising from the declaration and much recrimination after the recess.[88]

[86] S. Lambert, 'The Beginning of Printing for the House of Commons, 1640–1642', *The Library*, 6th ser., III (1981), pp. 43–61; 'Proceedings in Kent', ed. Larking, pp. 80–100.

[87] *C.J.*, II, pp. 279–87; Brit. Lib., Harl. MS 164, fos. 888–90, 895–914. Rushworth, *Historical Collections*, IV, p. 385.

[88] *The Journal of Sir Simonds D'Ewes From the First Recess of the Long Parliament to the Withdrawal of King Charles from London*, ed. W. H. Coates (New Haven, 1942), pp. 5–6, 11, 12, 19–20, 35, 41; *Private Journals*, eds. Coates et al., pp. 136–7. See the pointed reiteration of the Lords' declaration and of Culpepper's amendment in the royal declaration on religion on 10 December 1641, Rushworth, *Historical Collections*, IV, pp. 392, 456–7.

This decisive debate revealed fully the basic split within the Long Parliament: there was an anglican party before there was a royalist party and a commitment to 'the reformation intended' before any recognition that non-negotiable constitutional issues would arise. The radicals who won the day 'expected' that 'the reformation intended' (i.e. licensed iconoclasm) would not occasion tumult. But they had already exonerated lay preachers and were soon to stay proceedings at common law against those who absented themselves from their own parish church.[89]

These assumptions of power over religion were, of course, pragmatic and piecemeal. But in debates that were often long and acrimonious, they were to lay the groundwork for a future church permanently and explicitly under gentry control. In June 1641, the Commons approved a scheme to set up a synod which would propose a permanent settlement of religion: meanwhile the Houses were to empower nine lay commissioners in every county, chosen by its parliamentary representatives, to discharge all ecclesiastical jurisdiction, and both to run the church and to supervise a massive redistribution of episcopal and capitular wealth. Clergy who resisted the authority of these commissioners would incur the penalties of *praemunire*. Nominated clergy would ordain and assist in determining cases of heresy and schism. But powers of excommunication would lie exclusively with Parliament itself. At other times in 1641, the Commons proposed bodies of lay commissioners in each county to proceed against scandalous ministers (through jury trial), and to establish lay feoffees to handle alienated church land and impropriations.[90]

Not all parliamentarians were erastians;[91] but it is hard to believe that those who pushed through the bill 'for the abolition of archbishops, bishops', etc., on second reading on 27 May 1641 by 139 to 108 envisaged surrendering this gentrified church. In the spring of 1642, they did set up an assembly of divines to advise on a permanent solution.[92] This hand-picked assembly was as dependent on the Houses for the fate of its proposals as it was for its summons. The lack of commitment to a presbyterian scheme and the determination on secular control of the means to effect the building of Jerusalem does not make the religious imperatives any less vital.

Between 1640 and 1642 the Church of England collapsed, its leaders reviled and discredited, its structures paralysed, its practice if not yet proscribed, at

[89] *Private Journals*, eds. Coates *et al.*, pp. 302–3; Brit. Lib., Harl. MS 163, fo. 669.
[90] A. Fletcher, 'Concern for Renewal in the Root and Branch Debates of 1641', *Studies in Church History*, XIV (1977).
[91] Yule, *Puritans in Power*, pp. 149–208.
[92] *C.J.*, II, pp. 159, 579; *L.J.*, IV, pp. 595, 672–3; *Private Journals*, eds. Coates *et al.*, pp. 133–9; Brit. Lib., Harl. MS 163, fos. 475, 514.

least inhibited. In the years to follow, yet worse was to befall it. And yet in every year of its persecution after 1646, new shoots sprang up out of the fallen timber: bereft of episcopal leadership, lacking any power of coercion, its observances illegal, anglicanism thrived.[93] As memories of the 1630s faded and were overlaid by the tyrannies of the 1640s, by the attempts of Zerubbabel and Zachariah to frogmarch the nation to the site of the Temple, the deeper rhythms of the Kalendar and the ingrained perfections of Cranmer's liturgies bound a growing majority together. In April 1660, three weeks before the Declaration of Breda and the proclamation of Charles II, Easter, a forbidden Festival, was celebrated in most parish churches up and down the country. It was the collapse of the old church which presaged the downfall of the monarchy: and it was to be the church's survival which was to herald the Restoration.

[93] J. S. Morrill, 'The Church of England 1642–9', in *Reactions to the English Civil War*, ed. J. S Morrill (London, 1982), pp. 89-114.

Oliver Cromwell and the
Sin of Achan

BLAIR WORDEN

Oliver Cromwell knew that God had a special and surpassing purpose in the civil wars. The Lord 'hath been pleased to make choice of these islands wherein to manifest many great and glorious things', 'such things amongst us as have not been known in the world these thousand years'.[1] For 'reasons best known to Himself', God had wonderfully raised up Cromwell, a 'weak instrument', 'not worthy the name of a worm'. Under his leadership 'the poor despised people of God', now miraculously delivered from the persecution of the 1630s, and 'by providence having arms', laid low the mighty in victories which, won as they were by 'an army despised by our enemies, and little less than despaired of by our friends', confounded all human calculations.[2] When Cromwell and the saints sought to comprehend the size and the meaning of those mercies, they turned to the Old Testament, which they knew so intimately. There they found the figurative models, the 'parallels', which came to dominate their political imaginations and to shape their interpretations of political and military events. In the divine plan of history, they believed, the deliverance of 'God's peculiar' in England might have a place equal in importance to the salvation of the people of Israel. They had passed out of an Egypt, through a Red Sea, towards a Promised Land.

Their progress constituted in Cromwell's mind a 'remarkable series' or 'chain' of 'providences'. The saints 'were never beaten; wherever they engaged the enemy they beat them continually. And truly this...has some instruction in it.'[3] There was Marston Moor, which Cromwell believed to have 'all the evidences of an absolute victory obtained by the Lord's blessing

[1] *A Declaration of his Highness the Lord Protector and the Parliament...for a Day of Solemn Fasting and Humiliation in the Three Nations* (London, [September] 1654); W. C. Abbott, *Writings and Speeches of Oliver Cromwell*, 4 vols. (Cambridge, Mass., 1937–47), III, p. 592 (hereafter cited as Abbott).
[2] Abbott, I, p. 697, II, p. 483; Stephen Marshall, *A Sacred Record* (London, 1645), p. 30.
[3] Abbott, IV, p. 471.

upon the godly party principally'. There was Naseby, where, inspecting the cavalry on the morning of battle, he 'could not...but smile out to God in praises, in assurance of victory, because God would, by things that are not, bring to naught things that are'. Then, in 1648, when royalist risings seemed certain to crush the godly party, the New Model was vouchsafed the spectacular triumphs of the second civil war. Cromwell cried out in astonishment at those 'wonderful works of God, breaking the rod of the oppressor, as in the day of Midian...Wherever anything in this world is exalted, or exalts itself, God will put it down, for this is the day wherein He alone will be exalted.'[4]

Still greater mercies were to come. In 1649, the year when 'providence and necessity' directed Cromwell to kill the King, and when the Irish then threatened to destroy the infant Commonwealth, God bestowed 'astonishing', 'marvellous great', 'unspeakable mercies' at Dublin and Drogheda and Wexford. Those victories, wrote Cromwell to Parliament, were 'seals of God's approbation of your great change of government'. In a private letter he rejoiced that God still prospered

His own work in our hands; which to us is the more eminent because truly we are a company of poor, weak and worthless creatures. Truly our work is neither from our brains nor from our courage or strength, but that we follow the Lord who goeth before, and gather what He scattereth, that so all may appear to be from Him... What can we say to these things? If God be for us, who can be against us? Who can fight against the Lord and prosper? Who can resist His will?

In 1650, now Lord General, Cromwell invaded Scotland. On the day after Dunbar, where the army together with the godly cause had seemed doomed to extinction, Cromwell wrote to Parliament to report 'one of the most signal mercies God hath done for England and His People, this war...It would do you good to see and hear our poor foot go up and down making their boast of God.'[5] The outcome was especially significant because both sides had 'appealed' to 'the God of battle' to decide between them.[6] 'The Lord hath heard us', proclaimed Cromwell, 'upon as solemn an appeal as any experience can parallel.' A year later the royalists were finally vanquished by that 'crowning mercy', the 'marvellous salvation wrought at Worcester'.[7]

How could the magnitude of those deliverances be measured? How could they be sufficiently praised? Cromwell said a great deal about the central

[4] Ibid., I, pp. 287, 365, 619, 638.
[5] Ibid., II, pp. 103, 124, 173, 235–6, 324–5.
[6] Original Letters and Papers of State...addressed to Oliver Cromwell, ed. J. Nickolls (London, 1743), pp. 19, 25, 73 (hereafter cited as Original Letters).
[7] Abbott, II, pp. 335, 463.

place of providence in his life, in his victories, in the making of his decisions. Yet however much he said, he could never feel that he had done justice to his theme. How, amidst the lengthy and autobiographical 'narratives of matter of fact' which he visited upon so many audiences, was he to communicate 'those things wherein the life and power of them lay; those strange windings and turnings of providence' which gave a thread of meaning to 'the lowest historical narration...there being in very particular...a remarkable imprint of providence set upon it, so that he who runs may read it'?[8] He was unmoved when men questioned whether God's will could truly be known from the results of battles, or when they reminded him how unsearchable are God's judgements, and His ways past finding out; when they protested that Christ's kingdom is not of this world; or when they remarked that since in Scripture God often prospered the wicked but only for a season, his confidence in the Lord's approval might be premature. His knowledge of God's favour came not from logic but from experience, and not so much from the victories themselves as from the spiritual 'manifestations of His presence' among the saints in arms. The Lord declared His 'approbation and acceptance...not only by signal outward acts, but to the heart also'.[9] Victory was an aid to the sanctification of His elect: it strengthened the believer's assurance and assisted the workings of grace upon his heart. 'I think, through these outward mercies,' Cromwell told his friend Lord Wharton after the victories of 1648, 'faith, patience, love, all are exercised and perfected, yea, Christ formed, and grows to a perfect man within us.'[10]

Cromwell's trust in God's providence was the 'rock', the 'sure refuge', the 'sun and a shield' of his life. Even in adversity 'I can laugh and sing in my heart when I speak of these things.'[11] Through the fear of God he conquered the fear of men. When providence led him into unknown political territory he followed unflinchingly, and took his weaker brethren with him. And yet, within all the joy and confidence and wonder of his providentialism, there was always room for anxiety, perhaps even for doubt. What happened when, as in 1646–8 and again from 1651, peace afforded no military successes to fortify the saints, or to help them discern God's will amidst the complexities of political negotiation and compromise? What should His elect think when God 'mingled the cup' of triumph by dividing them among themselves, or by marking them out for private affliction and grief? And there was a further, graver possibility: that the God of battle, who had brought so many victories, would one day bring defeat.

8 *Ibid.*, III, pp. 53–4.   9 *Ibid.*, II, p. 190.
10 *Ibid.*, I, p. 646. Cf. *ibid.*, I, p. 698, II, p. 103; John Bond, *Ortus Accidentalis* (London, 1645), p. 34.   11 Abbott, III, p. 590

Of course, the saints expected setbacks. They expected God to send them 'rebukes', 'trials' and 'corrections', in order to preserve them from the 'security', the 'drowsiness', the 'sloth' which unbroken prosperity might bring. Although God loved to melt the soul with mercies, He sometimes needed to scourge it with judgements. So adversity might be a sign of grace. Yet other, less assuring explanations were possible. God was known to abandon and exchange his imperfect 'instruments' when they began 'to fail, and fall off like untimely fruit'.[12] Might not the saints' difficulties signify the withdrawal of His presence from them? Might He not be angry with them? That a wrathful God providentially punishes sin, and takes vengeance upon it in order to vindicate His honour, was a seventeenth-century common-place, which Cromwell's mentor and friend Thomas Beard wrote a long and famous book to illustrate. 'Sin causes wrath', John Preston succinctly explained; 'sin and wrath are knit together, they are inseparable'. 'Wrath for sin! Who knows not that?' Henry Ferne asked the civil war royalists.[13]

God's punishments could visit communities and nations as well as individuals, and the sins which provoked Him must be repented collectively as well as individually, on days of solemn fasting and humiliation. Yet collective sins were the sum of individual sins; and just as the believer looked into his soul to divine the meaning of military success, so must he search inward to discern God's purpose in public adversity. The Puritan imagination observes a series of God-given correspondences and interactions between external events and the inward motions of faith: between the showers which end drought in the fields and the waters of grace upon the barren soul, or between the trials and deliverances of the traveller and the pilgrim's inner progress towards salvation. To the Puritan, reformation of the world begins with reformation of the heart. Politics are a public projection of the struggle which lust, will and passion wage against God's grace for dominion of the soul.

When God was provoked by transgression, He could be appeased only if the offending sin were identified and purged. The force of that conviction is evident in the belief, which justified much civil war killing, that an afflicted land must be cleansed of the blood which has been shed in it (Numb. 35, 33). But at least blood-guilt could be laid at the door of the saints' enemies. What if the sin was among the believers themselves? In the dread of that thought Cromwell and the saints, individually and collectively, devoted many hours

---

[12] *A briefe Relation*, 25 June–2 July 1650, p. 30. Cf. A. S. P. Woodhouse, *Puritanism and Liberty*, 2nd edn (London, 1974), p. 19; *The Parliamentary or Constitutional History of England*, 24 vols. (London, 1751–62), XIX, p. 180.

[13] John Preston, *The Saint's Qualification* (London, 1637), p. 252; H. F., *A Sermon preached at the Publique Fast, the twelfth day of April* (Oxford, 1644), p. 15.

and many days to intensive self-examination. We shall now see something of the politics of iniquity to which that preoccupation gave rise.

In late April 1648, as the second civil war approached, Parliament and army reflected on the imminent perils before them. On 25 April Parliament ordered a national fast day to be held. For

> whatsoever dangers are threatened or feared, either by divisions amongst ourselves, or practices from enemies abroad, we have assurance, out of the Word of God, that we are not in the least danger, if God Almighty be not incensed against us for our sins and wickedness; which our consciences testify that He is exceedingly, against every one of us in particular, and the kingdom in general: yet we believe that, if we do heartily and sincerely humble ourselves, and turn to the Lord, crying mightily to Him in fervent prayer, with a lively faith in Christ, we shall certainly be delivered from all evils and dangers, and enjoy all needful blessings and benefit to the whole state and kingdom.

Parliament resolved to suppress the vice and the blasphemy wherewith the land was defiled, so that God's 'heavy judgements' might be 'diverted from us' and the Roundhead cause saved.[14]

Four days later, on 29 April, the New Model produced its own response to the crisis. The General Council of the army met at Windsor Castle 'to search out...our iniquities, which, we were persuaded, had provoked the Lord against us'. The army leadership often turned to prayer to help restore unity and direction to its counsels. In the Putney debates of 1647 the New Model had sought, through a 'prayer-meeting', to recover the spirit and the purpose which had sustained it in battle, but which in the post-war peace had made way for 'carnal' and 'fleshly strivings'. Cromwell spoke for his colleagues at Putney when he dwelt on the necessity 'to recover that presence of God that seems to withdraw from us', to root out 'false deceit', and to reflect that 'God will discover whether our hearts be not clear in this business'. 'I think the main thing', concurred Ireton, 'is for everyone to wait upon God, for the errors, deceits, and weakness of his own heart.'[15]

The army leaders were still divided and downhearted when they gathered at Windsor in April 1648. A party among them seems to have yielded to political despair and to have wanted the army to lay down its arms. The Windsor meeting lasted three days, of which the first evidently produced

---

[14] *Journal of the House of Commons*, 25 April 1648; Keith Thomas, 'The Puritans and Adultery: The Act of 1650 Reconsidered', in D. Pennington and K. Thomas (eds.), *Puritans and Revolutionaries. Essays presented to Christopher Hill* (Oxford, 1978), pp. 263, 277; *Severall Proceedings in Parliament*, 16–23 May 1650.

[15] Abbott, I, pp. 521, 523, 524; Woodhouse, *Puritanism and Liberty*, pp. 19, 22.

no answer to the army's prayers. On the second day, when 'many spake from the Word and prayed', Cromwell

did press very earnestly on all there present to a thorough consideration of our actions as an army, as well as our ways particularly as private Christians, to see if any iniquity could be found in them; and what it was, that if possible we might find it out, and so remove the cause of such sad rebukes as were upon us by reason of our iniquities.

William Allen, who was present and who later drew up a large account of the meeting, described how it then conducted 'a long search into all our public actions as an army', to inquire why 'the presence of the Lord' was no longer 'amongst us'.[16] At length 'we were, by a gracious hand of the Lord, led to find out the very steps (as we were then all jointly convinced) by which we had departed from the Lord, and provoked Him to depart from us'. Those 'steps', it was agreed, were the 'cursed, carnal conferences' which 'our own wisdoms, fears, and want of faith had prompted us in the year before to entertain with the King and his party': in other words the negotiations which Cromwell and Ireton had held with Charles I in 1647 and which had aroused so much resentment among the army radicals.

At this stage of the meeting a decisive lead was given by William Goffe, who had instigated the prayer-meeting at Putney. He now 'made use of that good word, Prov. 1, 23, "Turn you at my reproof"'. In that chapter God threatens to 'laugh at your calamity; I will mock when your fear cometh; when your fear cometh as desolation, and your destruction cometh as a whirlwind; when distress and anguish cometh upon you'. But if the elect of Israel – and so of England – will 'turn at my reproof', 'behold, I will pour out my spirit unto you, I will make known my words unto you'. Goffe's speech

begot in us great sense, shame and loathing our selves for our iniquities, and justifying the Lord as righteous in His proceedings against us. And in this path the Lord led us not only to see our sin, but also our duty; and this so unanimously set with weight upon each heart, that none was able hardly to speak a word to each other for bitter weeping.

Thus 'we were led and helped to a clear agreement amongst ourselves, not any dissenting'. Two historic decisions were taken. The army resolved, first, to fight the royalists; and secondly, 'if ever the Lord brought us back

---

[16] Allen's account, published in 1659, is reprinted in *A Collection of Scarce and Valuable Tracts...of the late Lord Somers*, ed. Sir Walter Scott, 13 vols. (London, 1809–15), VI, pp. 498–504 (hereafter cited as *Somers Tracts*). I believe that Allen's document, despite its late appearance, is likely to be broadly reliable. For the date of the Windsor meeting see S. R. Gardiner, *History of the Great Civil War*, new edn, 4 vols. (London, 1897–8), IV, p. 117.

again in peace, to call Charles Stuart...to an account for that blood he had shed'.

The Windsor meeting was a critical moment in the Puritan Revolution – and in the career of Oliver Cromwell. His previous unhappiness, and his vulnerability to the reproaches of radicals, can be glimpsed at Putney, where his advocacy of moderation, of the practicable, was countered by men ready to match his claims to divine illumination, and to argue that there could be no half measures in the service of the Old Testament God: to claim that Cromwell's caution on the franchise betrayed a 'distrust of providence', or to report that God had 'providentially' indicated, through the medium of prayer, a liking for the Levellers' *Case of the Army Truly Stated*.[17] Cromwell never supposed that radical programmes were necessarily more pleasing to God than moderate ones. He knew that the Lord required His instruments to work through political means and to be wise as serpents in His cause.[18] Yet he also knew God's way of blasting the 'politic contrivances' of men who, professing to serve Him but missing the path He had marked for them, stooped to 'carnal' political calculation. Within Cromwell's providentialism, which could lead him in such various political directions, there lay always a radical imperative, which asserted itself at times of crisis and uncertainty. In a swift and decisive change of course he would find sudden release from the strains and the doubts which negotiation and compromise invariably imposed upon 'my inward man'. So it was in April 1648. His decision to 'turn at God's reproof'[19] was to have massive consequences. The army recovered its unity and its fire; and the period which followed the Windsor meeting, the time of the second civil war and of regicide, proved in Cromwell's words 'the most memorable year...that ever this nation saw;...and this by the very signal appearance of God Himself, which, I hope, we shall never forget'.[20]

There were to be many more occasions when the army saints gathered to seek the root of iniquity among themselves.[21] In 1650 God 'mixed' their military successes in Ireland and Scotland with a series of afflictions: with

---

[17] Woodhouse, *Puritanism and Liberty*, pp. 70, 98–100, 439.

[18] Cf. William Carter, *Israel's Peace with God* (London, 1642), p. 14; *Works of John Owen*, ed. W. H. Goold, Banner of Truth reprint, 16 vols. (Edinburgh, 1965–8), VIII, p. 348.

[19] Cf. Abbott, II, p. 340 (l.5); *A Collection of State Papers of John Thurloe*, ed. T. Birch, 7 vols. (London, 1742), VII, p. 367 (hereafter cited as *Thurloe State Papers*).

[20] Abbott, III, p. 54; cf. *ibid.*, II, p. 20, III, p. 73. (Strictly speaking the 'year' to which Cromwell referred began in March; but see *Somers Tracts*, VI, p. 501 (ll.32–3, 39–43).)

[21] See e.g. *The Clarke Papers*, ed. C. H. Firth, 4 vols. (Camden Soc., 1891–1901), II, pp. 58–9; Worcester College, Oxford, Clarke MSS., XXI, fo. 73v, XXIV, fo. 98v.

grave demoralisation and acute division within the government; with differences within the army about the justice of invading Scotland;[22] with outbreaks of plague in garrisons in England and Ireland; with the deaths of 'many choice instruments'. The forces in Ireland, having earnestly 'inquired into' the 'meaning' of God's 'chastisements',[23] provoked the Lord by ceasing to interrogate themselves after Cromwell's departure for England in May. Fresh afflictions followed, until 'at last', as Cromwell later learned from Ireton and his colleagues,

by all these sad strokes from heaven we were raised out of that sleepy secure condition to call upon His name, seek His face, and beg to know His mind in these His judgements, which while we were doing He both discovered the sin, which was our departure and backsliding from Him,...and on a sudden, whilst He was discovering His mind to us, in answer to our desires, He was also pleased to abate...that heavy stroke of the pestilence.[24]

As in England in 1648, so in Ireland in 1650, the army was promptly restored by its self-examination to its accustomed course of victory. Meanwhile army headquarters in England had circulated regiments and garrisons throughout the country to arrange a day of coordinated prayer, when the saints were to seek the cause of their travails. The Lord was besought 'to grant that this may be a cleansing day', and to 'enable us to turn at His reproof'.[25] Even Dunbar in September 1650 did not wholly assure the chosen of God's contentment with them. Oliver St John, rejoicing in the triumph but remarking too on the plague and the threat of famine, wrote to Cromwell that God, by 'mingling water with His wine, tells us that something is amiss amongst us, and calls upon us to search and try our ways'.[26]

The battle of Worcester in September 1651 brought a reversion to peace – and to its anxieties. Cromwell, who now returned permanently to civilian politics, warned Parliament not to permit 'the fatness of these continued mercies' to 'occasion pride and wantonness, as formerly the like hath done to a chosen nation'.[27] The regime must acknowledge its victories to have come from the Lord alone, for 'God will curse that man and his house that dares to think otherwise'.[28] And Parliament must 'improve' God's 'mercies'

[22] For those differences see *Original Letters*, pp. 21, 29, 58, 73.
[23] *A briefe Relation*, 1–8 January 1650; *A Perfect Diurnall...in relation to the Armies*, 7–14 January 1650; Bulstrode Whitelocke, *Memorials of the English Affairs*, 4 vols. (London, 1853), III, p. 151.
[24] *Original Letters*, p. 72.
[25] *Perfect Diurnall*, 20–27 May 1650; cf. *ibid.*, 10–17 June, 24 June–1 July 1650.
[26] *Original Letters*, p. 26.
[27] Abbott, II, p. 463.
[28] *Ibid.*, II, p. 173. Cf. *ibid.*, I, p. 621, III, p. 583 (ll. 4–8), 591 (ll. 18–22), IV, p. 707; Edmund Calamy, *God's Free Mercy to England* (London, 1642), pp. 14–15; Ps. 28.5; Jer. 17.5.

by righteousness and reform, for 'the eyes of the Lord run to and fro; and as
He finds out His enemies here, to be avenged on them, so He will not spare
them for whom He doth good, if by His loving kindness they become not
good'.[29] The nation's want of gratitude for God's glorious dispensations, and
its failure to give 'a worthy return of all the blessings and mercies you have
received',[30] were to trouble Cromwell all his days. How often, in his speeches,
he would recall the encouragement which after Worcester the army had given
Parliament to reform, and the frustration which had eventually driven him
to expel the Commons by force in April 1653. What had gone wrong?

No doubt the immediate blame lay with the notorious 'corruption' and
'self-seeking' of Parliament. But might not the failure of reform be a rebuke
to the army saints themselves? Since Worcester, they observed in January
1653, 'the work of the Lord' had 'seemed to stand still, and all the instruments thereof to have been of no might'. In that month they accordingly
spent 'several days waiting at the throne of grace', where they 'humbled
ourselves at His feet, for those evils which might cause Him to withdraw
His presence from us, and to manifest tokens of His displeasure against us'.[31]
Once more their self-examination produced vigorous action. They announced
a bold reform programme, and made it clear that Parliament's survival depended on its implementation.

In the saints' new-found resolution lay a challenge not only to Parliament
but to Cromwell himself. Since September 1651 he had sought to build
bridges between Parliament and army, a policy which exposed him to suspicion and rebuke from the radicals. As early as December 1651 'the private
churches begin to call his Excellency an apostate', while by the spring of
1653 he was 'daily railed on by the preaching party, who say they must
have a new parliament and a new general before the work be done'.[32]
Although such acute hostility is likely to have been confined to the extreme,
the psychological pressure exerted on Cromwell by the army and the congregations was intense. They kept him informed of their constant prayers on
his behalf; instructed him not to 'consult with flesh and blood'[33] or to
succumb to the bait of compromise; listed the biblical heroes on whom they
expected him to model his conduct; intimated to him his failure to meet
their political hopes; and scrutinised his public statements for radical com-
mitments or implications with which they could subsequently confront him.[34]
In 1651 the officers in Ireland, Ireton among them, had urged him to

29 Abbott, II, pp. 130, 433; cf. *ibid.*, II, pp. 215, 325, 506, 588, III, p. 56.
30 *Ibid.*, IV, p. 270; cf. *ibid.*, IV, p. 25.
31 *The Moderate Publisher*, 28 January–4 February 1653.
32 B. Worden, *The Rump Parliament 1648–1653* (Cambridge, 1974), pp. 291, 379–80.
33 *Original Letters*, p. 80. Cf. *Works of John Owen*, VIII, p. 349; Gal. 1.16.
34 The best source for such pressure is *Original Letters*.

'remember Hezekiah's fate and judgement' and 'take heed of making it your own'.[35] Hezekiah, we may remember, had 'rendered not again according to the benefit done unto him; for his heart was lifted up: therefore there was wrath upon him, and upon Judah and Jerusalem' (2 Chron. 32. 25). The parallel made a point which was to acquire an added force once Cromwell became Protector in 1653: that a whole people might be punished for the sin of its leader.

Cromwell, whose bond with his radical followers was so important to him, was not well equipped to bear their admonitions. Why, he asked, had the godly cause become so dependent upon so weak an instrument as himself?[36] Although he had long known himself to be among the chosen, to have found 'acceptance' among 'the congregation of the firstborn', he retained a sense of spiritual inadequacy which can be glimpsed in his private letters, in his artless acknowledgements there of 'my corruptions', 'my weaknesses, my inordinate passions, my unskilfulness and every way unfitness to my work'.[37] In 1651–3, as he manoeuvred among the parliamentary factions, he found politics a lonely business. He yearned to re-create the broad-based godly party which had been destroyed by Pride's Purge, and to persuade his intimate saintly friends among the parliamentary middle group, whom he believed to 'have helped one another to stumble at the dispensations of God', to return to the fold.[38] He missed other allies too. In September 1652, when the breach between Parliament and army was widening, he wrote to an intimate colleague, 'Have I one friend in our society to whom I can unbowel myself? You absent; Fleetwood is gone; I am left alone...Lend me one shoulder. Pray for me.'[39]

In April 1653 he bowed to radical pressure. Having 'sought the Lord day and night', he once more cut through 'carnal' politics, suddenly expelled Parliament by force, vituperatively attacked its members for their personal and political corruption, and assured his army colleagues after the coup that he had 'consulted not with flesh and blood at all'.[40] His action restored his position among the churches, who told him that his expulsion of Parliament had removed their 'fear of God's presence withdrawing from you'.[41] Yet the new mood did not last long. The members of Barebone's, that hand-

[35] *Original Letters*, pp. 74–5. [36] See Abbott, II, p. 421, IV, p. 872.

[37] *Ibid.*, I, pp. 96–7, 696, II, pp. 289, 329, 400, 404–5, 483.

[38] *Ibid.*, I, pp. 574–5, 577–8, 646, II, pp. 189–90, 328–9, 425–6, 453.

[39] *Ibid.*, II, pp. 575–6.

[40] Worden, *Rump Parliament*, p. 356; cf. Abbott, I, p. 698 (1. 21). I believe that in essence the explanation of the dissolution given in *The Rump Parliament* survives the searching and courteous criticism of it in Austin Woolrych, *Commonwealth to Protectorate* (Oxford, 1982).

[41] *Original Letters*, pp. 91, 93.

picked assembly of the chosen which met in July 1653, were soon quarrelling among themselves, and in August, 'unbowelling myself' to Fleetwood, he confessed that 'I never more needed all helps from my Christian friends than now.' In December he took the title of Protector, 'which place I undertook not so much out of the hope of doing any good, as of a desire to prevent mischief and evil'.[42] He was to retain the position until his death in 1658.

Repeatedly he and his supporters would claim that providence had declared in favour of his elevation, and that the evidence of God's approval obliged the nation to accept the new constitution. Yet he faced a persistent chorus of accusation from men who had been among his closest and most trusted spiritual counsellors. Ousted from government by his 'usurpation', they held him to be a traitor who had sacrificed the cause on the altar of his own ambition, and without whose removal God's purpose could never be fulfilled. He was the scapegoat upon whom all future political failures and disappointments could be blamed. His problems were magnified in January 1655, when the first Protectorate Parliament collapsed and when he sensed that the godly cause might collapse with it. In the months which followed, a siege mentality is evident in Whitehall. Cromwell now seems to have abandoned the conciliatory policies he had pursued, in politics and in religion, since December 1653. He had not lost his faith in God's approbation: indeed, he defiantly reaffirmed it in his magnificent angry speech at the Parliament's dissolution. In March 1655 'the good hand of God going along with us' enabled the government to put down Penruddock's rising, and in April the Lord 'was pleased to appear very signally' in Blake's victory at Tunis.[43] Three months later, however, in July 1655, news arrived of a catastrophe: of the abject defeat of the expedition sent by Cromwell to the Caribbean island of Hispaniola to launch the conquest of Spanish America. An ill-prepared, ill-disciplined force had been shamefully routed by a handful of Spaniards. There had been nothing in Cromwell's career to parallel that disaster. When the news came through he shut himself in his room for a whole day.[44] The defeat at Hispaniola was to have a profound and lasting effect on him. Indeed it may be that he never fully recovered from it.

Cromwell had sent the expedition to the West Indies because 'God has not brought us hither where we are but to consider the work that we may do in the world as well as at home... Providence seemed to lead us hither, having

---

[42] Abbott, III, pp. 88–9, IV, p. 470.   [43] *Ibid.*, III, pp. 672, 745.
[44] S. R. Gardiner, *History of the Commonwealth and Protectorate*, 4 vols. (London, 1893), IV, pp. 142–3.

160 ships swimming.' Spain, 'the great underpropper' of 'that Roman Babylon', was 'providentially' England's enemy. Citing Thessalonians and Revelation, Cromwell told the Parliament of 1656 that 'except you will deny the truth of the Scriptures, you must needs see that that state is so described in Scripture to be Papal and anti-Christian'. To those who questioned the justice of the war he opposed Genesis 3. 15, 'I will put enmity between thy seed and her seed', a text 'which goeth but for little among statesmen, but it is more considerable [than] all things'.[45] Yet could Cromwell be certain that God favoured his policy? In October 1656, when news of the capture of Spanish treasure ships had given an urgently needed boost to government morale, the Cromwellian preacher John Rowe told Parliament that the exploit had 'silenced the secret thoughts and reasonings of some, touching the engagement in this war; and who are too apt to say, that God never owned you since you undertook this business'.[46] In the same year Sir Henry Vane taunted Cromwell about the 'great silence in heaven' since 1653.[47]

The debacle at Hispaniola could be blamed partly on 'instruments', on the leaders of the expedition, who were duly punished. But Cromwell knew the need to look deeper. Not only had the invasion force lost a battle: it had plainly been a godless army, untouched by the spirit of the New Model. Its cowardice was itself evidence of God's displeasure, for Cromwell knew that in the course of battle God gave and withdrew courage as it pleased Him.[48] He knew that sinful armies were their own worst enemies.[49] The expedition remained spiritually (and militarily) wanting even after it had proceeded to take Jamaica. 'The hand of the Lord hath not been more visible in any part of this rebuke', Cromwell told the commanders of the forces there in 1656, 'than in taking away the hearts of those who do survive amongst you, and in giving them up to ... sloth and sluggishness of spirit.'[50] Whatever wickedness had been at work, it would not have been confined to the expeditionary force. When God humbled soldiers he also punished their rulers, or their countrymen, or both. What had provoked the Lord?

To find out, the government in November 1655 invited the nation to a day of solemn fasting and humiliation, when 'we may everyone be searching out the plague of his own heart' in the hope of discerning God's purpose in

---

[45] *Clarke Papers*, III, p. 207; Abbott, III, pp. 860, 879, IV, pp. 261–2, 274.

[46] John Rowe, *Man's Duty Magnifying God's Work* (London, 1656), p. 20; cf. *A True Narrative of the Late Success...upon the Spanish Coast* (London, 1656).

[47] Vane, 'A Healing Question Propounded', *Somers Tracts*, VI, p. 313; cf. Rev. 8. 1.

[48] Abbott, II, pp. 127, 164, 235, 324.

[49] That, like much else in Cromwell's providentialism, was not a peculiarly Puritan or Roundhead view. Cf. William Chillingworth, *A Sermon preached to his Majesty at Reading* (Oxford, 1644), p. 13.

[50] Abbott, IV, p. 193; cf. *ibid.*, p. 385.

'the late rebukes we have received'. Evidently the nation's prayers went unanswered in the months which followed, for in March 1656 the government tried again. The declaration for a further fast day acknowledged that 'the Lord hath been pleased in a wonderful manner to humble and rebuke us, in that expedition to the West Indies'. The disaster 'gives us just reason to fear, that we may have either failed in the spirit and manner wherewith this business hath been undertaken, or that the Lord sees some abomination, or accursed thing, by which He is provoked thus to appear against us'. In September 1656, after Cromwell's speech at the opening of Parliament had lamented the failure of the West Indian expedition, a declaration was passed by Protector and Parliament for another fast day, on which 'a people laden with iniquity', who had 'provoked the holy one of Israel to anger', was to strive 'to appease His wrath...that He will remove whatever accursed thing there is amongst us'.[51]

The Puritan readership of the declarations of March and September 1656 will have recognised, in their allusions to an 'accursed thing', a clear signpost to the seventh chapter of the Book of Joshua. In 1650 the despondent forces in England had explored that text when they inquired into God's chastisements of that year.[52] Now Hispaniola gave the text a much sharper application. To appreciate it, we may need to reacquaint ourselves with the story which Joshua 7 relates. It concerns the catastrophe which afflicted the children of Israel after the fall of Jericho, that miracle to which the Cromwellian saints often compared their own mercies of 1642–51. After the victory 'the children of Israel committed a trespass in the accursed thing...and the anger of the Lord was kindled against the children of Israel'. The consequence was the shattering defeat of an expedition which had been confidently dispatched by the Israelites from Jericho to the east side of Bethel. The troops 'fled before the men of Ai', who (like the Spaniards on Hispaniola) were 'but few'. Joshua was devastated. He 'rent his clothes, and fell to the earth upon his face before the ark of the Lord until the eventide, he and all the elders of Israel, and put dust upon their heads'. To what purpose had God brought His people over Jordan, only 'to deliver us into the hand of the Amorites, to destroy us'? What could Joshua say to neighbouring nations 'when Israel turneth their backs before their enemies'?

[51] *Ibid.*, IV, p. 274 (ll.30–1); *A Declaration of his Highness, with the advice of his Council, inviting the People of this Commonwealth to a Day of Solemn Fasting and Humiliation* (London, [November] 1655); *A Declaration of his Highness, inviting the People of England and Wales to a Day of Solemn Fasting and Humiliation* (London, [March] 1656); *A Declaration of his Highness the Lord Protector and his Parliament for a Day of Solemn Fasting and Humiliation* (London, [September] 1656). The declarations will hereafter be cited by their dates.

[52] *Perfect Diurnall*, 20–27 May 1650.

And the Lord said unto Joshua, Get thee up; wherefore liest thou thus upon thy face? Israel hath sinned, and they have also transgressed my covenant which I commanded them: for they have even taken of the accursed thing, and have also stolen, and dissembled also, and they have put it even among their own stuff. Therefore the children of Israel could not stand before their enemies, but turned their backs before their enemies, because they were accursed: neither will I be with you any more, except ye destroy the accursed from among you. Up, sanctify the people, and say, Sanctify yourselves against tomorrow: for thus saith the Lord God of Israel, There is an accursed thing in the midst of thee, O Israel: thou canst not stand before thine enemies, until ye take away the accursed thing from among you.

One particular man, God intimated, had 'taken of the accursed thing'; and for his wickedness all Israel was punished. He was identified by an investigative process which, in its ritual, revealed the extension of guilt from the sinner to his household, from the household to the tribe, from the tribe to the nation. The sinner was Achan, the son of Carmi, the son of Zabdi, the son of Zerah, of the tribe of Judah. His confession identified the accursed thing:

When I saw among the spoils a goodly Babylonish garment, and two hundred shekels of silver, and a wedge of gold of fifty shekels weight, then I coveted them, and took them; and, behold, they are hid in the earth in the midst of my tent, and the silver under it. And they took them out of the midst of the tent, and brought them unto Joshua, and unto all the children of Israel, and laid them out before the Lord.

Achan, as God instructed, was stoned and burned to death in the valley of Achor. Only now that the accursed thing had been found and cast out was the hand of God's blessing laid once more upon His chosen people. The men of Ai were duly smitten, and the conquests of the Israelites resumed.

The saints did not expect the parallels between Israelite and English history to be exact.[53] But when there were so many literal and figurative parallels, divine instruction was clearly visible. Civil war Puritans had traditionally equated the sin of Achan with the ceremonialism of Archbishop Laud.[54] After Hispaniola there was a closer target. In 1656 Sir Henry Vane, who had been one of Cromwell's most intimate friends until in 1653 Cromwell bitterly accused him of betrayal, circulated a treatise, *A Healing Question Propounded*,[55] for which he was brought before Cromwell and the Council. Vane's document answered the passage in the fast-day declaration of March 1656 concerning the 'accursed thing'. The 'accursed thing', he suggested, was the motive of 'self-interest and private gain' hidden beneath the Protectorate.

---

[53] See e.g. John Arrowsmith, *England's Eben-ezer* (London, 1645), p. 21.

[54] Paul Christianson, *Reformers and Babylon* (Toronto, 1978), pp. 141, 186, 190. Cf. William Hunt, *The Puritan Moment* (Cambridge, Mass., 1983), pp. 188–9.

[55] *Somers Tracts*, VI, pp. 303–15.

Cromwell's elevation sprang from the 'private and selfish interest of a particular spirit...which sin (Joshua 7) became a curse in the camp, and withheld the Lord from going any more amongst them, or going out with their forces'. The 'Babylonish garment' which Achan 'saved from destruction' signified the 'tyrannical principles and relics' of government by a single person.[56] Cromwell after the civil wars, like Achan after Jericho, 'brought not in the fruit and gain of the Lord's treasure, but covetously went about to convert it to his own use'. 'This' observed Vane, his eye turning to Hispaniola, 'caused the anger of the Lord to be kindled against Israel, and made them unable to stand before their enemies.' So only when England had been purged of Cromwell's selfishness would God again 'become active and powerful in the spirits and hearts of honest men, and in the works of his providences, when...they go out to fight by sea or by land'. Vane's *Healing Question* was not the only saintly tract to portray Hispaniola as God's punishment upon the cause for Cromwell's usurpation, and to tell the Protector that 'you are not able to bear the reproofs of the Lord';[57] but to Cromwell it must have been the most disconcerting of them.

Cromwell responded uneasily and defensively to the charges which the defeat at Hispaniola elicited against him. He acknowledged, even more fulsomely than the proprieties of Puritan self-abasement required, that his own sins had 'justly...incurred' the disaster 'and much more'. He professed before the nation his desire 'first to take the shame to himself and find out his provocation'. Yet why should the blame lie with him alone? By what right, he asked, was the iniquitous people 'imputing the cause only to the work of the magistrate' and 'charging sad miscarriages upon instruments... when every individual hath helped to fill up the measure of those sins'?[58] Cromwell, belonging in this as in so much else to the mainstream of the Puritan tradition, was certain that God punished nations for vice and for blasphemy.[59] In March 1654 he had summoned a fast day to implore an end to 'the present rod of an exceeding and unusual drought', an affliction provoked, he ruled, by 'the common and notorious sins so boldly and impenitently practised amongst us'. He was to respond almost identically when

---

56 That may have been a shrewd blow, for there are hints that the disturbing image of the 'spotted garment' may have made an impression on Cromwell's mind: Abbott, I, p. 619 (cf. Isa. 9. 5), IV, p. 473.

57 *The Proceeds of the Protector (so called) against Sir Henry Vane, Knight* (London, 1656), p. 8; *A Perfect Nocturnall of Several Proceedings, between Hiel the Bethelite, and... Madam Policy* (n.p., n.d.), pp. 4, 6.

58 Declarations of March and September 1656 (above, n. 51); cf. Abbott, III, p. 858 (l. 33).

59 Abbott, II, p. 110, IV, p. 237 (ll. 23–4). For Cromwell as a zealous 'godly magistrate' see too *ibid.*, I, p. 278, III, pp. 400, 436, 589, 845, IV, pp. 25, 112, 274, 493–4.

God visited the nation with sickness in 1657 and again in 1658.[60] Why, in 1655–6, should the sin of Achan not be supposed to lie in the same moral territory?

Of one thing, at least, Cromwell professed himself confident. At Hispaniola God had punished the English, not declared 'in favour of the enemy'. Although England's rulers should, like Joshua, 'lay our mouths in the dust, yet He would not have us despond', for 'undoubtedly it is His cause... Though He hath torn us, yet He will heal us...After two days He will revive us, on the third day He will raise us up.'[61] Did Cromwell remember, when he thus alluded to Hosea 6, how in 1650, after Dunbar, he and his friends had derided the very similar biblical explanations of defeat which were then advanced by the Presbyterians?[62] We cannot say. Yet there are indications that Hispaniola taught Cromwell to think less boldly and less simply about the ways in which God reveals His purposes to men. In the days of Cromwell's triumph, providence had been 'clear and unclouded'; but in the later Protectorate he came to refer to 'the dark paths through the providence and dispensations of God'.[63] Although the Lord might still appear in battle, as in the 'very signal' and 'very wonderful' mercy vouch-safed to Blake off Santa Cruz in 1657, Cromwell's reading of such events became more tentative. 'We have been lately taught', he reminded Blake in April 1656, 'that it is not in man to direct His way. Indeed all the dispensations of God, whether adverse or prosperous, do fully read that lesson.'[64] The dynamic providentialism of the civil wars had become a part of Cromwell's past, to be remembered and praised and yearned after in speech after speech, but finding no parallel among current events. When he now reflected upon the present or the future, his tone was distant from army providentialism. It resembled instead the more conventional and more stoical approach to providence taken by moderate and Court party politicians like John Thurloe and Henry Cromwell. He came to speak, as they did, of the need to become 'submitted' or 'resigned unto' providence.[65]

Did God forgive His people in England for the accursed thing? Cromwell's anxiety on that subject is indicated by his preoccupation, during the last two years of his life, with Psalm 85, which on three occasions he urged upon the consideration of his second Protectorate Parliament. In September 1656

[60] Abbott, III, p. 225 (cf. ibid., pp. 290–1); Mercurius Politicus, 13–20 August, 10–17 September 1657, 29 April–6 May 1658.
[61] Abbott, III, pp. 859–60, 874. Cf. Original Letters, p. 26.
[62] Original Letters, p. 23; Abbott, II, p. 335.
[63] Abbott, I, p. 697, IV, pp. 472–3.
[64] Abbott, IV, pp. 148, 549. Cf. An Order in Parliament...for a Day of Thanksgiving... the third of June next (London, 1657).
[65] Thurloe State Papers, VI, p. 243, VII, pp. 153, 376, 579, 680; Abbott, IV, p. 148.

he recited it almost in full before the Commons, whose members he encouraged to 'peruse' that 'very instructive and significant' Psalm, which 'I wish...might be better written in our hearts'. It seems at first a Psalm of wholehearted thankfulness. The Lord 'hast been favourable unto thy land', 'hast forgiven the iniquity of thy people', 'hast taken away all thy wrath', 'hast turned thyself from the fierceness of thine anger'. Yet a sudden change of tense and of mood makes the meaning of the Psalm ambiguous. The Psalmist begs God to 'cause thine anger toward us to cease. Wilt thou be angry with us for ever? Wilt thou draw out thine anger to all generations?' While Cromwell is glad to infer from the Psalm that 'sometimes God pardons nations', and hopes for a time when Englishmen can 'say as David, thou...hast pardoned our sins, thou hast taken away our iniquities', he evidently believes the nation to remain under the penalty of its wickedness.[66]

I shall suggest in the concluding part of this essay that Cromwell's concern with iniquity – with his own and with the nation's – may help us to understand what was perhaps the most important (and perhaps the most disastrous) decision he made as Protector: his refusal in May 1657 of Parliament's offer of the title of King.

Cromwell could have taken the Crown had he wanted to. It is true that, by his hesitations and delays over three months, he gave the opposition in the army and the churches the chance to mobilise resistance. Yet even when it had done so, the challenge to Cromwell looked no stronger, and was probably weaker, than opposition which he had brushed aside before. The title was an attractive prospect. It would give his rule the parliamentary sanction he had long wanted for it, and would boost the hopes of settlement and stability. Yet those arguments, pressing as they were, might be 'carnal'. Had God led His chosen of England through the Red Sea of civil war merely in order to effect a change of dynasty? Had not 'the providence of God', asked Cromwell, 'laid this title aside'?[67] As Protector, he did not like to think of himself as King in all but name. He had accepted his elevation in 1653

well looking, that as God had declared what government He had delivered over to the Jews, and placed it upon such persons as had been instrumental for the conduct and deliverance of His people; and considering that promise in Isaiah, that God would give rulers as at the first, and judges as at the beginning, I did not know but that God might begin, and though at present with a most unworthy person, yet as to the future it might be after this manner, and I thought this might usher it in.[68]

[66] Abbott, IV, pp. 277–8, 706–7, 720.   [67] *Ibid.*, IV, p. 473.
[68] *Ibid.*, III, p. 589; Isa. 1. 26.

Parliament in 1657 had an altogether less biblical purpose. It aimed
to break the army's hold on Cromwell, and to surround him with *politique*
courtiers.

While Cromwell prayed for guidance, the radicals 'wearied him with
letters, conferences, and monitory petitions'.[69] One letter was from Colonel
Thomas Wilkes in Scotland. In the black month of January 1655 Cromwell
had written to Wilkes a letter[70] which discloses the anxieties so often evident
at Cromwell's times of trial: his dismay at his 'wounds' and 'reproaches'
from 'such as fear the Lord, for whom I have been ready to lay down my
life, and I hope still am';[71] his concern to convince the saints that in becoming
Protector he did not 'make myself my aim';[72] his awareness that, but for
the strength which his adherence to God's path gave him, 'the comforts of
all my friends would not support me, no not one day'.[73] Now Wilkes urged
him to 'stand fast, in these ... apostatising days', and, rather than yield to
parliamentary persuasion, to await 'that crown which the Lord of righteous
judgement gives' in heaven.[74] The congregations of Gloucestershire, ever
ready with advice to Cromwell, warned him to keep 'close to God, His cause
and His people', and to resist the 'temptations' wherewith 'you are encompassed'. Acceptance of the title would 'rejoice the hearts of the profane
party', and expose the saints to the charge 'that they fought not for the
exalting of Jesus Christ, as they pretended, but themselves'. The crowning
of Cromwell would 'generally sadden, and endanger your losing room in
the hearts of, the saints in England'. He should 'search your heart', and
beware that 'such as have prayed, wept, fought, followed on with you...
may never have occasion to sit down by the rivers of bitter waters, lamenting
for your sake'. In London the Baptists, the religious group which had been
so close to Cromwell, alerted him to 'the fearful apostasy which is endea-
voured by some to be fastened upon you, upon plausible pretences, by such
who for the most part had neither heart nor head to engage with you'.
The Baptists ventured an allusion, which Cromwell would not have
missed, to the words of Mordecai to Esther: 'Think not with thyself
that thou shalt escape in the King's house, any more than the Jews'
(Esther 4. 13).[75]

In his diffuse and anguished speeches to Parliament during the kingship
crisis, Cromwell longingly recalled the certitudes of civil war: the victories,

---

[69] *Ibid.*, IV, p. 448 (from Bate).   [70] *Ibid.*, III, pp. 572–3.

[71] Cf. *ibid.*, I, p. 429, III, pp. 89, 756 (ll. 5–6), IV, p. 272.

[72] Cf. *ibid.*, III, pp. 289, 452.   [73] Cf. *ibid.*, IV, p. 146.

[74] *Thurloe State Papers*, VI, pp. 70–1.

[75] *Original Letters*, pp. 139–43. John Lilburne, likewise alive to Cromwell's susceptibili-
ties, had reminded him of the same text when Cromwell frustrated the Levellers in
1647: Abbott, I, p. 434.

and the manifest presence of God with his saints. The opponents of the title were eager to keep his memories alive. John Owen, a firm enemy to kingship, had once remarked that the rhetorical question 'Where is the God of Marston Moor, and the God of Naseby? is an acceptable expostulation in a gloomy day.'[76] In 1657 the saints expostulated accordingly. 'We beseech you in the bowels of Christ', the London Baptists warned Cromwell, 'remember what God did for you and us, at Marston Moor, Naseby, Pembroke, Tredah, Dunbar and Worcester, and upon what grounds.' William Bradford, writing as one who had 'gone along with you from Edgehill to Dunbar', urged that 'the experiences you have had of God at these two places, and between them,...should often make you shrink' from the title. Cromwell should 'remember you are but a man, and must die, and come to judgement...Those that are for a Crown, I fear you have little experience of them: the other, most of them, have attended your greatest hazards.'[77]

The opponents of kingship did not have all the providentialist arguments. John Thurloe and Henry Cromwell encouraged the Protector to make his decision as God directed him. It was their hope that God had given him 'the clearest call that any man had' to accept the title.[78] Throughout the Protectorate Cromwell had been described as the instrument of providence by men who welcomed the return to relative political stability under his rule. God had given England 'those lovely twins, peace and plenty (the unexpected issue of cruel wars)'.[79] A part of Cromwell concurred with that view. The arrival of peace seemed to him a 'miracle', while liberty of conscience, which in his eyes was a tangible and precious gain of civil war, could take root only beneath the shelter of stability. Had not a time come for consolidation rather than advance? In 1655 Cromwell told Parliament that, before it had wrecked the Instrument of Government, 'we were arrived ...at a very safe port, where we might sit down, and contemplate the dispensations of God and our mercies'. Next year he and Parliament concurred in lamenting the nation's sin 'in being more dissatisfied that we have not obtained all that we aimed at, than thankful that we have obtained so much as through mercy we now enjoy'.[80]

---

[76] *Works of John Owen*, VIII, p. 88. Cf. Obadiah Sedgwick, *A Thanksgiving Sermon, preached...April 9* (London, 1644), p. 21; Mathew Barker, *The Faithful and Wise Servant* (London, 1657), pp. 14–15.

[77] *Original Letters*, pp. 141–3.

[78] *Thurloe State Papers*, VI, pp. 183, 219, 222–3; cf. *Original Letters*, p. 144.

[79] *Original Letters*, p. 134. Cf. *ibid.*, pp. 105–6, 138–9, 147, 150–2; *Thurloe State Papers*, VI, p. 431; *Mercurius Politicus*, 8–15 February 1655, 11–18 March, 17–24 June, 8–15 July 1658.

[80] Abbott, III, p. 579; *Declaration of September 1656* (above, n. 51).

Images of rest and peace, of 'sitting down in quiet under our vines', could sometimes appeal powerfully to the army saints.[81] Yet the radicals soon became restless and unhappy when providence 'stood still'. At best, the England of the Protectorate was but half reformed. Surely God had not led His people out of bondage for so limited a purpose. The rivalry between that radical perspective and the outlook of the kingship party produced some contrasting biblical allusions. From the regiment of Henry Cromwell's favourite Anthony Morgan, the Protector learned that 'after our long and troublesome and dangerous pilgrimage through the Red Sea of blood, and wilderness of confusion, we have obtained to some prospect, nay some taste and enjoyment of Canaan, the resting place of God's people'. The Gloucestershire congregations were outraged by such parallels: 'surely He speaks to us (as once to His people in the wilderness), "This is not your rest". It is not for us to call our wilderness Canaan.' The choice before Cromwell in the kingship crisis was between the 'Canaan' view and the 'wilderness' view of the Protectorate.[82]

His speeches indicate the difficulty of the decision and the strain which days of fruitless prayer created in him. Ill, wretched with uncertainty, acknowledging 'the abundance of difficulty and trouble that lies upon me', he spoke repeatedly of the 'burden', the 'weight', on 'my back'.[83] Courteously conceding the political force of Parliament's arguments, he concluded that 'I am not able for such a trust and charge': that 'what may be fit for you to offer, may not be fit for me to undertake...At the best I should do it doubtingly. And certainly what is so [done] is not of faith; and whatsoever ...is not of faith, is sin to him that doth it.' He must 'give an account to God' for a decision which, he said again and again, must be taken within his 'conscience'.[84] He must follow the guidance which providence gave him; 'and though a man may impute his own folly and blindness to providence sinfully, yet that must be at my peril'. If the title should 'fall upon a person or persons that God takes no pleasure in, that perhaps may be the end of this work': the end of the cause to which Cromwell and the saints had committed their lives.[85]

---

[81] See e.g. Woodhouse, *Puritanism and Liberty*, p. 403.
[82] *Mercurius Politicus*, 8–15 April 1658; *Original Letters*, p. 146. Cf. Richard Vines, *The Happinesse of Israel* (London, 1645), pp. 4–5; Richard Baxter, *True Christianity* (London, 1655), p. 204; George Smith, *God's Unchangeableness...wherein is clearly demonstrated and proved that Oliver Cromwell is by the Providence of God Lord Protector* (London, 1655), p. 55; Abbott, III, pp. 434–5, 442; *Thurloe State Papers*, VI, p. 401, VII, p. 295; Owen Watkins, *The Puritan Experience* (London, 1972), p. 167; Deut. 12. 9.
[83] Abbott, IV, 443, 482; cf. *ibid.*, III, p. 756.
[84] For 'conscience' see Abbott, IV, pp. 446, 454, 470, 472, 473, 513.
[85] *Ibid.*, IV, pp. 446, 454, 472–3, 513; cf. *ibid.*, IV, p. 277 (ll. 20–3).

Was it possible that Cromwell had become 'a person that God takes no pleasure in'? Might the Lord be exchanging His instruments once more? Cromwell's first biographer, writing in 1659, recorded that near the end of his life the Protector 'twice a day...rehearsed the 71 Psalm of David, which hath so near a relation to his fortune and to his affairs, as that one would believe it to have been a prophecy purposely dictated by the Holy Ghost for him'.[86] What was it that drew Cromwell to Psalms which fail to sustain their initial confidence? The opening verses of Psalm 71, like those of Psalm 85, have a message of hope and strength and faith. With the Psalmist, Cromwell could call God 'my rock and my fortress', 'my trust from my youth'. Yet we must wonder whether he did not also follow the Psalmist's ensuing supplication: 'Cast me not off in the time of old age; forsake me not when my strength faileth. For mine enemies speak against me; and they that lay wait for my soul take counsel together, saying, God hath forsaken him...'

Cromwell's salvation was not alone at stake in the kingship crisis. The fate of God's people rested on his choice. He feared that if he took the Crown wrongfully he might be made 'a captain to lead us back into Egypt'. Beside the risk of sinful leadership he saw another and perhaps a greater danger: the danger of contagion. To take the Crown without the light of God's approval might, in the manner of Achan's iniquity, 'prove even a curse to... these three nations'. 'If I undertake anything not in faith, I shall serve you in my own unbelief, and I shall then be the unprofitablest servant that ever a people or nation had.'[87] It was in the knowledge of that peril that he alluded to the warning which Joshua had given to the Israelites between the fall of Jericho and the disaster wrought by the sin of Achan: 'Cursed be the man before the Lord, that riseth up and buildeth this city Jericho' (Josh. 6. 26). 'I would not seek', said Cromwell to Parliament, 'to set up that that providence hath destroyed and laid in the dust, and I would not build Jericho again.'[88]

[86] R. S. Paul, *The Lord Protector* (London, 1955: Michigan, 1964), pp. 300–1 (quoting Carrington).

[87] Abbott, IV, pp. 263, 446, 472–3, 513, 729. Cf. *Works of John Owen*, VIII, p. 448; Numb. 14. 4.

[88] *Ibid.*, IV, p. 473. For Cromwell and the 'accursed thing' see too *ibid.*, I, p. 677. For the hold of the story of Achan on the Puritan mind see also, e.g., *Diary of Thomas Burton*, ed. J. T. Rutt, 4 vols. (London, 1828), I, p. 39 (where James Nayler is compared to Achan), IV, p. 458; Chillingworth, *A Sermon preached*, p. 14; John Goodwin, *Theomachia* (London, 1644), pp. 2–4; *A Seasonable Word: or, Certain Reasons against a Single Person* (London, 1659), title-page; *The Complete Prose Works of John Milton*, ed. D. M. Wolfe *et al.*, 8 vols. (New Haven, 1953–82), VII, p. 328; *The Political Works of James Harrington*, ed. J. G. A. Pocock (Cambridge, 1977), pp. 629–31; *Mercurius Politicus*, 3–10 July 1651; Conrad Russell, in *London Review of Books*, 4–17 October 1984, p. 21. Cf. Deut. 17. 5.

Tithe in eighteenth-century France: a focus for rural anticlericalism

JOHN McMANNERS

The Church in eighteenth-century France was as rich as the Crown, its total income being about twice as large as the yield of the basic land tax, the *taille*. This wealth was derived from two sources, landed property and tithe, and it was commonly said that, of the two, tithe brought in rather more. But the balance between the two branches of revenue varied throughout France. There was an infinity of local differences and one broad contrast: in the North, where there were vast tracts of ecclesiastical property, tithe played a lesser part than in the South, where in some dioceses it was the primary and indispensable support of the clergy. It formed three-quarters of their revenues in the dioceses of Albi, Castres and Lavaur;[1] the canons of the cathedral of Toulouse and the bishop of Pamiers would have been in penury without it.[2] Where there were no alternative sources of income, the clergy naturally would tend to be more exacting, and to insist on the letter of the law; not surprisingly, therefore, the great tithe agitations of the last twenty years of the *ancien régime* came mainly in the south of the country.

In theory, the levy was a tenth of the crop; in practice, said Arthur Young, it was less.[3] This was indeed the case in many areas; in Maine, Berry and Champagne, it averaged one thirteenth, around Orléans only one thirtieth, even less in parts of Dauphiné and Provence.[4] On the other hand, there were places where tithe outran the fraction implied by its formal definition, reaching one seventh in Lorraine and one eighth sometimes in Gascony. Such cases of an unusually high proportion need analysis, however: they may

[1] H. Marion, *La Dîme ecclésiastique en France au 18e siècle et sa suppression* (Bordeaux, 1912), 116.
[2] G. Frêche, *Toulouse et la région Midi-Pyrénées au siècle des lumières* (Paris, 1975), 531.
[3] A. Young, *Travels*, Fr. trans. H. Sée, 3 vols. (Paris, 1931), with excellent notes, III, 1038.
[4] P. Gagnol, *La Dîme ecclésiastique en France* (Paris, 1910), 137–51; M. Marion, *Dict. des institutions de la France au XVIIe et XVIIIe siècles*, 2 vols. (Paris, 1923), I, 174.

represent a composite levy, including other dues of a seigneurial kind.[5] Local custom sometimes reduced the formal burden; there were villages where it was understood that the *curé* must accept less than his legal entitlement,[6] and others where the community was accustomed to buy off the tithe by paying a lump sum annually. This is what happened in the little town of Gap,[7] in two villages in the diocese of Lodève, and commonly in mountain hamlets in Auvergne, where the rugged terrain made direct collection difficult.[8] Where such commutations were made, the payers got off lightly (and, according to a government tax official in 1778, their land was always more efficiently cultivated).[9] Even so, when all corrections have been made, there were wide disparities between the highest fractions levied and the lowest, all the more illogical and vexatious when they co-existed – as they often did – within a narrow area, even in adjoining parishes.

Tithes were of various kinds, according to the produce on which they were levied – the *grosses dîmes*, the 'great tithes' on the main cereal crops, the *menues dîmes*, the 'small tithes', divided into the *dîmes vertes* on vegetables and fruits, and the *dîme de sang* on animals and wool. Different provinces had different rules about what was included under each heading, and within each category the tariff could vary.[10] There were places where there was a due paid to the clergy as an alternative to the tithe. In Brittany, it was a tax collected by *recteurs* on the inheritance of moveable property, the so-called *neûmes*.[11] In some parishes in the *bocage* country and coastal marches of Bas Poitou, chiefly in the diocese of Luçon, the place of tithe was taken by the *boisselage*, an unjust levy paid at a fixed amount of grain by all households, irrespective of the extent of their property or of the state of the year's harvest (in 15 parishes, it was a supplement to the tithe, not a substitute for it). When a Royal Edict of 1769 replaced the *boisselage* with a tithe at one sixteenth, the inhabitants protested so vehemently that the reform was withdrawn (the rich liked the old system because they got off cheaply, the poor because it was so unjust that the *curé* dared not make them pay).[12] In some places, there

---

5 A. Poitrineau, *La Vie rurale en Basse-Auvergne au XVIIIe siècle, 1726–1789*, 2 vols. (Paris, 1965), I, 351.

6 G. Lefebvre, *Les Paysans du Nord pendant la Révolution française* (Lille, 1924), 108.

7 Gagnol, 151–3.

8 E. Appolis, *Le Diocèse civil de Lodève* (Paris, 1951), 124–5; Poitrineau, I, 353.

9 Appolis, *loc. cit.*

10 Gagnol, 35–9; Marion, *Dict.*, I, 174.

11 Potier de la Germondaye, *Introduction au gouvernement des paroisses suivant la jurisprudence du Parlement de Bretagne* (St Malo, 1777), 146–8.

12 M. Faucheux, *Un ancien droit ecclésiastique perçu en Bas Poitou: le boisselage* (La Roche-sur-Yon, 1953), 19–21, 44, 57, 63, 66; J. Deharge, *La Bas Poitou à la veille de la Révolution* (Paris, 1963), 102.

was an extra little tithe over and above the usual ones, like the *prémice* occasionally found in Brittany and the diocese of Lodève (one sheep in every sixty or so, or a piglet from the first litter of the season).[13] Voltaire also cites the *droit de moisson* in Franche Comté, paid by villagers to their *curé* in parishes where the orthodox *grosses dîmes* had fallen into the hands of monastic houses.[14]

The tithes within a parish were often levied by several different tithe owners. They might include – though not always – the parish priest himself, a bishop, chapter, monastery, priory or other ecclesiastical foundation or, maybe, a layman. The *dîmes inféodées*, tithes held by lay proprietors, were an old-established anomaly, and the law was strict about them: to prove his title, a layman had to demonstrate no less than 100 years' prescription. Hence, one of the few victories of the clergy over Voltaire. When he bought his *seigneurie* at Ferney, he inherited a *dîme inféodée*, coming to the lord of the manor from the Bernese confiscation of ecclesiastical property at the Reformation, but not recognized by the Parlement of Dijon when the Pays de Gex came under French overlordship. In spite of influence at court and well-organized litigation, the Patriarch of Ferney had to agree to an inglorious compromise with his *curé*. As ever, he made the best of his discomfiture, adjuring the warring factions of Geneva to make peace by instancing his own sweet reasonableness, meeting with his parish priest to settle their differences over a friendly glass of wine.[15] Strict though the law was, a goodly proportion of the tithe of France – perhaps a twelfth, was held by laymen; had this been exclusively in the hands of the *seigneurs* descended from the founders of churches, the position would have been easier to justify, but by dint of having been sold and subdivided, the *dîmes inféodées* had passed to all sorts of people[16] – they had become property, just as feudal dues were property. Tithes held by churchmen other than the parish priest were open to similar censures whenever, as was often the case, the bishops, canons or monks concerned enjoyed excessive riches. More than a third of the *curés* of France were paid the officially prescribed dole, the *portion congrue*, by the holders of the great tithes; and throughout the century, their complaints

---

[13] Appolis, 126; H. Sée, 'Les Classes rurales en Bretagne du XVIe siècle à la Révolution', *Ann. de Bretagne*, XXI (1905), 507.

[14] *Dict. philosophique*, 'Impôt' (*Oeuvres*, ed. L. Moland (Paris, 1883–5), XIX, 444).

[15] F. Caussy, 'Voltaire et ses curés. Lettres sur les dîmes', *Rev. de Paris*, XV (1909), 254–6, 619–35. (His parish priest was not the one in the tithe dispute.)

[16] P.-J. Guyot, *Répertoire universel et raisonné de jurisprudence, civile, criminelle et bénéficiale*, 64 vols. (Paris, 1775–83), further 14 vols. (1786), XIX, 509–17.
L. Michel, 'La dîme et les revenues du Clergé d'Anjou à la fin de l'ancien régime', *Ann. de Bretagne*, LXXXVI (1979), 570.

about the misappropriation of ecclesiastical wealth became more insistent, and received increasing popular support.[17]

In many parishes, the division of the tithes had reached an astonishing complexity. In one place near Sedan, the *curé* was entitled to two-fifths, the Prior of Donchery, the chapter of Reims and the local *seigneur* to one fifth each. In the nearby parish of Torcy, the *curé* had half, the Prior of Donchery thirteen thirty-seconds, another prior one sixteenth and a *seigneur* one thirty-second.[18] In the little village of Courbesseaux in Lorraine, the *curé* collected a quarter, a seminary seven twenty-fourths, an abbot five twenty-fourths, a prior one eighth and two lay lords three forty-eighths each.[19] In the diocese of Toulouse, of 109 parish priests who owned tithes, only three were the exclusive collectors; 60 had half shares, 29 had thirds, and so on.[20] Confronted with problems of division, some tithe owners made peace among themselves by adopting a system of rotation, whether chronological (the *curé* to levy every third year, and his lay rival in the other two),[21] or geographical (the parish divided into halves with the two tithe owners collecting in alternate years in each).[22] In the diocese of Châlons-sur-Marne and in odd places elsewhere, a custom of division prevailed which must surely have been invented by lawyers anxious for fees: the right of the *suite de fer*. The *curé* of a parish in which a farmer stabled his horses or oxen during the winter had a right to collect half the tithes (and the whole of the tithes on animals and wool) in fields of another parish where these animals were used to do the ploughing. There were conditions, however: the boundaries of the parishes must run alongside at some point, the plough must be able to cross the border without encountering a stream or other natural obstacle, and the farmer must be self-employed.[23] In a tiny parish near Reims, this right to 'follow the plough' was divided equally between the *curé*, another parish priest and the cathedral chapter, with the two *curés* owing small fractions of their portion to three different monastic institutions.[24] A whole history of

[17] A major subject of eighteenth-century study. See, e.g., E. Préclin, *Les Jansénistes du XVIIIe siècle et la Constitution civile du clergé, 1713–91* (Paris, 1928); and J. McManners, *French Ecclesiastical Society under the Ancien Régime: A Study of Angers in the Eighteenth Century* (Manchester U.P., 1960).

[18] G. Hubrecht, 'La région Sedanaise à la veille de la Révolution', *Ann. hist. Rév. fr.* (1937), 33.

[19] D. Mathieu, *L'Ancien régime dans la province de Lorraine et Barrois* (Paris, printed Macon, 1907), 140.

[20] Frêche, 521.

[21] Marion, *La Dîme*, 20.

[22] A. Girault, *Les Biens d'église dans la Sarthe à la fin du XVIIIe siècle* (Laval, 1953), 379.

[23] Guyot, XIX, 429–32.

[24] G. Laurent, *Reims et la région rémoise à la veille de la Révolution* (Coll. docs. inéd. dépt de la Marne, 1st ser., V, Reims, 1930), cclxiv–viii.

distrust and litigation lay behind these confusions. Yet the story of such labyrinthine arrangements was not always a sordid one. In one Angevin parish a simple tripartite division had prevailed, until a great nobleman listened to the stirrings of conscience, and complicated everything by giving a ninth of his third share to the *curé*, and an eighth of it to maintain a local chapel.[25]

Whether there were various tithe owners or just one, the whole business of collection might be leased to a *fermier*. Since prices tended to rise and leases to be traditional, an entrepreneurial family which established itself in the tithe-farming business was likely to do well.[26] Collecting for a modest nunnery, then on to service with more opulent institutions, and eventually farming the *taille* for the government – this was how Cardinal Fleury's family had climbed up into the world of finance in the seventeenth century.[27] The list of *fermiers* who undertook to collect the archbishop of Albi's tithes shows that it was not artisans or peasants who competed for the contracts, but merchants and entrepreneurs, one third of them from Albi itself and the others from smaller towns. Frequently, in this area of France, within reach of the great canal crossing the whole country, it was the professional grain merchants who took up the collection; a typical case is at Calmont in 1770 where the auction stood at just over 6,000 *liv.* – a grain merchant took it up in alliance with an innkeeper and two other local worthies who would oversee the collection for him.[28] In the diocese of Auch, a fifth of the contractors were peasants, but always the richer, 'les plus aisés', of their villages. Most of the rest were bourgeois and, significantly, when collection became difficult because of 'strikes' of tithe payers towards the end of the *ancien régime*, it was the richer merchants and lawyers who were able to stay in competition for the contracts. In 1786, the archbishop of Auch farmed the whole of his tithes (in more than 300 parishes) to an *avocat* of Paris for the huge sum of 306,000 *liv.* and 706 sacks of barley. It is easy to see why the auction of the tithes of the bigger tithe owners should so often be won by the better-off bidders. To sign a contract, often for half a dozen years ahead, was too risky a business for a family without substantial resources, and a single rich entrepreneur could afford to finance a lawsuit against selected individuals, and could settle the matter of a rebate from the tithe owner for unpaid sums in one comprehensive negotiation.[29] To make the peasants fork

---

[25] L. Michel, 'La dîme et les revenues du Clergé d'Anjou à la fin de l'ancien régime', *Ann. de Bretagne*, LXXXVI (1979), 572.
[26] F. Évard, 'Les dîmes dans le parc de Versailles', *Révolution française* (1928), 115.
[27] E. Le Roy Ladurie, *Les Paysans de Languedoc* (Paris, 1966), 480.
[28] Frêche, 527–30.
[29] J. Rives, *Dîme et société dans l'archidiocèse d'Auch au XVIIIe siècle* (Paris, 1976), 57–60.

out, it was as well to have a man of influence accustomed to hobnobbing with lawyers, and if he lived out of the parish, so much the better for his peace of mind.

Instead of contracting out the collection, a tithe owner might decide to exercise a general oversight himself, but employ one or two professionals to share the odium of getting the produce safely into his barn. In Anjou, these characters, called *métiviers*, were substantially remunerated, retaining between a tenth and a sixth of all they garnered.[30] Even doing it oneself, collecting a tithe could be an expensive business. One *curé*, in a year when he took up 2,178 *liv.*'s worth of produce, reckoned that the operation had cost him 435 *liv.*: engaging two labourers and plying them with wine, hiring carts and extra help to unload them and getting in a threshing expert had run away with a fifth of his income.[31] This was a high proportion: according to an official record in the diocese of Clermont in 1763, the cost of collection was normally one tenth.[32] In 1786, a *curé* of the diocese of Comminges complained to his bishop about the alacrity of his parishioners in joining his rejoicing on the day his sheaves came home; by tradition, he had to furnish 12 jars of wine, 12 pounds of matured cheese and a dinner to the municipal officers – after deducting these expenses and other largesse which he had to furnish at Christmas and on All Saints Day, and the wages of a *vicaire*, he was left with only 512 *liv.* to live on.[33] Another peculiar obligation afflicted the tithe owners of Lorraine, who had to provide their villagers with stud animals, and these, like aldermen invited to a tithe-banquet, had voracious appetites. At Montiers-sur-Saulx,[34] in the diocese of Toul, where the tithe was shared between the *curé* and two abbeys, by tradition the parish priest provided the ram, the abbey of Ecurey the bull, and the abbey of Montier-en-Der the boar. But in 1714 the Benedictines of Ecurey refused to pay for a bull and persuaded the local court to order the *curé* to contribute towards it as he alone drew the *menues dîmes*. A new *curé* appealed against the verdict, and obtained a legal ruling obliging all three tithe owners to pay equally towards all three animals. The monks, on appeal to the *bailliage* court, got the *curé* condemned to pay one third towards the bull and to pay entirely for the ram and the boar. But in 1730 the parish priest finally turned the tables; the system of pre-1714 was restored, and the conspiratorial Benedictines, in addition to having to pay all the expenses of furnishing the bull, had to give costs and damages to the *curé* and the inhabitants.

30 Michel, 571.   31 Gagnol, 124–5.   32 Poitrineau, I, 352.

33 A. Saramon (ed.), *Les Paroisses du diocèse de Comminges en 1786* (Coll. docs, inéd. sur l'hist. écon. de la Rév. fr., Paris, 1968), 23.

34 R. Laprune, *Hist. religieuse de Montiers-sur-Saulx*, 5 vols. (dupl. Thesis, B. Nat. 4°Lk7 58305 (1–5), 1967), I, 25–6.

But the owner of the *grosses décimes* had obligations going far beyond the provision of cheese and wine, bulls and boars. Any tithe owner who drew the revenues to the exclusion of the *curé* had, as his first obligation, to pay the officially prescribed salary to the parish priest – the so-called *congrue*. The *gros décimateur*, whether he was the parochial minister or not, was also responsible for the repairs to the church, at one time solely responsible. The Edict of 1695 limited this obligation to the chancel and the choir, an injustice to parishioners which was not entirely forgotten in the *cahiers* of 1789.[35] In addition, if the parishioners were poor, chalices, ornaments and liturgical books had to be provided, possibly candles also, and laundry expenses. Royal Edicts of 1771 and 1772 made these obligations more precise. By contrast, an Edict of May 1768, purporting to excuse tithe holders from having to pay out more than a third of their annual profit on repairs, was sufficiently ambiguous in its wording to cause confusion.[36] There was, however, some safeguard for a parish priest, as distinct from other tithe owners: by tradition, he ought always to be left with a reasonable living wage.[37] Doubtful questions abounded, with corresponding scope for litigation. What redress was available if the tithe owner was the Crown, and the administrators of the royal demesne refused to provide 'what is necessary for the celebration of the holy mysteries'?[38] Could a parish sue for past negligence? – in 1740, a village in Dauphiné went to law for arrears of candles back to 1672.[39] Did 'what is necessary' include the salary of a parish clerk, as the Parlement of Toulouse was trying to prove in the mid-eighteenth century?[40] Did repairing responsibilities accompany the enjoyment of the *menues dîmes*? Generally not, and the matter was finally settled by a ruling of the Grand Conseil in 1748 – a verdict which rescued a country *curé* who was being haunted by the archbishop of Cambrai and the chapter of Notre-Dame of Paris (no less) to contribute to chancel repairs on the strength of a miserable tithe on beans and lentils and a mere bushel of grain allotted to him from the great tithes.[41] Towers and spires were ruinously expensive: if the tower was over the nave, the parishioners had to pay, if over the choir or chancel, the tithe owners. But what of the tower at Guyancourt, with two supporting pillars on one side and two on the other? It took lawsuits from 1769 to 1775 to get to the common-sense solution of dividing the cost.[42] What if the tower fell, damaging the nave? In 1751, the spire of Mortagne

---

[35] Gagnol, 86–9.   [36] Marion, *La Dîme*, 76–7.
[37] M. Piales, *Traité des réparations*, 4 vols. (Paris, 1762), II, 22.
[38] A. Playoust-Chaussis, *La Vie religieuse dans le diocèse de Boulogne au XVIIIe siècle* (Arras, 1976), 60.
[39] Marion, *La Dîme*, 154–5.   [40] Marion, *La Dîme*, 148.
[41] Guyot, X, 550.   [42] Évard, 122–3.

in Poitou was blown down, and the Benedictine monks who tithed there refused to rebuild it as 'unnecessary'. The parish went to law, alleging that it had been a landmark for travellers and a look-out post when the English had attacked La Rochelle; in the end, the Benedictines escaped their obligation on the aesthetic ground that the architecture had been Gothic, and therefore of dubious value.[43] The Edict of 1695 had favoured tithe owners, but it had not repealed certain provincial customs benefiting parishes, more especially, it had not changed the old jurisprudence of Flanders.[44] Here, the exploiter of the great tithes was responsible for the whole of the church building, and was obliged to allocate two years' revenue out of every six for the purpose. The Parlement of Flanders repelled all manoeuvres of the tithe owners to bring the province under the law of 1695; indeed, the magistrates went further, and in a series of lawsuits ruled that the salaries of curés and repairs to vicarages and churches were expenses which holders of the grosses dîmes had to pay however much they exceeded the compulsory two years' contribution.

Where the tithe of a parish went to the curé, his people looked to him to give proportionately to the poor. Whether by Christian charity or by the pressure of public opinion, most parish priests did something – and in times of famine, a great deal. But what of the absentee chapters, monasteries and laymen whose contractors' carts trundled off the sheaves or the wine jars at the appropriate harvest season? In some places, more especially in Dauphiné, the holder of the great tithe on cereals was, by custom, expected to hand over a fixed proportion to the curé for the poor.[45] In others, the courts had intervened to make custom into obligation. In this way, great abbeys had been saddled with compulsory alms; Lessay in Normandy, for example, was under the orders of the Parlement of Rouen to pay 6,000 liv. to 7,000 liv. a year 'without prejudice to ordinary almsgiving as circumstances require, or to the exercise of hospitality'.[46] When farming out its estates, an ecclesiastical institution might impose a tariff of charity on its contractor – in this way, perhaps, losing credit for its generosity among local people at the time and among historians subsequently.[47] In various other ways, friendly gestures were made by tithe owners to their villages; the collège of Pélegri near Cahors had set up exhibitions limited to the children of the three parishes where it collected half the tithe.[48] But except in crises of dearth, and not always then, the absentee tithe owners were rarely generous. 'I haven't received a sou

43 Piales, II, 133, 191–210.   44 Guyot, XI, 112–27.
45 Marion, La Dîme, 73.   46 Gagnol, 113.
47 Gagnol, 114–15.
48 E. Sol, La Vie en Quercy à l'époque moderne (le mouvement économique) (Paris, 1948), 99.

from anybody at all to help me to aid the destitute in my parish', said a *curé* of Guyenne in 1789, 'not even from le sieur Thyerri, who draws the great tithe... which Thyerri I must leave to the judgement of his own conscience.'[49] An enquiry, towards the end of the *ancien régime*, by the archbishop of Rouen throughout his diocese, was full of such complaints – the great abbey of Bec gives 72 *liv.* a year only, that of Jumièges nothing at all; 'the poor get more aid from the most insignificant of Protestant families than they do from a celebrated abbey which plunders 800 acres of my parish'. 'It appears to me to be simple justice', said another *curé*, 'that the holders of the *grosses dîmes* should contribute to helping their brethren, seeing they enjoy crops that have been fertilized by the sweat of the poor.'[50] Similar complaints abound in the *cahiers* of 1789. The villagers of Cumières, near Reims, had an ancient tradition that the tithe which they paid at one eleventh had, long ago, been as little as one sixtieth, until their ancestors, 'as honest and trusting as monks and ecclesiastics are sly and crafty', had agreed to an increased payment for the rebuilding of the abbey of Hautvilliers, an increase which had been illegally perpetuated. Even so, the abbey gave no alms. 'The abbot of Hautvilliers does nothing to help to pay for the expenses of religious services in Cumières. We tried to stir up his charity on behalf of the poor, but there has been no reply; his heart of bronze remains deaf – it hears only the chink of gold pieces.'[51]

The motivation to contest the levy of tithe was universal, and confusions and ambiguities providing grounds for litigation were legion.[52] Mines and quarries were exempt, so were woods, though under certain circumstances a major cut of trees became taxable. Fruit trees were exempt in most of France, but were all chargeable in Gascony, and certain fruits in some other places. Why, in Auvergne, should hemp pay so generally and hay so rarely, and why, when new crops in that province were mostly exempt, did turnips and sainfoin occasionally slip into the tithe gatherer's net?[53] The produce of hunting escaped, so too of fishing, except in certain Norman ports. Crops cut before due time were free if used to feed the working animals, but not if used to fatten beasts for sale to the butchers. An enclosed private garden adjoining a house was free, but not if it was newly created from land that had once been ploughed and sown. Needless to say, there were regulations to stop the laity enclosing whole fields and calling them gardens; logical in injustice, the Parlement of Bordeaux allowed one size of garden to a man who ploughed with two oxen, and double this amount to one who ploughed

[49] Gagnol, 15.
[50] C. Bloch, *L'Assistance et l'État en France à la veille de la Révolution* (Paris, 1908), 273–6.
[51] Laurent, ccxlv–vii.   [52] Marion, *La Dîme*, 35–8.   [53] Poitrineau, I, 352.

with four. Private parks did not pay tithe, but if they were created from arable land, compensation had to be paid; Louis XIV gave annuities to *curés* and the abbey of Sainte-Geneviève when he created the Trianon park in 1668 – these fell steadily in value and were a cause of complaint in the eighteenth century.[54]

Odd local circumstances could intensify ill-will and provide occasions for tragi-comic feuds and litigation. Not every village had an established, clear procedure for allocating the tithe owners' share – like Blairy in Burgundy, where each proprietor had to stack his sheaves in a straight row, so that the *dixmeur* could start counting at any one he chose and collect every thirteenth sheaf thereafter,[55] or Heuilley, where the payment was a fixed measure of grain according to the amount of land under cultivation, the area to be declared by the proprietor, with the *curé* having the right to challenge (surveyor's fees paid by the party which was mistaken).[56] In some places, the size of sheaves was argued about, in others, whether they were properly tied, whether the necessary warning of the harvesting date had been given, whether the sheaves had remained available long enough in the field for inspection.[57] What of new crops – clover, potatoes, maize? What of crops planted between rows of vines?[58] Who was to dictate which of two alternative local measures of grain should be used – like the bushel of Falaise, marginally bigger than that of Briouze?[59] What if a crop of rye had been harvested green to be used as ties for the bundles of ripe grain later on? What of windfall fruit, fallen to the ground before it was ripe?[60] One thing was sure; if the tithe owner let things slip, a precedent would be created against him, and what was allowed to one individual in one year would be demanded by everyone the next. In 1770, a canon of Saint-Omer sued a proprietor of Helfaut for tithe on a few tobacco plants; a derisory sum was involved, but the crop might have become significant in a few years time.[61] And in any case, there was the whole principle of tithe to be upheld, so that even the most improbable windfall was worth pursuing. In 1747 the *curé*

---

[54] Évard, 58–9.

[55] P. de Saint-Jacob, *Les Paysans de la Bougogne du nord au dernier siècle de l'ancien régime* (Paris, 1960), 271.

[56] P. de Saint-Jacob, *Documents relatifs à la communauté villageoise en Bourgogne* (Paris, 1962), 146–8.

[57] Gagnol, 128; Marion, *La Dîme*, 97.

[58] L. and G. Trenard, *La Diocèse de Belley* (Paris, 1978), 114.

[59] Marion, *La Dîme*, 144.

[60] Guyot, XIX, 404–7.

[61] G. Coolen, *Helfaut: essai sur l'administration d'une paroisse sous l'ancien régime*, Mems. Soc. Antiquairies de la Morinie, XXXVII (St Omer, 1939), 24.

of Issy won a lawsuit before the Parlement of Paris for 'la dîme des sangliers élevés dans les maisons' – the severe winter had driven wild boars into the village for refuge. 'It is true', said the lawyers, 'that there is no custom of tithing wild boars, but that is not an argument for saying the claim is unfounded, because up to now there has been no custom of rearing wild boars in houses.'[62] It was important to seize the right moment for litigation, and also to choose the appropriate adversary. In 1788, a *curé* wrote to the abbot of the Cistercian abbey of La Ferté-sur-Grosne proposing a joint onslaught on 'le sieur Grassart', evidently a man of substance, who had been stirring up the parishioners to refuse a tithe which the abbey and the parish priest shared between them.[63] This was the strategy of staking everything on breaking through the enemy's centre. But it might be safer to begin with an attack on the flank, to pick off some miserable peasant, thus establishing a legal ruling to be used against the richer ones. The poor, we must remember, ran the danger of ruin if they contested a lawsuit, since they might have to pay the costs of the other side. In Voltaire's correspondence we read of the fate of five peasant families who foolishly disputed a tithe of 30 *liv.* a year which came to them as a charity, in opposition to the grasping *curé* of Monëns, only to find themselves condemned to pay 1,300 *liv.* in costs, including the *curé*'s lodging and wine bills during the hearing of the case in Dijon.[64] In 1767, the *recteur* of Saint-Denoual noted in his journal that his tithe of one fleece from each flock invariably brought him in the most mangy specimens: 'on vole le Recteur en tout'. Though nobles were the meanest of all in this respect, he dissimulated his ire; the only way to proceed was to look out for a chance to cite before the *présidial* someone too poor to fight back, then to publish the sentence of the court (at a cost of ten *écus*, he notes gloomily), in the hope of frightening the others.[65]

One standard device for evading tithe which the richer cultivator could resort to was to change to a different crop – one which the lawyers recommended as having a chance to qualify for exemption. Thus Restif de la Bretonne's father, smarting at the rapacious forays of the bishop and canons of Auxerre among his corn sheaves, planted part of his non-ploughable hill

---

[62] P. de Vaissière, *Curés de campagne de l'ancienne France* (Paris, 1933), 88–9.

[63] G. Guillot and A. Amic, 'Le dernier abbé de la Ferté-sur-Grosne', *Rev. Mabillon*, III (1907), 367–9.

[64] Voltaire, *Corresp.*, ed. Th. Besterman, revised complete edn., 51 vols. (1968–77), XIX (1971), 299–30, 312 (Nos. D7996 of 25 December 1758 and D8011 of 29 October 1758). When the *curé* got into a fracas, Voltaire got his revenge by stirring up a legal enquiry (F. Caussy, *Voltaire, seigneur de village* (Paris, 1912), 53–6).

[65] P. Lemarchand, 'Journal d'un curé de campagne au 18e siècle', *Soc. Émulation Côtes du Nord*, LXXXVIII (1960), 63–4.

terrain with vines, and in seven years was producing wine, a commodity not titheable by local custom.[66] M. de Goupillières, directeur of the Mint at Caen, was not so lucky. In 1734 he went down in person to his *seigneurie* of Saint-Hilaire to supervise the change of some arable to pasture (catching a cold in the process), and wrote a smooth letter to the *curé* – 'Mon Révérend Père' – pointing out that he was within his legal rights since he had left two-thirds of his land under the plough. After four years of litigation, however, he was condemned to pay an annual compensation.[67] His lawyers had not done their homework. True, a declaration of 1657 protecting tithe owners against loss of revenue when meadows were created, had never been registered, and the Parlement and the Grand Conseil had ruled that a tithe owner could claim compensation only if he was losing more than a third of his revenue. But the essential point was – it was a third of the *whole* tithe from the parish which mattered; thus, landowners who were quick to create meadows might get away with it, but not the later ones.[68] In this same year, 1734, M. Grandjean de Lespine planted trees on a stretch of his arable land in Crevecoeur-en-Brie. In this case the *curé* failed in his lawsuit as his losses, on all heritages taken together, still did not total a third.

Disputes of a like kind arose from Government Edicts[69] to encourage the extension of the area of cultivation by granting a limited suspension of tithe. In 1761, an exemption for ten years was offered for wasteland brought under the plough; three years later this was raised to fifteen. As for land reclaimed from marsh, this would enjoy an exemption of twenty years, with tithe thereafter pegged at the low figure of one fiftieth. Foolishly, the clergy of the province of Guyenne protested. 'The saying, you must sow before you can reap, is unknown to them', complained Quesnay, the Physiocrat.[70] Most ecclesiastics were more enlightened, and saw these concessions as a source of future profit: a minor waiving of principle in the present, and an increase of revenue in the long run. The chapter of Notre-Dame of Paris and the clerical representatives at the Estates of Brittany were willing to improve on the Government's regulations and offer a twenty-one years' immunity in the areas where they tithed. But what was 'wasteland'? Inevitably, any weedy patch that had escaped the plough for a while was claimed to be such

---

66 Restif de la Bretonne, *La Vie de mon père*, *Oeuvres*, ed. M. Bachelin, 9 vols. (Paris, 1930–2), IV, 81.

67 V. Gourdet, 'Saint-Hilaire-de-Briouze', *Bull. soc. hist. arch. de l'Orne*, XIII (1894), 78–9.

68 Guyot, XIX, 421–6, and for what follows.

69 Marion, *La Dîme*, 48–53.

70 G. Weulersse, *Le Mouvement Physiocratique en France de 1756 à 1770*, 2 vols. (Paris, 1910), I, 462. See II, 185–6, where it is said most dioceses had accepted.

by its owners, so an *arrêt* of 1766 laid down a definition of 40 years without cultivation. The Assembly General of Clergy still had to go on protesting, however; the Parlement of Bordeaux was allowing proprietors to plough waste without giving the tithe owner notice of intent, thus obliterating evidence of previous cultivation, while in the *landes* the sand performed the function anyway. And what of the crafty estate managers who ploughed up old-established meadows and switched some of their old titheable arable to pasture in exchange? In Gascony and Quercy, it was the nobles who led the way in manipulating the code concerning wasteland and marshes to evade the tithe owner's levies; bourgeois *entrepreneurs* tended to be mixed up in the business of collection, and therefore sided with the clergy.[71] A Breton nobleman wrote to the Controller General in 1783 pointing out that the fifteen-year exemption granted in 1766 was now running out for many proprietors.

The peasant proprietor, the *laboureur* [no doubt it was convenient not to mention the drainers and enclosers among the nobility], panic-stricken, can already see the Church annexing the fruit of his toil, and is deciding to abandon the cultivation of land he had enclosed from the waste, and on which he has become agreeably accustomed to pay nothing more than taxes to the State.

Thus, he concluded, the king is going to lose revenue, simply because the clergy are being allowed an unearned windfall – was there not a Royal Edict in 1749 forbidding them to acquire new property, and what is tithe but property of a sort?[72]

Given this atmosphere of suspicion, fraud and litigation, tithe was inevitably hated. It was all the more grudgingly paid when the peasant made comparisons. If he paid tithe at a high rate, he would compare his burden with the lighter burden borne by others. Of a group of 36 parishes in Champagne,[73] 21 paid a global sum equal to one third of all State taxation levied, but four paid fully two-thirds of the total exactions of the Crown; an enormous disparity. The peasants were narrowly confined, physically and intellectually, within the boundaries of their village community, but where paying out was concerned, they knew when they were being unequally treated. In Brittany, where tithe in adjoining parishes could vary from one tenth to one thirty-sixth, this was a general complaint in the *cahiers*. That of the village of Comblessac asked for some reduction in its one twelfth, 'seeing that the parishes around owe it only on the fiftieth or thirtieth sheaf,

---

[71] J. Rives, 'Dîme et défrichements en Gascogne et Quercy au XVIII siècle', *Ann. du Midi*, XCII (1980), 57–66.
[72] Pierre de Vaissière, *Gentilshommes campagnards de l'ancienne France* (Paris, 1928), 356–7.
[73] Marion, *La Dîme*, 112–13.

and their land is better quality than ours'.[74] Another comparison to be made
was with the privileged few who escaped paying tithe altogether. A man
whose income consisted solely in an official salary or house rents, would pay
nothing. Mills were exempt and forests often escaped, and these were mostly
owned by the privileged classes. In Provence nobles paid at a lower rate
than commoners, even on non-noble lands which they might have pur-
chased. The orders of Malta, Cîteaux, Cluny, the Prémontrés and the
Chartreux held exemptions granted to them by popes, though there was a
developing jurisprudence in the eighteenth century to limit their privilege.
Oddly enough, some Protestants in Alsace were not liable, since the lawyers
of Louis XIV had failed to list all provincial peculiarities that needed to be
changed on annexation.[75] And finally, there was the most devastating comparison of all, between the poverty of the payer of tithe and the wealth of
some great ecclesiastical institution which levied it – and if this institution
collected seigneurial or other dues locally as well, the cumulative effect was
overwhelming. Richeprey, touring the South, investigating inequalities of
the taxation system, noted the nuns of Saint-Sernin (Rodez) tied up in lawsuits with a parish in which they levied a *champart* of one quarter or one fifth
along with the tithe.[76] The cathedral chapter of Beauvais, in twelve parishes
of its estates, enjoyed a tithe and a *champart* which together took 18 per cent
of the peasants' crops; the *cahiers* of this area in 1789 overflow with bitterness.[77]

The peasant, enviously reflecting on his misery, was well aware that the
true rate at which he paid his tribute to the Church was always higher than
the ostensible official figure. As the villagers of Saint-André-du-Double in
Périgord said in their *cahier*, they paid twice over when they paid a tithe on
potatoes, then another one on the pigs that were fed on them; similarly
when they paid on grain used to feed chickens. Furthermore, they were not
allowed to deduct anything to cover the seed corn which they planted.[78]
This was an important point, for the yield of grain was often only one in
four; that is, a tithe which appeared to be one eighth would in fact be one
fifth.[79] Dupont de Nemours, drawing up the *cahier* of the Tiers Etat of his

[74] H. Sée, 'Les classes rurales en Bretagne du XVIe siècle à la Révolution', *Ann. de Bretagne*, XXI (1905), 506–7.

[75] Marion, *La Dîme*, 10–13; Gagnol, 49–50.

[76] J. F. Henry de Richeprey, *Journal des voyages en Haute-Guienne*, ed. H. Guilhamon (Arch. hist. du Rouergue, Rodez, 1952), 300.

[77] P. Goubert, *Beauvais et le Beauvaisis de 1600 à 1730*, 2 vols. (Paris, 1960), I, 180.

[78] L. Ampoulange, *Le Clergé et la convocation aux États Généraux de 1789 dans la séné-chaussée principale de Périgord* (Montpellier, 1912), 47–9.

[79] G. Lizerand, *Le Régime rural de l'ancienne France* (Paris, 1942), 175. Cf. Register of the commune of Artiguelouve, 'Une commune rurale des Pyrénées au début de la Révolution', *Rev. hist.* XLI (1889), 97.

bailliage, declared that proprietors were paying as much as a third of their crop if all expenses were taken into account. 'You imagine, O complaining farmer, that it's one sheaf in ten they are taking out of your field', said a pamphleteer of 1789, *L'Iniquité de la dîme*, 'Great is your error; they are taking one in five. Half of your crop goes in covering your advances, your cost of cultivation, your seed corn.'[80] And an important item in this cost of cultivation was the manuring of the fields. Carting seaweed or the fragrant contents of municipal cesspits to the land was a toilsome expedient available only to those who lived near the seashore or suburbs. For the most part, the fields were fertilized by the dung-impregnated litter which had bedded the animals, more especially during the winter months. But straw was so often in short supply: 'la paille est toujours ce qui manque', said an agricultural reformer in a treatise of 1763.[81] To collect tithe 'au champ' instead of 'dans le sac' (that is, taking the stalk along with the grain) was a notable device of seigneurial oppression – used, for example, by a Catholic seigneur against a Protestant village in Alsace to force it to conversion.[82] Some of the Parlements made regulations compelling tithe owners to sell back their straw to the inhabitants at low prices fixed by the local judicial officials.[83] This arbitrary intervention of the magistrates was not unreasonable. The least wealthy chapters and monasteries could do was to refrain from hampering the cultivators who grew the crops which paid their tribute.

If tithe was collected by a contractor, it was likely that enforcement would be harsher, and if the contractor was from outside the village, no one was satisfied. The richer peasants saw a lucrative job escaping them, and the poorer saw wealth leaving the parish that might have provided them with employment or charity. In Flanders, by a cherished local custom, the job of collecting tithes was auctioned annually in separate details, enabling even humble peasants to have a chance to try their hand at this minor capitalist enterprise. By contrast, in the areas where the archbishop of Cambrai left his tithe collection in the hands of the manager who ran all his estates, there was a general clamour in the *cahiers* of 1789 for tithe to be farmed to parishioners only.[84] There was an exception – an illogical one – to this preference for a local contractor. Some parish priests held the tithe in their own hands and collected it: this was accepted as an inevitable evil, and it was satisfying, at

---

[80] Marion, *La Dîme*, 117–22.

[81] Duhamel du Monceau, *Éléments dé'agriculture*, 2 vols. (Paris, 1763), I, 200.

[82] L. Châtellier, *Tradition chrétienne et renouveau catholique dans l'ancien diocèse de Strasbourg, 1650–1770* (1981), 287.

[83] F. Mourlot, 'La convocation des Etats Généraux de 1789 dans le bailliage de Vire', *Révolution française*, XXXI (1896), 421.

[84] Lefebvre, 112.

any rate, to reflect that the profits stayed in the parish. But there were *curés* who did not enjoy the tithe, but who nevertheless volunteered to collect it, to obtain the contractor's percentage.[85] Thus, the abbey or chapter which had usurped the *curé*'s true patrimony (for this was how everyone regarded it), and which now paid him a mere pittance, was able to make use of his local knowledge in levying its dues. What was worse, here was a man of God stepping out of his spiritual rôle to usurp a job which a layman of the parish might have hoped for. 'By taking holy orders, he had become the protector and father of the flock confided to his care; but he takes the bread from the hands of the hard-up individuals who used to collect the tithes, work which used to help them to earn a living and to pay their taxes' – this concerning the *curé* of Marche-Maisons near Alençon, in the village *cahier*.[86] Another variant of the pastor as professional collector is when he shared a tithe with others, drawing a fraction which, perhaps, was too small to be economically levied on its own. In this case, it was only common sense to offer to collect the lot and to arrange the share-out. In his memoirs, Marquis-Ducastel, *curé* of Sainte-Suzanne, describes how he inherited a comfortable arrangement of this kind, handing over two-thirds to the abbot of Evron, less 360 *liv.* collector's charges. A new abbot, however, put the business into the hands of the city slickers – 'intriguers from Laval' – who farmed his estates; Marquis-Ducastel lost something like 800 *liv.* a year by having to hire a separate barn for storing his third.[87] He does not tell us what was the attitude of the parishioners of Sainte-Suzanne; there was no doubt about that of the inhabitants of Rumegies, in the diocese of Tournai, earlier in the century. Dubois, the *curé*, tells us how the abbey of Saint-Amand enjoyed a tithe of seven hundredths in his parish, and he himself one of one hundredth, a fraction too small to levy effectively; how in 1702 he bought the right to levy the abbey tithe as well as his own – 'using the same collector, the same cart and the same efforts as before!'. He soon wished he had not been so efficient.

On every side nothing was heard but threats – to burn him out, to kill him, to insult him, to drive him out of his cure. And even his best friends in the parish all made war on him. And unless God in his goodness touches their hearts, they will never pardon him! Indeed, if the *curé* had had the least inkling that he'd become so unpopular, he'd never have thought of taking over this tithe collecting.[88]

---

[85] Hubrecht, 33–4; Girault, 318.
[86] Gagnol, 122.
[87] *Vie de M. Marquis-Ducastel, doyen rural d'Évron et du Sonnois*, ed. E. Pichon (Le Mans, 1873), 57–8.
[88] *Journal d'un curé de campagne au XVIIe siècle*, ed. M. Platelle (Paris, 1965), 88.

The lawyers who grew sleek by conducting the tithe suits of the laity had accumulated theoretical and historical arguments; anticlericals in search of ammunition did not need to go further than the law dictionaries. Was tithe of divine institution? In his Edict of 1657, Louis XIV had repeated this claim, but the Parlement of Paris had refused to register it. The lawyers insisted that here was a simple tax 'for the maintenance of the ministers of the Church'.[89] True, the Levites had enjoyed their tithes, as recorded in the Books of Leviticus and Numbers. But the Gallican Church was in a different situation, having its own landed endowment. St Paul was much concerned about the maintenance of preachers of the Gospel, yet he was silent about this Levitical precedent, so too were the laws of the first six centuries.[90] Christians, unlike Jews, are not obliged to pay a fixed tribute, St Augustine had boasted. St Thomas Aquinas does not accept the principle of divine institution. Indeed, the argument ran, the variations in the rate at which tithe was levied suggest an accumulation of practical concessions rather than the imposition of a theoretical obligation. The Parlement of Franche Comté used these arguments in 1725 to prevent a *curé* from levying tithe on a tiny hamlet. Even though the rest of the parish paid, the inhabitants of Boismurie were held to be exempt on grounds of prescription – they had evaded payment for a long time. No tithe was levied in the early centuries, the Eastern Church has never had it, it has not been paid in India or America, said the Parlement; therefore it has arisen purely by custom, and as it arose, so let it die, beginning maybe in the hamlet of Boismurie.[91] Montesquieu added learning and Voltaire irony to the concept of tithe as a purely human institution which the law of the land could modify. Payment of a tenth among the Jews, said Montesquieu, had been 'part of the plan of the foundation of their republic', while in France it was a 'charge independent of those involved in the estab-lishment of the monarchy'. Before Charlemagne, tithe was 'preached...but not established', and for long after him payment was episodic. And tithe, as Charlemagne had devised it, was divided between the bishop, the clergy, the church building and the poor. Since he had considered his gifts to the Church less as a religious than as a 'political dispensation' there is every reason to believe that the tithe is not exclusively for the clergy; in its primi-tive allocation, half went to the church fabric and the indigent.[92] Voltaire, as ever, had fun with the arrangements of the Old Testament. The Levites tithed in the wilderness of Cades, and Abraham gave to Melchizedeck the

---

[89] P. Viard, 'La dîme en France au 17e siècle', *Rev. hist.*, CLVI (1927), 243.
[90] Guyot, XIX, 399–400; L. F. Dejouy, *Principes et usages concernant les dixmes* (1761), 4.
[91] Guyot, XLVII, 162–7.
[92] Montesquieu, *L'Esprit des Lois*, XXXI (12), *Oeuvres complètes* (Pléiade, 2 vols. (Paris, 1966)), II, 960–2.

tithes of Sodom; let us pack off our modern tithe owners to collect their revenues in those distant, insalubrious places. This applies, however, only to the rich monks and canons, who drink choice vintages, eat pheasant and partridge, and sleep, not unaccompanied, on feather beds; by contrast, Voltaire laments (probably sincerely) the lot of the country *curé* 'obliged to dispute a sheaf of corn with his poor parishioners...to be hated and to hate'. Surely, these unjust exactions do not spring from the Christian Gospel: 'did God come down to earth to award a quarter of my income to the...abbot of Saint-Denis?'. In northern Europe, ministers of religion are paid from public funds, and everyone is happier.[93] These were hard words; even so, the clergy were to be officially maintained. But why should this maintenance be official? According to a more radical view – rarely found – the laity should be left to contribute of their own free will. In his journal, the abbé Véri explored the unavowed, subconscious cause of the intolerance of the Gallican Church towards Protestants: the fear that tithe would be lost. 'As soon as the exercise of religion is freely allowed, each believer then ought to allot the tithe of his field to the actual minister who exercises pastoral care over him.'[94] There is a logical further step which Véri does not mention. Unbelievers might keep their crops for themselves; once this was allowed, their numbers would be legion.

Criticism of tithe on grounds of history or principle was reinforced by solid economic arguments from the Physiocrats. The theories of this dominant school of French economic thinkers were dubious enough; they were mistaken about the declining population; they oversimplified when they made agriculture the sole source of real wealth; their theoretical insistence that grain must be allowed to rise to its natural price level disregarded the misery of the common people. But they saw clearly what was wrong with the French countryside; as a result of conspicuous waste, heavy taxation, tithe and the purchase of offices investment in agriculture was inadequate. So they proclaimed a new slogan, 'the inviolability of agricultural capital'[95] – much discussed by provincial Agricultural Societies. The owner of land ought not to push up the farmer's lease to the limit, ought not to pass on to him the unpredictable burden of State taxation. The actual tiller of the soil should enjoy a surplus, growing in proportion to the intensity of his own efforts, and which, in every sense of the word, he would plough back into the business. Tithe clearly was a major drain of capital away from the land, and a discouragement to enterprise and to the extension of the area of culti-

93 Voltaire, *Dict. philosophique*, 'Curé de campagne' (Moland, XVIII, 303–5).
94 J.-A. de Véri, *Journal*, ed. J. de Witte, 2 vols. (Paris, n.d.), I, 255–6.
95 Weulersse, I, 454–5.

vation. To the peasants' complaint that the true fraction of the crops taken was greater than the apparent one, the Physiocrats added a further argument. The costs of agricultural production were greatest in the least fertile areas, so that their tithe absorbed a greater fraction of the net crop than elsewhere: it was a levy falling most heavily on the poor.

The arguments of lawyers, *philosophes* and Physiocrats were but dimly grasped in rural France. Yet the peasants understood perfectly the basic principle at issue. Tithes were meant to pay the parochial ministers, to maintain the church building and keep divine service going; but they had been diverted to other purposes. Properly used they ought to provide a liberal maintenance for the *curé*, leaving him well enough off to feed the poor in time of dearth, and freeing him from the need to collect surplice fees at weddings and funerals. *Dîme* and *casuel* (tithe and surplice fees) were linked in the minds of the peasants: given the burden of the one, the other was unjustified. Representatives of the community of Gignac in the diocese of Aix-en-Provence in 1775 described how they paid tithe to the tune of 2,000 *liv.* a year, and all they got back was 200 *liv.* to pay a priest so ignorant that he did not know how to baptize; they applied, therefore, to be allowed to keep their money and use it to build up a real parochial life.[96] The *cahier* of Rougeon (diocese of Blois) gave a ruthless summary of peasant grievances:

We lament to see our parish priests in abjection, misery and necessity, while...a horde of monks of various sorts, abbots and canons take away our tithe and swindle our *curés* out of what is their due. The [tithe owners] on whom the benefice depends do not blush to see our churches without books, linen, ornaments, and on the verge of falling down, and dirtier than stables. Let their riches be cut back, and let our churches and our *curé* – the inspiration and support of our families – be properly endowed. And let us hear no more of surplice fees – the tithe is sufficient to pay for the administration of the sacraments...[97]

In the last twenty years of the *ancien régime*, a revolt against tithe was smouldering in the South of France. In 1775, the Assembly General of the Clergy of France accused the Parlement of Toulouse of an underhand design to encourage refusal to pay the *menues dîmes*. According to the magistrates, these could only be demanded if there was a clear title or long prescription, with proof that at least two-thirds of the inhabitants had been paying over at least two-thirds of the area of the parish, and that all had been paying at precisely the same rate (variations would show that the tribute was voluntary). Furthermore, these details had to be established by the testimony of witnesses other than the actual collectors. Since these were impossible

---

[96] E. Lavaquerie, *Le Cardinal de Boisgelin, 1732–1804*, 2 vols. (Angers, 1920), I, 230–1.
[97] Marion, *Dict.*, I, 175.

conditions, the Government issued declarations to rescue the clergy, declarations which the magistrates refused to register.[98] To the assembly of the clergy of the ecclesiastical province of Auch in 1780[99] (one of the areas of France where tithe was levied at a high rate), the archbishop reported widespread refusals to pay any more than the literal tenth, and to pay anything at all on maize, which was regarded as a new and exempt crop. 'This revolt is winning support from parish to parish, to the point that, if the approaching Assembly General of the Clergy fails to act in this respect, or acts unsuccessfully, payments will become purely a matter of individual choice, and refusals universal.' The Parlement of Toulouse backed M. de Saint-Géry's defiance of the bishop of Lectoure over the payment of a tithe of 2/17 on millet, and other cases were on the way. At another assembly of the clergy of his province in September 1782, the archbishop of Auch spoke of 'an evident conspiracy', with 500 lawsuits pending before the Parlement, and little doubt as to what the verdicts would be. The crisis came when the magistrates of Toulouse considered the plea of the villagers of Mouchez, who had refused to pay a tithe of 4/31 on wheat, offering to pay at 1/10. The *curé* had won his case when he cited the three chief recalcitrants before the court of the *sénéchausée* of Auch, but on appeal, the Parlement reversed this verdict in March 1781. From then onwards there was a torrent of refusals. By December 1784, more than half the parishes of Auch and Comminges were offering to pay at a strict tenth and no more. The tensions are evident in the complaints of the *curés* to the bishop of Comminges in 1786. They spoke of 'fire' and 'fermentation' and 'visible' threats; the old days when the tithe owners could be brusque with their peasants were over – 'il faut les traiter comme à des noces: de cette façon, ma portion est toujours petite'.[100] Not surprisingly, the clergy backed away from the desperate confrontation that seemed to be developing. Instead of 500 lawsuits being prosecuted, possibly only a dozen were fought through to a conclusion. Tithe owners avoided coming to a legal crunch unless they were confident about their documentary evidence; the *curés* urged the archbishop and chapters to be moderate and were themselves willing to negotiate. In most places there was a 'transaction'; on the main cereal crops the payment was reduced to the strict one tenth, and by way of compensation the clergy might be allowed peaceful possession of the *menues dîmes* in areas where these had been contested.[101] Other sovereign

[98] Marion, *La Dîme*, 141–3. In fact, so far as the great were concerned – bishops and Chapters – the Parlement was often inclined to favour them (Frêche, 539–40).

[99] A. Degert, 'Les Assemblées provinciales du Clergé Gascon', *Rev. de Gascogne*, NS, XX (1925), 87–184.

[100] Saramon (ed.), *Les Paroisses*, 66.

[101] Rives, *Dîme et société*, 147–156.

courts began to follow the example of Toulouse. In 1774, the Parlement of
Normandy declared that only the tithe on the four basic grain crops, wheat,
rye, barley and oats, could be levied as of right: tithes on all other crops were
'insolites', that is, proof of 40 years' possession was required.[102] The Parlement of Burgundy had been accustomed to decide cases in favour of tithe
owners; from 1770, it tended to find against them and in 1775 issued an
arrêt modelled on that of Normandy.[103] These were years of rising prices
and of agricultural diversification. From both these developments (somewhat
paradoxically coinciding) the tithe owners were gaining an enhanced income.
Hence, given the pervasive anticlericalism of the countryside, an envious
alliance of magistrates and cultivators formed against them.

At first sight it seems astonishing that the reformers of the early years of
the Revolution abandoned their original idea of confiscating tithe for the
coffers of the State, and simply suppressed it, thus making a handsome
present to all landowners at a time of national bankruptcy. Yet it is not
difficult to see why the intention of 4 August 1789[104] was never carried into
effect. For long, there had been a vast, undeclared conspiracy over the whole
of France to evade and outwit the tithe holders. On this issue landowners
had become pathologically conditioned to be deaf to reason and religion,
and, if need be, patriotism. The history of the guerilla war against tithe
waged for so long in the law courts is essential evidence in any study of rural
anticlericalism in France. A formula for calculating its intensity in any
particular areas may be suggested. Start with a standard, inevitable figure,
then slightly adjust it for the worse in years of very bad or very good
harvests, when tithe becomes especially hated as either a confiscation of the
bread of the poor or a theft from the profits of diligence and enterprise.
To this, add extra points of discontent if an ecclesiastical institution holds
the tithe to the exclusion of the *curé*, more points still if that institution is
scandalously rich, and still more if it levies seigneurial dues on the same
people from whom it takes tithe, and a substantial bonus if it gives only
derisory alms locally. All this to be multiplied by a coefficient based on the
rate at which tithe is levied as compared with other places. The suppression
of tithe by the representatives of the nation went far beyond what was suggested in the *cahiers*, yet was entirely compatible with them. Tithe had lost

---

[102] Marion, *La Dîme*, 140–1.
[103] P. de Saint-Jacob, *Les Paysans de la Bourgogne*, 374–6.
[104] It was then resolved that arrangements for buying off tithe would be made. Earlier
proposals would have made tithe a permanent tax, see [G.-F.-R. Molé, *avocat*], *Voeu
d'un citoyen pour la conversion des dîmes en un impôt territorial qui sera perçu au profit de
l'État* (1788). For the injustice to *métayers* involved in this gift to landowners see
S. Aberdam, 'La Révolution et les luttes des métayers', *Études rurales*, LIX (1975), 73ff.

all religious overtones and associations, and had become just a set of dues authorized by the State and levied by a minority of citizens on all the others. As Condorcet said, it was 'un véritable revenu indépendant de tout service religieux'.[105]

[105] Condorcet, *Sur les Assemblées provinciales*, *Oeuvres*, VIII, 160. The fluctuations in the yield of tithe are being studied as an indicator of agricultural progress. (E. Le Roy Ladurie and J. Goy, *Les Fluctuations du produit de la dîme. Conjoncture décimale et domaniale de la fin du Moyen Age au XVIIIe siècle* (Paris, 1972).) For the eighteenth century, the findings are: around Toulouse and Bordeaux and along the Pyrenees, the tithe yield was rising slowly, but there was no improvement in Brittany. (Summary in E. Le Roy Ladurie and J. Goy, 'La dîme et le reste, XIVe–XVIIIe siècles', *Rev. hist.*, CCLX (1978), 123–38; but the whole thesis of growth is denied by M. Morineau, in *Les Faux-semblants d'un démarrage économique: agriculture et démographie en France au XVIIIe siècle* (Paris, 1971); see also 'La dîme et l'enjeu', *Ann. hist. Rev. fr.* (1980), 162–80). In some areas, the rise of population must have cancelled out any improvement of living standards which might have been expected from the increased yield of agriculture, in contrast to the extra income which ecclesiastical institutions received from the tithe; it would be interesting to know if these were areas of more intense rural anticlericalism. But at the moment the whole subject bristles with difficulties and disagreements.

Christians and 'philosophes': the case of the Austrian Enlightenment

DEREK BEALES

How influential were the great men of the French Enlightenment, the *philosophes*, outside France? Or, how typical were they of the Enlightenment as a whole? These questions have been much discussed, not least by Owen Chadwick.[1] This essay is a small contribution to the debate, from what I think is a fresh standpoint: a consideration of the concept *philosophe*, as understood by the leaders of the French Enlightenment, in relation to the attitudes of some prominent figures associated with the Austrian Enlightenment. Although this standpoint appears so restricted, I think that what is visible from it has wider significance.

I

The concept *philosophe* needs some elucidation. It has been well studied – in English, for example, by Commager, Dieckmann, Lough, Shackleton, Wade, White and Wilson.[2] But for my purposes their work must be brought together and given a particular emphasis.

[1] E.g. O. Chadwick, *The Popes and European Revolution* (Oxford, 1981), pp. 406–7 and *passim*.

I am grateful for help and references given me by my wife, Dr T. C. W. Blanning, Prof. J. A. Crook, Dr J. C. McKeown, Prof. H. B. Nisbet, Dr S. O'Cathasaigh, Dr R. S. Porter, Mr S. P. Salt, Prof. Q. R. D. Skinner, Mr R. C. Smail, Dr E. Wangermann and Dr R. L. Wokler. Dr Blanning and Dr Wokler have very kindly read and commented on the text, but they are of course not responsible for it.

I should also like to acknowledge that this essay has benefited from the opportunities I have had to lecture on a similar theme at the Universities of Leeds and Newcastle and at Clare College and Trinity Hall, Cambridge.

I was assisted, in carrying out some of the research for this essay, by grants from the British Academy and the Leverhulme Trust.

[2] H. S. Commager, *The Empire of Reason* (London, 1978), esp. Appendix, 'The Term "Philosophe"', pp. 236–45; E. Dieckmann, *Le Philosophe: Texts and Interpretation* (St Louis, 1948); J. Lough, 'Who Were the *Philosophes*?', in *Studies in Eighteenth-Century French Literature Presented to Robert Niklaus*, ed. J. H. Fox, M. H. Waddicor

Unlike the term Enlightenment,[3] the word *philosophe*, used roughly as modern scholars use it, was current in the eighteenth century itself. The great men of the French Enlightenment – or most of them, most of the time – took pride in calling themselves, individually and collectively, *philosophes*. They can with plausibility be described as a party under that name, at least from the early 1750s. Even before that, but especially from the late 1750s, they were attacked as such, notably by their former comrade, Rousseau, and in Palissot's play of 1760, *Les Philosophes*.

One of Palissot's shafts, clearly well-aimed, was that they sought to mono-polise the concept *philosophe*. In so doing they were trying to eradicate its original and accepted meanings. Before the late seventeenth century, *philosophe* had two usual senses, both of them equally applicable to the word 'philosopher' in English and to the corresponding words in other languages: first, the man who seeks wisdom through abstract thought and by reasoning from first principles, perhaps erecting an intellectual system supposed to explain the universe in all its aspects – the metaphysician; secondly, the thinker who withdraws from ordinary affairs, probably in a morose temper, to contemplate with detachment the follies of his fellow-men and to suffer with resignation the outrages of fortune – loosely, the Stoic. In 1694 a third meaning was acknowledged by the *Dictionnaire de l'Académie française*: 'a man who, through waywardness of mind, puts himself above the ordinary duties and obligations of civil and Christian life. It is a man who denies himself nothing, who does not restrain himself in any way, and who leads the life of a philosopher.'[4] This definition, of course, pejoratively recognised the use of the word by *esprits forts* like Bayle in anti-Catholic if not anti-Christian connotations. His *Commentaire philosophique* dates from 1686. From this third sense stems the usage of the great *philosophes* themselves. It never became fully established in any language other than French.

---

and D. A. Watts (Exeter, 1975), pp. 139–50; R. Shackleton, 'When Did the French "Philosophes" Become a Party?', *Bulletin of the John Rylands Library* [*BJRL*], vol. LX (1978), pp. 181–99; I. O. Wade, '*The Philosophe' in the French Drama of the Eighteenth Century* (Princeton, 1926); R. J. White, *The Anti-Philosophers* (London, 1970), esp. ch. 1; A. M. Wilson, *Diderot* (Oxford, 1972), esp. pp. 70–2, 181–2, 210, 221–2, 245–6. The next few paragraphs derive mainly from these works.

3 Cf. O. Chadwick, *The Secularization of the European Mind in the Nineteenth Century* (Cambridge, 1975), esp. p. 144. *Aufklärung* is of course an eighteenth-century usage.

4 Quoted in Dieckmann, *Le Philosophe*, p. 72: 'un homme, qui, par libertinage d'esprit, se met au dessus des devoirs et des obligations ordinaires de la vie civile et chrétienne. C'est un homme qui ne se refuse rien, qui ne se contraint sur rien, et qui mène une vie de Philosophe'. It seems right to give the original French version of quotations whose precise phrasing is important to a study of the *philosophe*, while noting that it is always difficult to decide whether to render the word in English as 'philosopher' or as *philosophe*.

Christians and 'philosophes'

The *Encyclopédie* contains the classic statement of the concept *philosophe* in the article under that title in volume XII, published in 1765. This is a late appearance for a document so fundamental to the French Enlightenment. However, the article is in fact Diderot's version – much shortened but essentially faithful – of an essay first printed in a collection called *Nouvelles Libertés de penser*, published in 1743. This compilation was the work of radicals and free thinkers; its component pieces had previously circulated in manuscript; and its publication 'inaugurated...a period of intense intellectual activity'.[5] Voltaire wrote of the original essay *Le Philosophe* when he in his turn republished it in 1773: it 'has been known for a long time and has been kept to hand by all inquiring persons; it dates from the year 1730'. Its author was probably Dumarsais.[6] So the article in the *Encyclopédie* has a very good claim to have embodied the view of the *philosophe* held by most writers of the French Enlightenment over a period of half a century.

It explicitly rejects both the traditional meanings of *philosophe*. The original essay included a lengthy critique of universalist systems of thought. Although Diderot cut this section severely, he left the essential points: the *philosophe*, though a rationalist, relies on proven observed facts and does not expect to be able to explain everything.

Rather more survives in the *Encyclopédie* article of the critique of Stoicism. For example,

Our *philosophe* does not imagine that he is in exile in this world; he does not suppose himself to be in enemy country...He seeks pleasure from the company of others;... he is an *honnête homme* who desires to please and to make himself useful.

...it is easy to grasp how far removed the unfeeling sage of the Stoics is from the perfection of our *philosophe*: such a *philosophe* is a man, and their sage was only a phantom. They blushed for humanity, and he glories in it.[7]

By very strong implication, the *philosophe* is represented as anti-Christian. For instance, in Diderot's version: 'Reason is in respect to the *philosophe* what Grace is in respect to the Christian...Civil society is, so to speak, a

---

[5] Shackleton, *BJRL*, p. 189. Cf. M. C. Jacob, *The Radical Enlightenment* (London, 1981), p. 217.

[6] The quotation from Dieckmann, *Le Philosophe*, p. 7. A. W. Fairbairn, 'Dumarsais and *Le Philosophe*', *Studies on Voltaire and the Eighteenth Century*, vol. LXXXVII (1972), pp. 375–95. I am most grateful to Dr Fairbairn for giving me a copy of this article.

[7] Dieckmann, *Le Philosophe*, pp. 44, 60: 'Notre *philosophe* ne se croit pas en exil dans ce monde; il ne croit pas être en pays ennemi...Il veut trouver du plaisir avec les autres;...c'est un honnête homme qui veut plaire et se rendre utile...il est aisé de conclure combien le sage insensible des stoïciens est éloigné de la perfection de notre *philosophe*: un tel *philosophe* est homme, et leur sage n'était qu'un fantôme. Ils rougissaient de l'humanité, et il en fait gloire.'

divinity on earth for [the *philosophe*]; he worships it...'[8] It seems plain that this rejection of Christianity is integrally related to the rejection both of *esprit de système* and of Stoicism. Roman Catholic theology had come to terms with Cartesianism, the reigning metaphysical system; and the resulting hybrid now dominated the teaching of philosophy in French Universities.[9] Similarly, the neo-Stoicism of the late sixteenth and early seventeenth centuries, especially associated with the writings of Lipsius, had been easily reconciled with Catholicism. The Jesuits themselves became the chief promoters of 'Christian Stoicism', and one of them published in 1637 a volume entitled *Seneca Christianus*.[10] The *philosophe* naturally could not countenance any tendency of thought that subserved *l'infâme*.

However, as the article illustrates, his attitude to *esprit de système* differed from his attitude to Stoicism. Whereas he totally condemned the former, he applauded aspects of Stoic thought – or Stoicism understood in a certain sense. Only five historical figures are mentioned in the article, four of them Roman, of whom two were Stoics. Cato the Younger receives praise for having always acted in a manner true to his character, and Marcus Aurelius is quoted with approval for having remarked: 'How happy peoples will be when kings are philosophers, or philosophers kings!'[11] This, of course, must rank as a disingenuous quotation, first since it originally derives from the arch-metaphysician, Plato, and secondly since Marcus Aurelius hardly meant by 'philosopher' what Diderot and his friends understood by *philosophe*. But the citation from Marcus Aurelius is heavy with significance. While the most Christian, servile and respectable authors admired him, and no exception could possibly be taken by minister or censor to the glorification of his name, yet for the *philosophes* he counted as one of themselves, an enemy of superstition and a persecutor of Christianity. This was the guise under which

---

[8] *Ibid.*, pp. 32, 46: 'La raison est à l'égard du *philosophe* ce que la grâce est à l'égard du chrétien...La société civile est, pour ainsi dire, une divinité pour lui sur la terre; il l'encense...'. The original essay is less categorical in the first passage, more so in the second, and contains lengthy aspersions on superstition, dogma, religion, etc., that Diderot largely omitted.

[9] L. W. B. Brockliss, 'Philosophy Teaching in France, 1600–1740', *History of Universities*, vol. I (1981), pp. 131–68. Cf. O. Chadwick, *From Bossuet to Newman: The Idea of Doctrinal Development* (Cambridge, 1957), p. 55.

[10] In English, G. Oestreich, *Neostoicism and the Early Modern State*, eds. B. Oestreich and H. G. Koenigsberger (Cambridge, 1982), esp. pp. 63–4, 99–109; N. O. Keohane, *Philosophy and the State in France* (Princeton, 1980), esp. pp. 129–33; R. J. W. Evans, *The Making of the Habsburg Monarchy, 1550–1700* (Oxford, 1979), esp. p. 113. T. Zielinski, *Cicero im Wandel der Jahrhunderte* (3rd edn, Leipzig, 1912).

[11] Dieckmann, *Le Philosophe*, p. 56. The other individuals named in the article are Velleius Paterculus for the information on Cato, and Terence and La Rochefoucauld, also for quotations.

they praised him, and the same applied to Stoicism as a whole. As Peter Gay has argued, the *philosophes* were deeply influenced by Stoicism – but it was by Stoicism conceived as pagan and anti-Christian. Moreover, for their purposes it had also to be separated from its connotation of morose detachment. The true Stoic, the Stoic who was to be admired, played his part in society and politics, trying to give practical effect to his philosophy – like, they claimed, Marcus Aurelius.[12]

Voltaire's article *Philosophe* in the second edition of his *Dictionnaire philosophique* (1765) reinforces the argument. Unlike the article in the *Encyclopédie*, it contains no carefully stated definition. But it offers a wider variety of examples of *philosophes*, who are chiefly commended for the supposed purity of their morals. Those that receive the greatest praise are Confucius; Bayle and Fontenelle; and, bracketed together, Epictetus, Marcus Aurelius and Julian. Further, one of the less orthodox seventeenth-century neo-Stoics, Charron, qualified for a favourable reference on the ground that his life had been threatened by pious persecutors. In addition, 'Julian the *philosophe*' was honoured with a special article in which his hostility to Christianity was excused.[13]

So it formed an essential part of the programme of the *philosophes* to impose their new meaning on the word in place of older meanings. In particular, Stoicism had to be condemned if it was understood as unsocial and quietist or if it was treated as compatible with Christianity, and especially with Roman Catholicism.

II

In trying to assess the influence of the *philosophes* outside France, we can use as an index – though only one index among many – the way in which the concept *philosophe* was employed and Stoicism was regarded. White claimed that the new meaning of *philosophe* had won the day by the middle of the eighteenth century; and Oestreich, the author of notable studies of neo-Stoicism, asserted that by the same period 'the influence of Lipsius in

---

[12] P. Gay, *The Enlightenment: An Interpretation*, 2 vols. (London, 1967–70), esp. vol. 1, pp. 50–1, 120–1, 300–4, 320.
   On Marcus Aurelius and the Stoics themselves I have found most useful, apart from the *Meditations*, *Lives of the Later Caesars*, ed. A. Birley (Harmondsworth, 1976), see esp. p. 135; A. S. L. Farquharson, *Marcus Aurelius, His Life and His World*, ed. D. A. Rees (Oxford, 1951); A. Birley, *Marcus Aurelius* (London, 1966); and P. A. Brunt, 'Stoicism and the Principate', *Papers of the British School at Rome*, vol. XLIII (1975), pp. 7–35.
[13] Voltaire, *Dictionnaire philosophique*, ed. J. Benda (Paris, 1954), esp. pp. 342–7. English translation ed. T. Besterman (Harmondsworth, 1971), esp. pp. 334–8.

Germany was played out'.[14] These propositions can be tested in studying the attitudes of prominent figures associated with the Austrian Enlightenment. It is natural to begin with the reign of Maria Theresa (1740–80) and with the royal family, taking first Francis Stephen, her husband, emperor from 1745 to his death in 1765. Born and brought up in Lorraine, he married Maria Theresa in 1736. It was from this event that the prince de Ligne, an exemplar of Enlightened French culture and one of the few men who had standing both with the *philosophes* and at the Court of Vienna, dated the adoption there of French as 'the common language, which greatly contributed to the spread of urbanity'.[15] Ligne exaggerated, of course. French had been much used at Court before the marriage or accession of Maria Theresa. Further, Francis Stephen was an imperfect advertisement for French culture: he shocked the more sophisticated by his tolerance of German comedies; and his spelling in French embarrassed even his wife.[16] But he brought a number of French artists and *savants* to Vienna; and the pre-eminence of the French language there seems to date from the early years of Maria Theresa's reign.[17]

Students of the early Radical Enlightenment seize on Francis Stephen as proof of its influence in bigoted, benighted Austria, since he was initiated as a Freemason by Walpole at Houghton in 1731 and is believed to have practised the craft privately in Vienna even after it had been banned there by his wife.[18] But his surviving writings give no encouragement to such students. He left two sets of instructions for his children, of 1752 and 1765, which urge on them sobriety, modesty and economy, together with regular prayer, communion, confession and self-examination. He also composed two tracts, whose dates are unknown, entitled 'The Hermit in the World' and 'Christian Reflections and Short Prayers'. The burden of these pieces is that the ruler, though enveloped in business, pomp and flattery, must keep his soul secret and entire for the service of God and in preparation for death.

---

14 White, *Anti-Philosophers*, pp. 6–7; Oestreich, *Neostoicism*, p. 101.

15 Prince de Ligne, *Fragments de l'Histoire de ma Vie*, ed. F. Leuridant, 2 vols. (Paris, 1927–8), vol. I, p. 264n.

16 A. Wolf, 'Relationen des Grafen von Podewils, Gesandten K. Friedrich's II. von Preussen, über den Wiener Hof in den Jahren 1746, 1747, 1748', *Sitzungsberichte der kaiserlichen Akademie der Wissenschaften*, vol. v (1850), p. 499; H. L. Mikoletzky, 'Kaiser Franz I. Stephan in Briefen' in *Études européennes: Mélanges offerts à Victor Tapié* (Paris, 1973), pp. 270–1.

17 Information about French influence in Vienna is brought together usefully by J. Schmidt, 'Voltaire und Maria Theresia', *Mitteilungen des Vereines für Geschichte der Stadt Wien [MVGSW]*, vol. xi (1931), pp. 73–115 – a much broader article than its title suggests. See also H. Wagner, 'Der Höhepunkt des französischen Kultureinflusses in Österreich', *Österreich in Geschichte und Literatur [ÖGL]*, vol. v (1961), 507–17. I am grateful to the Librarian of the Austrian Cultural Institute in London for supplying me with a copy of this article.

18 E.g. Jacob, *Radical Enlightenment*, p. 111.

They seem to depend on writers of Jansenist tendency like Pascal, Fénelon and Muratori – and on Cicero and Marcus Aurelius. It is evident that the Stoic element is completely assimilated to Catholic Christianity and retains its connotation of withdrawal from the world. If the emperor, with his French background and Masonic affiliations, was aware of the attitudes associated with the new meaning of *philosophe*, he rejected them completely.[19]

During the 1750s he and his wife superintended, with much assistance from ministers and other advisers, an elaborate programme of education designed to fit their heir, the future Joseph II, for the throne. He was two years of age when *Nouvelles Libertés de penser* was published, seven when *De l'Esprit des Lois* came out, and ten when the first volumes of the *Encyclo-pédie* appeared. But the French Enlightenment had little part in his studies: the only major work by a *philosophe* to figure in them was the *Esprit des Lois*, and that very selectively. Further, the Stoics, unless Cicero is counted among them, scarcely appear. On the other hand, Pufendorf dominated Joseph's education in political theory, and the Natural Law school that Pufendorf belonged to owed much to the Stoics.[20] But it is the prince's education in philosophy that is most interesting here. This was entrusted to a Jesuit, Father Frantz. The 'little treatise' he wrote in Latin for his pupil avoided 'the disputations of the schools' and 'all the subtleties that are more ingenious than useful, like categories, universals...' – the formula comes from the Jansenist popularisation of Descartes, *L'Art de penser*. In other words, it claimed to reject, in the Renaissance tradition, Aristotelianism and Scholasticism. But it dealt with logic, deductive reasoning and metaphysics. *Esprit de système* imbued it, and its system was Descartes', Christianised or Catholicised. Such few later writers as are mentioned are almost all criticised, like Leibniz. Insofar as it comes to grips with sceptics, it is with Spinoza, who had died as long ago as 1677.[21] There is no sign of any awareness of the French *philosophes* whether as individuals or as a class of philosophers.

The Jesuits retained their monopoly of theological teaching at the University of Vienna until 1759. It was only in 1735 that they had been instructed to teach Cartesian metaphysics; they had previously been identified with Scholasticism. But Father Frantz was one of their most progressive scholars,

[19] A. Wandruszka, 'Die Religiosität Franz Stephan von Lothringen', *Mitteilungen des österreichischen Staatsarchivs* [*MÖSA*], vol. XII (1959), pp. 162–73.

[20] See my article 'Writing a Life of Joseph II: The Problem of His Education', *Wiener Beiträge zur Geschichte der Neuzeit*, vol. VI (1979), pp. 183–207; R. F. Tuck, *Natural Rights Theories: Their Origins and Development* (Cambridge, 1979), p. 17; Oestreich, *Neostoicism*, esp. pp. 123–4.

[21] 'Das Lehrbuch der Metaphysik für Kaiser Josef II., verfasst von P. Josef Frantz', ed. T. M. Wehofer (Paderborn, 1895), in supp. vol. II of *Jahrbuch für Philosophie und spekulative Theologie*, with a valuable commentary. Beales, *Wiener Beiträge*, p. 190.

concerned not only with the reform of the University curriculum but also with mitigating the rigours of the censorship. Both these processes advanced during the 1750s under the aegis of Gerard van Swieten, the empress's physician. One of his most notable successes was to secure the admission into the Monarchy of the *Esprit des Lois*.[22] So Joseph's education fell during a decade of reform. But it was painfully slow reform and, by European standards, from a remote starting-point. To prince Albert of Saxony, brought up as a Catholic but in a Protestant state, Joseph's education in logic and metaphysics was indistinguishable from 'peripatetic philosophy'.[23]

In 1760 Joseph married Isabella of Parma, whose intelligence and personality were to make a profound impression on him and on the whole Court during her three remaining years of life. Her mother was a French princess, Louis XV's daughter, and their personal ties were with France rather than with Spain, where Isabella had been born. In the late 1750s the duchy of Parma became heavily dependent on France. In 1758 Condillac was summoned from Paris to tutor the heir to the throne; and in the next year its ruler appointed a prime minister of French extraction and reformist views, Du Tillot.[24] Isabella had received an unusually sophisticated education: she not only played the violin well and patronised Gluck's new brand of opera; she also read such books as *La Nouvelle Héloïse*, and herself wrote with some distinction. But her temperament was 'sombre', she yearned for an early death, and her remarkable writings are suffused with religious melancholy. After she died, her *Christian Meditations* were published by Maria Theresa.[25]

One of Isabella's essays was entitled 'The true philosopher'. 'I have developed the habit', she wrote, 'of considering what affects me personally without any emotion.' But she finds that she does not always succeed. Where her friendships are concerned, she cannot remain indifferent. She – and, she believes, all other self-styled 'philosophers' – are 'philosophers *manqués*'. Nonetheless, she is emphatic that 'The principles that a philosopher sets up for himself...can be summed up as follows: indifference to all the

---

[22] E. Winter, *Der Josefinismus* (2nd edn, Berlin, 1962), p. 41. G. Klingenstein, *Staatsverwaltung und kirchliche Autorität im 18. Jahrhundert* (Vienna, 1970), esp. pp. 165, 176–8. Wehofer's edn of Frantz (see previous note), p. 102.

[23] Quoted from Albert's MSS memoirs by A. von Arneth, *Geschichte Maria Theresias*, 10 vols. (Vienna, 1863–79), vol. VII, p. 532.

[24] U. Benassi wrote a long series of excellent articles on 'Guglielmo du Tillot, un ministro reformatore del secolo XVIII' in *Archivio storico per le province parmensi*, new series, vols. XV–XVI (1915–16), XIX–XXV (1919–25). The rise of Du Tillot is described in vol. XVI, esp. pp. 193–213, 334–68. More accessibly, F. Venturi, *Settecento riformatore*, II (Turin, 1976), pp. 214–16. On the cultural side, in English, A. Yorke-Long, *Music at Court* (London, 1954), esp. pp. 19–32.

[25] J. Hrazky, 'Die Persönlichkeit der Infantin Isabella von Parma', *MÖSA*, vol. XII (1959), pp. 174–239.

chances of life...and absolute disinterestedness, which makes [him] love
what is good by reference only to good itself...'.[26] Her idea of a philosopher
corresponds exactly to the Stoicism rejected by the *Encyclopédie*.

However, she also wrote a treatise called 'On fashionable philosophy'.
Unfortunately, only its table of contents seems to survive. From this it
appears that she knew a good deal about some other brand of philosophy,
presumably that associated with the French *philosophes*, in particular Condillac, but that she rejected it almost wholly:

1. The Principles are varied
2. The Principles are extreme
3. The Principles are false
4. The Principles are dangerous
5. The Attitudes are not consistent
6. The Attitudes are culpable
7. There is, however, some good in them
8. This is what leads them astray
9. This is what gives them their reputation
10. What use ought to be made both of the good and the bad that they contain.[27]

Maria Theresa herself considered French the appropriate language for her
family correspondence, promoted the alliance of 1756 with France and employed a number of officials who were influenced by the French Enlightenment. In the early 1750s Voltaire sent her copies of his historical works and
in 1752 received from her for the *Siècle de Louis XIV* a watch and a snuff-box.
The Diplomatic Revolution no doubt accounts for Voltaire's two uncharacteristic effusions of 1756, a contribution to the *Festschrift* compiled to
celebrate the opening of the new Aula of the University of Vienna, and the
following 'quatrain' commemorating the empress's visit to Carnuntum:

> Marc-Aurèle autrefois des princes le modèle
> Sur le devoir des Roys écrivoit en ces lieux;
> Et Marie Thérèse fait à nos yeux
> Tout ce qu'écrivoit Marc-Aurèle.[28]

Voltaire can hardly have supposed that Maria Theresa resembled his vision
of Marcus Aurelius, and this verse is clearly inconsistent with his usual attitude.
Equally, Maria Theresa's graciousness towards him at this period was un-
natural. It is notorious that she frequently denounced *philosophie* and the
philosophes, and particularly dreaded the prospect of Joseph's visiting Voltaire
during the journey to France planned for 1774 and eventually undertaken
in 1777.

---

[26] *Ibid.*, p. 194.
[27] Haus-, Hof- und Staatsarchiv [HHSA], Vienna, Familien-Archiv, Sammelbände 68.
[28] Schmidt, *MVGSW*, esp. pp. 91–7; Wagner, *ÖGL*, esp. pp. 509–13.

The precise terms of her denunciations bear examination. Her first on-slaught on *philosophie*, like most of them, refers to Joseph. On 27 November 1768 she wrote about her younger son, Ferdinand:

He will not have Leopold's great industry, but more charm, and will be fonder of pleasures, if the emperor doesn't turn him, as he puts it, into a philosopher. I'm not worried on this score, since I see no attractions in this so-called philosophy, which consists of avoiding close ties and of enjoying nothing, whether theatre, hunting, cards, dancing or conversation.[29]

In May–July 1772 she and Ferdinand exchanged letters about philosophy. She declared:

All these titles so fashionable at the moment, hero, *savant*, *philosophe*, are simply the inventions of *amour-propre* to cover up weaknesses. Those who are so called do not deserve it; they just want to cut some sort of figure.

Again,

It is better to feel too much than too little. Honest men can be attracted by sentiment alone, but not by philosophy, which is so fashionable at present, and which is only refined *amour-propre* and harshness towards others. Don't let yourself be carried away...If we accept worldly things as Christian philosophers, we feel the same in all situations, in adversity as in prosperity.

And finally she compliments him on quoting the adage 'neither philosophy nor reason stands when the heart speaks'.[30]

In 1774 she corresponded with her ambassador in Paris, the comte de Mercy-Argenteau, about Joseph's projected visit to France and especially his 'idea of returning through Switzerland to see Voltaire, Tissot, Haller and all these extremists'. Mercy replied:

I think [the project] will not materialise; first because it would take H.M. too much out of his way, secondly because there will be objections to be made against Voltaire which might dispel the desire to make his acquaintance. Tissot is a doctor, Haller a poet, neither of them so exceptionally famous that they deserve the emperor's atten-tion. Further, I shall make a point of showing H.M. here a sample from which he will be able to judge the worth of these modern *savants* and *philosophes* who, in their private lives, their works and their detestable principles, set a pattern calculated to overturn society and introduce trouble and disorder.

The empress answered:

It is true that even here people can't stop praising these wretches as great men and superior geniuses, but I hope you'll succeed in bringing home to the emperor all that is base, inconsistent and contemptible in their characters and behaviour.[31]

[29] Maria Theresa to Maria Beatrix, printed in *Briefe der Kaiserin Maria Theresia an ihre Kinder und Freunde*, ed. A. von Arneth, 4 vols. (Vienna, 1881), vol. III, p. 99.
[30] *Ibid.*, vol. I, pp. 125, 130, 135 (Maria Theresa to Ferdinand, 22 May, 11 June and 9 July 1772).
[31] Maria Theresa to Mercy, 1 Jan. and 3 Feb. 1774; Mercy to Maria Theresa, 19 Jan.

Later in the same year, she sent her youngest son, Maximilian, a similar diatribe:

If I saw these self-styled *savants*, these *philosophes*, achieving more success in their enterprises and more happiness in their private lives, I should be able to charge myself with bias, pride, prejudices, obstinacy for not following them. But...no one is weaker, more easily discouraged than these *esprits forts*, no one more cringing, more frantic at the least slight. They are bad fathers, sons, husbands, ministers, generals, citizens. Why? They lack the essential foundation. All their *philosophie*, all their maxims derive simply from their *amour-propre*.[32]

These statements of 1774 show that Maria Theresa thought she knew what the French *philosophes* stood for, and purveyed a crude critique of their position as she understood it. But she evidently had not grasped the implications of the new meaning of *philosophe*; and her indiscriminate bracketing of Voltaire with Haller and Tissot reveals her ignorance of their work. Her earlier attacks on 'philosophy' seem directed against the sort of unfeeling and misanthropic Stoicism that the *Encyclopédie* itself denounced. But in her mind the chief ex-emplar of this outlook must surely have been Frederick the Great – together with Joseph II, insofar as he was modelling himself on her great enemy.

It is 'Christian philosophers' she applauds. The use of the phrase in her letter to Ferdinand can be matched in several others. When Joseph's only daughter died in 1770, she wrote: 'He feels this loss very deeply, but as a Christian philosopher.' She spoke in 1772 of Gerard van Swieten dying 'as a philosopher the death of a saint, a great consolation for me'. Seven years later she said her son Maximilian bore his painful illness 'as a philosopher, but Christian'. Most tellingly, when in April 1778 she was praising Joseph for his letters to Frederick about the Bavarian crisis, she announced: 'I love my Cato, my Christian philosopher.'[33] Her ideal remained the neo-Stoic, Catholicised.

1774. In *Marie-Antoinette: Correspondance secrète entre Marie-Thérèse et le comte de Mercy-Argenteau*, ed. A. von Arneth and M. A. Geffroy, 3 vols. (2nd edn, Paris, 1875), vol. II, pp. 89, 101–2, 105.

[32] Maria Theresa's instructions for Maximilian, Apr. 1774: *Briefe der Kaiserin an ihre Kinder und Freunde*, ed. Arneth, vol. IV, p. 322. The empress's references to *amour-propre* must be related to the important tradition of writing on this theme discussed in Keohane, *Philosophy and the State*, esp. pp 184–97, 255, 294–302, 427–32. In this connexion she appears to follow Bossuet – or Rousseau – rather than the Jansenists.

On French influence at the Court of Vienna under Maria Theresa and Joseph II, from a rather different standpoint but using some of the same material, see A. D. Hytier, 'Joseph II, la cour de Vienne et les philosophes', *Studies in Voltaire and the Eighteenth Century*, vol. CVI (1973), pp. 225–51.

[33] To Maria Beatrix, 23 Jan. 1770 and 12 Apr. 1779; to countess Enzenberg, 15 June 1772. *Briefe der Kaiserin an ihre Kinder und Freunde*, ed. Arneth, vol. III, pp. 107, 354; vol. IV, p. 506. Cf. also her letter to Ferdinand, 14 Aug. 1779. To Joseph, 21 Apr. 1778, in *Maria Theresia und Joseph II. Ihre Correspondenz*, ed. A. von Arneth, 3 vols. (Vienna, 1867–8), vol. II, p. 214.

III

While Maria Theresa lived, she ensured that the Monarchy was insulated from many aspects of French cultural influence. Contemporary travellers found her regime bigoted, superstitious and intolerant. They were astonished to have their books impounded at the frontier.[34] Even ambassadors had difficulty in bringing in their libraries.[35] The Monarchy's index of prohibited books was longer than the pope's.[36] Wraxall, who spent some months in Vienna in 1778–9, made the severest judgment. He was 'inclined to believe, that fewer persons of extensive reading and information are found [here], proportion observed, than in any of the German Courts'. 'The Austrian youth of rank or condition are in general insupportable... distinguished only by pride, ignorance and illiberality.' He met no learned women at all. 'Natural philosophy has scarcely made greater progress in Vienna, than sound reason and real religion.' He estimated that 3000 persons were engaged in seeking the philosopher's stone.[37]

Yet, according to one notable scholar, Hans Wagner, the latter part of Maria Theresa's reign marked 'the highpoint of French cultural influence in Austria'.[38] This judgment can be sustained, if at all, only by placing great emphasis on the attitudes of a small circle of wealthy nobles and officials. However, it must be acknowledged that among this group was to be found a remarkable awareness of the latest developments in the French Enlightenment and an extraordinary freedom in discussing them. The empress, while enjoining bigotry on the vast majority of her subjects, would permit a few trusted servants to defy it and would even, within strict limits, listen to advice founded on progressive views.

A special place must be accorded to count (from 1763 prince) Kaunitz, who after a spell as Austrian ambassador in Paris returned to Vienna to direct the Monarchy's foreign policy in 1753, and continued to do so for the next

34 E.g. *Journal d'un Voyage en Allemagne, fait en 1773, par G. A. H. Guibert* (Paris, 1803), pp. 248, 276–7; [J. Moore], *A View of Society and Manners in France, Switzerland and Germany*, 2 vols. (London, 1779), vol. II, p. 300; [C. A. Pilati], *Voyages en differens pays de l'Europe en 1774, 1775 & 1776*, 2 vols. (The Hague, 1777), vol. II, pp. 103–4.
35 Arneth, *Geschichte Maria Theresias*, vol. VII, pp. 197–8.
36 [Pilati], *Voyages*, vol. I, p. 6. Cf. L. Bodi, *Tauwetter in Wien* (Frankfurt, 1977), esp. pp. 47, 51.
37 N. W. Wraxall, *Memoirs of the Courts of Berlin, Dresden, Warsaw and Vienna, in the years 1777, 1778, and 1779*, 2 vols. (3rd edn, London, 1806), vol. II, pp. 246–7, 249, 257–9, 278–89. I am very grateful to Dr L. Colley for helping me to obtain from Yale the MSS. of this work on microfilm, which tends to confirm its value as a record of the years of Wraxall's stay in central Europe, despite the fact that the book was not published until 1799.
38 Wagner, ÖGL. Cf. E. Wangermann, *The Austrian Achievement, 1700–1800* (London 1973), pp. 80–8, 130–4.

forty or so years. It was not long before he became a force in internal politics too, especially from the foundation of the Staatsrat in 1760.[39] He was known for his admiration of France both as a potential ally and for her culture. He was in touch with Voltaire.[40] From the middle 1760s he became a ruthless promoter of ecclesiastical reforms which he justified by reference to many sources, including the *Encyclopédie*.[41] But in fact he never accepted the *philosophes'* approach to traditional philosophy. Professor Klingenstein, who has studied his early life and work, writes of him:

Perhaps there was no Enlightened statesman in whom the mathematical-deductive method in political thought was so strongly rooted as in [Kaunitz]. The statement of political premises *more geometrico*, the deductions following logically from them about the possible decisions and actions available to the various European states within the European state-system, the related bases for making predictions about future trends and events – the deployment of this method gave Kaunitz that superiority and self-assurance among Maria Theresa's ministers which...brought [her] under his spell.

The thinker to whom he owed most was not Descartes, but nor was it any *philosophe*. It was Wolff, in whose method he had been schooled at Halle.[42] He drew upon the work of the great men of the French Enlightenment, but within an alien metaphysical framework. Moreover, contrary to what has often been claimed, he was not a Freemason, and he was some sort of Catholic.[43]

One especially valuable source enables us to observe the French Enlightenment percolating into aristocratic and bureaucratic circles in Vienna after 1761. Count Karl von Zinzendorf arrived there in February of that year prospecting for a career in government service. Every day he recorded in his diary what he had read and talked about and with whom. He immediately gained the *entrée* into the highest social circles because his brother was already an established official. As early as 16 March 1761 he was discussing Voltaire and the *Encyclopédie* at princess Esterházy's. In January 1762 he came across in his reading the problem of defining 'philosopher' – though not in a recent work.

[Fontenelle's] *Dialogue between Anacreon and Aristotle* [1683] pleased me very much, when Anacreon says that the name 'Philosopher' is nowadays given only to astrono-

39 F. Walter, 'Kaunitz' Eintritt in die innere Politik', *Mitteilungen des österreichischen Instituts für Geschichtsforschung*, vol. XLVI (1932), pp. 37–79.
40 Schmidt, *MVGSW*, p. 115. See *Voltaire's Correspondence*, ed. T. Besterman, 107 vols. (Geneva, 1953–65), e.g. vol. CLIII, p. 128, Voltaire to Kaunitz, 25 Nov. 1763.
41 F. Maass, *Der Josephinismus*, 5 vols. (Vienna, 1951–61), vol. I, esp. pp. 94n, 347.
42 G. Klingenstein, *Der Aufstieg des Hauses Kaunitz* (Göttingen, 1975), esp. pp. 170–1.
43 H. Wagner, 'Die Lombardei und das Freimaurer Patent Josephs II.', *MÖSA*, vol. XXXI (1978), p. 143; A. Novotny, *Staatskanzler Kaunitz als geistige Persönlichkeit* (Vienna, 1947), pp. 145–71.

mers and physicists, while the Philosopher ought to think only of himself; but since no one would want to be a Philosopher on this condition, people had banished Philosophy as far as possible from themselves.

In 1763 we find him at the French ambassador's talking about Rousseau and Helvétius, and reading some Hume and the *Contrat social*.[44] In the following year, having obtained a permanent post in the administration, he travelled to Switzerland at government expense and met both Rousseau and Voltaire. He had been recommended to the latter as travelling *en philosophe*.[45] Among his numerous later references to advanced writings two may be singled out. Discussing *L'Esprit de l'Encyclopédie* enlivened one of his flirtations in 1771; and at almost the same time he was much impressed by Voltaire's *Questions sur l'Encyclopédie*, the enlarged version of the *Dictionnaire philosophique*.[46]

It is tempting to present this remarkable record as evidence for the unadulterated influence of the *philosophes* in the Vienna of Maria Theresa. But the context makes this impossible, even insofar as Zinzendorf's own thinking is concerned. He arrived in Austria a devout Pietist. But his brother, Kaunitz and the empress herself made it clear that if he wished for a prosperous career in the bureaucracy he must become a Roman Catholic. The issue came to a head in the early months of 1764. On 10 January he wrote that he would convert only in 'ultimate despair', and two days later he thought of fleeing the country. On 1 February he prepared a letter of resignation from his temporary post, heard count Philipp Sinzendorff and the French ambassador vying with each other in satirising the Christian religion, but – on the recommendation of this same count Philipp – began reading Bossuet. He found 'both good and bad' in Voltaire on toleration.[47] On 1 March he decided that one of his great misfortunes was never to have taken a course in philosophy, which meant that he lacked 'the philosophical and geometric spirit'. He had been put off the subject, presumably in his Pietist youth, as effacing 'from the heart those tender feelings which the great truths of the Christian religion have implanted there'. He finally made his general confession to Müller, the Jansenist abbot of St Dorothea, on 13 March, and his confession of faith the next day – but on the 15th did not dare acknowledge

---

[44] The diary is in HHSA, Vienna. There is a volume a year. I give footnote references only where the exact date does not appear in the text. The discussion of Fontenelle is to be found under 18 Jan. 1762, the reference to Rousseau and Helvétius under 17 Jan. 1763.

[45] Zinzendorf's diary, 7–10 Sep. and 3 Oct. 1764. Zinzendorf's entries are reproduced in *Correspondance complète de Jean-Jacques Rousseau*, ed. R. A. Leigh, vol. XXI (1974), pp. 328–34. Louis Eugene, prince of Württemberg, to Voltaire, 28 Sep. 1764 (*Voltaire's Correspondence*, ed. Besterman, vol. LVI, p. 54).

[46] Zinzendorf's diary, 24 and 31 Dec. 1771, 7 Jan. 1772.

[47] *Ibid.*, 27 Feb. 1764.

himself a Catholic before Kaunitz's assembly. On the 23rd he read Isabella's *Christian Meditations*, where he found 'traces of the purest and soundest piety'. He later took vows of celibacy as a member of the Teutonic Order, although throughout his long life he hankered after the religion of his youth.[48]

Hence it is no wonder that, after his visit to Voltaire, he recorded that he could not trust everything the great man had said. And what he especially admired in the *Questions sur l'Encyclopédie* were Voltaire's attack on despotism *and* his defence of the existence of God.[49] It is clear that Zinzendorf saw his deep and broad interest in French Enlightened writing as compatible with strong religious feelings. He must have grasped the implications of the concept *philosophe*, yet rejected them.

The cosmopolitan prince de Ligne – great landowner in Belgium, prince of the Holy Roman Empire, grandee of Spain, etc., etc. – serving in the army of Maria Theresa, visited Voltaire in 1763. They corresponded regularly, and in 1772 the *philosophe* wrote to the prince: 'I prophesy that you will make wholesome *philosophie* known to minds still somewhat removed from it.' This has been assumed to mean that Voltaire expected Ligne to spread the gospel to the *philosophes* in Vienna.[50]

Ligne cut a figure at the Court of Vienna for sixty years, was a friend and general of Joseph II, and won a reputation all over Europe for intelligence, Enlightenment and self-indulgence. It has seemed impossible to associate this master of persiflage with serious, still less religious, opinions.[51] But of all my examples, he showed the clearest understanding of the issues raised by the new usage of *philosophe*. He composed – when seems unfortunately to be unknown – a dialogue between an *esprit fort* and a Capuchin. Both men pride themselves on their philosophy. For the Capuchin it is the crown of his religious development, and is both Stoic and metaphysical. He declares: 'I involve myself in nothing, because I am a philosopher.' He denies to the *esprit fort* the right to call himself a philosopher at all. But the *esprit fort* responds: 'I involve myself in everything, because I am a *philosophe*. I'm always writing; I study everything deeply; I remove from Divinity its thunderbolts, from kings their sceptres, from Europe its Balance of Power, and from the dead their immortality.'[52]

---

[48] Zinzendorf's religious difficulties are discussed in A. Wolf, *Geschichtliche Bilder aus Oesterreich*, 2 vols. (Vienna, 1880), esp. vol. II, pp. 265–7, 305–6.

[49] Zinzendorf's diary, 3 Oct. 1764, 7 Jan. 1772.

[50] E.g. by Schmidt, *MVGSW*, p. 98. See n. 55 below.

[51] See, e.g, the introduction by L. Ashton to *Letters and Memoirs of the Prince de Ligne* (London, 1927). Maria Theresa spoke of his *légèreté* (*Marie Antoinette*, ed. Arneth and Geffroy, vol. II, p. 485), Zinzendorf of his lack of *sens commun* (diary, 10 Nov. 1770).

[52] *Mémoires et mélanges historiques et littéraires, par le Prince de Ligne*, 5 vols. (Paris, 1827–8), vol. II, pp. 127–47. Quotation from p. 135.

His correspondence with Voltaire survives only in part, but what remains has considerable interest for the views of both men. Each flatters the other archly and wittily. In particular, Ligne often expresses his indebtedness to Voltaire's *philosophie*.[53] A letter of 20 November 1768 thanks the old man for sending by Gottfried van Swieten, who has just visited him *en philosophe*, 'all your new *gaietés philosophiques* – and thoroughly Christian of course. May the God of Abraham, if you like, or of the Rock, or of Socrates always treat you as favourably as you have treated us.' In his reply of 3 December Voltaire is triumphant over the rapid decay of superstition.[54]

It is never easy to determine what either writer really means. But behind the calculated flippancy some letters of 1772 seem to embody a serious clash of opinions. Ligne writes that he has been demonstrating to his friends that Voltaire has 'never denied the truths of religion', ranks indeed as a Father of the Church, 'only rather more amusing than your comrades'. 'The declamations of Diderot and the arid conversation of D'Alembert, that cold if perhaps able geometer, almost induce in me the desire to become a Capuchin.' Voltaire, he goes on, has a more salutary religious influence. He has 'blasted the seven or eight atheists of the great Frederick'. Ligne then imagines many Classical writers glorying in the role of bishops, praises the Roman Catholic Church for its patronage of the arts, denounces Jansenists, suggests that Voltaire quite likes Jesuits and enlists him to purify the Church:

I should like good *curés*, Christian magistrates, polite and politic, speaking only from the pulpit (without wishing to set up teachers of transfiguration, transubstantiation etc.) and always preaching morality and good sense on duty to family and to society and on the practice of religion. Unbelievers would have to be ridiculed.

Voltaire's reply contains his prophecy, already quoted, that Ligne 'will make wholesome *philosophie* known to minds still somewhat removed from it'. But in context the remark seems less than enthusiastic:

Since, then, you make me realise I'm a prophet, I predict for you that you will continue to be what you already are, one of the most amiable and one of the most respectable men in Europe. I predict that you will introduce taste and style to a nation which up to now has perhaps supposed that its good qualities ought to be a substitute for charms.

I predict for you that you will make wholesome *philosophie* known to minds still somewhat removed from it, and that you will be happy in cultivating it.[55]

53 E.g. Ligne to Voltaire, 30 Dec. 1763, 1 June 1766, ?June/July 1774 (*Voltaire's Correspondence*, ed. Besterman, vol. LIII, pp. 213–14, vol. LXI, pp. 122–3, vol. LXXXVIII, pp. 74–5).

54 *Ibid.*, vol. LXX, pp. 177–8, 197–8. See also Hennin to Voltaire, 2 Oct. 1768 (*ibid.*, pp. 84–5).

55 Ligne to Voltaire, ?Aug./Sep. 1772, and Voltaire to Ligne, 29 Sep. 1772 (*ibid.*, vol. LXXXII, pp. 188–91, and LXXXIII, p. 53). There is a difficulty about the text as well

It looks as though Ligne has gone rather too far in associating Voltaire with the defence of established religion. Certainly, what the prince has been advocating does not sound much like the *philosophe*'s usual brand of 'wholesome *philosophie*'.

So even these three luminaries of the Austrian Enlightenment, Kaunitz, Zinzendorf and Ligne, wore their *philosophie* with a difference. Kaunitz revelled in traditional, deductive philosophy; Zinzendorf remained at heart a Pietist; and Ligne understood, and felt the force of, Catholic neo-Stoicism.

IV

With the accession of Joseph II as sole ruler of the Monarchy at the end of 1780, the position was transformed. One of his advisers, Gebler, wrote exultantly to Nicolai in Berlin three years later:

For a man who thinks philosophically, no period is more remarkable than that which began in 1781. Such a rapid change in the general attitude – even among the common people, who put many obscurantist members of higher classes to shame – is, so far as I know, unexampled. The...abolition of the religious brotherhoods, of most so-called devotions and of all monastic sermons has now given the final blow to all superstition ...But freedom of the press, and still more, *freedom of reading* (for, practically speaking, there is almost no book left that is not openly for sale) also contributes greatly.[56]

This was the time of the 'pamphlet flood' in Austria – or of a sudden 'thaw' after a long chill winter.[57] Vienna could now be represented as 'the *philosophes*' homeland'.[58]

It is impossible to deal here with the immense range of writings published during Joseph's sole reign, the decade 1780–90, though a study from the standpoint of this article would surely be revealing. But it is instructive to consider two individuals, each in his own way of striking significance: the emperor himself, and one of the humbler supporters of his reforms, I. A. Fessler.

The *philosophes* had claimed Joseph for themselves since the 1760s. In 1769 Voltaire was assured that he was 'one of us'.[59] When the emperor visited Paris in 1777, Grimm's *Correspondance littéraire* declared: 'Only in this century

as the date of the Ligne letter, since it is known only in his later printed version; but it makes a very plausible provocation for this reply of Voltaire's.

[56] Gebler to Nicolai, 16 Nov. 1783 in *Aus dem josephinischen Wien*, ed. R. M. Werner (Berlin, 1888), p. 112.
[57] See the admirable recent treatment by Bodi, *Tauwetter in Wien*.
[58] [J. Pezzl] *Skizze aus Wien* (Vienna, 1789–90), p. 45. Cf. his *philosophischer Roman* of 1784, *Faustin*.
[59] Voltaire to D'Alembert, 28 Oct. 1769 (*Voltaire's Correspondence*, ed. Besterman, vol. LXXIII, p. 142), quoting Grimm.

has *philosophie* persuaded rulers to travel purely for instruction.' The same source recorded Joseph showing respect towards Buffon, attending a demonstration by Lavoisier, listening to D'Alembert and (less attentively) to Marmontel and La Harpe, asking why Diderot and Raynal were not members of the French Academy, and visiting Tissot and Haller in Switzerland.[60] He met Turgot and studied his state papers.[61] Next year, Le Bret, a prominent populariser of Enlightenment in Germany, remarked 'how benignly the Philosopher on the Viennese throne smiles on the Muses'.[62] The traveller Riesbeck called him 'a philosopher in the true sense of the word' – whatever that meant.[63] In 1781 Joseph won further favourable publicity from the *philosophes* by sitting down to dinner at Spa with Grimm and Raynal.[64] On his death the following famous manifesto was ascribed to him, and accepted very widely as genuine: 'I have made Philosophy the legislator of my Empire.'[65]

Most elaborately, there appeared in 1774 a three-volume work by Lanjuinais entitled *Le Monarque accompli*, 'The Accomplished Monarch, or Prodigies of Benevolence, Knowledge and Wisdom which redound to the Credit...of Joseph II'.[66] Voltaire docketed his copy of this astonishing production 'Roast Monarch'.[67] After it was banned in France as part of the battle between Turgot and his rivals in 1776, it became well known.[68] In it Lanjuinais, referring occasionally to some fact about the emperor, and more frequently inventing some myth about him, painted the portrait of an ideal king. This paragon in the guise of Joseph is favourably compared to the most respectable Roman emperors like Trajan and Marcus Aurelius, and to the most notable kings of France. He is wise, tolerant, humane, 'enlightened' and *philosophe* – *ad nauseam*. Towards the end of the third volume Lanjuinais

[60] *Correspondance littéraire, philosophique et critique par Grimm, Diderot, Raynal, Meister etc.*, ed. M. Tourneux, 16 vols. (1877–82), vol. XI, pp. 468, 471–4, 526, 529.

[61] H. Wagner, 'Die Reise Josephs II. nach Frankreich 1777 und die Reformen in Österreich', in *Österreich und Europe. Festgabe für Hugo Hantsch zum 70. Geburtstag* (Graz, 1965), pp. 224–6. This useful article much exaggerates the influence of the visit on Joseph.

[62] Le Bret to Bertolà, 7 Jan. 1778, in J. U. Fechner, *Erfahrene und erfundene Landschaft: ...Bertolà's Deutschlandbild* (Opladen, 1974), p. 230. On Le Bret, M. L. Pesante, *Stato e religione nella storiografia di Goettingen* (Turin, 1971).

[63] C. Riesbeck, *Travels through Germany*, trans. Maty, 3 vols. (London, 1787), vol. I, pp. 255–6.

[64] *Correspondance littéraire*, ed. Tourneaux, vol. XIII, p. 6.

[65] See my article, 'The False Joseph II', *Historical Journal*, vol. XVIII (1975), esp. pp. 467, 471–2, 493.

[66] J. Lanjuinais, *Le Monarque accompli, ou prodiges de bonté, de savoir, et de sagesse qui font l'éloge de...Joseph II*, 3 vols. (Lausanne, 1774).

[67] *Voltaire's Correspondence*, ed. Besterman, vol. XCIV, p. 165.

[68] See E. Faure, *La Disgrâce de Turgot* (Paris, 1961), pp. 505–6.

embarks on a disquisition about philosophy. No one, he asserts, knows better than the emperor how *l'esprit philosophique* differs from *philosophie*. Philosophy is just one branch of knowledge, whereas *l'esprit philosophique* embraces all branches. The basis of *l'esprit philosophique* is 'enlightened metaphysics'. According to Lanjuinais, Joseph has reacted against 'modern peripatetics', finds Voltaire instructive but is very judicious in appraising his, Rousseau's and Montesquieu's works. Surprisingly, the emperor turns out also to be 'pious' and 'Christian', a prince who wants the clergy better educated, an enemy of *libertinage* and a man proof against the blandishments not only of Greeks and Romans but also of 'contemporary unbelievers, modern blasphemers'.[69]

Lord Acton pronounced, in one of his maddening displays of fantastic erudition, that 'Joseph II borrowed his ideas from the *Monarque accompli.*'[70] But any resemblance between Lanjuinais' paragon and the living emperor, whether before or after the book was published, seems accidental. It is true that his knowledge of Voltaire passed muster with Frederick the Great;[71] that a close friend wrote of his weakness for the ideas of Holbach and Helvétius;[72] and that the French strategist, Guibert, having met him in 1773, claimed that the word *philosophie* was often in his mouth.[73] Moreover, Joseph was violently opposed to many of his mother's policies, and soon after he gained power embarked on the reform programme which Gebler partly described in his letter to Nicolai.

Yet Joseph ostentatiously drove past the gates of Voltaire's estate in 1777, and in 1789 refused to permit the circulation within the Monarchy of a German translation of his works on the ground that 'in this tawdry dress, as always in a translation, the wit is lost, and the bald result becomes all the more harmful to religion and morals'.[74] Unlike Frederick II and Catherine II, he carried on no correspondences with *philosophes*. Writers as a breed excited his scorn.[75] He explicitly denied the influence on him of theoretical approaches. He wrote in 1765: 'I have learned nothing more firmly than to fear intelligence and all its subtleties. I recognize no argument which comes

[69] Lanjuinais, *Monarque accompli*, esp. vol. III, pp. 250–62, 284–91. Joseph is a 'monarque philosophe' from vol. I, p. 1. Comparison with Trajan and Marcus Aurelius is reached on vol. I, p. 6.

[70] Lord Acton, *Essays on Church and State*, ed. D. Woodruff (London, 1952), p. 355.

[71] Frederick the Great to Voltaire, 18 Aug. 1770 (*Voltaire's Correspondence*, ed. Besterman, vol. LXXVI, pp. 112–13).

[72] Countess Leopoldine Kaunitz to princess Eleonore Liechtenstein, 1782, in A. Wolf, *Fürstin Eleonore Liechtenstein* (Vienna, 1875), p. 165.

[73] *Journal d'un Voyage en Allemagne, fait en 1773, par G. A. H. Guibert*, vol. II, p. 250.

[74] Quoted in O. Sashegyi, *Zensur und Geitesfreiheit unter Joseph II.* (Budapest, 1958), p. 117.

[75] Beales, *Historical Journal*, p. 489.

from the ancient Greeks or the modern French.'[76] Zinzendorf thought him 'very well versed in the maxims that are at present being applied [by the government], and very ignorant of any kind of principles'.[77] Although both these remarks referred specifically to financial affairs, they have wider relevance.

As for Guibert's statement that the word *philosophie* was always in Joseph's mouth, if it relates to the new meaning of *philosophie*, it is not borne out by the emperor's surviving writings. He never said he had made philosophy the legislator of his empire – or anything like it.[78] He did employ the word quite often, but in senses that can loosely be called Stoic. 'One must be content,' he wrote, 'with the smallest of blessings, that is what we learn from Philosophy, and unfortunately from experience as well.'[79] This, like several other instances, occurs in a discussion of the limitations of women – in one of which he says his 'system. . . is close to Epicurus'.[80] But, even when writing to Mercy about his projected visit to France, with the *philosophes* in his mind, he called them *savants* and spoke of himself as being 'pretty philosophical about the chapter of accidents'.[81] He refers at least once to an *encyclopédiste*, but calls Voltaire 'the self-styled *philosophe*'.[82] This is his longest passage of self-conscious philosophy:

The idea of being able to do good and render one's subjects happy is undoubtedly the finest and the only attractive aspect of power, as it is the most powerful spur for any feeling and honest man. But when one knows at the same time that every false step is counter-productive, that evil is so easily and quickly done, and good is of its very nature so difficult and slow, and cannot (except slowly) impress itself solidly on a vast state – then this comforting illusion is much weakened, and there rests only the satisfaction that one has inside oneself, which makes one uniquely contented through knowing oneself in good company when one is alone and through seeking, without the least regard to any personal consideration, to do only what the general good of the State and the great number requires.

It is rarely possible to look after the happiness of individuals without spoiling the whole, and it is apparent that under good laws and a good system, founded and regulated in accordance with the spirit and character of the nation as well as the

---

[76] Memorandum of 1765 (*Maria Theresia und Joseph II.*, ed. Arneth, vol. III, p. 338).

[77] Zinzendorf's diary, 27 Oct. 1773.

[78] Beales, *Historical Journal*.

[79] Joseph to Lacy, 12 June 1773 (HHSA Familien-Archiv, Sammelbände 72).

[80] Joseph to Leopold, 28 July 1768 (Arneth, *Maria Theresia und Joseph II.*, ed. Arneth, vol. I, p. 228).

[81] *Correspondance secrète du Comte de Mercy-Argenteau avec l'Empereur Joseph II et le Prince de Kaunitz*, eds. A. von Arneth and J. Flammermont, 2 vols. (Paris, 1889–91), vol. II, p. 446: Joseph to Mercy, 4 Apr. 1774.

[82] W. C. Langsam, *Francis the Good: The Education of an Emperor, 1768–1792* (New York, 1949), p. 38. Joseph to his circle of ladies, 16 July 1777 (Czechoslovak state archive, Litoměřice – pobocka Žitenine: LRRA – P – 16/22–3 (copies)).

geographical position of the State, each citizen ought to find a way of being happy if he has intelligence and is willing to take the trouble – the sovereign being the upholder of the laws and the shield protecting them against any violence, administering the money entrusted to him by his subjects simply and solely for this purpose.

If there is too much philosophy in all that, if I have gone too far in laying aside the royal mantle, the crown and the sceptre, and shown the sovereign *déshabillé* and in front of his *valet de chambre*, please forgive me for having always held the principles of going back to the primitive source of everything and of trying to see every person and thing in its natural state, plain and unadorned. I don't on that account feel more unhappy. No, every individual, I say to myself, is created to occupy a position in the world for a certain span of years. Well, I am one of those marionettes that Providence, without my being able to choose, ask or seek it, has been pleased to put in the place I occupy so that I can complete my term. She has given me only the intelligence and abilities that she intended, she will offer me only such opportunities and conditions as she pleases for being or appearing to be of some consequence; and when she has had enough, the curtain will fall and the farce will be over for me, as for all those who have preceded me.[83]

This is certainly not *philosophes' philosophie*. But it breathes the spirit of Stoicism.

However, it is not specifically Christian, still less Catholic. In this respect it gives a misleading impression of Joseph's attitude. When he was disputing with his mother about her treatment of Moravian Protestants, he said both that he favoured 'complete freedom of worship' and that he would 'give what I possess if all the Protestants of your states could become Catholic'.[84] One of the principles of his legislation was that much of the proceeds from his suppressions of contemplative monasteries should go to funding more parish clergy. He was not atheist, deist or Protestant, but a Catholic reformer.[85]

As well as the *philosophes*, their opponents had tried to claim his allegiance. He was eulogised in Italy during his visit of 1769 as a 'Christian hero', 'the true Catholic Marcus Aurelius'.[86] In 1781 Belgian propagandists urged him to keep the influence of *philosophie* at bay.[87] Joseph contrived to hold at the same time opinions that were sponsored by both groups and were considered by them mutually incompatible.

---

[83] A. Beer and J. von Fiedler, *Joseph II. und Graf Ludwig Cobenzl: Ihr Briefwechsel*, 2 vols. (Vienna, 1901), vol. II, pp. 391–2: Joseph to Grand-Duke Paul of Russia and his wife, 24 Feb. 1781.

[84] Joseph to Maria Theresa, 20 July 1777 (*Maria Theresia und Joseph II.*, ed. Arneth, vol. II, p. 152).

[85] The best evidence for these statements is to be found in Maass, *Josephinismus*, vol. II; Winter, *Josefinismus*, pp. 100–14; and in H. Schlitter, *Die Reise des Papstes Pius VI. nach Wien*, 2 vols. (Vienna, 1892–4).

[86] HHSA Familien-Akten, Hofreisen 1: report from Naples, 8 Apr. 1769.

[87] E.g. Delobel, *A S.M.I. Joseph II. père de la patrie* (Mons, [1781]).

Ignatius Fessler was born in Hungary in 1756. He was destined for the Jesuit Order and educated in its schools, but with its suppression in 1773 he became a novice of the Capuchins under the name Innocent. However, the views of his superiors and the discipline they exercised alienated him. He made contacts with the Church reformers who looked forward to the accession of Joseph II and who thereafter supported his programme. In the early 1780s he left the cloister for the University of Vienna, published the first two parts of what was intended to be a massive disquisition on the emperor's rights in ecclesiastical matters, *What is the Emperor?* and was appointed by Joseph to a Chair of Old Testament and Oriental Studies in the University of Lemberg in Austrian Poland. Fessler's views meanwhile fluctuated between atheism, deism and Jansenism. After 1787 he became disillusioned with the emperor's policies, and in 1788 he left the Monarchy. He converted to Lutheranism and henceforth called himself Ignatius Aurelius Fessler. Both before and after his departure from Lemberg he was an active Freemason. While in Prussia he fell in and out of love with the philosophy of Kant, and was much influenced by Herder. He ended his days in 1839, after a spell teaching at a Russian Orthodox seminary, as the Lutheran bishop of Saratov on the Volga. In 1824 he had published an autobiography, *Dr Fessler's Retrospects on his Seventy-Year Pilgrimage*.[88]

His special interest for this essay arises from his enthusiasm for Stoics. His novice-master recommended him to study Seneca's philosophical works with the words: 'Learn from the pagan Christian humility, mortification of the flesh, and resignation.' Fessler revelled in Seneca, in whom he 'discovered a certain mysticism' which he thought could only have derived from divine inspiration. When he read writings of Jansenist spirit like Fleury's *Church History* and Muratori's *True Devotion*, his dedication to the monastic life was shaken. But he was held back from abandoning his profession, and from moral depravity, by the influence of Seneca. Fessler always took with him on his journeys an edition of the Stoic philosopher's works. Further, he wrote, 'As for what is *called* Philosophy, I had enough in Plato, Cicero, Seneca, Bacon of Verulam, Stanley, Malebranche and Brucker. Of what Philosophy *is*, I had as yet no inkling.'[89]

He continued to love Seneca, but his exile and conversion were associated with study of Marcus Aurelius. In 1790 appeared the first three volumes of what Fessler called his 'psychological novel' about the Stoic emperor, which

[88] *Dr. Fessler's Rückblicke auf seine siebzigjährige Pilgerschaft* (Breslau, 1824) can be supplemented by the works of P. F. Barton, esp. *Jesuiten, Jansenisten, Josephiner. Eine Fallstudie zur frühen Toleranzzeit: Der Fall Innocentius Fessler*, part 1 (Vienna, 1978). *Was ist der Kaiser?* was published in Vienna in 1782.
[89] *Fessler's Rückblicke*, esp. pp. 35–6, 43–5, 158, 324n.

went into three editions and achieved considerable notoriety. As the author acknowledges, anyone who took the work for an attempt at history found it 'bad'. The emperor is represented, for example, as a model of the constitutional monarch. According to Fessler, 'the whole book is written, not with art as its midwife, but with feeling as its inspiration, that is, from a heart steadfast and peaceful in God. If I have written anything good and true, it comes from God, the source of all goodness and truth.' He was at pains to deny that he had desired 'to be counted among those who in our day have arrogated to themselves the titles of Philosophers and Men of Enlightenment'.[90] Through all the changing scenes and attitudes of his bizarre 'pilgrimage', Fessler clung to a view of Stoicism as essentially Christian.

V

So, in the Austrian Monarchy during the Age of Enlightenment, there were few who grasped the significance of the redefinition by Diderot and others of the term *philosophe*; and even those few did not fully accept it. For many, not only of the older generation like Francis Stephen and Maria Theresa, but also of the younger like Joseph II and Isabella, the word remained for ordinary purposes a synonym for Stoic or Stoical – understood more or less loosely. For the empress 'Christian philosopher', as used by neo-Stoics, was a natural expression. For her children 'philosophy' and Catholicism were perfectly compatible. Even to her more advanced ministers like Kaunitz and Zinzendorf, and to the prince de Ligne, the new usage was for differing reasons and in varying degrees unpalatable. Whereas the writings of Seneca helped to inspire Rousseau's ideas on education, and Diderot devoted years of labour to rehabilitating the philosopher's reputation as an Enlightened minister of state,[91] for Fessler he ranked as a forerunner of Christian mysticism, the stern teacher of morality who held him to his monastic obligations.

It would not be difficult to widen the range of evidence in support of the argument of this essay. Here are a few further examples. In Fessler's homeland, Hungary, Lipsius was twice reprinted in the vernacular after the date when Oestreich considered his influence at an end.[92] Leopold II, younger

---

[90] *Ibid.*, pp. 241–4, 487, 489.
[91] G. Pire, 'De l'Influence de Sénèque sur les théories pédagogiques de J.-J. Rousseau', *Annales de la Société Jean-Jacques Rousseau*, vol. XXXII (1953–5), pp. 57–92; W. T. Conroy, Jr, *Diderot's 'Essai sur Sénèque'*, Studies in Voltaire and the Eighteenth Century, vol. CXXXI (1975).
[92] Evans, *Making of the Habsburg Monarchy*, p. 113n.

brother and successor of Joseph II, though patron of the second Italian edition of the *Encyclopédie*, still used the word *philosophe* in the traditional sense, and combined with deep interest in the French Enlightenment dogmatic zeal for the reform of the Roman Catholic Church.[93] In the 1780s the great monastery of Strahov in Prague, spared from dissolution by Joseph because of its proven usefulness, began building a second, 'philosophical' library to match its theological collection. When frescoes were applied to the new building in the 1790s, the incorrigibly Baroque painter, Maulbertsch, was asked to depict, in a scheme that glorified divine revelation, along with other ancient and modern philosophers, the Encyclopaedists.[94]

According to Peter Gay, 'neither Gibbon nor the other *philosophes* could ever grant that philosophical Christians or Stoic Christians were men with a coherent world view'.[95] Historians have been inclined to feel the same. On the one hand, all Josephists have been condemned as heretical by some modern Catholic scholars;[96] on the other, signs of Enlightenment and Jacobinism within the Monarchy have been studied out of their Christian, generally Catholic, context.[97] The combinations of influences acknowledged at any one time by, say, Francis Stephen, Zinzendorf and Fessler seem as mutually irreconcilable as the Catholicism, Classicism, astrology and alchemy that jostled together at the Court of Rudolf II. But the latter *mélange* has recently been studied with sympathy, among others by Robert Evans.[98] It is unhistorical not to accord the same respect to the mentality of the Austrian Enlightenment.

The study of intellectual influences is notoriously treacherous ground. An obvious pitfall, not always avoided, is to assume that in the period roughly from 1740 to 1790 French influence meant Enlightened influence. The vogue of the French language and of French thought at the Court of Maria Theresa, and even under Joseph II, gave as much scope to the ideas of Bossuet, Pascal, Descartes and Fénelon – not to mention Mesmer[99] – as to those of Voltaire and Diderot. Jansenism was primarily a French movement,

[93] A. Wandruszka, *Leopold II.*, 2 vols. (Vienna, 1963–5), esp. vol. I, pp. 219–26, 279–87, vol. II, part IV.
[94] K. Garas, *Franz Anton Maulbertsch 1724–1796* (Budapest, 1960), pp. 154–7, 276.
[95] Gay, *Enlightenment*, vol. I, p. 320.
[96] Explicitly by H. Rieser, *Der Geist der Josephinismus und sein Fortleben* (Vienna, 1963), who divides Joseph's subjects into those who were *Romtreu* and the rest. See e.g. p. 82 for a denial that the Josephists' reforms were Catholic reforms.
[97] This seems to be true e.g. of E. Wangermann, *From Joseph II to the Jacobin Trials* (2nd edn, Oxford, 1969), though not of his more recent writing.
[98] R. J. W. Evans, *Rudolf II and His World* (Oxford, 1973).
[99] R. Darnton, *Mesmerism and the End of the Enlightenment in France* (Cambridge, Mass., 1968).

and the height of its influence in Vienna coincided with the age of Enlighten-ment.[100] Yet for Voltaire Jansenists were worse even than Jesuits.[101]

No doubt the Monarchy was peculiar by the standards of Enlightened Europe as a whole. But these considerations apply, at least to some extent, everywhere. Voltaire usually saw himself as embattled against *l'infâme*, and did not always imagine that he was winning. He complained in 1769 that he had not found three *philosophes* to follow him, while 'a madman and an imbecile like St Ignatius' had found a dozen.[102] His full doctrine – like the redefinition of *philosophe* – won few converts. On the other hand, his many ferocious enemies did not include all Roman Catholics, all priests and all Austrians. It was the king of England, where Voltaire thought everyone was a *philosophe*, who talked to Zinzendorf 'of burning Voltaire with his books, and said he would never permit him to come to England'.[103] More typical than the strident and self-conscious French *philosophes* or their rabid opponents were Lutheran *Aufklärer*, Enlightened Italian clergy like pope Benedict XIV and Muratori, and even the *abbés* who contributed to the *Encyclopédie*.[104] A *curé* of Mouzay, though he read and recommended to others writings critical of Voltaire and Rousseau, paid the two *philosophes* the unique compliment of incorporating funeral eulogies for them in his parish register.[105]

One does not usually expect to find in Bentham's work penetrating insights into ecclesiastical history. But allowing for his prejudices, one may regard the following remarks, published in 1789, as impressive evidence for the interrelationship between religion and Enlightenment with which this essay has been concerned:

Happily, the dictates of religion seem to approach nearer and nearer to a coincidence with those of utility every day. But why? Because the dictates of the moral sanction do so: and those coincide with or are influenced by these. Men of the worst religions, influenced by the voice and practice of the surrounding world, borrow continually a new and a new leaf out of the book of utility: and with these, in order not to break with their religion, they endeavour, sometimes with violence enough, to patch together and adorn the repositories of their faith.[106]

---

[100] See P. Hersche, *Der Spätjansenismus in Österreich* (Vienna, 1977).

[101] R. Pomeau, *La Religion de Voltaire* (Paris, 1956), esp. pp. 25–7.

[102] Voltaire to Frederick the Great, 30 Oct. 1769 (*Voltaire's Correspondence*, ed. Bester-man, vol. LXXIII, p. 145).

[103] Zinzendorf's diary, 28 Apr. 1768.

[104] Cf. T. C. W. Blanning, *Reform and Revolution in Mainz* (Cambridge, 1974), pp. 23–32; Chadwick, *Popes and European Revolution*, esp. pp. 395–402; R. Shackleton, *The 'Encyclopédie' and the Clerks* (Zaharoff lecture, Oxford, 1970). More generally, *The Enlightenment in National Context*, ed. R. Porter and M. Teich (Cambridge, 1981).

[105] Pomeau, *Religion de Voltaire*, p. 343 and n.

[106] J. Bentham, *An Introduction to the Principles of Morals and Legislation*, ed. W. Harrison (Oxford, 1948), p. 241.

Like Bentham, Peter Gay, while recognising this development, sees it as 'treason of the clerks', 'doing the philosophes' work'.[107] But the Christian, even the Catholic, philosopher, though he could hardly become a full-blown *philosophe*, could adopt, even promote, some elements of French Enlightened thinking, not merely without doing violence to his religion, but under its banner and to its perceived advantage.

[107] Gay, *Enlightenment*, vol. I, p. 22.

The role of religion in European counter-revolution 1789–1815

T. C. W. BLANNING

The spectre of religion haunted the French revolutionaries, both at home and abroad. Inside France, from 'the first important manifestation of counter-revolutionary activity'[1] – the *bagarre de Nîmes* of June 1790 – to the White Terror of 1815, resistance expressed in religious forms was a constant reminder of the tenacity of old regime values and institutions. Abroad, religion was invariably obtrusive in counter-revolutionary agitation, in the Italian risings of 1796, in the Belgian *Boerenkrijg* and the Luxemburg *Klöppelkrieg* of 1798, in the revolt of the Swiss cantons of the same year, in Cardinal Ruffo's reconquest of Naples in 1799, in the Spanish War of 1808, in the Tyrolean revolt of 1809 – just to mention some of the more intense manifestations. From Cadiz to Moscow, the counter-revolutionaries adopted the Cross as their standard in the struggle against what they believed to be the atheism of their adversaries.

In recent decades, however, writing on counter-revolution has been dominated by historians who ascribe to religion only a minor and essentially superficial role. All those religious slogans and symbols which clerical historians of the nineteenth century regarded as testimony to the universal and eternal power of their faith have been reassessed as retrospective justification. The true motivation of those apparently religious manifestations has been relocated, not in the abstract world of the spirit but in the concrete realities of society. Particularly influential has been Paul Bois' study of counter-revolution in the Sarthe – *Paysans de l'Ouest* – first published in 1960. This is concerned with material problems such as conditions of land-tenure, relations between town and country, the sale of *biens nationaux*, the role of manufacturing, the seigneurial regime and the like. When religious forces do make an appearance, they do so only as symptoms of a more fundamental social reality. A good example is his explanation of the striking correlation

---

[1] Gwynne Lewis, *The Second Vendée, The Continuity of Counterrevolution in the Department of the Gard 1789–1815* (Oxford, 1978), p. 25.

between areas of high support for counter-revolution and areas with a high percentage of non-juring priests. That, he argues, was simply the *expression* of social conditions: chameleon-like, the pliable priests were obliged to adopt the colour of their communities. Their parishioners were motivated not by devotion to Catholicism but by material deprivation. As the peasants of the Western Sarthe sallied forth to do battle with the Revolution, it was almost as an afterthought that they donned the protective cap of religion.[2] This view that religion's role in counter-revolution was one of retrospective justification rather than autonomous causation has dominated the field, despite certain nuances of expression.[3] Claude Mazauric, for example, criticised Bois for demoting religion too far, but he too saw it only as 'part of the superstructure'.[4] Even Charles Tilly, who wrote with sympathy about the religious loyalties of the Vendée and conceded that 'religious questions *were* important, the good priests *did* matter', arrived at the same conclusion: 'the beliefs about the virtues of the old regime and the intentions of the rebellion which have so often been retroactively imputed to the rebels actually emerged from the stress of battle', and 'the ideology of the "Catholic and Royal Army" emerged from the stress of battle and from the need of the combatants to explain to themselves and to others what they were doing'.[5]

Certainly scholars such as Bois and Tilly have put the methodological tools supplied by the social scientists – both Marxist and non-Marxist – to highly productive use. They have advanced our knowledge and understanding of resistance to the Revolution further and more rapidly than during any previous historiographical phase. Clearly there can be no return to the simple faith/counter-revolution, cause/effect nexus assumed by the clerical historians of the nineteenth century. Yet a nagging doubt remains. Can all those thousands – hundreds of thousands – of Europeans who rose in the name of their faith really have been the dupes of their own misinterpreted needs and/or the manipulated puppets of their selfish elites? Such a doubt about the exclusively materialist motivation of the counter-revolutionaries

---

[2] Paul Bois, *Paysans de l'Ouest. Des structures économiques et sociales aux options politiques depuis l'époque révolutionnaire dans la Sarthe* (Paris, 1971), pp. 292, 353.

[3] They have not gone entirely unchallenged, however. See especially Barrington Moore Jr, *Social Origins of Dictatorship and Democracy. Lord and Peasant in the Making of the Modern World* (London, 1967), pp. 93–100. For an earlier sharp exchange on the same subject, see A. Lajusan, 'Origines immédiates et lointaines de la Vendée', *Bulletin de la Société d'histoire moderne*, XXXVIII (1938), and the riposte from Georges Lefebvre which is printed immediately afterwards.

[4] Claude Mazauric, 'Vendée et Chouannerie', *La Pensée*, CXXIV (1965), p. 76.

[5] Charles Tilly, *The Vendée* (Cambridge, Mass., 1964), p. 260; Charles Tilly, 'The analysis of a counter-revolution', *History and Theory*, III, 1 (1963), p. 57; Charles Tilly, 'Some problems in the history of the Vendée', *American Historical Review*, LXVII, 1 (1961), p. 32.

of the Vendée, for example, arises when one reads accounts of events written by revolutionaries on the spot: 'This is true fanaticism, of a fourth-century variety. Every day they are executed and every day they die singing hymns and making their profession of faith', or 'They were made to get down on their knees and were ordered to shout "Long live the Republic!" All refused to do so, made the sign of the cross and were then shot.'[6]

Such a doubt is strengthened by the lack of understanding evinced by certain historians when reacting to evidence of religious conviction. *La saine raison* looks down on the masses trapped in their mythopoeic bog with an unappealing mixture of condescension, exasperation and contempt. A fine example is provided by Jean-René Suratteau's pitying and petulant comment on the obtuse loyalty of the people of Porrentruy to the Bishop of Basle: 'Clearly these simple people were unable to make the subtle distinction between temporal and spiritual.'[7] Moreover, Suratteau goes on, these bovine clodhoppers were not so much attached to religion as to their priests.[8] The spirit of that assertion is echoed in Jacques Godechot's equally unfounded generalisation: 'the peasant in western France was very attached to religious practice, if not to religion itself...The situation was the same in Calabria and Spain.'[9] It is indeed ironic that historians so quick to censure their clerical-conservative predecessors for uncritically assigning religious motives to their subjects should themselves write with equal confidence – and with an equal lack of support – on the same theme, albeit in a disapproving fashion. Gaetano Cingari's comments on the clergy of Calabria provide a good example:

their attitude was one of obscurantist fanaticism; deprived of any valid and soundly based culture and in general not motivated by any sincere religious vocation, the Calabrian priest was just the reproducer of sterile theological phrases...of the worst habits, prone to violence, a misfit in his social relations, secretly or openly more rakish than the libertine Jacobins.[10]

The coincidence of the style and terminology of this denunciation with those of Jacobin diatribes is by no means rare. The charge is often levelled that the basically good, if dim and ignorant, masses were *fanatisiert, fanatisés* or *fanatizzati* by their clerical svengalis.[11]

[6] Marcel Reinhard, *Religion, Révolution et Contre-Révolution* (Paris, 1960), pp. 226–7.
[7] Jean-René Suratteau, *Le Département du Mont-Terrible sous le régime du Directoire (1795–1800)* (Paris, 1965), p. 270.
[8] *Ibid.*, p. 227.
[9] Jacques Godechot, *The Counter-Revolution; Doctrine and Action 1789–1804* (London 1972), p. 205.
[10] Gaetano Cingari, *Giacobini e sanfedisti in Calabria nel 1799* (Messina, 1957), pp. 93, 303.
[11] Heinrich Scheel, *Süddeutsche Jakobiner: Klassenkämpfe und republikanische Bestrebungen im deutschen Süden Ende des 18. Jahrhundertes* (Berlin, 1962), pp. 9, 288, 439; Jean-René Suratteau, 'Occupation, occupants et occupés en Suisse de 1792 à 1814',

Doubts aroused by the neo-Jacobin tone of these and many other similar analyses have been fed by two recent studies which suggest that religion may yet reclaim an autonomous causative status. In an article published in the *Journal of Modern History* in 1982 Timothy Tackett presented new evidence 'to suggest that prior to the Revolution the religious configuration of this area [Western France] was indeed distinct from that in much of the rest of the kingdom; and that this particular religious culture may have been an important contributing factor to the counterrevolutionary tendencies throughout so much of the West after 1792'.[12] He was able to show that the rural clergy in the West were unusually well-off, enjoyed unusually high status, were unusually thick on the ground and to an unusually large extent were local men, with the result that the laity were strongly clericalist. In the *towns* of the West, on the other hand, the later eighteenth century was characterised by rapid social and cultural secularisation. As a result: 'the veritable collision of the particular religious conceptions of the westernmost of the two peoples with the strikingly different world view of the islands of the urban cultural elite in that region would be one significant factor in the origins and special character of the uprisings in the West after 1790'.[13] Tackett does not try to overstate the case; he does not seek to deny the importance of social forces in generating counter-revolution. But he does insist on the existence of an autonomous, independent cultural and religious dimension:

In the final analysis, there can be no denying the importance of economic relations, of patterns of land tenure, of the issue of military conscription as factors in the outbreak of the *Vendée* and the *Chouannerie*. Yet it seems clear that the socioeconomic clashes between town and country were paralleled and greatly reinforced by an independent cultural clash; and that the peculiar constellation of religious structures and attitudes rendered this clash as sharp and pronounced as in any other region of France. And we must seriously entertain the possibility that it was this very religious confrontation which served as a key catalyst in the relative cohesion and unity of so much of the rural West, galvanising and energising the diverse and sometimes contradictory patterns of social and economic conflict at the local level.[14]

Occupants-Occupés, 1792–1815. Actes du Colloque qui s'est tenu à Bruxelles, les 29 et 30 janvier 1968 (Brussels, 1969), p. 178; Gabriele Turi, '*Viva Maria*'. *La reazione alle riforme leopoldine (1790–1799)* (Florence, 1969), p. 254.

[12] Timothy Tackett, 'The West in France in 1789: the religious factor in the origins of the counterrevolution', *Journal of Modern History*, LIV, 4 (1982), p. 718.

[13] *Ibid.*, p. 740.

[14] *Ibid.*, p. 745. See also Maurice Hutt's conclusion in the introductory chapter to his massive study *Chouannerie and Counter-Revolution. Puisaye, the Princes and the British Government in the 1790s*, 2 vols. (Cambridge, 1983), I, p. 2: 'It was the Civil Constitution of the Clergy, voted in 1790, which served more than any other single public measure to hasten the process of explicit polarisation in Western France.'

A similar conclusion was reached by Donald Sutherland in a book on the *chouans* of Brittany published in the same year (1982).[15] He too took full account of the socio-economic origins of counter-revolutionary insurgency in the area, most notably the serious material deprivation suffered by tenant-farmers after 1789. Nor did he suppose that religious disaffection in itself produced *chouannerie*. But he did argue – persuasively – that religion played a vital role. Among other things, the conflict over the imposition of the Civil Constitution of the Clergy forced those groups which had neither benefited from nor had been harmed by the Revolution to take sides. Because of the special role and status of the Church in Brittany (for reasons similar to those identified by Tackett in the Vendée), this exercise propelled most of the rural population into the counter-revolutionary camp. As Sutherland puts it: 'Ideologically, *chouannerie* was a protest against the destruction of the moral unity of the peasant community' and 'The Civil Constitution of the Clergy was seen as an invasion of a community which was defined in moral and religious rather than in institutional terms.'[16]

With the debate on the role of religion reopened, this essay proposes to examine some of the ways in which it interacted with counter-revolution in various parts of Europe. On one point agreement can be reached without difficulty: the Revolution began with little or no trace of the anti-clericalism which was to prove so serious a handicap. The evidence of the *cahiers de doléance* suggests that religion was not a major issue in 1789: only 10 % called for abolition of the tithe, only 4 % for abolition of the regular clergy and only 2 % for the sale of all ecclesiastical land.[17] Far from forging a throne-altar axis, the Church called for change. The last clerical General Assembly of the old regime, which met in June 1788, gave full support to the Notables and to the Parlements, demanding the recall of the latter and the convocation of the Estates General.[18] The contribution made by the *révolte des curés* to the successful establishment of the Revolution in the course of 1789 is too well known to need rehearsing again here. But it was not long before the lack of political foresight displayed by these well-meaning but naive priests

---

[15] Donald Sutherland, *The Chouans. The Social Origins of Popular Counter-Revolution in Upper Brittany, 1770–1796* (Oxford, 1982).

[16] *Ibid.*, pp. 218, 311. In an even more recent article Sutherland has stressed the importance of the special grievances of tenant-farmers, but also shows how they fused with the religious issue to form a particularly combustible mixture – T. J. A. Le Goff and D. M. G. Sutherland, 'The social origins of counter-revolution in Western France', *Past and Present*, no. 99 (May, 1983), p. 72.

[17] Claude Langlois and Timothy Tackett, 'A l'épreuve de la Révolution (1770–1830)', *Histoire des catholiques en France du XVe siècle à nos jours*, ed. François Lebrun (Toulouse, 1980), p. 243.

[18] *Ibid.*, p. 244.

was brought home. The expropriation of church land, the savage reduction in the number of urban parishes, the secularisation of education and the lay election of bishops led to progressive alienation. The rift was then made irrevocable by a fatal act of revolutionary legislation. As John McManners has written: 'If there was a point at which the Revolution "went wrong", it was when the Constituent Assembly imposed the oath to the Civil Constitution of the Clergy, 27 November 1790. This marked the end of national unity and the beginning of civil war... This was the fatal moment in the history of the Revolution.'[19] The oath-taking exercise which followed was 'a genuine plebiscite for the population, for or against the Revolution'.[20] From that moment, the French clergy were divided into *constitutionnels* and *réfractaires*, revolutionaries and counter-revolutionaries.

Eighteen months were still to elapse before the outbreak of war on 20 April 1792. In the intervening period the Revolution's ever-accelerating drift to the left was accompanied by ever more overt anti-clericalism. It was dramatised for all Catholic – if not all Christian – Europe by the papal bull *Quod aliquantum* of 10 March 1791, in which Pius VI roundly condemned the Civil Constitution of the Clergy as an attempt to achieve nothing less than the destruction of the Catholic religion.[21] Inside France, the attempt to expel non-juring priests from their parishes and to enforce acceptance of more pliable replacements was provoking countless violent confrontations, most notably and ominously in the bocage of the West.[22] The result was an exodus of non-jurors, seeking refuge in Belgium, the Rhineland, Switzerland, Northern Italy and Spain. It has been estimated that between 30,000 and 40,000 Catholic priests left France[23] – or, in other words, between 30,000 and 40,000 supporters of counter-revolution. When they reached their respective places of refuge, not unnaturally the exiles broadcast flesh-creeping stories of revolutionary atheism and iconoclasm, thus lending first-hand confirmation to the blanket condemnation issued by Rome.

Consequently, by the time the French armies began their first great offensive, in the autumn of 1792, they were handicapped by the image of militant godlessness. Moreover, as if to prove that this image was supported by reality, the Parisian crowd chose just this moment to slaughter 3 bishops and 220 priests in the 'September Massacres'.[24] So the Belgians and the Rhinelanders, who were first in line for liberation, knew just what to expect.

[19] John McManners, *The French Revolution and the Church* (London, 1969), pp. 38, 46.
[20] Langlois and Tackett, 'A l'épreuve de la Révolution', p. 250.
[21] André Latreille, *L'Église catholique et la Révolution française*, vol. I: *Le Pontificat de Pie VI et la crise française (1775–1799)* (Paris, 1970), p. 109.
[22] Marcel Lidove, *Les Vendéens de 93* (Paris, 1971), p. 35.
[23] Langlois and Tackett, 'A l'épreuve de la Révolution', p. 253.
[24] McManners, *The French Revolution and the Church*, p. 67.

Their worst expectations were soon fulfilled, as hair-raising stories of blasphemy and iconoclasm began to make the rounds. That French soldiers really did commit all the atrocities ascribed to them is barely credible; that everyone believed that they did is certain. The following sample, drawn from a variety of eye-witness accounts and hearsay reports gives some impression of how they were regarded: they mutilated crucifixes, they emptied the ciborium and trampled the host on the ground, they subjected statues of the Virgin to sexual abuse, they stopped church services and forced organists to play revolutionary songs, they sang anti-clerical songs themselves, they performed blasphemous parodies of religious ceremonies, they pinned the host to their cockades, they seized and drank the consecrated wine during the Mass, they dressed up in clerical garments, they fed the host to their horses, they baited dogs on altars, they took prostitutes into church and fornicated with them, they lit their pipes from the eternal light, they defecated into tabernacles.[25] This violent anti-clericalism stemmed from the highly political nature of the French armies during the early stages of the revolutionary wars. Just as the Catholics associated the Revolution with atheism, so did the revolutionary soldiers associate Catholicism with royalism.[26] Once that reciprocal process of identification had begun, every act of hostility on either side could only intensify mutual hatred.

Official action – as opposed to the spontaneous excesses of the rank-and-file – did nothing to break this infernal circle. Certainly the various occupation authorities installed by the French were more diplomatic in intention. With France having to fight every major power in Europe at one time or another in the course of the 1790s, this was no time to be adding to one's enemies gratuitously. In 1797 General Bonaparte even insisted that his new satellite state, the Cispadane Republic, should reserve to Roman Catholicism the exclusive right to public worship.[27] Although his attitude towards religion was perhaps unusually elastic, he was not the only pragmatist to command an army or direct an administration. Yet neither he nor anyone else ever succeeded in achieving a durable accommodation. The wealth, power and pretensions of the Church were just too great to allow coexistence with the most powerful and demanding state the world had ever seen. From the start of the French revolutionary expansion until the final collapse of Napoleon's Empire, periods of uneasy tolerance were punctuated by bouts of active

[25] For a complete list of sources, see T. C. W. Blanning, *The French Revolution in Germany, Occupation and Resistance in the Rhineland 1792–1802* (Oxford, 1983), p. 221 n. 57.

[26] Richard Cobb, *Les Armées révolutionnaires. Instrument de la Terreur dans les départements avril 1793 – Floréal an II*, 2 vols. (Paris, 1961), II, p. 653.

[27] Jacques Godechot, *La Grande Nation. L'expansion révolutionnaire de la France dans le monde 1789–1799*, 2 vols. (Paris, 1956), II, p. 523.

persecution. There was certainly no steady dilution of revolutionary anti-clericalism: it was more vehement in 1794 than in 1792 and still more so in 1798. The arrest and imprisonment of Pius VI in 1798, for example, threw Italian democrats who were also Catholics into confusion, not to say despair.[28] Even the great Concordat of 1801 was soon succumbing to the forces which made Church and Revolution irreconcilable. It was a process which ended with the excommunication of Napoleon and the imprisonment of the Pope.[29] Those two events occurred in 1809, by which time Napoleon was involved in a war in Spain with a pronounced religious character.

In short, religion presented a counter-revolutionary threat to the French almost continuously and almost everywhere. In trying to understand how and why it played such a disruptive role, it is important to stress first that there is a strong line of continuity leading from the old regime. As several enlightened reformers had discovered to their cost, attempts to purify the excesses of traditional piety were resisted fiercely by the faithful. The same conservative religiosity which made life so difficult for the French had caused similar problems for the Catholic reformers before 1789. In the late 1780s the peasants of the Vorarlberg rioted against the allegedly heterodox reforms of Joseph II. Ten years later they rose again, this time against the French but once again marching under the banner of the true faith.[30] The same consistency is to be found in many other parts of Europe. In Tuscany rioters showed on several occasions in the 1790s that the slogan *Viva Maria!* could be applied with equal force to both revolutionaries and Habsburgs. In May 1790 the rioting in Livorno against the regime of Grand Duke Leopold began on the feast-day of the city's patron saint, S. Giulia. The insurgents revived ceremonies which had been prohibited, reopened churches which had been closed and restored images for public veneration. Six years later, a rising against the French occupation force was heralded by reports that the Pope had preached a crusade against the new regime and that an image of the Virgin had lent miraculous support by opening and closing her eyes. The major insurrection of 1799 was also preceded by a rash of miracles.[31]

In many parts of Catholic Europe the religious atmosphere had been intensified in the decades before the Revolution by the attempts to enforce Jansenist reforms. Ironically, the resulting tension which posed such problems for the old regime then came to its assistance when support was being mobilised

---

[28] Vittorio E. Giuntella, 'L'esperienza rivoluzionaria', *Nuove questioni di storia del Risorgimento e dell' Unità d'Italia* (Milan, 1961), p. 325.

[29] Owen Chadwick, *The Popes and European Revolution* (Oxford, 1981), p. 511.

[30] Reinhold Bernhard, *Die Geschichte Vorarlbergs von den Unruhejahren 1789 und 1790 bis zum Ende des Zweiten Koalitionskrieges im Jagre 1801* (Innsbruck dissertation, 1967), pp. 96–102, 372, 584–6, 752.

[31] Turi, '*Viva Maria*', pp. 8–10, 133, 244, 310.

against the French. When the revolutionary armies arrived in Belgium, the Rhineland or Italy, they found Catholic communities hypersensitive to any threat to their traditional faith. They also found Catholic communities with long-established traditions of expressing social discontents in religious forms. Thanks to the researches of Gabriele Turi, Gaetano Cingari and many others, it is now clear that behind the religious rhetoric there seethed all manner of material grievances. The Tuscan rioters of 1790 were protesting not just – or even mainly – against religious innovations but also against the sharp rise in the price of food which they blamed on the government's liberation of the grain trade.[32] Wherever social antagonism and material deprivation were acute, religious agitation acquired a correspondingly virulent intensity. That meant almost everywhere in the period 1792–1815. Such was the devastation inflicted by the French armies as they rampaged across Europe that there was always a seething brew of resentment seeking release. Once the local population had been alienated by the looting, murder and rape committed by the soldiers and by the levies, requisitions and billeting imposed by the military authorities, it was often only an act of iconoclasm by the former or an act of anti-clericalism by the latter that was needed to provoke an insurrection.

This material deprivation did not need to stem directly – or even at all – from the French to provoke a counter-revolutionary episode with religious forms. One of the most violent, widespread and successful insurrections erupted in an area largely untouched by revolutionary warfare. This was the conquest of the short-lived Neapolitan Republic by the *sanfedisti* in 1799. If ever there were a counter-revolutionary rising with a religious character, then this was surely it. It was led by a prince of the Church – Cardinal Ruffo; its rank-and-file took their name from the faith itself – *santa fede*; and it marched under the banner of the Cross.[33] Yet it is clear that what gave Ruffo's expedition its unique impetus – within just a couple of weeks his original band of 8 had swollen to 15,000 – was its social-revolutionary dimension. During the previous decades Calabria had been afflicted by almost every imaginable social disaster: earthquakes, overpopulation, economic recession, inflation, expropriation, banditry, increased taxation, pauperisation.[34] The potential violence engendered by this formidable combination might well have been mobilised for the Revolution by the new Neapolitan Republic, established in January 1799 following the French capture of Naples. The opportunity was missed, as the new regime, largely composed of noble

[32] *Ibid.*, pp. 9–10.
[33] Antonio Lucarelli, *La Puglia nel Risorgimento* (*Storia Documentata*), vol. II: *La Rivoluzione del 1799* (Bari, 1934), p. 375.
[34] Cingari, *Giacobini e sanfedisti*, pp. 15–102.

and bourgeois landowners, embarked on social reform too hesitantly and too late.[35] Instead, it was Cardinal Ruffo who seized the initiative, abolishing or reducing the most unpopular of the old regime's dues.[36] Deftly exploiting the raw unfocused resentment of the masses, he injected into his counter-revolutionary crusade the irresistible momentum of social violence. Yet the role of religion should not be assigned a merely rhetorical function. It was just the vitality of Calabrian (and Puglian and Campanian) religious life which allowed Ruffo to perform this dexterous manoeuvre.

The events in the kingdom of Naples in 1799 also illustrate one further striking characteristic of the relationship between religion and counter-revolution during this period: the laity were often more inclined to associate the Revolution with impiety than were the clergy. Of course most prelates and most priests rallied to the old regime, but with surprising frequency a significant minority of both welcomed and collaborated with the new order. At Taranto, Archbishop Giuseppe Capecelatro donned the republican cockade, removed the Bourbon insignia from his palace and began to sign himself 'Citizen Archbishop'. His colleague at Bari, Archbishop Guevera, solemnly blessed the new liberty tree erected by local Jacobins, while at Nicastro Bishop Carlo Pellegrino held a Te Deum to mark the foundation of the Republic but declined to perform the same ceremony for the royalists when they recaptured the town.[37] Cardinal Zurlo of Naples not only proclaimed the compatibility of republicanism with the faith but also condemned Ruffo's expedition.[38] In Spain, too, after 1808, the supporters of the French – the 'afrancesados' – included a number of prominent prelates, most notably the Archbishop of Toledo, Cardinal Luis de Borbón, a cousin of the deposed king Charles IV.[39] Indeed, Manuel Tuñon de Lara has written that *most* of the higher clergy in Spain changed their allegiance from Charles IV to Joseph Bonaparte after 2 May 1808 without much hesitation.[40]

Clerical support for French-sponsored regimes could lead to some bizarre spectacles when counter-revolutionary retribution arrived. At Molfetta in Puglia in 1799 a mob concentrated its attention on the house of the Dominicans, looting its contents, slaughtering two of the friars and dragging off a third to be lynched to cries not just of 'Die, Jacobin scum!' but also of

35 Giorgio Candeloro, Storia dell'Italia moderna, vol. 1: Le origini del Risorgimento (Milan, 1956), pp. 258–60.
36 Cingari, Giacobini e sanfedisti, pp. 190–2.
37 Ibid., p. 197; Lucarelli, La Puglia nel Risorgimento, II, pp. 150, 338.
38 Chadwick, The Popes and European Revolution, p. 474.
39 Gabriel H. Lovett, Napoleon and the Birth of Modern Spain, vol. 1: The Challenge to the Old Order (New York, 1965), p. 126.
40 Manuel Tuñon de Lara, La España del Siglo XIX (Paris, 1971), p. 15.

'Long live the King, the Church and the Faith!'[41] North of the Alps the situation was very different, for – outside France, at least – clerical collaborators of whatever rank were few and far between. The reasons for this difference are still not clear. It could be speculated that the various reform movements, both secular and religious, which had been implemented in the decades preceding the outbreak of the Revolution had persuaded progressive clergy that the best way forward was through cooperation with the existing authorities. Moreover, unlike their Spanish or South Italian colleagues, they had experienced early and at first hand revolutionary anti-clericalism in its most violent form. Those German, Belgian or Swiss priests who did embrace revolutionary ideology usually abandoned their clerical careers altogether – or were obliged to do so by their indignant parishioners. In short, the pious laity were not, as the French often maintained, mere putty in the hands of their priests.

Nevertheless, the influence of those priests was very considerable and in most cases it was exercised in a counter-revolutionary sense. The reasons are not hard to fathom. A parish priest's first acquaintance with the Revolution in action usually confirmed all his worst fears about the Revolution in theory. Typical was the experience of the parish priest of Haaren, a village just outside Aachen on the road to Jülich. He recorded in the parish register the following account of the first arrival of French soldiers in January 1793:

I shall pass over the irksome, grievous and hideous assaults perpetrated against my person. It would also take too long to describe how and in what fashion these atheists tormented, plundered and ill-treated the people, especially those living in isolated houses...or how they blasphemed against God, the Blessed Virgin Mary, and our dear saints, reviled the clergy, abused and disrupted church services and all other forms of Christian worship. Almost all of them were men (although in my view they were not human beings at all) *sine Fide, sine Religione, sine Lege et disciplina, sine Luce et Cruce.*[42]

Immediate and concrete discomforts of the kind inflicted on the priest of Haaren were then followed up by afflictions of a more intangible but no less keenly felt variety. Wherever the French established their rule on a permanent basis, the Church and its priests were moved from the centre of social life to its periphery. The introduction of toleration and the consequent intrusion of non-Catholics, the secularisation of education, censorship and marriage, and the prohibition of public religious ceremonies such as processions and pilgrimages – just to mention a few of the more important innovations – represented a drastic reduction in the priest's status. His material

[41] Lucarelli, *La Puglia nel Risorgimento*, II, p. 82.
[42] H. Schnock, 'Aufzeichnungen eines Haarener Kirchenbuches aus den Kriegsjahren 1792–1795', *Aus Aachens Vorzeit*, X, 3 (1897), pp. 36–7.

circumstances also took a sharp turn for the worse, as the proceeds of the tithe were diverted to the French war-effort and ecclesiastical land was expropriated. No wonder, therefore, that priests were to the fore in organising opposition to the French occupations, whether by sabotaging the elections held in Belgium and the Rhineland in February 1793, or by publishing pamphlets in Spain in 1794 calling for a Holy War against 'the regicide sons of Lucifer', or by agitating against the referendum held in the Cispadane Republic in 1797, or by financing a royalist band in Calabria in 1799 – or in 1001 other ways.[43] The Church militant achieved its finest – or at least its most active – hour in Spain after 1808. Even after allowances have been made for their natural tendency to exaggerate, the contemporary accounts do make it plain that the clergy were always in the thick of the guerrilla war and often in the van. Even if Father Santiago Sas, for example, did not account for 17 French soldiers single-handed during the general assault on Saragossa on 27 January 1809, he certainly made his mark, both on that day and throughout the rest of the epic siege. When the city finally fell to the French, he was caught, bayoneted to death and thrown into the Ebro, together with another warrior-priest, Don Basilio Bogiero.[44]

The Spanish War of Liberation was an exceptionally bloody affair – by their own admission the French lost 60,000 killed in action during the two sieges of Saragossa[45] – but the degree of clerical participation was much less unusual. Even those historians who deny religion a causative role in resistance to the French are agreed that the priests were both active and effective in organising that resistance. Recent work by Suratteau and Michaud on Switzerland, by Bernhard on the Vorarlberg, by Kolb on the Tyrol, by Turi on Tuscany, by Assereto on Genoa, by Lewis on the Gard, by myself on the Rhineland – just to mention a few – all draw attention to the counter-revolutionary role of the priests.[46] Only Soviet historians are reticent about

43 Suzanne Tassier, 'Les Belges et la Révolution française (1789–1793)', *Revue de l'Université de Bruxelles*, xxxix (1933–4), p. 466; T. C. W. Blanning, *Reform and Revolution in Mainz 1743–1803* (Cambridge, 1974), pp. 287–9; D. Carlos Seco Serrano, *Principe de la Paz: Memorias* (Madrid, 1956), p. xxv; Candeloro, *Storia dell'Italia moderna*, I, p. 227; Cingari, *Giacobini e sanfedisti*, p. 185.

44 Geoffroy de Grandmaison, *L'Espagne et Napoléon*, 3 vols. (Paris, 1908, 1925, 1931), II, pp. 5, 39, 46, 66. Even a historian as keen to analyse the war in social-revolutionary terms as J.-R. Aymes agrees that the clergy were actively involved in the armed struggle against the French – 'La Guerra de la Independencia (1808–1814) y las postrimerías del Antiguo Régimen: ¿Sucesión forzosa o sucesión abierta?', *Crisis del antiguo regimén e industrialización en la España del siglo XIX, VII Coloquio de Pau de la crisis del antiguo regimén al franquismo* (Madrid, 1977), pp. 69, 72.

45 Gunther E. Rothenberg, *The Art of Warfare in the Age of Napoleon* (London, 1977), p. 220.

46 Suratteau, *Le Département du Mont-Terrible*, pp. 227–9; Marius Michaud, *La Contre-Révolution dans le Canton de Fribourg (1789–1815)* (Fribourg, 1978), pp. 231–5;

the role played by priests, in their case in the 'war of the fatherland' (*otechest-vennaya Voyna*) of 1812. The standard modern account on the popular militias, by L. N. Bychkov, mentions religious matters only in the context of the iconoclasm committed by French soldiers.[47] It is possible, of course, that the orthodox clergy were just less bellicose for some reason than their Catholic counterparts, although this seems improbable. Every now and again, however, there is a tantalising hint in the voluminous modern literature on the partisan war that the clergy – 'even the clergy', as A. N. Kochetkov puts it – were actively involved.[48] As early as August 1812 a band of guerrillas led by Father Sakharov and operating in the Mosal'sky uezd claimed to have killed 30 soldiers of Napoleon's Grand Army and to have taken prisoner 190. The major credit for organising the defence of Veren and district was given to the priest Ivan Skobeyev.[49] But these are just straws in the wind and the subject remains a mystery.

In Russia, as in Spain, as in many other parts of Europe, religion can be disentangled only incompletely and only with difficulty from nationalist sentiments. This identification was naturally most intimate in areas marked by inter-religious or inter-denominational conflict. In Spain the old sense of being in the front-line of Christendom against the Moors in the Mediterranean, the heretics in the North and the pagans in the New World, was still strong. The association of the French Revolution with a new and peculiarly dangerous threat to the true faith – atheism – gave both the war of 1793–5 and the more intense conflict of 1808–14 a traditional crusading flavour.[50] The transfer of old fervour to a fresh target was neatly symbolised by a ceremony in Cadiz on 25 July 1808, the feast-day of Saint James. The procession to a specially venerated statue of the saint was conducted as usual, with one important difference – the Moorish captives depicted lying prostrate at his feet had been reclothed in the uniforms of French soldiers.[51]

Bernhard, *Die Geschichte Vorarlbergs*, pp. 189–90, 249; Franz Kolb, *Das Tiroler Volk in seinem Freiheitskampf 1796–1797* (Innsbruck, Vienna, Munich, 1957), pp. 89–112, 331, 609; Turi, '*Viva Maria*', pp. 50, 119, 203; Lewis, *The Second Vendée*, p. 127; Giovanni Assereto, *La Repubblica Ligure: lotte politiche e problemi finanziari (1797–1799)* (Turin, 1975), pp. 56, 88; Blanning, *The French Revolution in Germany*, pp. 226–30.

[47] L. N. Bychkov, *Krestyanskoe partizanskoe dvizhenie v Otechestvennoy Voyne 1812 goda* (Moscow, 1954), p. 24.

[48] A. N. Kochetkov, 'Partizanskaya Voyna', *1812 god. K stopyatidesyatiletiyu otechestvennoy voyny. Sbornik statey*, ed. A. V. Fadeyev (Moscow, 1962), p. 172.

[49] *Ibid.*, p. 173.

[50] On the popular and religious nature of the first war against France (1793–5), see Antonio Dominguez Ortiz, *Sociedad y Estado en el siglo XVIII español* (Barcelona, 1976), p. 509.

[51] Grandmaison, *L'Espagne et Napoléon*, II, p. 100.

This association between national identity and religion was as widespread as the fighting itself. Just a few days earlier, on 16 July, a Spanish force had cut the French line of retreat at the ford of the Menjibar, in the manoeuvres which were to lead to the French disaster at the battle of Bailén three days later. The commander reminded his men that it was the anniversary of the battle of Las Navas, the day on which six centuries before Alfonso of Castile had defeated the Moors, saving Christianity and founding national independence.[52] In a country so divided by geography, climate, particularism and even language a common sense of being God's favoured defenders of the true faith provided some much-needed centripetal stability. As Geoffroy de Grandmaison put it: 'religion gives birth to martyrs, patriotism to heroes; when the two causes are identified, their disciples believe themselves to be invincible'.[53] So, right from the start, the war against Napoleon was given a religious character, as the junta of Seville proclaimed:

We are going to fight in defence of the Fatherland and of Religion and our actions must show that we are true Spaniards and Christians. This junta therefore urges the armies, the towns and persons of all classes to improve their habits, to be modest and to endeavour to appease the righteous wrath of God through...virtue and by means of ceaseless prayer.[54]

As this injunction suggests, the war against the French was to be not just a crusade against foreign atheism but also a movement for moral regeneration at home. Certainly the Spanish were identified with the Israelites and Napoleon with Anti-Christ, Nebuchadnezzar, Goliath and all the other Old Testament villains. Certainly it was argued that a nation which had smitten the Arians, Moslems, Lutherans, Calvinists and pagans could deal with this latest batch of God's foes. But the preachers also warned that divine assistance could not be taken for granted: it had to be earned by godly living and propitiatory worship. Otherwise the awful possibility loomed that a vengeful God would punish his chosen people with a new Babylonian captivity more terrible than anything the children of Israel had suffered. It was thought that a warning shot had been fired in the shape of the Andalusian plague of 1799–1800 but that the lesson had not been heeded.[55] In short, in Spain at least the war against the French was not just a crusade, it was also a religious revival.

In many other parts of Europe too the same dual phenomena can be observed. Everywhere, it seems, there was an intensification of popular religiosity, expressed in the redoubled popularity of confraternities, processions

---

[52] *Ibid.*, I, p. 310. [53] *Ibid.*, p. 195. [54] Lovett, *Napoleon*, I, p. 166.
[55] The sermons of the period have been the subject of an interesting if rather long-winded study by Alfredo Martinez Albiach, *Religiosidad hispana y sociedad borbónica* (Burgos, 1969); see especially chapter 1, section 2.

and pilgrimages. Particularly striking was the rapid increase in the incidence of miracles, often with overtly political implications. An early sign that trouble was brewing for the Revolution in the Vendée was the appearance of the Virgin in a tree at Saint-Laurent-de-la-Plaine. Local supporters of the Revolution, outraged by this affront to reason, promptly felled the sacred oak, only to find that the apparition nimbly moved to another tree. At that point, very sensibly, they gave up.[56] In Italy, in particular, miracles were often explicitly counter-revolutionary. At Lecce in Puglia, for example, the foundation of the Neapolitan Republic was marked by local republicans with the erection of a liberty tree. Shortly afterwards the rumour spread that the statue of St Oronzo in the square had indicated disapproval of the proceedings by turning his head away in disgust and by making a gesture which suggested that he was about to leave the town for good. Alarmed that they might lose his protection, a crowd tore down the liberty tree, processed through the streets with an image of the saint to cries of 'Long live Saint Oronzo! Long live the King!' and attacked the persons and property of local republicans.[57] All over the peninsula – and indeed all over Catholic Europe – the French learned to their cost that talking, weeping, blinking Madonnas, or whatever, were usually the prelude to riots.[58]

At a rather more sophisticated level this heightened religious atmosphere was expressed in the flourishing of cults, often with distinct regional if not national overtones. In Italy it was to cries of 'Viva San Marco!' that the Venetians rose against the new order.[59] In Spain there was a surge of enthusiasm for the cult of Saint James – Santiago – patron saint of the country, founder and continuing symbol of the unity and integrity of Spanish Catholicism.[60] In 1812 the Cortes of Cadiz gave official support to another potent cult when they recognised Saint Teresa as a second patron saint of the country.[61] This association of a particular religious cult with national identity was repeated in the Tyrol. Here it was the Sacred Heart of Jesus which bound the two together. Long established in the province, the cult had been fostered by the Jesuits during their popular missions of the mid-eighteenth century, suppressed during the Josephist campaign against baroque

[56] Tilly, *The Vendée*, p. 255.
[57] Lucarelli, *La Puglia nel Risorgimento*, II, pp. 103–4.
[58] For other examples, see *ibid.*, II, pp. 238, 299; Turi, '*Viva Maria*', pp. 133–4, 244, 257–62; Assereto, *La Repubblica Ligure*, p. 179; Blanning, *The French Revolution in Germany*, pp. 235–9.
[59] Jean Georgelin, *Venise au siècle des lumières* (Paris, 1978), p. 781; Bortolo Belotti, *Storia di Bergamo e dei Bergamaschi*, vol. III (Bergamo, 1959), p. 21.
[60] Albiach, *Religiosidad hispana*, p. 35.
[61] Grandmaison, *L'Espagne et Napoléon*, III, p. 199.

piety in the 1780s but revived after 1790. As the Tyrolean estates prepared to do battle with the advancing French, in the summer of 1796, they invoked divine assistance with a promise to celebrate the feast of the Sacred Heart each year with a special service. Within a year it was being observed in almost every community and quickly gained recognition as the Tyrol's religious-cum-national festival.[62]

This potent combination of religious and nationalist fervour in the Tyrol blazed again with spectacular results during the great rising of 1809 led by Andreas Hofer. Certainly material grievances played an important part in alienating the Tyroleans from their new Franco-Bavarian masters, but religion was prominent throughout. As Hofer's first proclamation stated, it was a war for 'God, Emperor and Fatherland'. After every victory the insurgent armies conducted services, processions and pilgrimages to give thanks for divine assistance and to supplicate for further marks of favour. At the battle of Bergisel on 13 August 1809, when 15,000 Tyrolean peasants defeated 20,000 French and Bavarian regulars, it was a Capuchin Father – Joachim Haspinger – who commanded the left wing. Moreover, for the Tyrolean leadership, as for the Spanish, this was a campaign for religious revival and moral regeneration as well as a war to reestablish the old regime.[63]

The same sort of impetus can also be found in the partisan war against the French in Russia in 1812. Right from the start Tsar Alexander I sought to give resistance to the French the character of a popular crusade. From his camp near Polotska he issued a manifesto on 6 July 1812 calling on the Russian people to join the militias which were about to be formed:

May every nobleman be for the enemy a Pozharsky, every priest a Palitsyn and every citizen a Minin.[64] Nobles, you have always been the saviours of your fatherland! Holy Synod and Clergy! By your fervent prayers you have always induced the Almighty to bestow His blessing on Russia. Russian Nation! Brave successors of the brave Slavs! On many occasions you have broken the teeth of the lions and tigers who were rash enough to attack you: unite all of you, one with another, and with faith in your heart and weapons in your hands no human power will be able to withstand you.[65]

---

[62] Kolb, *Das Tiroler Volk*, pp. 108–11; Heribert Raab, 'Zur Geschichte der Herz-Jesu-Verehrung im Mittelrheingebiet des 18. Jahrhunderts. Ein Beitrag zum Problem "Katholische Aufklärung und Frömmigkeit"', in Franz Rudolf Reichert, ed., *Festschrift für Anton Philipp Brück zum 60. Geburtstag* (Mainz, 1973), pp. 179–86.

[63] Karl Paulin, *Andreas Hofer und der Tiroler Freiheitskampf* (4th edn, Innsbruck, 1970), *passim*.

[64] Avraami Palitsyn was a monk who had distinguished himself in wars against Poland during the early seventeenth century, especially during the campaigns of 1612 when he had helped a popular militia led by D. Pozharsky and K. Minin.

[65] L. G. Beskrovny, *Narodnoe Opolchenie v otechestvennoy voyne 1812 goda. Sbornik dokumentov* (Moscow, 1962), p. 15.

The government made every possible use of the religious issue. During the earlier war of 1805–7 the orthodox clergy had launched a campaign to identify Napoleon as Anti-Christ. Russo-French rapprochement at Tilsit had put an abrupt stop to that, of course, but as war loomed in 1812 the exercise was repeated.[66] Now the Tsar seized every opportunity to demonstrate his own support for the faith. As he returned to Moscow at the end of July 1812, for example, he was met at the village of Pokorvsky by a priest carrying a crucifix in a silver dish. At once Alexander stopped his carriage, dismounted, knelt on the ground and kissed the sacred emblem. On arrival in Moscow he went straight to the cathedral to celebrate the Ascension of the Virgin and then on to another service to give thanks for the recent peace with the Turks (another mark of divine favour).[67] This religious theme was taken up by Alexander's subordinates. Count Rostopchin's first proclamation as governor of Moscow, issued on 24 August 1812, concluded with a prayer:

O Lord God who art in Heaven! Multiply the days of our virtuous sovereign on this earth. Be merciful to our all-Christian Russia, bless the efforts of its pious army, succour the zeal which inspires the valiant Russian people! Let our warriors destroy the enemy, let their power be multiplied, so that, protected by your Holy Cross, they may be victorious through it and by it.[68]

The excited tone of this and many other similar proclamations was heightened by news from the front that Napoleon's soldiers were up to their old tricks of blasphemy and iconoclasm.[69] When they reached Moscow, in the middle of September 1812, they were quick to demonstrate that the rumours were well-founded. Andrei Karfachevsky, an official who lived out the French occupation at the general post office, seeking to protect it, recorded: 'After pillaging churches they stabled horses, slaughtered cattle, and lodged wounded soldiers there; and having stripped the sacred icons of their frames, they bayoneted them and poured filth on them; they also committed other abominations which the tongue cannot mention.'[70]

The Russian authorities took good care that the last detail of every anti-religious outrage should be brought to the attention of those fortunate enough not to have first-hand knowledge. At the same time, the opportunity was also taken to link religious enthusiasm to xenophobia and national pride.

[66] E. V. Tarle, *1812 god: Napoleon. Nashestvie Napoleona na Rossiyu. Mikhail Illarionvich Kutuzov – Polkovodets i diplomat* (Moscow, 1959), pp. 623–5.
[67] M. Bogdanowitsch, *Geschichte des Feldzugs im Jahre 1812, nach den zuverlässigsten Quellen*, 3 vols. (Leipzig, 1863), I, pp. 163–4.
[68] Comte A. de Ségur, *Vie du comte Rostopchine, gouverneur de Moscou en 1812* (2nd edn, Paris, 1873), p. 215.
[69] Bychkov, *Krestyanskoe partizanskoe dvizhenie*, p. 24.
[70] A. Brett-James, *1812. Eyewitness Accounts of Napoleon's Defeat in Russia* (London 1966), pp. 186–7.

In the words of Rostopchin, it was 'the foreign vermin', 'the foreign rabble, the filthy scum', 'the French monsters' who had committed all those dreadful acts of irreligion he had recounted in all their gory details.[71] More specifically directed at the army were the religious ceremonies and the religious propaganda organised by its chaplains. On the eve of the battle of Borodino the holy icon of the Madonna of Smolensk was paraded up and down the Russian lines for all the army to see. That was done on the orders of General Kutuzov who prostrated himself before the icon, an example which was then followed by his entire staff.[72] In the French camp this spectacle was watched with a mixture of contempt and apprehension, for it was appreciated that the religious exultation of the Russian rank-and-file promised fanatical resistance on the battlefield the following day. Napoleon's aide-de-camp, Ségur, recorded the scene as follows:

In the course of the day [before Borodino] Napoleon noticed an extraordinary activity in the enemy's camp. In fact the entire army seemed to be armed and on foot. In the midst of the troops Kutuzov was seen advancing, surrounded by all religious and military pomp. The commander-in-chief had had the popes [priests] and archimandrites put on their richest, most majestic vestments – a heritage from the Greeks. They preceded him, bearing their precious religious symbols, in particular the beloved icon from Smolensk, which, they claimed, had been miraculously saved from the profanation of the sacrilegious French.

After describing how Kutuzov then harangued the crowd, depicting Napoleon as Anti-Christ, Ségur observed that all this mumbo-jumbo made a deep impression on the Russians because they were so primitive. He continued:

They were proud through lack of comparison, and credulous through lack of knowledge, worshipping images, as idolatrous as Christians can be; for, in order to bring their faith within the reach of the most brutal understanding, they had transformed a religion of the spirit, purely intellectual and moral, into something physical and material. This solemn spectacle, the exhortations of the officers, the benedictions of the priests, finally aroused the courage of the spectators to a fanatical heat. Down to the simplest soldier, they believed themselves consecrated by God to the defence of Heaven and the sacred soil of Russia.[73]

The battle of Borodino on 7 September 1812 proved to be one of the most bloody in the history of warfare. The French certainly lost 30,000 in killed

---

[71] Bogdanowitsch, *Geschichte des Feldzugs*, II, pp. 378–9.

[72] *Ibid.*, II, 159; L. G. Beskrovny and G. P. Meshcheryakovy (eds.), *Borodino, dokumenty, pis'ma, vospominaniya* (Moscow, 1962), pp. 375–6; F. Glinka, *Ocherki Borodinskogo srazheniya (vospominaniya o 1812 god)*, 2 vols. (Moscow, 1839), I, pp. 38–42.

[73] Count Philippe-Paul de Ségur, *Napoleon's Russian Campaign* (London, 1959), pp. 66–8.

and wounded and may have lost as many as 50,000; the Russians lost at east 40,000.[74] Did religion play a part in promoting this carnage by strengthening the Russian army's collective will to resist? In view of Ségur's account – and the accounts of other eye-witnesses – it seems reasonable to conclude that it did, although of course it can never be proved. The same sort of observation can be made about the role of religion in the extraordinary success of the Russian militias. In just 2–3 months a truly formidable number of men were assembled: 233,919 from the provinces officially designated for the militia, to which must be added 74,255 volunteers from the Ukraine (including 23,358 Cossacks), about 15,000 from the Don militias and 97,123 from provinces not included in the official scheme – a grand total of 420,297.[75] To what extent these partisans were moved to enlist by a concern for the faith is, of course, impossible to determine, especially given Soviet historians' lack of interest in the subject. Just the odd scrap of evidence, however, does suggest that religion was important for some. In August, 1812, for example, General Bagration reported to Rostopchin that 8,000 militia infantry and 1,500 cavalry had joined his unit and were conducting a reign of terror against the French 'because they plunder churches and burn villages'.[76] What Soviet historians do not dispute is the contribution made by the militia to the Russian victory. As A. N. Kochetkov has written: 'The partisan war played an enormous part in the rout of the Napoleonic army.'[77]

The role played by religion in the Russian War of 1812 is just one aspect of resistance to the revolutionary-Napoleonic regimes which requires much more attention. As this review of some of the possible links between religion and counter-revolution has sought to show, to demote the former to the status of superficial superstructure is to impede a full understanding of the latter.[78] Of course it cannot be maintained that all men always acted out of

---

[74] David G. Chandler, *The Campaigns of Napoleon* (London, 1966), p. 807.

[75] V. I. Babkin, 'Organizatsiya i voennye deystviya narodnogo opolcheniya v otechestvennoy voyne 1812 g.', *1812 god. K stopyatidesyatiletiyu otechestvennoy Voyny. Sbornik statey*, ed. A. V. Fadeyev (Moscow, 1962), p. 145.

[76] *Ibid.*, p. 146.

[77] Kochetkov, 'Partizanskaya Voyna', p. 178.

[78] Limitation of space has ruled out a discussion of inter-denominational conflicts and the counter-revolution, about which there is now a substantial and distinguished amount of literature available; see especially Lewis, *The Second Vendée*, and the numerous articles of James N. Hood, especially 'Protestant–Catholic relations and the roots of the first popular counter-revolutionary movement in France', *Journal of Modern History*, XLIII, 2 (1971). In a general review of the Midi Colin Lucas has written: 'By far the most striking feature of southern counter-revolution...was its rapid acquisition of a popular base. The principal agency everywhere seems to have been religion' – 'The Problem of the Midi in the French Revolution', *Transactions of the Royal Historical Society*, 5th ser., XXVIII (1978), p. 12.

concern for their faith. Of course the interaction of every other kind of motive, unconscious as well as conscious, social, economic and political as well as ideological, must be examined. Of course it cannot be denied that the rioters who shouted *Viva la religione!* as they looted, burned and murdered were driven primarily by economic misery and social resentment. On the other hand, it is unacceptably reductionist to maintain that religion was *never* anything more than the symptomatic wrapping for material grievance and class hatred. As Walter Abell observed about Arnold Hauser's materialist approach to the history of art:

It reduces the interpretation of art [religion] to something like the mathematical certainty of $2 + 2 = 4$. Relations as subtle as those of art [religion] to society might be better conceived in the algebraic terms of $2 + x = y$. The whole mystery of psychic existence, individual and collective, must be taken into account as a middle term interposed between the economic foundations and their ultimate effects upon culture.[79]

79 Walter Abell, Review of Arnold Hauser's *The Social History of Art*, *The Journal of Aesthetics and Art Criticism*, XI, 3 (1952), p. 265. Some pertinent remarks along the same lines and of equal relevance for the relationship between religion and society can be found in Richard Wollheim, *Art and Its Objects* (Harmondsworth, 1975), especially section 62; see also Roland Mousnier, 'Réflexions d'un historien à la lecture d'un manuel de sociologie', *Revue historique*, MXXXIV (1980), p. 400.

The role of Providence in evangelical social thought

BOYD HILTON

The following conversation is reported to have taken place between Thomas Chalmers, veteran leader of the Free Church of Scotland, and Richard Oastler, Tory paternalist and pioneer of Factory reform. The year is 1847 – Chalmers's last – and the subject is a Bill then before Parliament to limit the maximum hours of labour for women and children in the textile industry to ten hours per day.

Chalmers: I see this Bill is contrary to the Principles of Free Trade.
Oastler: Decidedly. If Free Trade be right, the Ten Hours' Bill is wrong.
Chalmers: I am a Free Trader, and cannot support any measure that is opposed to it.
Oastler: That is very strange. I thought you were a Christian.
Chalmers: And so I am.
Oastler: What! a Christian and a Free Trader. You surprise me.
Chalmers: How so?
Oastler: Why, Dr. Chalmers, it was from you I heard that Free Trade was anti-Christian. When a youth I read your *Astronomical Lectures*, and in one of them you treated on the responsibility of the rich...
Chalmers: What has that to do with Free Trade?
Oastler: Everything.[1]

Oastler's 'surprise' was of course a case of disingenuousness, since he knew perfectly well that Chalmers was and always had been a convinced exponent of *laissez-faire* social theory and Free Trade. Nevertheless, this 'misunderstanding' between the two men touches on an interesting problem of interpretation. Here were two of the most prominent evangelical spokesmen of their day taking opposite sides on the central issues of social policy. Does this mean that the possession of evangelical beliefs tells us nothing about a man's likely social and economic attitudes? Such a view would no doubt appeal to Edward Norman, who has argued that the social attitudes of the

---

[1] Oastler's report of the conversation is in Cecil Driver, *Tory Radical. The Life of Richard Oastler* (New York, 1946), pp. 468–9.

nineteenth-century clergy 'derived from the surrounding intellectual and political culture and not, as churchmen themselves always seem to assume, from theological learning'.[2] His case is presented with great panache and is inherently far from implausible, but this essay will attempt to show that, at least within the English and Scottish establishments, there was some correlation between the social and theological views of evangelicals.

I

So many evangelicals were prominent in charitable missions and benevolent societies during the first half of the nineteenth century that many historians have used the word 'evangelicalism' as though it were simply synonymous with philanthropy and paternalism. In his recent study of attitudes to poor relief, for example, Raymond Cowherd has contrasted 'the sentimental benevolence of the Evangelical humanitarians' with the callous brutality of the Utilitarian 'natural law reformers', though he is forced to concede that the former became increasingly susceptible to Utilitarian social theory after the Napoleonic Wars.[3] Oastler's colleagues in the Ten Hours Movement, Lord Shaftesbury, Michael Thomas Sadler, and Parson Bull of Byerly, all presented this 'acceptable face' of evangelicalism to the world, being among the most outspoken opponents of the orthodox political economy of the period. Sadler denounced in turn the Law of Population, the New Poor Law, Free Trade, usury, and competition. The age was intoxicated with a 'passion for cheapness', which only benefited men on fixed incomes, while the fashionable Bullionism merely enabled rich capitalists to keep down aspiring members of the lower middle class by restricting paper credit. Sadler's biographer and *alter ego*, the paternalist Robert Benton Seeley, was if anything even more outspoken. Malthus's doctrine of the 'preventive check' to population, which held that the poor could limit their own numbers by abstaining from sex, was 'a direct inspiration of the Father of lies – of him whose grand occupation and delight it is, to render earth a foretaste of Hell'. Seeley preferred the political economy of the Chinese, based as it was on the desirability of human multiplication. Seeley and Sadler did not particularly wish to make the working class more moral, but they knew that the only way to do it was for morality to be 'supplied by hope, and inculcated by kindness'. If labourers were forced into despair, on the other hand, they would become ever more reckless. 'In short, deal paternally with your

---

[2] E. R. Norman, *Church and Society in England 1770–1970. A Historical Study* (Oxford, 1976), p. 10.
[3] Raymond G. Cowherd, *Political Economists and the English Poor Laws* (Athens, Ohio, 1977), pp. 38, 45, and *passim*.

people, and they will repay your care. Feel for them; supply those wants which they cannot supply for themselves; guard them from the oppression of those who would "make haste to be rich".[4] Oastler's paternalist rhetoric was similar. 'The Bible is put out, and Miss Martineau is come in', was his sour response to the New Poor Law. A 'Demon called *Liberalism*' was abroad in the land, comprising the 'March of Intellect, Political Economy, Free Trade, Liberal Principles', and it was 'destroying the peace of the cottage and the happiness of the Palace'. More vividly than anyone else he denounced the mechanistic, self-acting, atomistic philosophy of his day, which was divorcing the profit motive from the spiritual parts of human nature, and destroying the older view that men are all members of one another in an organic social harmony.[5]

Then there was Henry Drummond, an evangelical banker and Member of Parliament 1810–13 and 1847–60. He was a firm supporter of the Old Poor Law, especially the generous system of outdoor relief known by the name of 'Speenhamland', and considered that its extension to Ireland would provide '*the* cure for that country's problems'.[6] He preached and practised the virtues of landed paternalism within what he saw as an organic and hierarchical society, setting up allotments for labourers as early as 1818. Despite his decision to endow a Chair of Political Economy at Oxford University in 1825, the first incumbent of which was one of the most influential of the 'dismal scientists', Nassau Senior, Drummond himself vilified 'orthodox' political economy with its *laissez-faire* individualism. He was scornful of *economistes* like James Mill, who considered merchants – mere men of the world – to be more significant in the scale of national wealth than landlords, and was terrified that Britain might be on the way to becoming 'one Manchester or Birmingham'. Cain's ancestors, he liked to remark, had been merchants, whereas Seth's had been yeomen. When the Corn Laws were repealed in 1846, Drummond prophesied

the destruction of all those things which God has instituted in a Christian monarchy as certainly as those things have been overthrown in France: such as, the annihilation of entails, that is, of family and hereditary interests as distinguished from merely personal interests; the destruction of primogeniture; the ruin of many widows and orphans: the minute subdivision of lands as in France; an universal attack on tithes, and on the compulsory support of cathedrals and parish churches. It is now to be

---

[4] R. B. Seeley, *Memoirs of the Life and Writings of Michael Thomas Sadler* (London, 1842), pp. 610 and 621. See J. C. Gill, *The Ten Hours Parson. Christian Social Action in the Eighteen-Thirties* (London, 1959), pp. 131–2 and 178–93; J. C. Gill, *Parson Bull of Byerly* (London, 1963), pp. 62–77.

[5] Driver, *Tory Radical*, pp. 293–7 and 430–4.

[6] Henry Drummond to Robert Peel, 17 Dec. 1824, Peel Papers, British Library Add. MSS, 40371, fo. 159.

shown how by all these ways Britain becomes the head of that system which God has denounced by His prophets under the name of Tyre.[7]

But if some of the most prominent paternalists were evangelicals, the most prominent evangelicals – that is, the 'Saints' or Clapham Sect – almost all lent support, as well as an aura of righteousness, to orthodox political economy. They have often been castigated by historians for having shown humanitarian sympathies abroad and callous indifference at home, for condemning negro slavery and condoning wage slavery. There were about thirty 'Saints' in Parliament, and most of them clearly favoured Free Trade and 'little' government, while repudiating all forms of economic paternalism. This fact has been partially obscured by Wilberforce's vote in favour of the notoriously protective Corn Law of 1815, but in fact, most 'Saints' opposed that Law, despite their general loyalty to the Tory Government of the day, and Wilberforce's own support was given most reluctantly, after he had opposed the second reading.[8] By the 1820s most evangelicals who were not also Ultra Tories were in favour of Corn Law repeal, and the leading parliamentary advocate of Free Trade after Ricardo's death in 1823 was William Wolryche Whitmore, a Shropshire evangelical. The *Christian Observer*, the mouthpiece of the Clapham Sect, defended Free Trade as 'a truly Christian system of intercourse', and warmly applauded the 'Liberal Tory' tariff reforms of Huskisson and Robinson after 1823.[9]

Meanwhile the main hero of the movement for 'economical reform' between 1807 and about 1822 was Henry Bankes, a close associate of Wilberforce. He began as Chairman of the Finance Committee set up by Perceval in 1807 to inquire into salaries and sinecures, and was mainly supported in that work by his fellow evangelicals Henry Thornton and Thomas Baring. During the 1820s he deserted the 'Saints' in order to take up an extreme anti-Catholic stance, and left the leadership of the campaign for retrenchment to the Radical Joseph Hume, whose humourless pedantry and lack of moral fervour largely destroyed its appeal. Meanwhile the Resumption of Cash Payments in 1821, which was the complement of *laissez-faire* 'Liberal' commercial policy, was hailed by the *Christian Observer* as a 'triumph of truth and justice over clamour and prejudice, and sordid interest'.[10] The 'Saints' were also anxious to see the Usury Laws repealed, and were opposed to the Government dispensing financial aid to business firms which

---

[7] Henry Drummond, *Letter to the Bishop of Winchester on Free Trade* (London, 1846), pp. 17–18 and 23–4.

[8] Ian Bradley, 'The Politics of Godliness: Evangelicals in Parliament 1784–1832' (Oxford D.Phil., 1974), pp. 215–17.

[9] *Christian Observer*, XXII (1823), 131; *ibid.*, XXVI (1826), 191; Bradley, 'Politics of Godliness', pp. 158 and 215–18.

[10] *Christian Observer*, XVIII (1819), 342; Bradley, 'Politics of Godliness', pp. 139–47.

found themselves in temporary difficulties. In their view the middle classes, like the poor, should *stand on their own feet.*

Not surprisingly such moralists distrusted all forms of sentimental paternalism. Henry Thornton and Charles Grant showed their indifference by falling asleep while Robert Owen was outlining his scheme for New Lanark to them.[11] Hannah More argued that poverty was 'ordained' by Providence and that the poor were especially favoured in God's sight. Wilberforce countered the 'greatest happiness' principle by claiming that social inequality 'combines the greatest measure of temporal comforts and spiritual privileges'.[12] It is true that the elder Peel's Factory Act of 1802 has some claims to be considered an evangelical initiative but, as Ian Bradley points out, there is no clear evidence that the Staffordshire philanthropist was in fact an evangelical. Wilberforce and his associates seem to have opposed the attempts by Whitbread and Sheridan in 1795 to secure a minimum wage, and by George Rose in 1808 to maintain the earnings of cotton weavers.[13] Thomas Babington, who came from an important family of 'Saints', denounced the 'Speenhamland' system of wage supplements,[14] and most of his colleagues were in agreement. The general feeling was that poverty was the fault of those who suffered from it, as Gisborne opined in his so-called *Friendly Observations* to the poor,[15] and Wilberforce endlessly repeated. Then again, it was an evangelical who argued that those working-men who formed combinations 'insult the majesty of Heaven', by showing discontent with their divinely appointed lot, 'and bring down the curse of God among themselves'.[16] Only when there were obvious *villains* did these 'Saintly' evangelicals get excited about social reform, as Bradley points out.[17] Thus they were prepared to campaign on behalf of climbing boys and negro slaves, though even here one cannot be sure that their most urgent desire was not to save the souls of the chimney sweeps and planters, rather than the lives of their victims. They were anxious to curb royal extravagance and impeach corrupt ministers, prohibit bear-baiting and duelling, and the abuse of the Sabbath, improve the efficacy of judicial punishment, and generally

---

[11] R. I. and S. Wilberforce, *The Life of William Wilberforce* (London, 1838), IV, p. 91.

[12] Quoted in Basil Willey, *Nineteenth-Century Studies, Coleridge to Matthew Arnold* (London, 1949), p. 133.

[13] Bradley, 'Politics of Godliness', p. 218.

[14] *Hansard*, 1st ser., XXXII (1816), 1054.

[15] Thomas Gisborne, *Friendly Observations Addressed to the Manufacturing Population of Great Britain* (3rd edn, London, 1827), p. 15; Chalmers to Wilberforce, 9 Feb. 1818, *A Selection from the Correspondence of the Late Thomas Chalmers*, ed. William Hanna (Edinburgh, 1853), pp. 93–6.

[16] Quoted in E. R. Wickham, *Church and People in an Industrial City* (London, 1957), p. 106.

[17] Bradley, 'Politics of Godliness', pp. 192–3.

'suppress vice'. And of course they wanted to see new churches built in the industrial cities, for they believed that the poor could only benefit from *standing on their own feet* if the well-to-do were ready to provide them with moral suasion and spiritual exhortation. While *real* paternalists like Owen assumed that the characters of the poor would improve automatically with the conditions of their existence, *moral* paternalists like the 'Saints' saw the need to force morality on the lower classes, and considered that a state of poverty and suffering was most likely to make them receptive. At all events, it was man's soul rather than his body which members of the Clapham Sect sought to rescue. As one of the most outspoken parliamentary evangelicals of the late eighteenth century put it: 'How much more to be dreaded is a famine of the Word of Truth, than a dearth of earthly food.'[18]

'I should consider the salvation of a single soul of more value than the deliverance of a whole empire from pauperism', echoed Chalmers,[19] the most uncompromising of all opponents of legal relief to the poor. Mistakenly described by his latest biographer as a paternalist who was opposed to *laissez-faire* Liberalism and political economy,[20] Chalmers nevertheless thought that the 1834 Poor Law, with its workhouse test, 'less eligibility', and separation of the sexes, was too lenient towards the pauper.[21] As for the old 'Speenhamland' system, with its outdoor relief, rates in aid of wages, and family allowances, Chalmers considered it to be 'a moral nuisance, a bane, a burden, an excrescence on the body politic, a sore leprosy, which has spread itself over ten thousand parishes of England'.[22] In all this he was roundly supported, not only by Wilberforce, but by *most* well-to-do evangelicals including the future Archbishop of Canterbury, John Bird Sumner, whose *Treatise on the Records of the Creation* (1816) and *Encyclopaedia Britannica* article (1824) had greatly helped to popularise Malthusian population theory.[23]

18 Richard Hill to a clergyman, 10 Nov. 1800, Edwin Sidney, *The Life of Sir Richard Hill* (London, 1839), p. 472.
19 Chalmers to James Brown, 30 Jan. 1819, Edinburgh University Library, DC.2.57, fo. 62.
20 Stewart J. Brown, *Thomas Chalmers and the Godly Commonwealth in Scotland* (Oxford, 1982), pp. 189, 194–9, and 225.
21 Thomas Chalmers, *The Sufficiency of a Parochial System, without a Poor Rate, for the Right Management of the Poor* (1841), in *The Works of Thomas Chalmers*, 25 vols. (Glasgow, 1836–42), XXI, pp. 139–53.
22 Thomas Chalmers, *A Speech Delivered on the 24th of May, 1822, before the General Assembly of the Church of Scotland, Explanatory of the Measures which have been Successfully Pursued in St. John's Parish, Glasgow, for the Extinction of its Compulsory Pauperism* (Glasgow, 1822), pp. 22 and 48.
23 R. Soloway, *Prelates and People. Ecclesiastical Social Thought in England 1783–1852* (London, 1969), pp. 96–9; R. S. Dell, 'Social and Economic Theories and Pastoral Concerns of a Victorian Archbishop', *Journal of Ecclesiastical History*, XVI (1965), 196–208.

It was only in the 1830s, when evangelicals of a rather different stamp began to enter Parliament, that we can identify some of them with paternalism, with social rather than merely moral reform. These M.P.s are sometimes called *Recordites* after their popular newspaper, the *Record*, whose editor was James Haldane. They were galvanised to political action by the drift of 'Liberal' reform, in which the Clapham Sect seemed to be conniving, and were particularly hostile to Roman Catholic Emancipation in 1829. There is much evidence in Bradley's thesis to suggest that the shift to paternalism among parliamentary evangelicals after 1830 was linked to the growing prominence of *Recorditism* and crypto-*Recorditism*. Sadler, who tried eight times to secure Poor Laws for Ireland between 1830 and 1832, was not himself a *Recordite*, but he supported the *Recordite* campaign in Parliament, and was in turn backed firmly by its Scottish leader, John Briscoe. His Select Committee, which marked the effective starting-point of the 'Ten Hours' campaign, included the 'prophetic' *Recordites*, Spencer Perceval junior, Estcourt, and Inglis, as well as Weyland and G. H. Rose, both frequent supporters.[24] Seeley – who wrote for the *Record* – Bickersteth, and Bull all supported the Ten Hours Movement, and Ashley, who took over the leadership of the movement after Sadler's removal from Parliament in 1832, has been called a crypto-*Recordite*, though he sometimes found that newspaper's language a little too strong.

The Ten Hours Movement indeed shows up more clearly than any other the divergence within Anglican evangelicalism on social issues. Ian Rennie has demonstrated that most evangelicals disliked its paternalist implications, and that they preferred to salve their consciences with fresh appeals to 'No Popery', which they affected to believe was a greater evil than the industrial system.[25] The *Christian Observer* gave some grudging support to Sadler, while insisting that protection of women and children must not be seen as a precedent for overthrowing the 'sacred rule' of non-interference in such matters. There are even indications that, in those circles, concern for the souls of the exploiting factory owners was actually a more potent argument in favour of reform than the plight of the employees. As is well known, Ashley was to complain over and over again in the 1840s that he could win very little help from most of the evangelicals in Parliament.[26] 'If Free Trade be right, the Ten Hours' Bill is wrong': clearly Oastler's observation touched on a central split in the thought of Anglican evangelicals.

[24] Bradley, 'Politics of Godliness', p. 255.
[25] Ian S. Rennie, 'Evangelicalism and English Public Life 1823–1850' (Toronto Ph.D., 1962; typescript in Cambridge University Library), pp. 390–4.
[26] Edwin Hodder, *The Life and Work of the Seventh Earl of Shaftesbury*, 3 vols. (London, 1886), I, pp. 325 and 346.

II

Generalisations are always dangerous in the history of ideas, but it seems clear that most 'Saints' supported Chalmers's *laissez-faire* views, while most *Recordites* would have supported Oastler's condemnation of them. This suggests that the divergence may have had theological connotations, since 'Saints' and *Recordites* were on opposite sides of the only serious theological division within Anglican evangelicalism.

Doctrinally evangelicalism was a simple and rather mechanical religion, in which souls were thought to be suspended between opposing forces of Sin and Grace, and destined either for Heaven or for Hell, both very literally conceived. All evangelicals held that Heaven was won by being justified, that justification came through faith in Christ, and that Christ's Atonement was – in their own mechanical language – the 'hinge of Christian truth'. All evangelicals believed that Divine Providence governed the world, though there was some disagreement as to whether or not Satan was independent of it: whether the contest for each individual soul was between God and Satan or 'merely' between Christ and Satan. However, the really important division, which was not a clear-cut one doctrinally, was between the respectable Clapham Sect and its followers on the one hand, and the pentecostal, pre-millenarian, adventist, and revivalist elements on the other.[27] These can for convenience be termed the 'moderate' and 'extreme' factions within evangelicalism. As Edward Thompson has shown so memorably with respect to evangelical Methodism,[28] the emotion and enthusiasm of the 'extremists' slipped easily into a masochistic chiliasm, a revelling in pain as though it were a mark of grace. Their cult of leadership, and increasingly apostolic and ecclesiological attitudes, marked them off still further from the 'moderate' individualists of Clapham. Pre-millenarianism can be found in the pages of the Dissenting *Evangelical Magazine*, the *Morning Watch*, and the less 'extreme' but strongly Calvinist *Record*, which took over from the 'moderate' *Christian Observer* as the best-selling evangelical journal during the 1830s. Within middle-class Anglican circles, the 'extreme' evangelicalism spread rapidly from the mid-1820s onwards, thanks to economic alarms, Catholic Emancipation, the crisis over Parliamentary Reform, cholera, and other 'signs' of

---

[27] On this split see D. N. Hempton, 'Evangelicalism and Eschatology', *Journal of Ecclesiastical History*, XXXI (1980), 179–94; Elizabeth Jay, *The Religion of the Heart. Anglican Evangelicalism and the Nineteenth-Century Novel* (Oxford, 1979), pp. 88–105; David Newsome, *The Parting of Friends. A study of the Wilberforces and Henry Manning* (London, 1966), pp. 10–13. S. C. Orchard, 'English Evangelical Eschatology 1790–1850' (Cambridge Ph.D., 1969), especially pp. 75–104.

[28] E. P. Thompson, *The Making of the English Working Class* (London, 1965), pp. 350–400.

an impending Divine initiative. The antinomianism of these 'extremists', and their often apocalyptic other-worldliness, undoubtedly alienated many serious-minded evangelicals of the younger generation, and helped to push potential leaders such as Gladstone, Stanley, Acland, Newman, Manning, and Robert Wilberforce away towards the High Church.

Doctrinally the most important point of issue between 'moderate' and 'extreme' evangelicals was the question of whether Providence operates 'generally' and predictably through natural and immutable laws of cause and effect, or 'specially' by *ad hoc* and *ad hominem* interventions in terrestrial affairs.[29] Of course the distinction was not a rigid one, and many of those who thought of Providence as working neutrally through physical or secondary laws, also reserved a place for Special Interventions from time to time, especially in judgments on whole nations,[30] and also in the vital matter of securing individual conversions. But by and large, the Clapham 'Saints' believed that 'the judicial and penal visitations of Providence occur...in the way of natural consequence'.[31] God had instituted a permanent moral law on earth, a 'natural' and predictable in-built system of rewards and punishments appropriate to good and bad behaviour. Almost always in the case of individuals, and sometimes in the case of communities, suffering was the logical consequence of specifically bad behaviour. It could therefore incite as well as guide men to virtuous conduct in the future, but they must of course take the opportunity to examine their own actions in the light of their sufferings. As Chalmers put it:

It is the constancy of nature that gives such confidence to the experimental philosopher in the manipulations of chemistry. And it is just the same constancy in the world of mind, or because of the doctrine of necessity realized there also, that we enter with any comfort or confidence on the management of human nature. It is because of this, that in our treatment of the human spirit, we ply all those various elements of hope, and fear, and conscience, and a sense of interest, and everything else that we have found to be of efficacy in leading our fellows on to the determinations of prudence and of virtue.[32]

---

[29] See Jacob Viner, *The Role of Providence in the Social Order* (Philadelphia, 1972), pp. 1–26 on Providentialist thought in the eighteenth century.

[30] For examples see G. F. A. Best, 'The Evangelicals and the Established Church in the Early Nineteenth Century', *Journal of Theological Studies*, new ser., x (1959), 64–6; Owen Chadwick, *The Victorian Church*, 2 vols. (London, 1966–70), I, pp. 451–2.

[31] William Wilberforce to Earl Bathurst, 4 July 1816, *Report on the Manuscripts of Earl Bathurst, Preserved at Cirencester Park* (Historical Manuscripts Commission 76th report: London, 1923), p. 418.

[32] Thomas Chalmers, *Institutes of Theology*, 2 vols. (London, 1849), II, p. 337. See Josiah Pratt in *The Thought of the Evangelical Leaders. Notes of the Discussions in the Eclectic Society of London during the Years 1798–1814*, ed. J. H. Pratt (1856; repr. Edinburgh, 1978), pp. 468–9.

Pre-millennialists, however, regarded this sort of attitude as blindness to the workings of Providence: 'The irreligious world mocks at, and the religious world' – meaning especially the Clapham Sect – '*cannot see*, God's hand in anything, either in pestilence, state, or Church.'[33] For them, temporal misfortunes were always 'Special' or 'Particular' Judgments on men and nations, inflicted for unspecifiable spiritual offences, and requiring miraculous suspensions of natural law. One should react to suffering with resignation, even with masochistic gratitude, and also of course with redoubled devotions and spiritual self-abasement, but one was not to suppose that the pain was a consequence of our own mistakes (as distinct from our general sinfulness), or that one could prevent sufferings in future by acting in accordance with natural laws. Providence always acted miraculously, and it was presumptuous to expect to comprehend its dispensations, or to seek, by rational and prudential calculations of one's behaviour, to avoid its blows in future.

We can see this distinction at work in a debate conducted by the *Christian Observer* on the food shortages of 1800. For an age obsessed by Malthusian predictions of mass starvation, the most potent weapon of a wrathful Providence was obviously famine. Most contributors to the debate followed Adam Smith in blaming the shortages on the economic selfishness of forestallers, regraters, and monopolists, in whom was manifest the original depravity of mankind, but one correspondent (styled 'B.T.') objected that to blame men was to deny 'the hand of God so awfully displayed in the dispensation'. 'B.T.' argued that famine should be regarded as a special retribution for national sins, such as participation in the Slave Trade, whereas moderate evangelicals claimed that it was the 'probable' and predictable consequence of specific wrong behaviour on the part of individuals.[34]

Now it may be that these different attitudes to the way in which Providence operates can help to explain why evangelicals took different approaches to social and economic policy. 'B.T.' was one of the few contributors to the *Christian Observer* in 1802 who defended England's 'humane' Old Poor Law, and it seems to be the case generally that those who held an interventionist view of Providence, who saw God as constantly directing earthly affairs by special warnings and judgments, also believed that governments on earth should take a similarly interventionist approach to social and economic problems. 'Moderate' evangelicals, on the other hand, matched their *laissez-faire* or neutral conception of Providence with a similar approach to the 'condition of England'. They wished to make society operate as closely to 'nature' as possible by repealing interventionist laws. Then men could be left to work out their own salvation, to find their own peace, and joy, and

---

33 Henry Drummond to W. H. Blunt, Mar. 1832, MS. in my possession.
34 *Christian Observer*, 1 (1802), 226–30.

spiritual life in the course of their worldly duties. *Laissez-faire* and Free Trade were necessary in order to ensure that God's mechanical universe operated as He intended it to.

In other words, 'moderates' believed that ninety-nine out of a hundred events were predictable consequences of human behaviour. Governments should interfere with a man's life as little as possible, so that he can exercise 'self-help' – the only means to salvation, both spiritually and economically – in a world beset with temptation, and meant for trial and judgment. 'Extremists' saw no such predictability, but a perpetual (and to our mortal eyes, arbitrary) governance, and thought that those whom it had pleased God to place at the head of temporal affairs, should exercise a similar measure of control over society.

III

All the paternalist evangelicals cited above can be located on the 'extremist' side of the movement. Shaftesbury was a fervent pre-millenarian, obsessed with prophecy, the conversion of the Jews, and the imminence of the Second Advent.[35] Seeley was a prominent pre-millenarian prophet, convinced that Divine vengeance was about to strike the nation. Pauperism was 'God's scourge that our own hands are twisting, for the purposes of severe chastisement'. 'The season of sunshine and of calm is too palpably past: the rain is about to descend: the floods to come, and the winds to blow.'[36] He held the greatest contempt for Chalmers, while Chalmers in turn attacked Seeley with uncharacteristic bitterness: 'They who divorce Theology from Science are, in effect,... the enemies of both.'[37] Chalmers's Christian version of political economy was scientific, based on a theory of constant law in the universe, and therefore excluded the interventionist God of the paternalists.

Another paternalist, Henry Drummond, was even more passionately associated with the pentecostal wing of evangelicalism. In 1825–6, alarmed by the insane speculation that was taking place in Latin American mining shares, he began, in his own words, 'to direct attention to the events connected with the close of the Christian dispensation'.[38] He was a founder member of, and chief host to, Edward Irving's Catholic Apostolic Church, of which he became in turn an Apostle, Evangelist, Prophet, and finally Angel, and his

---

[35] Geoffrey B. A. M. Finlayson, *The Seventh Earl of Shaftesbury 1801–1885* (London, 1981), pp. 153–71, and *passim*.

[36] Robert Benton Seeley, *The Perils of the Nation. An Appeal to the Legislature, the Clergy, and the Higher and Middle Classes* (London, 1843), p. 399.

[37] *Ibid.*, pp. 144–8 and 399: [Thomas Chalmers], 'The Political Economy of the Bible', *North British Review*, II (1845), 3.

[38] Henry Drummond, *Abstract Principles of Revealed Religion* (London, 1845), p. iii.

main preoccupation henceforward was to interpret the meaning of Providence through 'Speaking in Tongues'. He now bitterly attacked his former friends, the 'moderate' evangelicals of Clapham, 'scribes and pharisees; lovers of their own institutions, and of wealth; boasters of their charitable, and missionary exploits'; complacent prigs who thought they could co-operate with God to bring about the millennium, instead of leaving all to the Divine initiative.[39] Possibly his decision to endow a Chair of Economics was one which he would not have taken after his conversion to 'Irvingism'. As early as 1826 he was admonishing a friend from Clapham that,

like other branches of Politics, [political economy] is a ticklish one for a Christian to meddle with: they cannot be conducted upon Christian principles, nor ever will be, till *The* King reigns in righteousness, Sin and its concomitant curse is removed from the earth, the Lion and the lamb lay down beside each other, this world has received its baptism of fire.[40]

His mentor Edward Irving and their *Morning Watch* newspaper frequently attacked the Clapham evangelicals for their indifference to the sufferings of the poor.

The one Prime Minister who can indisputably claim the title of 'evangelical' is Spencer Perceval. Assassinated in 1812, he was unable to participate in the main debates over social policy, but it is clear that he would have opposed the 'Liberal' and *laissez-faire* tendencies of the post-1815 period. He was sympathetic to proposals for minimum wage legislation, and wished to extend the elder Peel's Bill to protect cotton apprentices. Furthermore he was an Anti-Bullionist and a Protectionist. It is therefore not surprising to find that his theology, like that of his more florid son, veered towards the 'extremist' and that, 'like many of the "weaker vessels among the evangelicals",...he was a keen student of biblical prophecy',[41] identifying Napoleon as the harlot 'who rides upon the beast', and anticipating the end of the world in 1926. He wrote to a friend:

If you will take up your map, and look at the countries where the French power and opinions have made their greatest impression, I think you will be of opinion that they have been raised up by Providence for the overthrow of the Popish superstitions:

---

[39] Henry Drummond, *A Defence of the Students of Prophecy* (London, 1828), p. 116. On Drummond see W. H. Oliver, *Prophets and Millennialists. The Uses of Biblical Prophecy in England from the 1790s to the 1840s* (Auckland, 1978), pp. 107–10; Orchard, 'English Evangelical Eschatology', pp. 75–84.

[40] Henry Drummond to Zachary Macaulay, 15 Nov. 1826, MS. in Huntington Library, California, MY 218.

[41] Denis Gray, *Spencer Perceval. The Evangelical Prime Minister 1762–1812* (Manchester, 1963), pp. 18–19. On Perceval's son, see Charles C. F. Greville, *A Journal of the Reigns of King George IV and King William IV*, ed. Henry Reeve, 3 vols. (4th edn, London, 1875), III, pp. 41, 123, and 331–3.

for except with some few exceptions, *which may have been permitted to prevent this object of God's Providence from being too strikingly apparent,* you will find their progress most destructive where the Popish superstitions most prevailed.[42]

What is strikingly apparent about this comment is Perceval's evident belief that Providence operated in a discretionary manner. Unlike Wilberforce, Simeon, and Chalmers, for example, he did not share the natural theologian's confidence in the existence of constant laws at work in the universe, laws which would be less obscure if only governments did not interfere with ones of their own.

A more telling illustration comes from an interesting correspondence between the Scottish evangelical M.P., Sir George Sinclair, and the Tory *Quarterly* reviewer, John Wilson Croker. In 1840 Sinclair wrote a 'sentimental' – that is to say, a paternalist – pamphlet on poor relief, which he sent to his friend. Now Croker was a lifelong champion of prescription (the only way to keep 'everything in its place') and a scourge of Utilitarianism, which he thought would reduce society to 'a fortuitous concourse of atoms'. Yet this supposed opponent of *laissez-faire* took a much more robust view of pauperism than Sinclair, approving of the Utilitarian New Poor Law of 1834. His tone is grimmer than that of evangelical moralists like Chalmers, but the perspective is very similar:

It is the first Law of nature, the primal curse of an angry, but all-wise Creator, that we should earn our bread in toil and pain, and by the sweat of our brow...It is meet and right, and our bounden duty, to help the weak, and to alleviate distress, as far as our means allow; but to tell the working-classes that any power can relieve them from their state of *want and dependence* is to impugn, as it seems to me, the dispensations of Providence, and to disorder the frame of society.[43]

It would be foolish to suggest that Croker was a closet or unconscious evangelical, even though he *was* a friend of Drummond and Sinclair, and greatly admired Wilberforce's *Practical View*. Nevertheless his 'beautiful' deathbed realisation that 'the entire depravity of man and the eternal justice of God could never have been reconciled without a Mediator',[44] reminds us that in that period, even conventionally pious, 'High-and-Dry' Anglicans of the old school were susceptible to an evangelical view of man's condition.

More important in the present context, why did the devout evangelical Sinclair *not* subscribe to Chalmers's and Wilberforce's severe views on poor relief? A clue is provided by the comments of Sinclair's friend and biographer on his occasional religious doubts and dilemmas:

[42] Gray, *Spencer Perceval*, pp. 45–6.
[43] Croker to Sinclair, Aug. 1840, James Grant, *Memoirs of Sir George Sinclair* (London, 1870), pp. 219–24.
[44] *Ibid.*, p. 228.

At times his faith was clouded, and the prosperity of the wicked, and the preponderating mass of evil and suffering in the world, perplexed him sorely and disquieted his spirits, for he took to heart the sins and sufferings of others, and their lack of advantages and good moral influences, and his heart was full of pity even for the outcasts of society, whom he always regarded as objects of compassion.[45]

In other words, Sinclair's soft-hearted attitude to pauperism, his compassion for those who suffer, was linked to his indignation that wicked men often succeed. He thought that life was unjust or, as his biographer put it, 'at times he was not free from perplexities and painful feelings in regard to the moral government of God'. Croker had no such doubts, and neither did most 'moderate' or 'natural law' evangelicals. They were confident that *laissez-faire* policies would reveal a providential order, and that that order would be a *just* one. Sinclair took a more paternalist approach because he could not help doubting the efficacy or fairness of God's judicial machinery. It is no surprise to find, therefore, that he was a supporter of the *Recordite* campaigns in Parliament, and a close friend of such prophetic writers as George Mandeville, 3rd Duke of Manchester, and Robert Jocelyn, 6th Earl of Roden. It has already been suggested that *Recordite* evangelicalism was distinguished from the mainstream by its rejection of a Newtonian or 'natural law' conception of Providence. Its view was rather that God exercised a perpetual superintendence by means of 'Special Providences'. The task of temporal governments was to imitate the Divine, to exercise their own paternal superintendence in the light of these Providences – to interpret them, and legislate accordingly. Croker meanwhile had no patience with the doctrine of Special Providence, even though it once seemed that his health might have been miraculously affected:[46] 'To look for Special Providences in such trivial matters, seems to us to mistake wholly any individual man's share in the general distribution of God's infinite but equal dispensations.'[47]

'Infinite but *equal*': this was what Sinclair could not be certain about, but James Grant, his biographer, suggests that his prayers were finally answered, and that he too came at last to believe in the 'equality' of God's dispensations, in permanent laws of natural justice. This may explain why in the 1840s he switched to a more robust, *laissez-faire* approach to poverty. In a pamphlet of 1849 on the Poor Laws, Sinclair regretted having supported the extension of the Poor Law to Scotland, 'unmindful of the solemn warnings, inculcated ...by...Dr. Chalmers, who clearly saw and emphatically predicted the ruinous consequences which the Poor Law would necessarily produce'. Now he accepted that compulsory assessments were destroying all industry,

---

45 *Ibid.*, p. 468.
46 Myron F. Brightfield, *John Wilson Croker* (London, 1940), p. 116.
47 [J. W. Croker], 'Life of Wilberforce', *Quarterly Review*, LXII (1838), 247.

all prudence, temperance, contentment, gratitude, veracity, and natural affection in the workers, as well as all benevolence in the rich.[48]

IV

If anything, Chalmers's self-help philosophy hardened with age. In his last community experiment, the West Port scheme of 1844, he allowed even less *material* relief to be given to the poor than he had done at St John's during the early 1820s. However, he lived just long enough to witness the Irish Potato Famine, which struck in the autumn of 1845, and his response, elaborated in an article of 1847, was extremely interesting. He emphatically did not blame the starvation on political economy, nor did he relinquish the ideal of Free Trade. The Whig Government in general, and Sir Charles Trevelyan in particular, had, he thought, responded with humanity and intelligence. Chalmers did, however, make two important concessions to the critics of political economy. In the first place, he admitted that Free Trade could only operate beneficially so as to 'reveal the order of nature', where there was abundant competition and no possibility of monopoly or combination. Free Trade was therefore inapplicable in pre-capitalist Ireland, since there was simply not sufficient competition to ensure a providential rationing of food along the lines described by Adam Smith. In such circumstances it might be necessary to resort to relief committees, food depots, and requisitioning. Secondly, and of particular interest in the present context, Chalmers distinguished between scarcities which were spread lightly over the entire nation, as in 1800–1, and famines which attacked just one part of a nation virulently, as in 1845–7. In the former case, the principles of Free Trade remained inviolable, but in the latter 'a due liberality' was requisite from those parts of the country which were not suffering. In a general famine, corn dealers and other middlemen should be *left alone*, as agents of 'a higher hand, of Him...who can make even the selfishness of individuals work out a country's salvation'.[49] But the present was not a general famine, since the majority of Englishmen were enjoying 'wonted jollity and abundance' and 'all sorts of luxurious and even riotous indulgence':

Providence equalized the visitation of about fifty years back; and the consequent equality of distribution which laid the necessity of spare living upon all, might be regarded as the effect at once of a direct ordering from God. Providence has laid upon us now, not a heavier visitation than then, but has laid the full weight of it on

[48] George Sinclair, *Observations on the New Scottish Poor Law* (Edinburgh, 1849), pp. 17–26, 42–9, and 79.

[49] [Thomas Chalmers], 'Political Economy of a Famine', *North British Review*, VII (1847), 252.

the distant extremities of our United Kingdom; and left the task of equalization – if there be enough of wisdom and mercy below for the accomplishment of the task – to the ordering of man.[50]

So although such things should normally be left to private charity, the present abnormal situation required that the State should supplement such charity by donations of money to enable those who were starving to buy meat. Chalmers had always supported direct taxation, if only as a gesture of conciliation by the upper classes, and he now hoped that the Government would utilise taxation, rather than a public loan, for the purpose of transferring resources from one part of the nation to another.

Stewart Brown regards this article as an eleventh-hour repudiation of all that Chalmers had said before. 'Chalmers's godly commonwealth ideal succumbed to the grim realities of the Great Famine of 1846–7, which both devastated the Celtic population and destroyed his confidence in the sufficiency of purely voluntary benevolence...His social thought had finally run full circle...He returned to many of his 1808 views' in favour of paternalism and Protection.[51] Despite Brown's further assertions, however, Chalmers's only assault on the principle of Free Trade, and his only criticism of Trevelyan, was a wish that Government would suspend distillation from grain – and this, not because it used up potential foodstuff, but because it was morally abominable 'that the Scotch might luxuriate in spirits, and the English in their potations of beer as usual' while Irishmen starved.[52] The article closes with a repetition of all Chalmers had ever said on the degrading effects of compulsory state relief, and a further attack on the recent decision to extend such relief to Ireland. It might be thought, nevertheless, that his desire for state action practically contradicted his usual *laissez-faire* approach, even if he clung to it in theory. But a careful examination of his phraseology will show that his response to the Famine was less of a departure from evangelical economics than might be supposed.

The important point was that the Famine was not 'a direct ordering from God', as those of 1795 and 1800–1 had been. Now in modern parlance the word 'direct', as applied to Providence, seems to designate a 'special' or 'immediate' intervention by the Almighty in the affairs of his world. In the nineteenth century, however, 'direct' meant, not immediate, but 'straight', 'undeviating', or 'without intervening agency', and was applied to the motions of planets. 'Direct actions' were those 'which took effect without intermediate instrumentality', and the term 'direct-acting' was applied to the new steam-engines and pumps of the 1840s. A 'direct tendency', observed the evangelical Hugh McNeile, was one which went 'according to the

[50] *Ibid.*, pp. 259–60.   [51] Brown, *Thomas Chalmers*, pp. 367–9.
[52] [Chalmers], 'Political Economy of a Famine', 277.

known and ordinary course of events'.[53] So the term 'Direct Providence' implied a natural law, clockwork view of God's worldly government. It will now be clear that Chalmers regarded the 1795 and 1800–1 scarcities as examples of natural law, self-acting Providence, to which the appropriate governmental response was one of *laissez-faire* and Free Trade so as to let that Providence operate without hitch. 1845–7 was different: the fact that famine was restricted to Ireland and parts of western Scotland was evidence that it fell outside the ordinary, mechanical, natural law course of Providence. It must be a 'Special Providence' which, as we saw when discussing Sinclair, called for an interventionist response from the Government. Thus, in attacking the new Irish Poor Law, Chalmers asked,

Is such a season of perplexity and pressure, when extraordinary visitations should be met by means alike extraordinary – is this a time for building up another system for the ordinary relief of the poor? Better, we do think, that emergencies like the present were met by the operation of some such expedients as did not leave one trace of themselves upon the statute-book... The method of relief for the present should have been made as peculiar as the emergency itself is peculiar.[54]

Dr W. P. Alison, whose social thought was opposed to that of Chalmers in almost every particular, retorted that the Irish Famine 'ought not to be regarded *merely* as a visitation of Providence, calling for temporary aid from the rest of the nation, but as an indication of a previously unsound condition of the population'.[55] Sir Charles Trevelyan and his fellow ministers agreed that the Famine was a predictable outcome of circumstances rather than a case of Peculiar Providence, though unlike Alison they saw it as a retribution on the Irish *themselves* for their sloth and fecklessness. It was because he could not accept that the Famine *was* a part of the ordinary course of Providence, however, or a logical consequence of either distress or dissipation, that Chalmers was prepared to derogate from his usual role of *laissez-faire*.

V

Chalmers's response to the Irish Famine provides us with another insight into evangelical social theory. He and his followers were opposed to legislation for the compulsory relief of the poor, partly because the certainty of such relief interfered with the machinery of suffering and judgment which God had devised for the poor, but also because relief had to be provided

---

53 See *O. E. D.* Hugh McNeile, *The Famine a Rod of God* (1847), repr. in *British Eloquence. Sermons by Eminent Living Divines* (London and Glasgow, 1856), p. 87.

54 [Chalmers], 'Political Economy of a Famine', 280 and 284.

55 William Pulteney Alison, *Observations on the Famine of 1846–7, in the Highlands of Scotland and in Ireland, as Illustrating the Connection of the Principle of Population with the Management of the Poor* (Edinburgh and London, 1847), p. 9.

voluntarily if it was to count in the credit column of the rich man's spiritual balance sheet. One of Chalmers's favourite axioms was 'the superior blessedness of the giver to the receiver',[56] but this depended on the gift being 'a free will offering', not something extorted in the form of a parish rate. It was, after all, the rich who trembled in greatest spiritual danger, and the poor existed partly in order to provide a field for the operation of upperclass virtue. So in the case of the Famine, it is clear that, despite his compassion for the sufferings of the Irish, and his refusal to accept the Government's view that they were largely self-inflicted, Chalmers's main concern was with the *spiritual* significance of the event for the English. Several times in the article he implied that it was the stigma on England which most alarmed him about the Famine. Unless the British Government acted swiftly, 'we shall have again and again to incur the misery and disgrace of those hideous starvations which have scandalised the world'.[57] Acts of national charity, of England towards Ireland, might have all the atoning, redemptive effects that private benevolence confers upon its practitioners.

Now is the time for Britain to step forward...to acquit herself generously, openly, freely, towards Ireland – and by her acts of princely but well-directed munificence to repair the accumulated wrongs of many generations. The chastisements of this dreary period have not been joyous but grievous; but thus might they be made to yield the peaceable fruits of righteousness to those who have been exercised thereby –[58]

meaning, of course, the rulers in England, not the starving in Ireland. This is not the abandonment of voluntary benevolence in favour of state aid, as Brown avers, but a call for the English State to exercise, in an hour of Special Providence, a voluntary benevolence towards Ireland. Chalmers ended on a note of affirmation, one which reminds us again that it is better to give than to receive:

But with all the blunders of England's legislation, the heart of England is in its right place – bent with full desirousness on Ireland's large and lasting good...With the guidance and guardianship of the Holy Providence above, a harvest of good will ensue from this great temporary evil; and Ireland, let us trust and pray, will emerge from her sore trial, on a bright and peaceful career to future generations.[59]

'What has [the responsibility of the rich] got to do with Free Trade?', asked Chalmers, and Oastler answered, 'Everything'. Oastler thought that the responsibility of the rich could only be exercised through the State, by means of social welfare reforms, whereas Chalmers believed that state aid would undermine responsibility by coming between Providence and the individual sinner.

[56] Chalmers, *Works*, XI, pp. 399–435.
[57] [Chalmers], 'Political Economy of a Famine', 275.   [58] *Ibid.*, 282.   [59] *Ibid.*, 289.

The role of Providence in evangelical social thought

While there are many reasons for the rapid rejection of Providentialist social thought in the middle decades of the century, the Irish Famine undoubtedly played a part. It was clear to many, if not to Trevelyan, that the Irish nation had not been especially wicked. Evangelicals had always regarded the perfection of the system of retributive justice as a proof that God was in charge of the world, but now a High Churchman was forced to suggest that 'one of the most important and improving trials of our faith, is the *imperfect* state of retributive justice'.[60] Many evangelicals agreed with Gladstone that Ireland was not the object but the minister of God's wrath,[61] the real object being England; it was '*a visitation* – a chastisement for our national sins and crimes – for [our] gambling, monopolising, covetous spirit'.[62] England was indeed being munificent towards Ireland in terms of private charity, but there was not much sign of self-abasement. Money was often being raised by 'the bribe of a public ball... *Charity* the handmaiden of dissipation... To everything there is a season: a time to mourn and a time to *dance*.'[63] And if England did step in and relieve the Irish Famine, what then became of the doctrine of *standing on one's own feet*? Anyway, could one really believe that God would wield a scourge so horrible and so arbitrary?

Evangelicals, like economists, had believed in a hidden hand: unlike economists, they believed that the hidden hand held a rod. 'Moderate' evangelicals believed that the rod was wielded justly, in response to human behaviour. The Irish Famine, among other things, forced them to rethink their views and to re-examine their notion of the Almighty. In admitting that the Irish Famine must be a case of 'Special Providence', Chalmers was helping to undermine the appeal of Providence theory generally in respectable circles.

[60] Henry Phillpotts, *A Sermon Preached on the Day Appointed for a General Fast, and Humiliation before God* (Exeter, 1847), p. 12.

[61] W. E. Gladstone to his wife, 12 Oct. 1845, *Correspondence on Church and Religion of William Ewart Gladstone*, ed. D. C. Lathbury, 2 vols. (London, 1910), II, p. 98. Gladstone agreed with Chalmers that Providence normally acted predictably – the world was a 'moral order which carefully adapts reward and retribution to desert' – but that the Famine was a case of 'Special Providence' – 'legibly Divine' because there was 'a total absence of such second causes as might tempt us to explain it away'. Gladstone to Manning, 9 Mar. 1847, *ibid.*, pp. 275–6; Gladstone, 'True and False Conceptions of the Atonement', *Nineteenth Century*, XXXVI (1894), 317–31; see Boyd Hilton, 'Gladstone's Theological Politics', *High Politics and Low Politics in Modern Britain*, eds. Michael Bentley and John Stevenson (Oxford, 1983), pp. 36 and 42–4.

[62] Charles Vansittart, *A Sermon on Famine: The Expediency of a Public Fast, and the Duty of Personal Abstinence in the Present Time of Dearth* (London, 1847), pp. 1–9.

[63] Phillpotts, *A Sermon on the General Fast*, p. 18.

Cardinal Manning and the
Temporal Power

E. R. NORMAN

The subject of this essay is close to the teaching interests of Professor Chadwick in the later years of his work for the Faculty of History at Cambridge. His 'Specified Subject' course of lectures on 'Italy and the Papacy, 1814–1945' – which examined '"the Roman Question" in its historical development' – included a study of Manning and his attitudes to the temporal sovereignty of the popes. It is an appropriate subject for this compendium for another reason: it scans, from a particular perspective, the major theme of the collection – the interpenetration of the sacred and the secular in the motivations and ideological preferences of men. For the considerations that Manning offered, in his defence of the states of the church in Italy at a crucial moment of their dismemberment by the Italian liberals between 1859 and 1867, were a complicated mixture. Some were plainly religious, some historical, and some utilitarian and pragmatic. When closely scrutinized, however, they show an affinity to Manning's other opinions – opinions fashioned in relation to social and political issues in England, and opinions which were imbued with liberal criticism of traditional society. The Manning who upheld the hated civil rule of the papacy, which Gladstone once called simply 'the worst government',[1] was the same man who in 1864 wrote 'if I have any politics they are popular',[2] and who, ten years later, declared 'I claim for labour the rights of property.'[3] Contemporaneous European defenders of the papal states also employed a mixture of arguments, but Manning's peculiarly English blend of liberalism and religious traditionalism perhaps owed more than theirs to a dependence upon the political culture in which he was set. As that culture changed, especially in relation to the claims of Ireland – which, by the later 1870s, Manning had come to compare with Italy – so his defence

---

[1] John Morley, *The Life of William Ewart Gladstone* (London, 1905), I, p. 646.
[2] H. E. Manning, 'The Visit of Garibaldi to England' [1864], in *Miscellanies* (London, 1877), I, p. 126.
[3] H. E. Manning, 'The Dignity and Rights of Labour' [1874], *ibid.*, II, p. 81.

of the papal sovereignty began to give way to a realistic acceptance of historical change.

Manning's conversion to Catholicism was in 1851. Unlike Newman and W. G. Ward he had, at the time of this change, an extensive knowledge of the Catholic Church as an institution. For the next three years he studied in Rome at the Accademia Ecclesiastica, so deepening his knowledge, and then returned to England and to rapid promotion. In 1857 he was made Provost of the Chapter of Westminster. As amanuensis and counsellor to the ailing Cardinal Wiseman he was soon recognized as the authentic voice of ultramontanism in the central affairs of the English Catholic Church.[4] By an unhappy chance, the assault upon the papal states in Italy coincided with a domestic trial of strength between the 'Roman' party and the 'Old Catholics' in England: the two sets of events were consciously held in Manning's mind as he composed his defence of the papal Temporal Power in 1860. Since July 1858, he had been involved in controversy with the Chapter of Westminster over the affairs of the seminary at Ware, and over George Errington's leadership of the opposition to Wiseman's 'Romanizing' policies. Both matters were subject to appeals to Rome at the time of the Italian crisis. To Manning's ultramontane sensibilities there seemed little difference between a 'national' spirit in the English Catholic Church and the desire for a 'national' Italian Church expressed by Italian liberals. To English Catholics of the old school, however, Manning's sudden pre-eminence was distasteful. Some of them, with their sympathizers in Rome, were shortly to intrigue against Manning's defence of the Temporal Power. 'All this shows how careful you must be, as you have enemies in every quarter', Mgr George Talbot advised from Rome in 1861.[5] The question of the Temporal Power, indeed, was initially a sort of test among English Catholics – an indicator to 'soundness' on wider issues of ecclesiastical polity.[6] This was still the position when Manning was composing his first defence in 1860. By 1862 there had been a rally among even the most old of 'Old Catholics' to the papal cause in Italy, and by then, also, the internal threat to Wiseman's and Manning's view of Catholicism seemed less pressing.[7]

It was against this strife-ridden English background that the events in Italy after the Plombières agreement of 1858 came as an unwelcome complication: the very papal Rome to which Manning had dedicated himself

---

[4] Shane Leslie, *Henry Edward Manning, His Life and Labours* (London, 1921), p. 138.

[5] E. S. Purcell, *Life of Cardinal Manning* (London, 1895), II, p. 156.

[6] H. A. MacDougall, *The Acton–Newman Relations. The Dilemma of Christian Liberalism* (New York, 1962), p. 56.

[7] Sheridan Gilley, 'The Garibaldi Riots of 1862', in *Historical Journal*, XVI, 4 (1973), p. 723.

looked as if it was liable to disappear through force of arms. The Peace of Villafranca, in July 1859, envisaged an Italian confederation with the pope as titular head – 'a preposterous idea', according to Gregorovius.[8] In March 1860, Piedmont annexed the central states at the invitation of their revolutionary governments, and in May Garibaldi began his conquest of the Sicilian kingdoms. Pius IX had issued his first declaration on the sanctity of the Temporal Power as early as 1849 in the Allocution *Quibus quantisque*, and remained consistently attached to it. 'The policy of the Pope is unchangeable,' as Cardinal Antonelli explained to the British representative in Rome in January 1860, 'for it is subject only to the holy laws of religion.'[9] The policy of the pope, it seems, was actually delivered in a series of night-time visitations which Pius IX received from St Philomena[10] – an early martyr whose feast was suppressed by the Holy See (because of historical doubts about her real existence) in 1960.

The hostility of English public opinion to the papal cause in Italy was also in Manning's mind as he gathered the materials of his defence. 'There is a traditional animosity against the Holy See, especially in its relations to Temporal Power, which Englishmen draw with their first breath', he wrote in the preface to his published lectures.[11] Bishop Patterson of Emmaus, another exponent of ultramontanism, told Talbot in 1860 that English opinion was 'ignorant of the real state of things' in Italy.[12] Manning wrote to supply the necessary corrective; but it was, to say the least, an uphill task, and he never lost the sense, expressed to Gladstone in the following year, that 'England is simply duped.'[13] The sentiment of Protestant England was overwhelmingly behind the forces of the Risorgimento. The press was filled with denunciations of the Temporal Power and with highly partial accounts of the actual condition of the papal states. The Mortara case of 1858 – which involved a young Jewish boy who had been baptized and was in consequence removed from his parents by the papal authorities in Bologna and brought up as a Christian – was given European publicity for several years, and was treated by the *Times* as 'conclusive for abolishing the Temporal Power of

8 *The Roman Journals of Ferdinand Gregorovius, 1852–1873*, ed. Friedrich Althaus (London, 1911), pp. 62–3.
9 *The Roman Question. Extracts from the Despatches of Odo Russell from Rome, 1858–1870*, ed. Noel Blakiston (London, 1962), p. 75.
10 *Ibid.*, p. 95.
11 H. E. Manning, *The Temporal Power of the Vicar of Jesus Christ* (2nd edn, London, 1862), p. vi.
12 Archives of the English College, Rome: Talbot Papers, 572 (James Patterson to Talbot, 20 May 1860).
13 British Library, Gladstone Papers, Add. MS 44248, CLXIII, fo. 175 (Manning to Gladstone, 26 October 1861).

the Pope',[14] and as evidence of 'the incompatibility of canon law with civil and religious liberty'.[15] Many in England appeared to suppose that the success of the Italian liberals would lead to the conversion of the peasantry to Protestantism. Garibaldi had indeed given land in Naples for a Protestant Church, and during these years the papal states were flooded with copies of Diodati's Italian Bibles – usually at the expense of the English Bible Society.[16] There was, in England, a popular impression that Cavour had espoused 'a Protestant programme'.[17] Throughout the crisis successive English governments preserved an official neutrality, but the pro-Italian sympathies of both the Conservatives under Derby and the Liberals under Palmerston (after June 1859) were unmistakable.[18] 'It is not in Italy that the seeds of discord and revolt are to be sought,' Pius IX himself remarked early in 1860, 'but in the example of England, the speeches of her public men, and the policy of Lord Palmerston.'[19]

English Catholics were not alone in pointing to the dangers inherent in such public sympathy for 'the most revolutionary party in Europe':[20] Lord John Russell's famous despatch, of 27 October 1860, which tacitly legitimized revolutionary action against the papal states on the grounds that the civil authorities had provided inadequately for the material well-being of their inhabitants, drew some shocked Conservative responses. Sir James Graham observed that Ireland might apply the doctrine to herself.[21] In Ireland, in fact, the response to the crisis was more immediate. Already inspired to ultramontane fervour by the triumphant tour of the country by Cardinal Wiseman in the summer of 1858, Catholic Ireland made an enthusiastic response to the call of Mgr de Mérode (the papal Minister of War), in January 1860, for a volunteer army, recruited from all over Europe, to come to the assistance of the pope. The 'Irish Brigade of St Patrick', enlisted by the priests under the familiar guise of emigration, eventually numbered 1,300 men. They served at Ancona and Spoleto, and were in the end repatriated, at the expense of the British government, after the defeat of the papal army

---

[14] E. R. Norman, *The Catholic Church and Ireland in the Age of Rebellion, 1859–1873* (London, 1965), p. 42.

[15] *Dublin Review*, XLVI (June 1959), p. 319.

[16] *Roman Journals of Gregorovius*, pp. 95, 115.

[17] Derek Beales, *England and Italy, 1859–60* (London, 1961), p. 25.

[18] Since the writing of this essay Dr C. T. McIntire has published *England against the Papacy, 1858–1861. Tories, Liberals, and the Overthrow of Papal Temporal Power during the Italian Risorgimento* (Cambridge, 1983). He describes the Italian policies of the English governments and shows an essential continuity in their opposition to the papal states, and a common indebtedness to the ideology of anti-Catholicism.

[19] *The Roman Question*, p. 85.

[20] *Dublin Review*, XLIX (February 1861), p. 414.

[21] Morley, *Gladstone*, I, p. 650.

at Castelfidardo. Their presence in Italy was not an unmixed blessing. The pope himself disclosed a fear that the cheapness of wine in Italy might 'prove fatal to the Irish';[22] there were quarrels about wages and clothing. Then there was the problem of 'The Kerry Boys' – who 'had been sent out of their parish by their priest because he wanted to be rid of them'.[23] Cardinal Antonelli achieved some new insights: 'the Pope as well as himself had not known the Irish character to be so energetic', he told the British representative in Rome; 'he could now appreciate the difficulties experienced by the British government in dealing with Ireland'.[24] For Manning and for Wiseman, however, the Irish Brigade represented an authentic Catholic response to the crisis. It tended to enhance sympathy between English and Irish Catholics, and inside Ireland itself it consolidated papalism. 'To our brethren in Ireland', Wiseman wrote in a Pastoral Letter of 1860, 'whose hearts God has inspired with so much generosity in his cause, and whose hands he has strengthened in constitutional power, we leave the noble task of making Catholic feeling effectually respected.'[25]

Manning's defence of the Temporal Power came in a series of three Lectures delivered in 1860 at the Church of St Mary of the Angels in Bayswater – the home of the Oblates of St Charles. In 1861 he followed them up with a further two series. They were published together in 1861 under the title *The Temporal Power of the Vicar of Jesus Christ.* In 1862 a second edition was published, with a French translation in the same year.[26] The Lectures were widely reported and discussed in the press at the times of delivery and proved an armoury indeed (as Manning's biographer made plain) for enemies of the Temporal Power.[27] Purcell's assessment of the Lectures is defective. For Manning was not, as he wrote, 'unfamiliar with the subject' – although it may be that there is some substance to the judgment that 'his zeal outran his discretion'. Nor is it really true that he did not give himself time 'to weigh his statements or to define with perfect accuracy the propositions he laid down'.[28] Purcell wrote with the letters of Talbot before him, letters disclosing the intrigue at Rome against Manning and his Lectures.

22 *The Roman Question,* p. 44.

23 G. F.-M. Berkeley, *The Irish Brigade in the Papal Army of 1860* (Dublin and Cork, 1929), p. 21.

24 *The Roman Question,* p. 117 (July 1860).

25 *Pastoral Letter of His Eminence the Cardinal Archbishop of Westminster Enjoining a Collection throughout the Diocese for His Holiness the Pope* (London, 1860), p. 7.

26 In the published version, the original Lectures are entitled 'The origin of the Temporal Power' (Part First), and the later ones 'The Perpetual Conflict of the Vicar of Jesus Christ' (Part Second), and 'The last Glories of the Holy See greater than the first' (Part Third).

27 Purcell, *Manning,* II, p. 152.

28 *Ibid.,* pp. 152, 161.

Manning had speculated on the possibility that one day Antichrist might rule in Rome: an apocalyptic illustration of the relativity of all human claims to the permanence of institutions. Opponents seized upon it as evidence of ultimate Catholic disloyalty. But the pope, presented by Talbot with an Italian translation of the Lectures, was 'much pleased with them'.[29] Rumours that the Lectures were about to be censored were dispelled.

There is enough internal evidence in the Lectures themselves to show that Manning had studied the available literature in English on the Temporal Power. He was largely unacquainted with the European writings, but derived powerful draughts of them through the agency of W. G. Ward. Like Manning, Ward was a convert from Anglicanism. He became, though a layman (in his Catholic life), Professor of Dogmatic Theology at St Edmund's College, Ware, until 1858, and was thereafter editor of the *Dublin Review* – transforming that journal into a vehicle of tight ultramontane principles. Manning rejected Ward's condemnation of political liberalism but was otherwise 'almost entirely in harmony with Ward's general views'.[30] Ward had studied the works of de Maistre during his Oxford years and transmitted his conclusions to Manning. He was concerned with the consequences of intellectual perversions of Catholicism and the need for papal authority to curtail them, and so became preoccupied with the question of Infallibility; Manning's priority was the universal authority of the papacy itself, and the need to secure its institutional independence – and so was taken up, initially, with the issue of the Temporal Power.

From John Francis Maguire, Manning acquired a sense of the importance of the Temporal Power to the person and policies of Pius IX himself. Maguire was an Irish Catholic convert, Liberal member of parliament for Dungarven, and an articulate defender of ultramontanism – an Irish equivalent of Ward. In 1857 he published *Rome. Its Ruler and Its Institutions*, and dedicated it to Mgr Talbot. A second edition, which appeared in 1859, contained an additional, long chapter on the Temporal Power. Manning's own views about the origins of papal sovereignty were in some large measure derived from it. It was from Maguire, also, that he got some of his evidence that the papal states could be defended on the grounds of their good civil administration – but most of his opinions on that came from another source: an anonymous contribution to the *Dublin Review*. 'The Government of the Papal States', which appeared in the June 1859 number,[31] was a long review article of, among other works, Gladstone's translation of Farini's *The Roman State*, Ranke's *History of the Popes*, and Maguire's *Rome*.

---

[29] *Ibid.*, p. 153.
[30] Wilfrid Ward, *W. G. Ward and the Catholic Revival* (2nd edn, London, 1912), p. 167.
[31] *Dublin Review*, XLVI (March and June 1859), pp. 187ff.

The author was William Frederick Finlason,[32] a barrister and writer on legal and religious issues who had been received into the Catholic Church by Faber in 1849. He was perhaps best known for his sympathetic published account of Newman's defence in the Achilli trial, which had appeared in 1852. He had supported the Catholic hierarchy in their opposition to legislation on charitable trusts in the 1850s.[33]

Manning's Lectures of 1860–1 were supplemented by two published statements on the Temporal Power in 1867. *A Sermon at the Mass of Requiem for Those who Fell in Defence of Rome*, and *Rome and the Revolution*, were elicited by the defeat at Mentana of Garibaldi's attempt to seize Rome. Together with the earlier Lectures they represent the whole range of Manning's thought on the question of the temporal sovereignty. His arguments were internally linked but for purposes of analysis may be considered within three categories – religious, historical, and pragmatic.

The defence of the states of the church on religious grounds derived almost entirely from European and ultramontane sources, and contained no intellectual novelties. They were received by Manning through the filter provided by Ward. The states were given by God as a permanent inheritance for the Christian world to guarantee the independence of spiritual truth; they received their legitimacy, therefore, from divine revelation: 'He that sows in the hearts of others seeds of disloyalty towards the vicar of our divine Lord, that man is resisting the ordinance of God.'[34] The temporal sovereignty 'was conferred by direct act of our divine Lord' since it was 'inherent in the pontificate'. Although not essential to the survival of the church – which had for centuries existed before the endowment of the patrimonies – temporal and spiritual sovereignty are in practice interdependent: 'the Spiritual and Temporal Powers of the Supreme Pontiff have gradually become integral and inseparable ideas in the same divine order'.[35] The Temporal Power itself contains 'two distinct elements'. The first is the sovereignty existing in the pope's own person; the second is the local sovereignty over the actual states of the church. Both are derived from God and are inviolable. The opponents of the Temporal Power are therefore the enemies of Christ – a

---

32 *The Dublin Review, 1836–1936. Complete List of Articles Published* (London, 1936), p. 25. The author's name is here spelled as 'Finlayson'. His second Christian name is sometimes given as Francis (see *The Letters and Diaries of John Henry Newman*, ed. C. S. Dessain (London and Oxford, 1961–), index to vol. XIV, p. 544); but for the version and spelling used here, see W. G. Gorman, *Converts to Rome. A Biographical List of the More Notable Converts to the Catholic Church in the United Kingdom during the Last Sixty Years*, new edition (London, 1910), p. 103.

33 See *Dublin Review*, XXXIV (June 1853), p. 68.

34 Manning, *The Temporal Power*, p. 28, Part First, Lecture I.

35 *Ibid.*, Preface, p. xvi.

point made with particular emphasis by Manning in his sermon at the mass in St Patrick's, Soho, for the souls of those who died at Castelfidardo.[36] Manning was especially anxious to counter the contentions of those who believed that the spiritual functions of the papacy would be more felicitously performed if unencumbered by civil rule – an argument deployed by some Protestants and later popular with English Liberal Catholics. 'It is one of the tactics of our adversaries to profess that they do not attack the Spiritual Supremacy, but only the Temporal Sovereignty,' Manning declared.[37] The Temporal Power is 'the shelter of the spiritual'.[38] Its destruction might ultimately prove to be part of the divine scheme, however: here Manning moved into the controversial area sniffed out by his Roman opponents. As Christ was delivered to his enemies to fulfil Providence, so the Temporal Power may be ended by the foes of religion. Then, perhaps, the Vicar of Christ, 'when the times of Antichrist are come', will be given over 'to the powers of this world'.[39] He cited the prophet Daniel, and the lament of the Saviour over Jerusalem.[40] He pointed to the fragility of all human institutions, yet also to the paradox of divine sustenance. 'We may be told that they were but political and human agencies which protected the Holy Father,' Manning later observed, 'Be it so. God works through the politics and actions of men.'[41] Indeed, Manning applied a doctrine of development to the interrelationship of revealed truth and culture which, though lacking the rigorously systematic logic of Franzelin or Newman, was clearly of the same pedigree. The Temporal Power was not found in the antiquity of the church, and there were few references to it in pontifical theology; but it was inherent in the divine mission of the church from the beginning, and emerged as historical and cultural developments influenced the conditions in which religious truth unfolded itself. 'As in science, so also in theology, and in the history of every truth, certain periods are to be traced,' he noticed: 'first, the period of conception; secondly, of definition; and lastly, of application and scientific manifestation.'[42] In the mid-nineteenth century the Temporal Power was entering the period of 'fuller appreciation and manifestation'.[43] He drew a parallel with the definitions of the doctrines of the Holy Trinity and the Immaculate Conception – the second proclaimed as recently as 1854 – to show that the temporal sovereignty of the papacy, though not a dogma of faith, required long gestation.[44] It was an essential element in the authority of the universal church, the very means by which

---

[36] Purcell, *Life of Cardinal Manning*, II, p. 164.
[37] Manning, *The Temporal Power*, Preface, p. xv.   [38] *Ibid.*, p. 25, Part First, Lecture I.
[39] *Ibid.*, pp. 55–6, Part First, Lecture III.   [40] *Ibid.*, p. 162, Part Second, Lecture IV.
[41] H. E. Manning, *Rome and the Revolution. A Sermon* (London, 1867), p. 6.
[42] Manning, *The Temporal Power*, Preface, p. xxi.
[43] *Ibid.*, p. xxii.   [44] *Ibid.*, p. xxiv.

spiritual truth was able to declare itself without hindrance from the world. The intrusion of worldliness upon religious knowledge was a phenomenon which, to Manning as to most ultramontanes, was especially marked in his day. It pervaded his sense that some dreadful cataclysmic event was impending in the affairs of men; it accounted for the easy corruption, so it seemed to him, of Protestantism. Even as he wrote, and as the fearful events occurred in Italy, English Protestantism was absorbed in the controversy provoked by the publication, in 1860, of *Essays and Reviews*.

Manning's historical depiction of the Temporal Power as the preserver and guarantor of Christian civilization was, like the religious grounds of defence, a version of familiar ultramontanist arguments. He believed that historical evidence, if properly evaluated, would always sustain Catholic truth. Professor Chadwick has himself pointed, in his 1976 Hensley Henson Lectures, to Manning's support of Acton and others in applications to get the Vatican archives opened for study.[45] Though not by any means accomplished in historical learning, he did recognize the importance of following the conclusions of critical thought. Thus he declined to support the reality of a 'Donation' of Constantine as the title-deed of the states of the church – a notion he called 'a fable'. Constantine's removal from Rome, however, 'represented the providential fact of the donation of God'.[46] His authority here was Maguire, who had written of 'the gradual growth of the temporal power',[47] and Acton, whose *Rambler* article of January 1860, had shown that no record prior to the thirteenth century which could be cited as upholding temporal sovereignty was authentic – although he did affirm that 'the origin of the patrimony belongs to the very earliest ages'.[48] It is interesting that Paul Cullen, Cardinal Archbishop of Dublin, and the leading ultramontanist in Ireland, agreed with this assessment too. In January 1860, he had addressed a huge meeting at the pro-Cathedral in Dublin called in order to express sympathy for the pope,[49] and had spoken of the Temporal Power as 'an institution of human origin' which dated from the eighth century.[50] Manning, who was an admirer of Cullen's, and later cooperated with him in the promotion of Irish political reforms, must have been aware of his opinions on the issue.

---

[45] Owen Chadwick, *Catholicism and History. The Opening of the Vatican Archives* (Cambridge, 1978), pp. 58, 86.

[46] Manning, *The Temporal Power*, pp. 12–13, Part First, Lecture I.

[47] J. F. Maguire, *Rome, It's Ruler and It's Institutions*, second edition (London, 1859), p. 457.

[48] *Rambler*, new series, II (March 1860), 'The States of the Church', p. 292.

[49] Peader MacSuibhne, *Paul Cullen and his Contemporaries* (Kildare, 1965), III, p. 274.

[50] *The Pastoral Letters and Other Writings of Cardinal Cullen*, ed. P. F. Moran (Dublin, 1882), I, p. 710 (9 January 1860).

The broad concept of a European civilization upheld by the temporal sovereignty of the papacy was at the centre of Manning's preoccupation with the Italian question. 'The Temporal prerogatives of the Pontificate are the divine conditions whereby the Christian order of the world has been created and sustained', he said in the Lectures.[51] This scheme of historical values came, via Ward, from de Maistre's vision of the papacy as the great bond of Catholic unity and as the only and essential preserver of order against revolution. The central contention of *Du Pape* (1819) had been the maintenance of the church as the guarantor of civilization and of the popes as exemplars of the principle of legitimate sovereignty. The Reformation, as a revolt against Roman authority, fostered revolutionary disorder. This idea, also, is found in Manning's defence of the papal states. Protestantism, he believed, was 'a revolt against the supernatural',[52] and so liable to vitiate true principles of revealed religion; it cultivated 'rationalism, ignorance, indifference, and infidelity, the four evils of which we have too plentiful a harvest'.[53] Modern nationalism, too, 'this system of national supremacy' so destructive of Christian and human harmony, was the fruit of the Protestant Reformation. He affirmed, instead, that 'there is a unity higher than the unity of any nation, in which the welfare of all nations is bound up: the unity of the Christian world'.[54] Nationalism, furthermore, was inherently tyrannical; it was 'the deification of the civil power'.[55] Here was another of Manning's key themes – the despotism of the state when it was released from the moral constraints of religion. The background was the Siccardi Laws, and the secularization of government practised by Piedmont. The only check upon the abuse of civil power by governments was 'the independence of the spiritual'.[56] This merged with Manning's apocalyptic scenario: 'When the civil powers of the world shall desecrate themselves and lose their relation to Christianity, they will inaugurate the beginning of the last times, when Antichrist shall come.'[57] Ever since the beginnings of Christian Europe, he argued, 'the political order of the world has rested upon the Incarnation of our Lord Jesus Christ'.[58] But Europe was now apostatizing through acquiescence in the destruction of the only protector of that order – the independent pope, the Temporal Power. It was Maguire who had pointed out that, because of this, the preservation of the papal sovereignty was 'as much a matter of importance to the sovereign powers of Europe as it is to

---

[51] Manning, *The Temporal Power*, Preface, p. xxxix.   [52] *Ibid.*, p. vii.
[53] *Ibid.*, p. 225, Part Third, Lecture III.
[54] H. E. Manning, *Christ and Antichrist: A Sermon at the mass of Requiem for Those who Fell in Defence of Rome* (London, 1867), p. 6.
[55] *Ibid.*, p. 14.   [56] Manning, *The Temporal Power*, p. 60, Part First, Lecture III.
[57] *Ibid.*, p. 74.   [58] *Ibid.*, p. 129, Part Second, Lecture III.

the Church itself'.[59] Manning represented the urgency of the matter to Gladstone in the autumn of 1861 for precisely those reasons: 'I look upon the present crisis as decisive not of the Temporal Power of the pope, but of the Christianity of Europe.'[60] In the Lectures he had said plainly that 'the dissolution of the temporal power of the pope would lead to the dissolution of Christendom', and that 'the state of the world before Constantine would be reproduced' for the church would descend again 'into the catacombs'.[61] Wiseman had maintained, in his *Recollections of the Last Four Popes* (1858), that the restoration of the papal states by the European powers at the end of the Napoleonic wars was a recognition of the stability of European institutions which their existence secured.[62] Manning was anxious to reinforce this. Was the dissolution of European civilization a proper price to pay for sympathy with Italian liberalism? 'Rome is not the capital of Italy', he said, 'it is the capital of Christendom. God has so made it, and man cannot unmake it.'[63]

It was integral to Manning's defence, therefore, that the Temporal Power was recognized not only as the means of papal independence but as the moral and actual cohesive of Europe. The question was 'between the natural and the supernatural societies; between the civilization of the mere human will and the civilization which is perfected and sustained by grace'.[64] It was the popes who had made the very fabric of the European inheritance, he insisted – 'the history of civilization is the history of the Pontiffs'.[65] Yet he saw the difficulty in conveying this vision to Protestant Englishmen. 'You will also smile when I say that I believe the Temporal Power to be the "nexus" between the Revelation of God's Truth and Law, and the civil society of the world', Manning wrote to Gladstone in 1864.[66] Like Louis Veuillot, he regarded the church and the world as now locked in conflict; a war between the spiritual and the secularized culture was beginning. The end of the Temporal Power would extend the range of the conflict, and religious authority would retreat from its beneficial relationship with the vital affairs of human society. The pope would become 'like the Archbishop of Canterbury'.[67] It was a truly baneful prospect.

[59] Maguire, *Rome*, p. 465
[60] British Library, Gladstone Papers, Add. MS 44248, CLXII, fo. 152 (Manning to Gladstone, 4 September 1861).
[61] Manning, *The Temporal Power*, pp. 56–7, Part First, Lecture III.
[62] H. E. Cardinal Wiseman, *Recollections of the Last Four Popes and of Rome in Their Times* (London, 1858), p. 129.
[63] Manning, *Christ and Antichrist*, p. 5.
[64] Manning, *The Temporal Power*, Preface, p. xliii.
[65] *Ibid.*, p. 49, Part First, Lecture II.
[66] British Library, Gladstone Papers, Add. MS 44248, CLXIII, fo. 222 (24 October 1864).
[67] Manning, *The Temporal Power*, p. 58, Part First, Lecture III.

In the third category of his defensive proposition Manning disclosed some particular English attitudes. This was not a matter of tactical or cosmetic presentation – disguising the hated Roman items in acceptable wrapping – but an indication of Manning's own indebtedness to English liberalism. In this aspect of his defence of the papal states, more than in others, the convergence of the sacred and the secular pressed in upon his analysis. As could indeed be expected of one whose reformist politics were marked at the Oxford Union of his youth, whose affinity with Gladstone's developing liberalism was a feature of their life-long if intermittent relationship, and who, in later life, was able to declare that his 'radicalism' went 'down to the roots of the sufferings of the people',[68] his support of the Temporal Power was made to rest upon the claim that it derived its legitimacy – appearances notwithstanding – from the suffrages of the masses. So, too, there was a consistency in one who supported trade unionism, and who said 'the rich can take care of themselves...my politics are social politics',[69] that he should argue for the states of the church on the grounds of their good internal government and social enlightenment.

Manning's English politics encompassed the belief, common among nineteenth-century radicals and liberals, that Saxon society had enjoyed popular institutions. He came to suppose that universal suffrage was 'a real return to the spirit of our old Saxon monarchy'.[70] It was not therefore out of keeping for him to claim that the Temporal Power of the popes originated in 'the express demand, suffrage, and vote of the people', sometime in the fifth or sixth centuries.[71] 'This I conceive', he continued, 'to be the ultimate title of the Temporal Power of the Sovereign Pontiffs over the people.' It was a governance based on 'popular election'.[72] Regarded from this perspective, the defence of papal sovereignty on the ordinary grounds of legitimacy – in which Manning also indulged – has a quite different set of inferences from those associated with conventional ultramontanism. Pius IX himself, at the consistory of June 1859, had spoken of the legitimacy of his rule as resting upon 'heavenly disposition' and 'ancient possession', but not upon the suffrages of the people.[73] Cullen, in Dublin, defended the papal sovereignty, in whiggish style, as a means of 'protecting the rights of property' against revolution, not as a means of expressing the popular political will.[74] But Manning was not without a supportive source for his idea – Finlason in his Dublin Review article had written of the popes having temporal dominion 'thrust upon them', in the early centuries, 'on account of

[68] Purcell, Manning, II, p. 633. [69] Ibid., p. 635. [70] Ibid., p. 636.
[71] Manning, The Temporal Power, Preface, xxxii. [72] Ibid., p. xli.
[73] Text printed in Rambler, new series, I (September 1859), Part III, p. 427.
[74] The Pastoral Letters and Other Writings, I, p. 711.

the confidence which the Roman people felt in their wisdom and capacity for civil rule'.[75] Since the public opinion of England and Europe was clamouring to denounce the Temporal Power precisely because it appeared to lack popular sanction, and because of the unreformed condition of the civil rule actually meted out, this kind of defence must have seemed especially unrealistic to Manning's contemporaries. He went on to claim that the civil administration of the popes was 'the freest and most republican and the most popular in Christian Europe' and, while conceding that this involved 'paradox', proceeded to prove it, by showing that in the Roman state any man 'though the son of a peasant' could sit upon the throne of St Peter: 'the only elective throne that has ever endured'.[76] As final evidence of the continuing popularity of this popular government Manning rehearsed the familiar contentions, deployed most often at the Vatican itself, about the insurrectionary movements (then in progress against papal rule) being inspired from without – the promptings of an international conspiracy. The popular uprisings were not really popular; they were 'because the whole flood of external revolution has found its home there, and because of the flagrant ambition of neighbouring states'.[77] This was the case put at the numerous public meetings got up by the English Catholic bishops early in 1860 to inform their flocks about the evil designs against the pope. 'It is my duty tonight to expose a conspiracy', Bishop Ullathorne began his speech on one such occasion – at Birmingham – and referred to 'the secret societies' which were fomenting dissension: 'the great mass of the Pope's subjects had no wish or desire for revolution'.[78] Wiseman said the people of the states had been 'allured, impelled, and artfully guided into rebellion'.[79] Cullen pointed to the Irish lessons to be considered: those disturbing the papal subjects with revolutionary notions were of the same *genus* as those who sought violent upheaval in Ireland.[80]

It was as an exponent of English social reform that Manning surveyed the internal condition of the states of the church, and what he saw was enlightenment and progress. Nowhere was his vision so greatly in opposition to current English opinion. His immediate inspiration was Finlason, whose *Dublin Review* article had, like a verbalized set of Pugin's contrasts, placed social conditions in England and in the papal states side by side in order

---

[75] *Dublin Review*, XLVI (June 1859), p. 188.

[76] Manning, *The Temporal Power*, pp. 50–1, Part First, Lecture III.

[77] *Ibid.*, p. 70, Part First, Lecture III.

[78] *The Speech on the Question of The Pontifical State Delivered by the Right Rev. Bishop Ullathorne at the Town Hall, Birmingham, 14th of February, 1860* (London, 1860), p. 3.

[79] *Pastoral Letter of His Eminence the Cardinal Archbishop of Westminster Enjoining a Collection throughout the Diocese for His Holiness the Pope* (London, 1860), p. 4.

[80] *The Pastoral Letters and Other Writings*, I, pp. 712, 733.

'to meet the charges against the Roman government by contrasting them with the actual working of our much-lauded system'.[81] A dark picture of English life resulted. There were detailed illustrations of social and legal injustices – the recent case of a youth of twenty sentenced to ten years of penal servitude for stealing two pence,[82] a claim that the numbers of political prisoners in the Roman states did not exceed those in Ireland,[83] the laws of sedition which inhibited press freedom,[84] the general state of the criminal law in England as 'one mass of egregious anomalies and absurdities'.[85] The institutions and laws of the papal states, on the other hand, 'are in many respects vastly superior to our own'.[86] Most of all this passed into Manning's defence. He went even further, in fact, to remark, of the papal states, that 'if the prisons are full, it is because offences which in England are avenged with capital punishment are there treated in a milder way'.[87] From Maguire, too, Manning derived accounts of the beneficence of papal civil institutions – of the hospitals, schools, and houses of refuge; of female education, poor relief, and public utilities. Maguire had a chapter on 'The Pope as a Commercial Reformer'.[88] This was especially conducive to the sensibilities of an England suffused with Free Trade idealism, and Finlason, too, had taken the trouble to record Cardinal Antonelli's commercial treaty with England.[89] In Manning's grand summary, the popes emerged not merely cleansed from the taint of oppressive rule but luminous as the most enlightened administrators the world had seen: 'the line of Pontiffs stands alone for justice and mercy in the history and assembly of kings'.[90] The dissolution of their rule would 'let loose an irresistible spirit of revolution'[91] which would engulf the civilized world. Yet in England, Manning observed, every possible calumny about the nature of papal government was given credence – and he referred, as an example of this gullibility, to Gladstone's translation of Farini's *Roman State*: the work of 'a revolutionist'.[92]

Though important parts of Manning's defence of the Temporal Power derived from a peculiarly English liberalism they were not, in consequence, agreeable to Gladstone. The Italian controversy of these years, in fact, brought the two men once more into some sort of relationship – a more distant and formal one than had once existed between them but one which, nevertheless, has not only an inherent interest but also elicited, in both parties, a clarification of divergent opinion. Gladstone, at the Exchequer,

[81] *Dublin Review*, XLVI (June 1859), p. 251.   [82] *Ibid.*, p. 248.   [83] *Ibid.*, p. 295.
[84] *Ibid.*, pp. 323, 329.   [85] *Ibid.*, p. 383.   [86] *Ibid.*, p. 409.
[87] Manning, *The Temporal Power*, p. 71, Part First, Lecture III.
[88] Maguire, *Rome*, chapter XL.   [89] *Dublin Review*, XLVI (June 1859), p. 349.
[90] Manning, *Christ and Antichrist*, p. 16.
[91] Manning, *The Temporal Power*, p. 61, Part First, Lecture III.
[92] *Ibid.*, p. 67, Part First, Lecture III.

was one of a recognized group of three ministers in Palmerston's cabinet – the other two were the Prime Minister himself and Lord John Russell, Foreign Secretary – who were especially identified with sympathy for the Italian liberals. Ever since his famous visit to Naples, in the autumn of 1850, Gladstone had shown a periodic interest in Italian affairs, and was, indeed, acclaimed by Cavour (in 1859) as 'one of the sincerest and most important friends that Italy had'.[93] His attitude to the states of the church was not straightforward. He certainly disapproved, and that vehemently, of the existing nature of papal administration and of the idea of the Temporal Power in a fully territorial sense. When translating Farini's highly prejudiced account, in 1851, he had taken the opportunity to observe the lack of evidence, as it seemed to him, to show 'that Pius IX desired or intended, of his own free will, to establish anything like what we understand by Constitutional freedom'.[94] The evidence upon which he was working could hardly have suggested any other conclusion: Farini's volumes furnished 'in a formal and elaborate manner all the matters of complaint that can be urged against the Papal government', and, so many believed, was 'the staple of all the invective circulated against it'.[95] Gladstone's translation confirmed his position as a leading opponent of the Temporal Power; he remarked later that this work inspired him to 'think much more earnestly' about the matter.[96]

In his study of the question, Gladstone seems to have separated Catholicism from 'Romanism', and to have sought a release of the spiritual influence of the papacy from corrupting involvement with temporal government[97] – a view which corresponded to Newman's contention that the Temporal Power enhanced the spirit of the world in the church.[98] His opposition to ultramontanism, which grew in the 1850s, derived from a conviction that it was the enemy of liberty. Yet Gladstone did believe that the pope had to be independent, to be subject to no civil power, in order to direct the affairs of the church. He was also concerned with the relationships of the powers – seeking a check to French influence and some sort of European guarantee of the papacy in which all the states, Protestant as well as Catholic, would be participants. He came at length to suppose the centre of such an arrangement to exist in an internationally recognized personal sovereignty

---

93 Morley, *Gladstone*, I, p. 640.

94 Luigi Carlo Farini, *The Roman State from 1815 to 1850*, trans. W. E. Gladstone (London, 1851), I, Translator's Preface, p. vii.

95 *Dublin Review*, XLVI (June 1859), p. 204.

96 D. C. Lathbury, ed., *Correspondence on Church and Religion of William Ewart Gladstone* (London, 1910), II, p. 42.

97 H. C. G. Matthew, 'Gladstone, Vaticanism, and the Question of the East', *Studies in Church History*, XV (1978), pp. 421, 427.

98 Josef Altholz, *The Liberal Catholic Movement in England* (Montreal, 1962), p. 132.

(or *suzeraineté*) in the pope, with no civil jurisdiction beyond the immediate environs of the city of Rome.[99] This grand design, however, he did not think incompatible with moral support for the insurrectionary forces within the existing papal states. The de-stabilizing of the Temporal Power appeared an essential preliminary to a European settlement, provided the French could be dislodged from their protective role. The campaign for internal revolution was based, as he declared in 1854, 'upon the right of men, under every law divine and human, first to good government, and next to the institutions which are the necessary guarantees of it'. [100] A decade later this view was unchanged; he then wrote to Manning: 'my position is that Rome is inhabited by human beings, and that these human beings ought not to be taken out of the ordinary categories of human right to serve the theories of ecclesiastical power'.[101] By that time, too, Gladstone seems to have envisaged a sort of 'Protestantizing' of the liberated states of the church – by which he seems to have meant a mass modernizing of the intellect through liberal education and free institutions. He wanted to see the Italians become 'Christian believers', and feared that the continuation of the Temporal Power would in the end so alienate the religious sensibilities of the people that they would lapse from Catholicism into complete secularism. 'It is you, and not I', he wrote to Manning, 'who are helping on the anti-catholic movement in Italy.'[102] Manning had not unnaturally differed in his diagnosis – 'As to the protestantizing or Anglicanizing of Italy, they might as well try to make Italians Novatians or Montanists.'[103]

The last contacts between Manning and Gladstone had been in August 1853. On the 14th of March 1861, while walking in the passage between the Horse Guards and Downing Street with William Monsell, Liberal member of parliament for Limerick, Manning ran into Gladstone. It was an extraordinary meeting. In Manning's account the two men shook hands 'warmly' and Gladstone said 'I hope I shall see you again.'[104] Manning, anxious to renew their relationship, at once wrote to ask Gladstone if he had really meant it. Gladstone replied coldly that his greeting had been no more than 'an impulse of nature', and added: 'it was not that I had anything to say'.[105] Manning, however, persisted in his advances,[106] and the two men

---

99 Lathbury (ed.), *Correspondence*, II, p. 392; 'Memorandum on the Roman Question' (1863). 100 Morley, *Gladstone*, I, p. 646.
101 Lathbury (ed.), *Correspondence*, II, p. 36 (26 December 1864).
102 British Library, Gladstone Papers, Add. MS 44248, CLXIII, fo. 218 (Gladstone to Manning, 15 October 1864).
103 *Ibid.*, fo. 214 (Manning to Gladstone, 10 October 1864).
104 Purcell, *Manning*, II, p. 162.
105 British Library, Gladstone Papers, Add. MS 44248, CLXIII, fo. 147 (Gladstone to Manning, 15 March 1861).
106 *Ibid.*, fo. 148 (Manning to Gladstone, 16 March 1861).

agreed to meet. When they did, on 20 March, they conversed for two hours on the question of the Temporal Power, and Manning was sufficiently encouraged, in consequence, to inaugurate a correspondence on the matter which endured, intermittently, throughout the 1860s and was ultimately terminated only with the publication of Gladstone's pamphlet on the *Vatican Decrees* in 1874.[107] Gladstone's own observations about their meeting, that March day in 1861, were not so encouraging. 'Under external smoothness and conscientious kindness, there lay a chill indescribable', he confided in his diary.[108] A perusal of Manning's Lectures on the Temporal Power did not elevate Gladstone's expectations. The Lectures were, he noted, 'mournful indeed'.[109] To Manning, he wrote of the enormous distance they indicated between them.[110] Manning agreed. The Lectures, he wrote in reply 'express in the main what I fear is the gulf between you and me'.[111] And Gladstone, in turn, confirmed it, declining to expand on his objections to particular arguments because he disagreed with them all – as he did with 'the temper of mind' which had assembled them.[112] Manning, at last perceiving that the dialogue he had initiated was running into the sands, proposed a 'treaty' for the collection and exchange of their past correspondence[113] – a matter of importance to scholars since by this chance Manning's letters on the issue of the Temporal Power (unlike his other papers, which are not available[114]) are now accessible for historical scrutiny.

In 1864, however, and prompted by the visit of Garibaldi to England, the correspondence resumed, and the letters of the two men on the Italian question, in the ensuing two years, contain their fullest explorations of attitudes. Gladstone actually dined with Garibaldi in London during April. In May, Manning issued a pamphlet both denouncing the visit and regretting the reception Garibaldi had received from public men. His optimistic assessment of the good effects which might yet emerge were proved false: 'I believe

---

[107] McClelland noticed these letters when writing his study of Manning, but regarded the subject of the Temporal Power as falling 'outside the scope of the present work'; see V. A. McClelland, *Cardinal Manning. His Public Life and Influence, 1865–1892* (London, 1962), p. 176.

[108] *The Gladstone Diaries*, ed. H. C. G. Matthew (Oxford, 1978), VI (1861–8), p. 18 (20 March 1861).

[109] *Ibid.*, p. 28 (28 April 1861); see also p. 33 (19 May 1861).

[110] British Library, Gladstone Papers, Add. MS 44248, CLXIII, fo. 151 (Gladstone to Manning, 8 August 1861).

[111] *Ibid.*, fo. 152 (Manning to Gladstone, 4 September 1861).

[112] *Ibid.*, fo. 156 (Gladstone to Manning, 13 October 1861).

[113] *Ibid.*, fo. 162 and fo. 185 (Manning to Gladstone, 14 October 1861, and 27 November 1862).

[114] The Manning papers are in the custody of the Revd Professor A. Chapeau of the Université Catholique de l'Ouest at Angers, and are not open for study.

that the visit of General Garibaldi has opened the eyes of many to the mischievous action of Her Majesty's Government in Italy; and that a calm and firm return to higher and nobler principles of international law will be the result.'[115] It had been in the hope of influencing Gladstone away from identifying the English government with Italian liberalism that Manning had pursued their renewed contacts in the first place. The 'terrible hereafter' being prepared in Europe, through the subversion of Christian civilization, was, he told Gladstone in 1862, 'mainly by the influence of England'.[116] Gladstone, of course, was one of the designers of the government's pro-Italian sympathies. After Garibaldi's visit, Manning returned to his appeals with renewed vigour. England, he wrote in October, 1864, 'has been of late on the wrong side'. Of Gladstone himself he added, 'I am very anxious to see you on the right side.'[117] Further appeals repeated the defence of the Temporal Power as the basis of order – 'the great providential order of Christian Europe'. That, he told Gladstone, was the centre of his position, not some mere attempt to uphold 'class interests or the Divine Right of Dukes or Kings to govern badly'.[118] Writing from Paris in January 1865, on the way to Rome, Manning laid out his political creed for Gladstone's inspection. The maintenance of the Temporal Power was about the preservation of the union of church and state – an appeal to which Manning must have had every reason to suppose Gladstone sympathetic since he could not have foreseen, any more than Gladstone could, that within two years the question of the Irish Church was to adjust Gladstone's views on the whole matter of church and state relationships. 'My position', Manning continued, in reference to the Italian states, 'is that the will of a majority apart from justifying causes does not carry the right to change existing governments.' Such causes, he declared, did not exist in the case of the papal states. A change of government without them was a rebellion 'against the natural rights and justice on which that Government reposes'. There were, that is to say, constitutional bases which were fundamental laws: it was a view very much within English constitutional theory. He went on to criticize – as many others had done, including other members of Palmerston's administration – Gladstone's speech in 1864 on Baines's motion for parliamentary reform, the speech in which Gladstone had observed that every man 'who is not presumably incapacitated by some consideration of personal un-

---

115 H. E. Manning, 'The Visit of Garibaldi to England', *Miscellanies*, I, p. 146.

116 British Library, Gladstone Papers, Add. MS 44248, CLXIII, fo. 187 (Manning to Gladstone, 28 November 1862).

117 *Ibid.*, fo. 214 (Manning to Gladstone, 10 October 1864). See also fo. 240 (30 December 1864).

118 *Ibid.*, fo. 222 (Manning to Gladstone, 24 October 1864). See also fo. 232 (22 December 1864).

fitness or of political danger is morally entitled to come within the pale of the constitution'.[119] Manning wrote 'I have no fear of extended suffrage, but I have of the tone in which it seems you appeal to *numbers*.' Sovereignty, he continued, resides in the constitutional basis; it cannot be recalled by numerical majorities 'without justifying causes' – these he defined as 'such moral necessity as justify both war and homicide'. It was a conventional, liberal view. He added impatiently 'I think we live in days when men preach the change of Government as they talk of changing their coats.'[120] Gladstone was unimpressed: conditions in the papal states were, to him, so bad that they did amount to Manning's 'justifying causes'. He wrote of Manning's determination 'to fight in the name of religion against natural right and justice'.[121] The correspondence, however, continued, and when in the autumn of 1866 Gladstone visited Rome, with his wife and daughters, it was Manning who prepared his reception and arranged two audiences with Pius IX. Gladstone had assured him that the visit to Rome was benign: 'it seems to be imagined that I am to repeat in Rome the steps I took at Naples'.[122] The stay in Rome was not without problems. The Gladstones' apartment twice caught fire, with a floor burnt through each time. The audiences with the pope were mostly about Irish, not Italian questions.[123]

It is interesting that Sir John Acton – who was later to assist Gladstone in his opposition to the Vatican Council and so foster the next major break in the relations of Gladstone and Manning – in 1860 held very similar views about the Temporal Power to Manning's. Acton was convinced that the existence of the states of the church guaranteed the independence of the pontiffs and was necessary to the universality of Catholicism. He had little sympathy for the Italian liberals, supposing that their version of nationalism was essentially opposed to true principles of political liberty.[124] His anonymous articles of 1860 in the *Rambler* were a defence of the Temporal Power:[125] in January he published 'The Political System of the Popes', an historical account of the origins of temporal sovereignty, and in March 'The States of the Church', an argument in favour of the 'glorious spectacle' of papal civil power.[126] He wrote: 'The secularization of the Roman system is simply contrary to the notion of a state which exists as the property and for the benefit of the whole Catholic Church.'[127] But he was about to be turned

---

[119] Morley, *Gladstone*, I, p. 760.

[120] British Library, Gladstone Papers, Add. MS 44248, CLXIII, fo. 250 (Manning to Gladstone, 15 January 1865).

[121] Lathbury (ed.), *Correspondence*, II, p. 36.   [122] *Ibid.*, p. 37.

[123] *Ibid.*, p. 398, 'Memorandum of a Conversation with His Holiness Pope Pius IX on October 22, 1866'.   [124] Altholz, *Liberal Catholic Movement*, p. 134.

[125] MacDougall, *The Acton–Newman Relations*, p. 68.

[126] *Rambler*, new series, II (March 1860), p. 291.   [127] *Ibid.*, p. 322.

round. After a meeting with Döllinger in Munich, during the December of 1860, he changed his mind. Döllinger appeared to have persuaded him both of fatal defects in the actual government of the states of the church and of the inevitability of the end of the Temporal Power. In fact, Acton had misunderstood Döllinger, who still favoured the retention of the states but with radically reformed internal administration.[128] When Döllinger delivered his lectures on the question of the Temporal Power in Munich, in April, this became clear. They were an indictment of bad government, not of papal civil power as such. The *Dublin Review*, in a critique, pointed out that the lectures were intended for an academic audience in Munich and not for the world-wide coverage they actually received; it lamented that the 'frank and unsuspecting outpourings' of Döllinger, and his 'laborious impartiality', would inevitably and with 'but little ingenuity' equip the opponents of the papacy with new weapons.[129] The tone of the lectures was sufficiently antipathetic, however, to win the congratulations of Gladstone – who had first met Döllinger in 1845 and now wrote to say: 'you have exhibited the gradual departure of the States of the Church from all those conditions which made it tolerable to the sense and reason of mankind'.[130] Acton's changed opinions placed him alongside Newman. The latter, apart from expressing some vaguely hostile sentiments about papal governments and the general 'miserable state' of Italy, in two anonymous letters in the *Rambler*[131] (in the second of which he observed that the popes anyway had only 'the name and not the power' of independence, since their rule depended on French bayonets[132]), kept out of public controversy on the matter. But his known opinions were enough to encourage a belief in Rome that he was a 'Garibaldian', so adding to his disfavour with the papal court and assisting the Catholic bishops in their desire to secure the censure of the *Rambler*. The journal was anyway disliked by the ultramontanes because of its liberal atmosphere and its parade of intellectual independence. After first offending with Newman's article on consulting the laity in matters of doctrine, in July 1859, it was now, through Acton's conversion, becoming associated with disloyalty on the Temporal Power question. Both Manning and Talbot believed hostile articles in the journal in 1861 were aimed at Manning's own Lectures.[133] Newman was actually unaware of any such purpose, but the accumulating distrust between Manning and Newman was

---

[128] MacDougall, *The Acton–Newman Relations*, p. 75.
[129] *Dublin Review*, LII (April 1863), p. 469; 'The Church and the Churches; of the Papacy and the Temporal Power' [by C. W. Russell, President of Maynooth; published anonymously].
[130] Lathbury (ed.), *Correspondence*, II, p. 33.
[131] *Rambler*, new series, I (May 1859), p. 103.
[132] *Ibid.*, p. 112.   [133] Purcell, *Manning*, II, pp. 165, 348.

greatly added to by Manning's suspicions.[134] In the summer of 1861 Manning warned Acton that Rome would censure the *Rambler* if unfriendly views on the Temporal Power continued to appear in its pages, and in November 1861, Wiseman sent his complaints about the 'infernal sentiments' of the magazine to Propaganda.[135] In order to avoid formal proceedings the *Rambler* changed its name to the *Home and Foreign Review* after May 1862, but in October the Catholic bishops' Pastoral Letters warned the faithful against both publications. The issue of the Temporal Power, and Manning's establishment of a Catholic orthodoxy on it, had decisively split off the Liberal Catholics from the main body of the 'Roman' Church which Wiseman and Manning were fashioning in England.

After the mid-1860s Manning was never again so completely preoccupied by the question of the Temporal Power. The subsequent history of his opinions on the matter, however, shows his continued proximity to developments in the political society around him. With time, he became convinced of the moral connexion between the Irish and the Italian questions – especially early in the 1870s, when he was involving himself with the Irish bishops in their approaches to Gladstone's government over proposed reforms in higher education. 'I am altogether unable to maintain the justice of our holding Ireland if the Pope had not a just sovereignty over Rome', he wrote to Gladstone in 1872.[136] He had, in a pamphlet of 1868, referred to the 'just discontent of almost a whole people' in Ireland.[137] The eventual and radical shift in his position over the Temporal Power was directly linked to this view of Irish claims. But the transition was a painful one. In 1877 he was still, in response to the papal Allocution *Luctuosis exagitati* – about the persecution of the church under Italian rule – repeating all his old defences of the Temporal Power. *The Independence of the Holy See*, which he published in order to popularize the arguments conveyed in the Allocution, urged a restoration of the temporal sovereignty as essential for the pope's independence. In 1870 the Italians had seized the city of Rome itself. The papacy, he repeated, was 'the key-stone' of European civilization.[138] 'Rome belongs to the Pontiffs because the Providence of God gave that city to them',[139] he declared; the taking of Rome was 'a high crime against the whole of Christendom'[140], and 'a rejection of God'.[141]

Yet Manning came to accept the new arrangement of things, and to see

---

[134] C. S. Dessain, *John Henry Newman* (3rd edn, Oxford, 1980), p. 118.

[135] Archives of Propaganda, *Scritture Riferite nei Congressi, Anglia*, XVI (1861–3), fo. 309 (25 November 1861) [in Italian].

[136] McClelland, *Manning*, p. 126.

[137] H. E. Manning, 'Ireland. A Letter to Earl Grey' [1868], *Miscellanies*, I, p. 251.

[138] Cardinal Manning, *The Independence of the Holy See* (London, 1877), p. 39.

[139] *Ibid.*, p. 45.   [140] *Ibid.*, p. 51.   [141] *Ibid.*, p. 91.

that the prospect of a restoration was hopeless. The European powers did not desire it, nor did the former subjects of the pope. Indeed, of the Italians he came to realize, in the 1880s, that 'a new generation' was arising 'acclimatised to the Revolution, and powerfully attracted by the open careers of public life'.[142] At the court of Leo XIII Manning counselled the withdrawal of the Decree prohibiting Italian Catholics from participation in the political life of the new Italian state. He was, in consequence, regarded by the Vatican – as Newman once had been – as 'an Italianissimo'. He further urged the creation of a Catholic party to represent the religious life of the nation in the legislative assembly, and told the pope that he should trust the people. It was 'a practical view of things'.[143] The more he shifted ground the less he was found acceptable at Rome; Leo XIII was no more able than his predecessor to come to terms with the Italian revolution. The logic of Manning's evolving Irish opinions worked though: as English government in Ireland was wrongly maintained by force of arms, he believed,[144] so the restoration of the papal states by force seemed inappropriate. When in 1886 Manning declared himself in favour of Home Rule for Ireland his reasons were markedly similar to those of the Italian liberals who had demanded the end of the Temporal Power. He looked now to the day 'when the people of Ireland will be re-admitted, so far as possible, to the possession of their own soil, and shall be admitted, so far as possible, to the making and administration of their local laws'.[145] It was exactly what Farini had asked of the Italian situation; it was the adoption of Gladstone's views in relation to both countries. The personal as well as the political reconciliation of Gladstone and Manning was one of the results.

[142] Purcell, *Manning*, II, p. 616.
[143] *Ibid.*, pp. 612–13.
[144] *Ibid.*, p. 627.
[145] *Ibid.*, p. 621.

The Poor in Christ: peasants, priests and politics in the Cosenza general strike, November 1920

JONATHAN STEINBERG

Noi calabresi siamo gli ultimi nel mondo. *Michele Serra*

Nel cristianesimo, o meglio nelle applicazioni sociali del cristianesimo, lavorare voleva dire *liberarsi*.

Father Carlo De Cardona

In April 1921, an unusual thing happened in Cosenza, the capital of one of the three regions of Calabria. A general strike of peasants ended peacefully. There was no bloodshed and very little violence. The event stood out so markedly from the chronicle of killing, maiming, beating, and arson which in the early months of 1921 inflamed Italy that the Prefect of Cosenza, the highest local authority, decided to celebrate the 'cordial understanding between proprietors and peasants' by a public meeting. 'A common desire' for such an occasion had been expressed by all parties.[1]

It was a grand affair. The local deputy, the *onorevole* Tommaso Arnoni, spoke, as did the chairman of the provincial council and the president of the chamber of commerce, the mayors of Cosenza, Rende and Montalto, the president of the local court, the public prosecutor, representatives of the landlords and the peasants. The main theme of the speakers was summed up in the *Giornale di Calabria*: 'once more in contrast to other regions, among us there has triumphed the undeniable good sense (*buon senso*) of our stock...'.[2]

The principal negotiator for the peasants was a priest, who taught at the local seminary, and had founded the Catholic Lega del Lavoro Calabrese, Father Carlo De Cardona. Don Carlo, while not entirely satisfied with all the clauses inserted in the agreements, said that the peasants 'had to be happy about the triumph of their organisation'. But they had, he continued, even

[1] Guadagnini to the minister of the interior, 15 April 1921, Archivio Centrale dello Stato, Ministero dell'Interno, Direzione Generale di Pubblica Sicurezza (abbreviated below as ACS DGPS), C–1, 'ordine pubblico', busta 66.

[2] *Giornale di Calabria*, 21 April 1921; ACS DGPS, C–1, 'ordine pubblico', b. 66.

more reason to be pleased that 'unlike other regions, where for the same cause blood had been spilt and hatreds perpetuated, among us spirits had been pacified, agreement had been reached, and good sense had prevailed'.[3]

Buon senso is not common at the best of times. The period 1920–1 in the Kingdom of Italy was not the best of times. The two years since the end of first world war, the *biennio rosso*, the 'red two years', had been a period of turbulence, political effervescence, hopes, disillusion, and almost uninterrupted violence. Promises made in the patriotic euphoria of war had been forgotten, and the sombre prophecy of Antonio Salandra in the chamber of deputies in November 1918 had been fulfilled: 'Men and governments will be once more worn out and consumed. Codes and institutions will change and be transformed, old customs of life and social relations, old and venerated ideals will fall, overthrown and shattered.'[4] By October 1920, the wave of revolutionary socialism had ebbed and, although only a few far-sighted people saw it, a new wave of violence from the right was about to begin. In the province of Ferrara, as Paul Corner has shown, the final moment of the left wing advance was the local elections on the 7th of November 1920, which brought socialists into power in Ferrara and in about a quarter of the country's town halls. The Ferrarese landlords turned to the fascists. In the first week of November 1920, a leading article in the *Gazzetta Ferrarese* described the next step in the landlords' battle against the peasants:

New, young, courageous forces are needed. Fortunately the recent electoral struggle has shown us these fresh forces: the fascists. People for the most part veterans of the trenches, who have known every sacrifice and are ready for that extreme sacrifice of life for the good of this land which they love today more than yesterday because it has been saved by their blood. To these, to the fascists, falls the honour and the duty. Only they have the right to make claims on the future of Italy; only they, who love youth and force, can arrest the wave of madness which is breaking over Italy.[5]

The *mezzogiorno*, the Italian south, had its violence too, some of it overtly political, much of it traditional expressions of peasant despair and exasperation. Peasants in many areas of the south had not by 1920, and have not today, forgotten or forgiven the usurpations of the commons, the *usi civici*, carried out in the name of liberty, equality, fraternity, and progress by the French invaders of the 1790s and continued with enthusiasm by the local bourgeoisie. A new class of 'Barons' had emerged. In Calabria they were the Barracco, Berlingieri, Lucifero and Gallucio families who had accumulated thousands of hectares of property which peasants had from time

3 *Ibid.*
4 Antonio Salandra, 20 November 1918, in Luigi Salvatorelli and Giovanni Mira, *Storia d'Italia nel Periodo Fascista* (4th edn. 'Gli Oscar', Milan, 1972), vol. I, p. 13.
5 Paul Corner, *Fascism in Ferrara 1915–1925* (Oxford, 1975), p. 113.

immemorial regarded as 'theirs'. As the Calabrian sociologist, Pino Arlacchi, puts it,

The spread of the market economy in the nineteenth century literally liquidated countless ancient usages and customs, customary rights to the use of the soil and ancient systems of measurement and barter. The new bourgeois class, often installed by the abolition of what early nineteenth-century liberals condemned as 'feudalism', claimed to own land which had, in the bourgeois sense, never been owned before. Peasant communities were atomised. Competition for the remaining scraps of land, forest and pasturage, destroyed immemorial customary agreements, the so-called *usi civici*. There was no effective central point in peasant society to permit them to re-group, reorganise and regulate their affairs. There was no class, group, economic or political coterie which had the slightest interest in obtaining the organised consent of the peasants to the new order.[6]

The Great War made these problems worse. Peasants bore the brunt of the fighting. Of those called to arms, 45.9% (2,618,234 men) were officially classified as *contadini* or 'peasants' but of those killed in battle more than two-thirds were so classed.[7] The dislocation of southern life was made worse by the high proportion of adult males from southern Italy who had emigrated before 1914. The burden of conscription fell, then, on a male population already severely reduced. The war raised prices, brought short-ages, disturbed markets, and interrupted emigration and remittances from emigrants. In the south of Italy, especially in Calabria, the war mobilised a class of persons who knew little of politics. Illiteracy in the Kingdom of Italy still stood at 40% in 1911 but in Calabria, in this as in other indicators bottom of the league table, it stood at 70%.[8]

Land hunger, that ancient craving of the Italian peasant, became irresistible in post-war Italy. Veterans returning after three years on the Isonzo or the Altipiano had no intention of waiting while the *signori* in Rome made them homes fit for heroes. They organised into veterans' cooperatives and took the *terre incolte*. Landlords protested. Prefects and sub-prefects ordered in the various local police forces and pitched battles took place. Prices of food stuffs shot up at the same time and shortages of basic elements in the Italian diet, olive oil, pasta, or flour, increased the exasperation. In the province of Catanzaro in 1919 there were fifteen riots about food shortages or prices, and thirteen in the neighbouring province of Cosenza.[9] These were additional

---

6 Pino Arlacchi, *Mafia, Peasants and Great Estates. Society in Traditional Calabria*, tr. Jonathan Steinberg (Cambridge, 1983), p. 16.
7 Arrigo Serpieri, *Le Guerra e Le Classe Rurali Italiane* (Bari, 1930), pp. 51ff.
8 Tullio De Mauro, *Storia Linguistica dell'Italia Unita* (Bari, 1972), p. 95.
9 The police reports for the province of Reggio Calabria, the third Calabrian province, were missing in the Archivio Centrale dello Stato for 1919; for 1920, they record thirty riots or incidents, of which fifteen involved occupation of uncultivated land,

to the customary riots caused by electoral battles or what the police reports refer to as *odi tradizionali*, traditional hatreds. In 1920 the total number of riots remained more or less at the same level but now in the province of Catanzaro occupation of uncultivated land had become the principal cause, eleven such incidents occurring in the autumn of the year, while in the province of Cosenza the subjects of public wrath spread more generally to exasperation about the absence of roads, sewers, bus service, honest local government, and cheap food.[10]

The citizens of the city of Cosenza were not wrong to praise their 'good sense'. They were indeed 'unlike other regions', even in their own province. My table of popular protest for the province of Cosenza shows that of forty-six incidents of riot, protest, or popular violence recorded by the prefectures and sub-prefectures and sent to the ministry of the interior during the years 1919 and 1920, the city of Cosenza and the surrounding villages do not appear until August 1920, when the movement which led to the general strike began. The fierce mountain community of San Giovanni in Fiore, no doubt true to the utopian gospel of the medieval visionary, Joachim of Fiore, who founded it, with a population only a fraction of that of Cosenza, the province's capital city, managed to produce no less than seven full scale riots, including one in which the carabinieri were kept prisoners by peasant barricades for several days.[11]

What made the peasantry and for that matter the bourgeoisie of the city of Cosenza and its surroundings less violent than their fellow Calabrians on the other side of the Sila mountains? The answer which I hope to offer in the rest of this essay brings together economics, sociology, settlement patterns and geography, theology and Christian witness, high politics,

protests about the terms of the tenancy agreements, and three specifically based on claims about usurpation of commons (*usi civici*). It is worth noting that land seizures bunch in short bursts of activity, which suggests, unlike food riots which occur at times of shortage, the presence of organisations and planned campaigns. The evidence in detail is spotty and deducing motives from police reports is not the ideal method of assessing peasant grievances.

10 'Popular Protest in Calabria, 1919–1922', table of statistics drawn from ACS DGPS, C–1, 'ordine pubblico', for 1919; b. 95, b. 96, b. 109; for 1920: b. 82, b. 83; for 1921: b. 65, b. 66, b. 73; for 1922: b. 64, b. 65, b. 75.

11 San Giovanni in Fiore poses a peculiar historical problem. It appears in the archives disproportionately: for 1919 cf. ACS DGPS, C–1, 'ordine pubblico', b. 96, prefect to DGPS, 10 Feb. 1919, 21 Feb. 1919, 2 July 1919, 9 Sept. 1919, 29 Oct. 1919, 9 Dec. 1919; for 1920 cf. ACS DGPS, C–1, 'ordine pubblico', b. 83, 18 Mar. 1920, 6 Dec. 1920. In the March 1920 rising, some 2000 demonstrators took to the street and troops had to be sent in. Why was it known for its 'spirit of rebellion' and still is a 'red' town today with a communist majority on the city council? How can we account for centuries of popular protest without thinking about the legacy of the medieval visionary who made the place famous?

administrative practice and institutional structure, and some, not inconsiderable, element of ignorance. The non-violence of the Cosenza peasants and their successful general strike, precisely because its geographical and temporal limits are so strict, offers a perfect case for a kind of 'total history' or, more accurately, an instruction in the difficulty of historical explanation as such. It takes a lot of work to explain very little.

Geography is important. The city of Cosenza sits in a broad basin circumscribed by mountains on three sides and looks so like a conch shell that locals call it the *conca cosentina*. Most of the surrounding villages perch like little fortresses on the heights above the city and at night look like clusters of stars against the black bulk of the surrounding mountains. At the turn of the century George Gissing, against the advice of all his sensible Italian friends, decided to visit Calabria. He took the train from Naples and got off at Paola on the coast, something the traveller still has to do. Eventually he reached the summit of the winding road from Paola to Cosenza and saw the *conca cosentina* spread out below him.

At an unexpected turn of the road there spread before me a vast prospect; I looked down upon inland Calabria. It was a valley broad enough to be called a plain, dotted with white villages, and backed by a mass of mountains which now, as in old time, bear the name Great Sila. Through this landscape flowed the river Crati – the ancient Crathis; northward it curved, and eastward, to fall at length into the Ionian Sea, far beyond my vision.[12]

What Gissing could not see were the social habits and economic relationships of the 'white villages', and it is not easy now to reconstruct them. They were certainly very poor, as indeed the whole of Calabria was. Conditions in these villages, some without sewers, others without paved streets, most without light, were primitive. As always, even in misery, there are gradations. A 1926 survey of drinking water found that the province of Cosenza was rather better off than the other two Calabrian provinces. It had the highest number of inhabitants living in communes with water called 'good' and the lowest in the categories marked 'mediocre' or 'bad'. Good water had, of course, nothing to do with availability; it simply meant that the water would not kill you if you drank it unboiled. In fact between 1885 and 1926 the water supply situation had worsened. Whereas in the earlier period only 22% of all Calabrian communes complained that the supply ran out, by 1926 55% now claimed that their supply was insufficient.[13]

Diet and general conditions of health varied throughout Calabria. In

---

12 George Gissing, *By the Ionian Sea. Notes of a Ramble in Southern Italy* (London, 1901), p. 15.
13 Piero Bevilacqua, *Le Campagne del Mezzogiorno tra Fascismo e Dopoguerra. Il Caso di Calabria* (Turin, 1980), p. 89.

*The diffusion of 'colonia parziaria appoderata' in the three
areas, in Calabria and in the Mezzogiorno*

	% of tillable surface occupied by units held under *colonia parziaria appoderata*
Cosentino	30.0
Plain of Gioia Tauro	8.5
Calabria	8.3
Mezzogiorno	4.5
Crotonese	0.0

general the inhabitants of the coastal zones suffered more from the endemic malaria than mountain people and seem to have had less well-balanced diets. Gissing recorded his amazement on seeing a healthy person after his own bout of malaria in Crotone:

At one of the wayside stations entered a traveller whom I could not but regard with astonishment. He was a man at once plump and muscular, his sturdy limbs well exhibited in a shooting costume. On his face glowed the richest hue of health; his eyes glistened merrily. With him he carried a basket, which, as soon as he was settled, gave forth an abundant meal. The gusto of his eating, the satisfaction with which he eyed his glasses of red wine, excited my appetite. But who *was* he? Not, I could see, a tourist; yet how account for this health and vigour in a native of the district? I had not seen such a man since I set out upon my travels; the contrast he made with the figures of late familiar to me was so startling that I had much ado to avoid continuously gazing at him. His proximity did me good; the man radiated health.

When next the train stopped he exchanged words with some one on the platform, and I heard that he was going to Catanzaro. At once I understood. This jovial, ruddy-cheeked personage was a man of the hills.[14]

The villages of the Cosentino were inhabited by mountain people and, while there is no hard evidence, other indicators suggest that they were probably better off both in physical and social terms than most Calabrians. A peculiarity of the zone was its special form of agricultural tenancy, *colonia parziaria appoderata*, that is, leases or tenancies of entire farms as productive units complete with structures and implements. The harshness of oppressive tenancies, well known and remarked on in other parts of Calabria, existed much less frequently within the *conca cosentina*. Pino Arlacchi has argued that this form of tenancy gave the Cosentino its peculiar social structure. The figures in the table above show how different the Cosenza region was from others in the Italian south.[15]

[14] Gissing, *By The Ionian Sea*, p. 105. [15] Arlacchi, *Mafia*, p. 15.

Participation of women among those occupied full-time in the three
areas, in Calabria, in mainland Mezzogiorno and other regions

	Women per 100 occupied persons
Cosentino	34
Central Italy	30
Northern Italy	27
Italy	26
Calabria	22
Mainland Mezzogiorno	18
Plain of Gioia Tauro	14
Crotonese	3
Sicily, Sardinia	2

Annual average emigration from the 'latifondo', from the peasant
community of the Cosentino, from Calabria and from the
Mezzogiorno from 1884 to 1915

Area	Emigration per 1,000 inhabitants
Cutro/Isola di Capo Rizzuto (Crotonese)	7
Figline Vegliaturo/ Piane Crati (Cosentino)	41
Calabria	18
Mezzogiorno	11

The family enterprise employed all its members, especially women, and
it is characteristic that the Cosentino should top the list in percentage of
women employed for the whole of Italy, as the table above shows.[16]

The countryside of the Cosentino was dotted with individual homesteads
or small villages instead of the typical southern Italian 'rural city', from
which the labourers went out to fields where nobody lived. In the 'rural
city' labour and life, man and woman, home and work were more strictly
divided than in the family farm and it is easier to think of class and functional
divisions than in the peasant holding where everybody did every job under
the joint supervision of the parents as employers.

Piero Bevilacqua provides a table of tenancy by size which shows that
Cosenza had many more medium-sized holdings than either the provinces

[16] *Ibid.*, p. 26.

of Catanzaro or Reggio Calabria. It also had the lowest number of micro-holdings under 1 hectare. Of tenancies in Cosenza, 27.1% lay between 5 and 50 hectares, as opposed to 18.1% in Catanzaro and only 5.3% in the province of Reggio. If measured by surface under cultivation, the figures show that Cosenza tenancies of 5 to 50 hectares covered 56.7% of all land cultivated by tenants, compared to 43.9% in Catanzaro and 29.6% in Reggio.[17] It is not far-fetched to speak of the Cosentino then as an area of 'middle' peasant cultivation.

The Cosentino social order rested on the family enterprise, a special kind of tenancy, and some solidity of economic well-being. It was this solidarity and what sociologists call 'reciprocity' that made it also, paradoxically, the area of emigration. The Italian emigrant went abroad then, as he does now, to come home, to buy that strip of land or to build that *palazzo*. A visitor to a southern Italian town today sees ghostly building sites on the edges of each village where, when the emigrant can spare the odd Deutschmark or Swiss franc, he adds another wall or brick course to the dream home that he and his children and children's children will occupy some day. In San Giovanni in Fiore today, a third of the total population and much more than half of those of working age live 'fuori'. To emigrate costs money; to come back costs money. The Cosentino peasant had access to both. The outward journey in the late nineteenth or early twentieth centuries was often paid by the dowry of the future wife, a curious transformation of peasant custom into modern steamship tickets. The figures given by Professor Arlacchi in the table on p. 263 for a typical village of the Cosentino make the point very clear.

[17] *Number and surface area of tenant farms by province in Calabria by size of unit*

	Catanzaro				Cosenza				Reggio Calabria			
	No.	%	Surface	%	No.	%	Surface	%	No.	%	Surface	%
below 1	1045	29.6	605.24	5.4	1736	20.5	946.05	1.8	8315	55.2	4469.53	16.6
1 to 3	1314	37.3	2581.72	22.9	2803	33.1	8621.61	10.8	4891	32.5	8885.69	32.9
3 to 5	510	14.5	2029.66	18.0	1529	18.1	6194.90	11.9	1041	6.9	4110.80	15.3
5 to 10	388	11.0	2716.01	24.1	1256	14.8	8924.58	17.3	578	3.8	4004.37	14.8
10 to 20	189	5.3	270.44	2.4	712	8.4	9920.75	19.2	186	1.2	2557.92	9.5
20 to 50	63	1.78	1957.26	17.4	335	3.9	10433.05	20.2	47	0.3	1440.09	5.3
50 to 100	11	0.31	751.30	6.7	70	0.8	4786.20	9.3	6	0.03	515.30	1.9
100 to 500	3	0.08	359.94	3.2	22	0.2	3797.10	7.4	2	0.01	350.00	1.3
over 500	—	—	—	—	1	—	1000.00	1.9	1	—	600.00	2.2
Total	3253	100	11271.57	100	8464	100	5162.24	100	15067	100	26933.70	100

The statistics in the table are drawn from Bevilacqua, *Le Campagne del Mezzogiorno*, p. 55. Professor Bevilacqua gives the absolute figures as drawn from the *Catasto agrario* of 1929 and I have calculated the percentages. There is some discrepancy in Professor Bevilacqua's figures since there are addition errors in two of his columns so that my figures rest on corrected calculations. It is possible, of course, that the sums are correct but misprints have occurred in the figures themselves. The general conclusions are not likely to be affected very much.

They also show how impossible emigration was for the *braccianti*, the desolate landless poor, of a typical village in the area of the great *latifondo* estates of the Crotonese. Isola di Capo Rizzuto is even today, perhaps, the grimmest rural community in Calabria, a legacy of the oppression of 'barons' so mean and avaricious, that the old adage could say, 'not even smoke comes out of the baron's house'.[18]

How the Italian peasant lived in 'the land of the free' has been memorably described by an American social scientist, R. F. Foerster, who in 1919 published one of the really great studies of emigrant experience, *The Italian Emigration of Our Time*.

'Men, women, dogs, cats, and monkeys eat and sleep together in the same hole without air and without light.' They buy stale beer at two cents a pint from a rascally Italian in a basement, and they break into endless brawls. During the summer they work on the railroads and in the fields; 'in the winter they return to fill the streets of New York, where the boys are bootblacks and the men either are employed at the most repulsive tasks, scorned by workmen of other nationalities – carrying offal to the ships and dumping it in the sea, cleaning the sewers *et similia* – or they go about with sacks on their shoulders rummaging the garbage cans, gleaning paper, rags, bones, broken glass'...

'And while the workmen fag from morning to evening, the bosses smoke tranquilly and superintend them with rifles at their sides and revolvers at their belts. They seem – and are – real brigands.' Whoever tells these natives of Avellino, of the Abruzzi, of Basilicata, that they are being cheated, loses his words. '*Signorino*', they reply, 'we are ignorant and do not know English. Our boss brought us here, knows where to find work, makes contracts with the companies. What should we do without him?' The Camorra flourishes as in the worst Bourbon times and 'the Italian, illiterate, carrying the knife, defrauded and fraudulent, is more despised than the Irish and the Chinese'.[19]

Miserable and oppressed as these people were, they had one force which not even the most despicable *camorrista* could suppress: their power to save money. Giorgio Amendola in his autobiography describes the astonishment of the communist prisoners on the island of Ponza when they went to complain about the inadequate sums they were given for food. The prison governor replied with a shrug that however inadequate it might have been for the peasant of the Po Valley or worker from Turin, the prisoners from the Mezzogiorno managed to save half.[20] The money sent by emigrants and fascist prisoners to their families in the south can literally be called their 'life's blood'.

Young Father Carlo De Cardona, still in his twenties when in 1895 he

[18] Arlacchi, *Mafia*, p. 175.
[19] R. F. Foerster, *The Italian Emigration of Our Time* (Cambridge, Mass., 1919), p. 326.
[20] Giorgio Amendola, *Un'Isola* (2nd edn, Milan, 1981), pp. 130–1.

was appointed by Archbishop Camillo Sorgente as his private chaplain, saw that truth. For the next forty years he tried to harness the peasants' urge to save and, rather like a social hydro-electric project, to use that tenacious energy to transform the way those peasants lived. His experiment combined the teachings of Marxism with those of St Thomas of Aquinas. From the beginning of his ministry, as parish priest in Moranno Calabro, as teacher of philosophy in the diocesan seminary and Archbishop's chaplain, he worked to mobilise and, by mobilising to civilise, the peasants. One device was the *Cassa rurale*, the rural bank. In 1902, the Cassa Rurale di Cosenza was founded, 'a cooperative society in collective name with unlimited liability but non-profit making'. The idea was simple:

Money there is in our province. Post offices and the savings bank are full of money which arrives from America, sweated money, saved with who knows what sacrifice. Now all that money, and we are talking about millions, is in the hands of the rich. It's money sweated from the workers, it's money of the people that ends in the hands of the rich, of the capitalists. And behold! The people's an ass. Not just your labour but your savings...take them to the banks where you are the bosses.[21]

These banks were not simply banks, but skeletal elements of the Christian community of love and brotherhood. To love, the peasant had to be free; to be a brother, he had to cease to be a slave. In 1916, when some scandals had occurred in what was by now a federation of rural savings banks, Don Carlo had to remind his peasants for the *nth* time what the purpose of the enterprise was:

Remember, friends, that the *Casse* are not banks, that you have not been called to play bankers. The function of the *Cassa* is limited to agricultural workers and to labourers, and not all labourers, but only those who normally live in the commune... but let us also remember what the immediate scope of our *Cassa* is. It is not just to make loans, no, because the *Cassa* is the most serious and most effective form of organisation; the shareholders of the *Cassa* really share, being tied to each other by the sacred bond of unlimited liability, all for one and one for all. Let us so behave that in the *Casse* the shareholders gradually acquire the consciousness of that solidarity which is in their state, and then in every little village we shall have created not only a little credit institution but the most solid and fruitful organisation. We shall have created the bases for a *new life* in the village – a new life economically but also morally ...If we have the patience and the courage to remain true to our constitutions, with the passing of time and with the benediction of God, we shall have done a great deal for our poor Calabria.[22]

[21] Ferdinando Cassiani, *I Contadini Calabresi di Don Carlo De Cardona, 1898–1936* (collana di storia del movimento cattolico, Rome, 1976), p. 96.
[22] 'Le nostre Casse Rurali – Badate Bene!', *Il Lavoro*, 27 Feb. 1916, in S. and G. Cameroni, *Movimento Cattolico e Contadino, Indagine su Don Carlo De Cardona* (Milan, 1976), pp. 154–5.

This solidarity required, and Don Carlo saw it from the beginning, self-government in other branches of life. There must be a peasants' newspaper. In due course he founded *La Voce Cattolica* in 1898 and later *Il Lavoro* in 1905. Workers and peasants had to learn to read and write, so he organised night classes. They needed to organise economically so in 1901 he set up the Lega del Lavoro Calabrese, an agricultural trade union run for and by the peasants themselves. He founded consumers' and producers' cooperatives to market crops and buy tools and seed. From the beginning too the fierce young priest set out to stir the consciences of the Catholic bourgeoisie. In a blistering leading article called 'Sorgiamo' of August 1898, he wrote:

While Christ in his church climbs Calvary again, you are content to tick off the rosary in some side room, deploring with a sigh the badness of the times. It's cowardice. It's treason...You say you don't want to get involved in politics but do you really know the limits which distinguish it from religion? Where does politics end and religion begin?[23]

A further consequence of his position was an outspoken and rigid *classismo*. If the peasants and workers were to rise and free themselves, they had to do it separately and on their own. Their politics must be theirs, not denatured with bourgeois compromise or made eloquent by the traditional loquacity of the southern *galantuomo*. 'If today we are forced to take on the struggle against the bourgeoisie, it is not through hate but for our own very necessary defence, to defend the rights and interests of the working classes against the unjust preoccupations and fierce hatred of the bourgeoisie.'[24] The intransigence of his position complicated the politics of the Catholics of Cosenza, as such attitudes were, after the first world war, to complicate the politics of the national party of Catholics, the Partito Popolare Italiano. For it is in the nature of confessional parties to be genuine *Volksparteien*, uniting the believers whether they are workers or employers, peasants or landlords, rural or urban. Such parties end up at an inner equilibrium in the dead centre of political struggle, where, as Don Carlo knew, nothing happens. He ran his own slates of candidates in Cosenza and the other surrounding villages and was elected both to the provincial and city councils.

The movement spread. By 1905, it began to get national notice. Ercole Casazza, writing in *L'Osservatore Cattolico*, commented that '...the Catholics of the Cosentino have understood how to conquer for themselves an eminent position in the public life of their city, thus constituting in the

---

[23] 'Sorgiamo !', *La Voce Cattolica*, 21 Aug. 1898; S. and G. Cameroni, *Movimento Cattolico*, p. 49.
[24] *Il Lavoro*, 26 May 1906; Cassiani, *I Contadini*, p. 80.

whole of Southern Italy an oasis of activity in a modern democratic sense...
breaking the crust of clientelism and corruption'.[25]

Once again, if by a different route, we come back to the fact that the
Cosentino was 'different', 'an oasis', 'anomalous' in the context of southern
Italy. Its land tenure system, its family solidity, its settlement patterns, made
it the appropriate environment for the communal Christianity which Don
Carlo preached. He was, after all, a Calabrian too. On the other hand, the
conca cosentina was not immune to the besetting vice of the *mezzogiorno* as
a whole, what Don Carlo called the *temperamento balcanico*, that fierce,
fragmented egocentricity which makes the southern peasant keep her own
house immaculate but throw rubbish onto the street. What is everybody's
is nobody's. The public good has no meaning and there is an almost complete absence of those civic virtues which sustain communal life. A shrewd
American observer, A. Lawrence Lowell, summed it up well toward the
end of the last century:

The causes of this last tendency run far back into mediaeval history. The long-
continued oppression in southern Italy, and the lack of a firm and stable authority
that maintained social order and administered justice between man and man, made
the people look on every government as a natural enemy instead of a protector; and
hence society disintegrated, and there developed a want of mutual confidence, and a
general absence of social cohesion. The community was reduced to its first elements,
and men did just what they have always done when there was no higher power to
which they could appeal. They banded themselves together for mutual assistance.
The process was precisely the same as that which gave birth to the feudal system, after
the fall of Rome had plunged Europe into a state of anarchy. Each man, feeling his
weakness and isolation, joined himself to another man or body of men stronger than
he, and rendered service on condition of receiving protection. This is the origin of
the relation of patron and client in southern Italy; and indeed, the only ties that seem
to be thoroughly natural there are those of the family and of patronage.[26]

Don Carlo saw that the cooperative to market figs, for example, was more
than a means to raise prices; it was a rudimentary civil society, a form of
primitive social contract. Cooperation in all activities might teach the peasants
the civic virtues and ultimately overcome the *temperamento balcanico*.

Don Carlo identified with 'his' peasants. They became in time the very
substance of his being. In a diary entry of August 1935, by which time the
fascists had destroyed his life's work and a compliant, philo-fascist archbishop had sent him into exile, he recorded these words:

[25] Ercole Casazza, *L'Osservatore Cattolico*, 3 Oct. 1905; S. and G. Cameroni, *Movimento Cattolico*, pp. 87–8.

[26] A. Lawrence Lowell, *Governments and Parties in Continental Europe* (Cambridge, Mass.,
1896), vol. I, p. 215.

After celebrating Mass, I saw in me with a vividness and a precision never before so sharp, the countryside, the villages, the people, the streets, the mountains...all of Calabria, where I have travelled and lived intensely during forty years of my ministry: I *was* all those people, the whole world, physical, social, human...And I said to the Lord present to my spirit: behold how many people, how many souls, how many faces...I am. In this social form, I have 'built' myself with labour, disinterested, continuous, hard, bristling with suffering and crowned with misfortune and dishonour; so, O Lord, the I who is no more I comes before you.[27]

The poor whom he served were more than the sum of suffering humanity. They were the very image of Christ. During the terrible year of 1935, when his life's work unravelled knot by knot,

there came to my door a 'poor' peasant of Carolei, to ask me for an extension of his debt. 'In a month I can get it together', he said. He had hurt his hand at a forge. He was dressed like a beggar, and had on his features the sad but gentle expression of the poor in Christ. It is Christ himself then who comes to ask me to give Him time to pay. Does He not know that I have been beaten to death by the mistrust, avarice and hardness of the patrons of wealth? How can I help the poor whom He sends to my door?[28]

The passages from Don Carlo's diary are not ordinary historical documents. They bear witness to a life of sacrifice and devotion to which few aspire and which few can comprehend. Nor is there much doubt that he had always been that way. A former student recalled years later his first impressions of Don Carlo De Cardona:

I saw him for the first time in 1895 alongside Don Camillo Sorgente, our grand and unforgettable Archbishop Monsignor Sorgente, and the figure of that slender priest with burning eyes made an enormous impression on me. I was in front of a force, contained in that long lean body, a concealed power which wanted to spring out, a flame which wanted to blaze. Monsignor Don Camillo Sorgente, by the side of that ardent young idealist whom he loved tenderly, relived, I would say, his own youth anew and smiled with pleasure and blessed the sometimes tumultuous manifestations of that youthful energy. Professor of philosophy, he infused us with a love of severe studies by his profound lessons and brought into the old seminary of Cosenza a breath of new life, a light which lit us all. Through his hands the latest works of philosophy passed to his disciples.[29]

Others recalled Don Carlo at the head of a band of peasants marching with a great walking stick in his hand, like some biblical patriarch, to register the latest complaint or protest. Still others remembered him coming home late at night from the house of some poor peasant to whom he had ministered.

[27] *Diario*, 16 Aug. 1935, Todi (Perugia), in Cassiani, *I Contadini*, p. 31.
[28] *Diario*, 19 Mar. 1935, in *ibid*.
[29] F. Cozza, 'Maestro e Lottatore', Mar. 1958, quoted in S. and G. Cameroni, *Movimento Cattolico*, p. 41.

Saintliness is not normally one of the 'forces and factors' that the historian considers in attempting to explain an event. Yet the evidence in this case is hard even for the queasiest secular sensibility to evade. Here was a brilliant charismatic leader who was also and always a devout, suffering, and praying Christian, whose work in every way, from keeping the books of a rural credit bank to leading demonstrations, became a continuous manifestation of his own Christian witness.

The *conca cosentina* was different not only in its social and economic realities, those 'forces and factors' with which modern historiography, post-*Annales*, finds itself at home, nor just in the forms of organisation which its peasants adopted, but also in the personality – prophetic, charismatic, and saintly – of the leader of these peasants. Yet all these factors cannot explain why the little general strike of Cosenza in late 1920 ended in peace and congratulations in April 1921. After all, the same peasants and the same priest were frustrated after 1922 by a state which rejected their aspirations; the same peasants and the same priest were betrayed by the very church they claimed to serve when the climate changed with the signing of the Lateran Pacts in February 1929. In 1935, Don Carlo was exiled: 'I have been expelled, removed – "I give you permission to depart", said the Archbishop on Passion Sunday – from the place where I have lived for forty years...'.[30] Such an order could have come at any time during those forty years and often nearly did, for the work of Carlo De Cardona was not popular with the hierarchy of the church. Indeed in 1906, at the fifth anniversary of the foundation of the peasant leagues, only two bishops, the Archbishop of Rossano, Monsignor Orazio Mazzella, and the Archbishop of Cosenza, Monsignor Camillo Sorgente, blessed and supported them.[31]

Archbishop Sorgente made the work of Don Carlo possible. The first rural credit bank had rooms in the archiepiscopal palace. Don Carlo worked in the archiepiscopal seminary and served as the archiepiscopal chaplain. Don Camillo, who lived to a great age and was Archbishop of Cosenza from 1874 to 1911, was the necessary but not sufficient condition for Don Carlo's enterprise.

High ecclesiastical politics must be followed a step further. It was the promulgation of the encyclical *Rerum Novarum* on 15 May 1891 which made the social gospel possible at all. Leo XIII declared in the encyclical that wages were not to be treated as any other commodity, fixed solely by market forces. For young priests like Don Carlo this opened the way to a new formulation of the gospel for industrial society. The Lega del Lavoro Calabrese celebrated the 15th of May each year along with the 1st of May as the days

---

[30] *Diario*, pencil notes, 1936, in Cassiani, *I Contadini*, p. 181.
[31] Cassiani, *I Contadini*, p. 70 n. 7.

which marked the liberation of the working classes. How far Archbishop Sorgente might himself have been able to protect Catholic social action in his diocese, had there been no encyclical, cannot be measured; he certainly protected it against the counter-attack launched under Pius X when after 1903 modernism and radicalism came to be associated in the minds of many prelates and when in 1907 Don Romolo Murri, the most prominent of the Catholic radicals, was suspended.[32]

The equivocal position of the church in Italy worked in favour of Don Carlo's brand of Christian socialism, since the church continued in theory and practice to boycott the liberal state until in 1922 it ceased to be liberal. Don Carlo attacked the bourgeois–liberal–masonic–radical ruling class of Cosenza in the name of all Catholics and in that sense took some part of the Catholic bourgeoisie and clergy with him. They might differ on *classismo* but not on the importance of religious education in schools nor their opposition to crude anticlericalism, masonic intrigues, and attacks, both verbal and physical, on the clergy. Catholics of Don Carlo's generation lived in a cultural ghetto, alienated in their own homes from the ideals of the Risorgimento and the secular Kingdom of Italy which had fulfilled them. As Arturo Jemolo put it, the generation of Catholic politicians born in the 1870s had not experienced in their own lives the bitterness of the struggles of 1848, 1861, and 1870, the hatred and suspicions on both sides and, therefore, 'had the unusual task for young people of speaking to their elders in the voice of moderation, of good sense and of possibilism'.[33] The younger, flexible, politically accommodating generation wanted to get into politics, to take seats on local and provincial councils, and to serve in parliament. To do that, the *non expedit*, which forbade Catholics to recognise the godless liberal state by being 'electors or elected', had to be lifted. Their desires, very different from Don Carlo's, nevertheless flowed together where local elections gave Catholics a chance to win power. The high politics of the church, on the whole, favoured the growth of Catholic social action, though often with anxiety and misgiving, and the war gave to such work the general aspect of Christian charity. By 1918 Don Carlo was a national figure, a founder member of the Partito Popolare and an example of what could be achieved.

By November 1920 local authorities and local politicians would have experienced more than two decades of agitation and organisation. The sight of Don Carlo at the head of a cortège of peasants would not have sent the

---

[32] A. C. Jemolo, *Chiesa e Stato in Italia negli ultimi cento anni* (Turin, 1963), pp. 381ff; Cassiani, *I Contadini*, pp. 49–58, for a discussion of the crisis of modernism and radicalism on both national and local levels.

[33] Jemolo, *Chiesa e Stato*, p. 360.

local bourgeoisie to the barricades or even to close their shutters. They had seen it all before and knew that the revolution was not at hand. On the other hand, the claims made by peasants in the post-war era had become, the land-lords felt, more and more exorbitant. The local landlords sent a telegram to the prime minister in November 1920, which put their fears into bold relief: 'The requests made by the organisation of tenant farmers which is led by the priest De Cardona, aim to supplant radically the bases of landed property ...Urge action be taken against priest Cardona, considered the person directly responsible for agitation, to recall him to all due respect for public institutions...'.[34]

Giolitti, the prime minister, took no action, for it was not his policy to act. As early as 1904, in his first major industrial crisis, he had taken the line that the government had a duty to maintain order but not to take sides in the conflicts between capital and labour. When the old wizard of Italian politics formed his fifth ministry on 15 June 1920, he saw no reason to change that line. In his speech to the Senate of 15 July 1920, he set out his views on the course that the government ought to take. The government intended 'to constrain those proprietors of land by very energetic means who do not cultivate them as they can and should be cultivated, even to the point of expropriation if the proprietor will not recognise his duty...'.[35] The new minister of labour, speaking for the first time for the newly created ministry of labour, was a well-known socialist, Arturo Labriola. He took an equally striking position on the right to property. In his maiden speech to the Senate, he defended the veterans' cooperatives which had occupied un-cultivated lands all over the south of Italy.

I fear that many criticisms have been levelled at the *Opera* [i.e. the Veterans' organisa-tion] because it has developed a very radical policy of expropriating land. It has not stopped before rights of property or acquired rights...The marquis X, count Y, the honourable senator Z or the honourable deputy A have been upset by ruthless activity of the *Opera*...We live in a period in which rights of property must give way to social exigencies...Like it or not, we shall go on, towards a social constitution in which the social principle will preponderate over the individual principle at least in matters economic.[36]

On 31 August 1920, the employers in the metal and engineering industries of Turin locked out their workers. The workers responded with a call for a general strike. The Under Secretary of the Interior telegraphed the news to

---

[34] Consiglio Generale dell'Agricoltura to Giolitti, 6 Nov. 1920, ACS DGPS, C–1, 'ordine pubblico', b. 83.
[35] *Atti Parlamentari*, Senato del Regno, Legislatura XXV, 1. Sessione, Tornata, 15 July 1920.
[36] *Atti Parlamentari, ibid.*, 19 July 1920.

the prime minister: 'The workers are occupying the factories as a reaction to the lock-out. Declarations made to me personally by the industrialists reveal their desire to go to extremes. I confirm that the Government does not intend to interfere in the conflict, responsibility for which is almost exclusively theirs.'[37] Lest there be any doubt that this was government policy, Giolitti said it once again very clearly three weeks later. Turin might be paralysed by the most serious general strike in the history of the country but the government would not budge:

I believe that when it is a question of a simple conflict of interest between capital and labour, the state should remain neutral, a vigilant neutral, but neutral nonetheless... The factories will be released. It's a matter of days. The work of the General Confederation of Labour is showing itself effective in gaining a hold on the mass of workers and on this point, with the exception of the occasional incident which will have no more social importance, I believe that we shall see work begin again. The public authorities and police will resume their normal functions. I must declare as minister of the interior that prefects, functionaries and agents have done their duty according to instructions given by the government. The responsibility therefore rises directly to the government itself.[38]

It was a courageous statement, perhaps even a wise one, and certainly an accurate prediction of what was to happen, but for factory or landowners it was exasperating. The state, 'their' state, did nothing in the face of blatant violations of the law and the rights of property. It is no wonder that owners sought to find other ways to assert their rights, some in the fascist squads, others by organising their own self-defence. In Cosenza the landlords reacted to threats of the Lega del Lavoro by organising their own Lega di Resistenza. On 4 November 1920, a general assembly of agricultural proprietors met 'to constitute themselves as a League of Resistance for the protection of the rights of private property and to assure respect for the prevailing laws'. The mood of the proprietors came through the exasperated words of Signor Carlo Campagna, a Cosenza lawyer and landowner (incidentally a common double identity in a region where the larger estates tended to be owned by bourgeois, professional people):

For some time now armed bands – the so-called white guard – have been the scourge of the countryside, abandoning themselves to every act of violence under leadership urged on by professor De Cardona. He has succeeded in arresting the normal and peaceful work of the fields, disturbing public order and the peace of families.

One has had to suffer, watching helplessly, manifestations of violence of all sorts, proper acts of thuggery, encouraged by the indolent attitude of a prefect who is not up to the demands of his high office. The time has come to rise against such a state of

[37] Martin Clark, *Antonio Gramsci and the Revolution that Failed* (New Haven and London, 1977), p. 156.
[38] *Atti Parlamentari*, Senato, 26 Sept. 1920.

things! It is necessary to reestablish the rule of law by every means, with persuasion and pacification first but with violence later if it should be shown that good manners are not enough.[39]

Exasperation mounted on the other side as the Cosenza socialists began to count the cost of the failure of the Turin general strike. The proprietors could not have been encouraged by the appearance in 1920 of the first newspaper in the province to call itself 'communist', nor by the fact that the editor and moving spirit behind the new paper, *La Vita Nuova*, was Nicola De Cardona, the 'red bolshevik' younger brother of the 'white bolshevik' Carlo. In the midst of the mounting tension Nicola De Cardona demanded that the socialists choose their way forward:

We have published above the programme of the Italian Communist Party which is about to constitute itself so that every Socialist section, convened urgently by the comrades, may discuss and deliberate its unconditional adhesion to the Communist Party, sending notice to Bologna and publishing such notice in this journal. In this moment of crisis and intensive labour for the revolutionary movement, it is no longer possible to go on floating indecisively or to equivocate. You have to decide: with the reformists or with the communists.[40]

The prefect, Commendatore Giuseppe Guadagnini, was in the words of the leader of the Cosenza socialists, Pietro Mancini, 'very shrewd and therefore very dangerous'.[41] He needed all his shrewdness, for his position had become difficult. The landowners blamed him for the failure to enforce the law, that is, to send in the carabinieri to expel peasants and to break strikes, but a prefect in the Kingdom of Italy had to think of his future. If he caused violence, the prime minister, who was also the minister of the interior and hence the prefect's direct superior, might be displeased and banish him to a prefecture even more remote from civilisation than Cosenza: Sassari in Sardinia, for example. Negotiate a settlement that pleased the prime minister or use force with delicacy, and the handsome prefectoral palace in Milan or Bologna or Turin beckoned. The centralised structure of rule which the Piedmontese copied from the Napoleonic regime and then imposed on all of Italy gave the prefect dictatorial powers. He could suspend markets, fix prices, seize assets, remove duly elected city or provincial councillors, but above all he could use the Royal Carabinieri, the national police force. His reports went right to the director general of public security in the ministry or in urgent cases to the prime minister himself. Prefects had to avoid what

---

[39] 'L'Imponente Riunione del 4. Novembre' *L'Agricultura Calabrese*, 12 Nov. 1920, cited in F. Cordova, *Alle Origini del PCI in Calabria 1918–26* (Rome, 1977), p. 29.

[40] *Vita Nuova*, 18 Nov. 1920, in Cordova, *Alle Origini del PCI*, p. 43.

[41] Pietro Mancini, *Il Partito Socialista nella Provincia di Cosenza 1904–1924* (Cosenza, 1974), p. 138.

Bismarck once called *furor consularis*, that tendency to blow up local incidents, to puff out the importance of their posts. Guadagnini had, in short, to get it right, stay neutral in conflicts between capital and labour, yet ensure that the law was obeyed. He had to force both sides to settle without, too overtly, using force.

On the 18th of November, Don Carlo and the 'whites', joined by a large number of the 'reds', formed a giant procession which marched to the prefecture and demanded an end to the employers' expulsions of tenants from the land, and better terms of tenancy. At the public meeting which followed the Lega del Lavoro declared a general strike, and fruit and vegetable supplies and milk and butter deliveries from the surrounding villages of the *conca cosentina* were blocked. The proprietors, very agitated, took the train to Rome and demanded to see the prime minister. It is not clear from the archives if they actually saw Giolitti but the lawyer Palmieri, 'one of the most excited', as Guadagnini reported drily, 'assures people publicly to have obtained from Your Excellency a promise to send the *Guardia Regia* and in that expectation urges the proprietors to resist to the last'.[42] By the 23rd he could report that the general strike of the peasants had now spread to fourteen communes and that the proprietors were divided between the 'intransigent and those who would like to negotiate'. Most marked was the fact that the 'strike remains in general bland'.[43]

On the 25th of November the council of the Agricultural Association voted by 9 to 5 to resist to the end and 'to refuse to negotiate' and on the 30th, the prefect telegraphed that the situation was still 'stationary. The peasants' strike still mild, the proprietors inert and divided...Dissident group of proprietors has published manifesto in which they declare themselves ready to reach accord with peasants but without recognising the League.'[44] As the tension began to subside, the prefect decided to act, and under the authority of the Royal Decree of 14 September 1919, article 1, he ordered the proprietors to send representatives to negotiate a settlement or he would nominate representatives in their name. The peasant strike had begun to 'droop' and on the 3rd of December, the leaders of the League informed the prefect that they 'had ordered a return to the sowing and assure me that this evening they intend to unblock the city'. The general strike was over.

During the month of December the prefect chaired nine meetings between representatives of the Lega del Lavoro and the proprietors but got nowhere in spite of 'cordial exchanges of views'. When the talks resumed in the new year, progress began to be made and by the end of March 1921,

---

[42] Guadagnini to minister of the interior, 18 Nov. 1920, and 23 Nov. 1920, ACS DGPS, C–1, 'ordine pubblico', b. 83.
[43] *Ibid.*, 23 Nov. 1920.   [44] *Ibid.*, 25 Nov. 1920, 30 Nov. 1920.

the two sides initialled the heads of a printed 'concordat', *Nuovi Patti Agrari* (the new agricultural contracts). Among the terms were the abolition of personal services as parts of tenancy contracts and the fixing by agreement of the precise shares of the crop to be paid to the owner under each type of tenancy in the three main market areas of Cosenza, Rende, and Montalto. While the peasants undoubtedly gained better terms and greater liberty of contract and above all the establishment of norms, 'which, as has been said, could be adopted for those other villages where there might be still other agricultural questions to define',[45] there is no mention whatever of the Lega del Lavoro. Indeed the concordat makes plain that the parties shall enjoy maximum individual liberty of contract both as to type of tenancy and to terms within each type. The Lega had won better terms but not 'recognition'. The *conca cosentina* was not to be unionised. Commendatore Giuseppe Guadagnini had his reward. He was transferred to Bologna.

This, then, was the Cosenza general strike of 1920, not, perhaps, a great historical event but in its features worthy of some reflection. In the first place, the historian notices even in the documents much evidence of the *buon senso* which speakers praised after the signing of the agreement. Again and again, the prefect describes the strike as *blando*, mild or bland. The owners, too, while occasionally 'excited', avoid confrontation. This little affair, not unlike the dog that did not bark in the night, raises some very interesting issues. Here in a country and time full of violence, we have an exception. The *conca cosentina*, it turns out, was exceptional in all sorts of ways: its settlement patterns, its type of tenure, its level of emigration, the high proportion of women employed, the local Archbishop, the evolution of successful cooperatives and credit institutions, the presence of a charismatic, dedicated, and saintly priest, and the discipline and devotion of his followers. Yet all that evidence painfully assembled before the weary reader would not have guaranteed the peaceful outcome of the strike had the constellation of high ecclesiastical and secular politics not been favourable. Had Giolitti not been prime minister with his explicit commitment to neutrality in labour disputes, Commendatore Guadagnini might have called for the police and not for the conference table. Once Mussolini took power, no prefect would have dared to grant peasants equal rights before the law, nor would, as we saw, the church after its own concordat with fascism tolerate any more 'turbulent priests' and their works. Yet even after all that, some elements of the outcome of this little event do not easily reveal themselves from the documents alone. It helps to know the area and its people today. I have been the guest of the grandsons of those proprietors who fought against the Lega

[45] *Nuovi Patti Agrari* (Cosenza, 1921), pp. 3–4, ACS DGPS, C–1, 'ordine pubblico', b. 83.

276

del Lavoro. When I look at the eight names who signed the concordat for the proprietors, I see lawyers, teachers at the local *liceo*, and only one 'barone'.[46] I suspect that like their descendants they ate large lunches in flats full of over-stuffed furniture. The Cosentino bourgeoisie were professional people, not the rapacious barons of the Crotonese nor like Baron Rotunno in *Christ Stopped at Eboli*, riding about on his little motor bike, wearing his pince-nez, and squeezing the last penny from his suffering peasants. The historian has to know that among Cosentino bourgeoisie ideology has little place, that some comfortable lawyers and engineers today call themselves communists and others are outspoken and unrepentant fascists. Such landlords may get 'excited' but they are unlikely to become violent.

Persons skilled in the methodology of the social sciences might feel that the outcome of the general strike in my analysis had been 'over-determined', a view no doubt shared by any readers who have got this far, that is to say, that it takes an astonishing amount of evidence to 'explain' even the smallest historical event. But what does 'explain' mean here? It means that accumulation of evidence and conjecture which makes the outcome that we know happened seem plausible. I believe that I know why Cosenza was 'different' from other regions and that knowledge arises from both the analytic and the narrative sides of historical understanding. I need the sociologist like Arlacchi, the economic historian like Bevilacqua to show me the structural characteristics of the area, but I need to read texts like the diary of Don Carlo De Cardona as one human being listening to another. For we historians have the problem that the objects of our study are subjects, people like ourselves, whose voices, though stilled, reach our inner ears and whose hopes and fears can move us.

But in the end I cannot explain Don Carlo De Cardona nor why he became a priest and his brother a communist nor why the De Cardona family, of all comfortable bourgeois families of Moranno Calabro, should have had a burning commitment to social justice. What is clear is that without Don Carlo there would have been no Lega to carry out the general strike. He had ministered to the peasants for more than twenty years, helped 'his' peasants found reading circles and consumer cooperatives, trade unions and political parties. Nobody then doubted that the Catholic social action in the *conca cosentina* was his work, and I do not doubt it now. Nor can I as an historian explain, or even put into words, that curious strand of utopianism that links the prophets of the Calabrian mountains to their people, from Joachim of Fiore through Thomas Campanella to Don Carlo De Cardona.

---

[46] Avv. Pasquale Campagna, Barone Diego Miceli, Avv. Michele Caruso, Prof. Vittorio Catanzaro, Prof. Annibale Mari, Avv. Giovanni Stancati, Avv. Raffaele Palmieri, Avv. Vladimo Zagarese, *Nuovi Patti Agrari*, p. 1.

Hume says in *A Treatise of Human Nature* that 'nothing is more requisite for a true philosopher, than to restrain the intemperate desire of searching into causes', and on those grounds alone I ought to rest contented with what I know.[47] There is, then, that element in the writing of all history which we cannot know nor explain. At that point the historian is reduced to his oldest function, the most ancient justification for his trade: to remember the sufferings and experiences of those now gone. 'Some there be which have no memorial,' says *Ecclesiasticus* in Chapter 44, 'who are perished as though they had not been and are as though they had not been born.' The historian who remembers them is, in a way, setting up a little memorial, in this case, to Don Carlo De Cardona and his 'Poor in Christ'.

[47] David Hume, *A Treatise of Human Nature*, ed. P. H. Nidditch (2nd edn, Oxford, 1980), p. 13.

Britain, 1940 and 'Christian Civilization'

KEITH ROBBINS

Spring in Cambridge in May 1940 was poignantly beautiful. It was noted that the rich promise of the blossom contrasted strikingly with the destructive activities of men.[1] Some dons sought relief from exposed East Anglia in the land of Lyonesse and asked themselves whether they should send their children to Canada.[2] All over the country, indeed, questions of life and death became urgent. Harold Nicolson advised his wife to flee to the security of his brother's Dartmoor farm. He sent his own will westwards as a precaution. It was indeed late, 'late in the afternoon of the city', but if invasion and conquest should come, was it the end of 'Christian Civilization' or was such a concept merely a lingering piece of exhausted rhetoric? This essay explores meanings and mentalities in various segments of English society at a time when national survival seemed at least in jeopardy. Kenneth Clark, future guide to *Civilisation* who was, at his end, to receive the sacraments of the Roman Catholic Church, directed the pictures from the National Gallery into a vast and disused slate cavern near Blaenau Ffestiniog in North Wales. It was known locally as 'the Cathedral'. It might be an unanticipated symbol.[3]

There was no especially Christian aura to be associated with Churchill's incoming government. However, the Prime Minister found it appropriate, on occasion, to use language which had religious connotations. There were references, allusive to be sure, to the defence of home and altar. 'The Battle of Britain', he declared in June 1940, 'is about to begin. Upon this battle depends the survival of Christian civilization.'[4] Such dogmatic language,

---

[1] A. S. F. Gow, *Letters from Cambridge, 1939–1944* (London, 1945), p. 41.
[2] B. Willey, *Cambridge and Other Memoirs* (London, 1968), pp. 100–1.
[3] K. Clark, *The Other Half* (London, 1977), pp. 4–5.
[4] Robert Rhodes James (ed.), *W. S. Churchill: Complete Speeches, 1897–1963* (New York, 1974), vol. VI, p. 6238. It should be noted that the remit of the Religious Division of the Ministry of Information was to impart 'a real conviction of the Christian contribution to our civilization and of the essential anti-Christian character of Nazism'. Cited in I. McLaine, *Ministry of Morale* (London, 1979), p. 151.

however, came from an undogmatic mind. It was no part of his purpose to define the term at such a juncture or to express a personal conviction. He stood in relation to the Church of England as a flying buttress – supporting, but external. Archbishop Lang was not for him the epitome of Christian civilization and these public sentiments did not presage an intimacy with the episcopate. It was Destiny that he was content to walk with. Some of his closest associates were not even sure that all their past lives had been but a preparation for the present. Anthony Eden allowed references to *Pilgrim's Progress* and McNeile Dixon's Gifford Lectures on *The Human Condition* to give an elevated tone to some of his speeches and even referred, in August 1940, to a belief that Britain would achieve the kind of peace she believed in 'by God's help', but he was not explicit about Christian civilization.[5] Although Nelly Cecil was later to describe Attlee as 'the most Christian-living P.M. in our time', he himself had no religious experience and disliked 'mumbo-jumbo'. He did not know whether he was an agnostic.[6] About the ailing Neville Chamberlain there remained only vestigial traces of ancestral Unitarianism. Ernest Bevin could only bring the spiritual dowry of a long-lapsed Baptist. Lord Beaverbrook was at best a devious propagandist, though there was more life in the Presbyterian pedigree of Sir John Anderson. Lurking in the distance was Lloyd George who seems sometimes to have thought that a last stand against the Teutons might be made in *Festung* Gwynedd. Meanwhile, he sought solace in the unlikely combination of William Carey's *Missionary Sermons* and Boccaccio's *Decameron*. He also strengthened the defences of Bron-y-de.[7]

As a body, the Cabinet did not trouble itself with Christian civilization, apart from discussing the propriety of ringing church bells should a victory occur. The diaries of Sir Alexander Cadogan, Permanent Under-Secretary at the Foreign Office, do not disclose any change of atmosphere after the advent, a little later, of William Temple to Canterbury. The archbishop is recorded as 'bleating' rather than 'talking'. On Easter Saturday 1943 Cadogan conceded that religion no longer played the part in society that it had once had. Moral atrophy, he thought, might be avoided 'by setting ourselves to some form of common endeavour, some kind of sacrifice – our duty to our

---

5 A. Eden, *Freedom and Orders: Selected Speeches, 1939–1946* (London, 1947), pp. 18 and 81.

6 K. Rose, *The Later Cecils* (London, 1975), p. 181. Attlee came from an active Anglican household and had siblings who remained committed Christians. He believed in 'the ethics of Christianity'. K. Harris, *Clement Attlee* (London, 1982), p. 218.

7 C. Cross (ed.), *Life with Lloyd George: The Diary of A. J. Sylvester, 1931–1945* (London, 1975), pp. 269 and 274.

neighbour, to the State, to the world'.[8] This objective smacked of the burning faith in the high ideals of the British people which Eden sought to kindle, since he apparently believed it was 'not enough merely to preserve Christian civilization, now in such deadly peril...'. While the Prime Minister's immediate reaction to Temple's death – 'There's a total abstainer died of gout. How right we all are' – cannot be taken as a rounded appreciation, it betrays a determination to keep the church in its place.[9]

There were, however, other currents. The news of the fall of France reached Lord and Lady Halifax when they were walking in the Yorkshire Wolds near their home. Gazing at the Vale of York, they thought it sad to contemplate that the 'Prussian jackboot' might force its way into this true fragment of 'the undying England'. They thought of the villages where, for generations, men and woman had knelt in worship and prayer.[10] From his lofty standpoint, Halifax had made no secret of his Christian belief and had made a number of public statements. Broadcasting on the Christian attitude to war in July 1937 he had spoken of the danger that in every war the original motives became overlaid with others less worthy. It could be the duty of the Christian man 'constantly to be searching the possibilities of concluding a righteous peace'. The true model of international peace ought to be a relationship between nations comparable to that which 'ought to obtain between Christian individuals as members of Christ's body'.[11] In November 1939 he broadcast an address on *The Purpose of the Struggle* – his remarks owed little to Foreign Office advice – arguing that in the war 'as indeed in all life, it is finally the spiritual side that counts'. Physical force could not in itself destroy the evil which was the source of war but if 'we rest inert before action which we hold evil, we are surely surrendering to annihilation the expression of spiritual values which have inspired and guided all human progress'.[12] Speaking as its Chancellor, he told the University of Oxford in February 1940 that the wounds inflicted on 'our' civilization need not be mortal 'but I do think we are fighting for its life'. He was certain that there was 'an active force of evil which, unless we fight it, will rapidly reduce our

---

[8] D. Dilks (ed.), *The Diaries of Sir Alexander Cadogan* (London, 1971), p. 523.

[9] Dilks, *Cadogan Diaries*, p. 675. Although Temple was a supporter of the Labour Party, Churchill told Attlee that he had recommended his appointment to Canterbury because 'he was the only half-a-crown article in a sixpenny bazaar'. Harris, *Attlee*, p. 218. See also M. Cowling, *Religion and Public Doctrine in Modern England* (Cambridge, 1980), pp. 284–312.

[10] Lord Birkenhead, *The Life of Lord Halifax* (London, 1965), pp. 457–8.

[11] H. H. E. Craster (ed.), *Viscount Halifax: Speeches on Foreign Policy* (London, 1940), pp. 102–3.

[12] *Ibid.*, p. 334.

civilization to a desert of the soul'. It rested with the 'British race', with all its faults, to wage that struggle.[13]

Such sentiments were close to those articulated by Lord Lloyd. He believed that the defence of 'Christian civilization' was an integral aspect of 'the British case'. Pre-war failings of policy had stemmed from a failure to bring before the British people the view that national endeavour should be 'shaped and determined by the requirements of Christian morality' since 'we are still, I believe, a Christian people'. He was distressed by signs of a reluctance 'to go on with the task of building up a Christian civilization in Africa and Asia, in our facile and foolish assumption that any other civilization is likely to be just as good'.[14] After 1939, he had no hesitation in claiming that the European conception of freedom derived directly from Christianity. Greece and Rome were slave civilizations whereas Man redeemed by Christ could never again be enslaved to man. Hitler's actions against Poland were 'not only an outrage against the public law of Europe, but an affront to every Christian conscience'. These were not merely the passing thoughts of an ex-Governor of Bombay. Lloyd played a vital role in the 'projection of Britain'. His own *The British Case* contained an introduction by Halifax himself.[15] He was nearer the centre of power, however, than old Lord Salisbury who could only take comfort in January 1940 from an Oxford Group conference in Bournemouth where it was revealed that, in Papua, Christian tribesmen covered their eyes with their hands as battle approached, whereupon their war-painted neighbours faded away.[16] Even so, Churchill took no risks with the Christian peers and knights. Sir Samuel Hoare, another prominent High Churchman, was banished to that recently reclaimed fortress of Christendom, Madrid. Lloyd died and Halifax went to Washington. In the United States, the new British Ambassador would be further away from Lord Baldwin and his visions. It was to Halifax that the former Prime Minister had communicated his experience of July 1940 when he had heard a voice speaking (and felt himself to see with extraordinary and vivid clarity). The purport of the message was 'You have now one upon whom to lean and I have chosen you as my instrument to work with my will.' It was to be hoped that this could be interpreted to mean that England would survive.[17]

The defence of Christian civilization had been undertaken in the Washington Embassy even before Halifax's arrival. His predecessor, Philip Kerr,

[13] *Ibid.*, pp. 362 and 368.
[14] Lord Lloyd, *Leadership in Democracy* (Oxford, 1939), pp. 16–17.
[15] Lord Lloyd, *The British Case* (London, 1939), pp. 14 and 48. For Lord Lloyd's connection with the British Council see P. M. Taylor, *The Projection of Britain: British Overseas Publicity and Propaganda 1919–1939* (Cambridge, 1981), pp. 283–4.
[16] Rose, *Later Cecils*, p. 101.
[17] K. Middlemas and J. Barnes, *Baldwin* (London, 1969), pp. 1058–9.

Marquis of Lothian, a Christian Scientist of Roman Catholic extraction, had stated, before sailing for the United States on the eve of the war, that the Christian tradition of praying for governments was more useful than criticizing them. He added that the only way that the reign of international morality might be secured was by 'Federal Union'. His capacity to pick up the latest contemporary fad and invest it with an intolerable significance was to be further demonstrated in public speeches during his short but critically important mission. 'At bottom,' he told the American Pilgrims in October 1939, 'we are fighting a defensive struggle. We are trying to prevent the hordes of paganism and barbarism from destroying what is left of civilized Europe.' A Swarthmore audience was told more explicitly in November that the war was becoming 'a struggle between the totalitarian and the democratic and Christian way of life'. The ultimate foundations of 'our civilization, were indisputably true', he claimed, but 'we' were in our present troubles 'because we have allowed religion to fall from its high estate, and allowed politics and economics to take its place'. His purpose, he said, was not to talk about theology, but he did so at some length. He also advocated 'a single constitution' for the world. It was the function of religion to change the hearts of men towards universal brotherhood and thus make possible such a political development. In April 1940, as the picture darkened, he told the St Louis Chamber of Commerce that 'a truce with Nazi Germany now would be the end of most of the civilized values which Christianity and Western democracy have laboriously built up in recent centuries'. In what proved to be his last speech, in December 1940, he claimed that Britain was not in the least dismayed by her circumstances. She would win decisively, by 1942, if not before. That confidence had a spiritual basis since the core of Hitlerism was 'moral rottenness' and all history proved wrong the belief that ruthless power led to greatness. 'The Sermon on the Mount is in the long run much stronger than all Hitler's propaganda or Goering's guns and bombs.'[18] Lothian died before he was able to ascertain what might happen in the short run.

Lothian's language betrayed an association with Lionel Curtis. His *Civitas Dei. The Commonwealth of God*, a volume of nearly one thousand pages, had appeared in 1938, sections of it having already been published in 1934 and 1937. Embedded in his survey of man's development was his claim that 'Belief, in the true sense of the word, is not the assertion of knowledge, or dogma, but courage to act on the best hypothesis we are able to conceive. Unbelievers are those too timid or idle to guess at the truth and to act on the guess.' That was a message for 1940. Curtis could not think of a time

[18] J. R. M. Butler, *Lord Lothian* (London, 1960), p. 256; *The American Speeches of Lord Lothian, July 1939 to December 1940* (London, 1941), pp. 10, 23, 34, 71, 139.

which appeared 'so fraught with disaster to the human race as a whole as the present'. However, from the Christian story he drew the message that 'From that moment of utter despair there sprang the movement which has gone some way to create, and in the ages before us will bring to fulfilment, the Kingdom of God upon earth, the Divine Commonwealth...'. In his view, Our Lord 'was trying to convince the world that men can grow to perfection, but only in so far as they mould their relations one to another on the principle that each man owes an infinite duty to God, and therefore to all his fellows'. He wanted to discover the means of passing from the national to the international state. Here was a role for religion. He felt that once the Protestant churches came to regard the creation of a world commonwealth as an 'all-important' aspect of their work 'an international commonwealth in the English-speaking world would come into being in a few generations'.[19] The outbreak of the war neither served to modify his convictions in these matters nor to discipline his prose. The history of civilization was now seen as a war between freedom and despotism. Amidst no paucity of proposals for reconstructing the world came the cry 'Who, indeed, would wish to have lived in the days of Agincourt or the Armada, or Trafalgar or Waterloo rather than here in England today with her ruined hearths and her broken shrines?'[20]

Arnold Toynbee noted that a cross dangled from Curtis's watchchain. He had no such emblem himself, but it was almost inevitable that when he came to Oxford in May 1940 to lecture in the Sheldonian it should be on *Christianity and Civilisation*. His message was not straightforward. Christianity might be conceived historically as either the destroyer of civilization or the humble servant of civilization. If religion was a chariot, he suggested, 'it looks as if the wheels on which it moves towards Heaven may be the periodic downfalls of civilisations on Earth'. It was obvious that 'we' had been living, for a number of generations, on spiritual capital, clinging to Christian practice without possessing the Christian belief. Practice unsupported by belief was a 'wasting asset', as had been suddenly discovered 'to our dismay, in this generation'. He considered that 'if our secular Western civilisation perishes, Christianity may be expected not only to endure but to grow in wisdom and stature as a result of a fresh experience of secular catastrophe'.[21]

Brisker, less qualified, but doubtless more acceptable thoughts flowed from other pens for less refined audiences. Having once believed in *Peace*

19 L. Curtis, *Civitas Dei. The Commonwealth of God* (London, 1938), pp. 288, 822–4, 953.
20 L. Curtis, *Decision* (London, 1941), pp. 75–6.
21 A. J. Toynbee, *Christianity and Civilisation* (London, 1940), pp. 22–7.

with Honour, A. A. Milne was now converted to war to end war. Seeking 'victory by any end and every means, victory regardless of any other consideration whatever', he concluded that 'In fighting Hitler we are truly fighting the Devil, Anti-Christ, the negation of every spiritual value which separates mankind from the rest of creation.' The British people would have to be ready to suffer and to inflict death 'to bring salvation to the rest of humanity'.[22] This was no mere international conflict. It was a struggle between Good and Evil. Hitler was a crusader against God, 'just that'.[23] Addressing a wider audience than the readers of the *Children's Newspaper*, Arthur Mee shared this vision. He had little doubt that 1940 would be remembered in all history as 'our finest hour'. Disasters, betrayals, risks, burdens, humiliations and grief were all experienced but 'we carried on. Guided by the Hand of God and sustained by our own right arm, we came through the shadows of defeat into the sunlight of a nobler dawn.' It was his conviction that 'If for one day the common people of these islands lost their faith in God the cause of Freedom must perish.' Dunkirk was an indication that 'we are part of some sublime event to which the whole Creation moves'. He concluded that never in the history of civilization was the ordinary life of a man or woman of such solemn account. 'If we are generous, ardent, patient, believing, refusing to despair, confident in right, upholding truth and loving justice more than all, we are fighting for God's kingdom and the island in which He has set us.'[24] It was this spirit which Vincent Massey broadcast back to Canada on Dominion Day, 1 July 1940. The spectacle of Empire troops, together with other soldiers of freedom, French, Polish, Norwegian and Dutch, reminded him inescapably 'of the warfare against the infidel, when Christian men from every part of Europe were gathered together to fight for the deliverance of the Holy Sepulchre'.[25]

The Times turned to 'Religion and National Life' in February 1940. Barrington-Ward, its new editor, had recorded in 1934 'a sense of liberation in worshipping Christ without miracles. His message is for us on earth and in our own day, to build or to build towards his earthly commonwealth...'. Time would expose the emptiness of the Fascist and Nazi 'philosophies'. It was a comment which revealed that he had been reading Curtis's *Civitas Dei*.[26] Ten years later, he remained convinced that a moral purpose had to

---

[22] A. A. Milne, *War Aims Unlimited* (London, 1941), p. 31.
[23] A. A. Milne, *War with Honour* (London, 1940), pp. 16–17.
[24] A. Mee, *Nineteen-Forty: Our Finest Hour* (London, 1941), pp. vi, 27, 60, 118–19.
[25] V. Massey, *The Sword of Lionheart* (London, 1943), p. 25.
[26] D. McLachlan, *In the Chair: Barrington-Ward of The Times, 1927–1948* (London, 1971), p. 276.

be rediscovered in the nation: 'To have any true vitality it must be rooted in religion, and our present-day religion lags behind the needs of the age, cluttered up with intellectual difficulties.' The problem was that the 'restatement' which might deal with such difficulties would shatter the churches as organizations.[27] However, in a leader of 17 February 1940, his newspaper was eloquent, declaring that it would be of little use to fight 'as we are fighting today, for the preservation of Christian principles if Christianity itself is to have no future, or at immense cost to safeguard religion against attack from without if we allow it to be starved by neglect from within'. It seemed odd that a country which was 'staking its all in defence of Christian principles' should have a national educational system 'which allows the citizens of the future to have a purely heathen upbringing'.

This comment sparked off a lengthy and vigorous correspondence. Writers concerned themselves with the paradox, not to say hypocrisy, of a situation in which it was claimed 'that we are fighting for a faith to which most of us appear to be completely indifferent'.[28] The Bishop of St Albans was quick to point out that both Stalin and Hitler ensured that 'the faith' was properly taught. 'They take no chances; we do. They see to it that every generation as it comes along is taught "the faith" and converted to it (if possible)... When shall we learn?'[29] The Bishop of Southwark appealed for better instruction for he agreed that without better teaching of religion there would be 'an increasingly secularist outlook among our people, which will render them less and less capable of standing up to ideologies such as those which are enslaving the people of Russia and Germany'.[30] The Dean of Winchester added his support to the view that Scripture teaching in all schools should be inspected like other subjects. Such a step would show that 'the State was in earnest about the character of our country's civilization in the future'.[31] Writing as President of the Boys' Brigade, Lord Home declared that the European tragedy would not have been in vain 'if we are led as a nation to a new realization of the primary place which should be given to the Christian faith in the education of our young people'. It was vital to ensure that the next generation 'in this Christian country' was helped to grow in favour with God and man.[32] The pressure of correspondence was very heavy, drawing in the President of the Mother's Union, the British and Foreign Bible Society and a host of clergymen and laymen.

[27] Ibid., p. 243.
[28] Sir Edward Cadogan in The Times, 20 February 1940.
[29] The Bishop of St Albans in ibid., 21 February 1940.
[30] The Bishop of Southwark in ibid., 23 February 1940.
[31] The Dean of Winchester in ibid., 24 February 1940.
[32] The (13th) Earl of Home in ibid., 28 February 1940.

The Times itself returned to the subject in a leader on 9 March. It noted that its original comments, published in pamphlet form, had excited great interest. Nearly four hundred thousand copies of the leaflet had been sold in twelve days. It took this concern to be an indication that the question was not merely one for specialists in religious education. The topic was seen 'to affect the whole future of our national life'. In proportion as the spiritual principles at stake in the war were clearly discerned, 'the greater will seem the need not merely of defending but of developing those principles by a national system of education which is definitely Christian'. Recognizing that the role of the home would be central, it concluded 'Almost the chief gain that will follow the reform of our national system of education will be its development of Christian children who in due course will become Christian parents. By this means the old order will be restored, when the task of the school will be to continue, instead of having to replace or even to combat, the teaching that has been begun in the home.' It would be difficult to envisage a more comprehensive endorsement of Christian civilization.

Confronted by such eminent wisdom from so many quarters, church leaders and committed Christians found themselves in an embarrassing position. The allegedly unreflective and strident patriotism of the churches during the First World War had been frequently criticized in the years that followed, not least, as George Orwell noted, by those who had no respect for the Christian principles which had supposedly been ignored. In part, the enthusiastic espousal of 'pacifism' by influential figures in the major denominations sprang from a determination that church and state should never again be so closely entangled.[33] Yet, by the late 1930s, it became increasingly evident that, if war should come, the issues at stake might entitle the government to wholehearted support. It would be a struggle for 'Christian civilization' in a deeper sense than had been true in 1914. The elderly Hensley Henson, writing in 1940, saw the struggle as 'au fond a civil war fought out on the fundamental principles on which Christendom, in so far as it is an effective unity at all, must needs stand'. Secular politicians talked about a 'war of ideologies' but he was prepared to call it a Crusade which had to

---

[33] M. Ceadel, *Pacifism in Britain, 1914–1945* (Oxford, 1980). In 1938, for example, Charles Raven argued that 'The last war produced Communism and the Treaty of Versailles, Fascism and the new Paganism. The next will leave no victors, will inevitably destroy freedom and, as many think, the Church.' *War and the Christian* (London, 1938), p. 158. In 1940 he was still a pacifist and found himself at loggerheads with the B.B.C. on this account. F. W. Dillistone, *Charles Raven: Naturalist, Historian, Theologian* (London, 1975), pp. 343–7. Bishop Barnes of Birmingham found himself unable to support the war. J. Barnes, *Ahead of his Age* (London, 1979), pp. 361–3.

be 'fought out to the bitter end. There can be no compromise or patched up peace.'[34] And, significantly, it was in the Temple Church on 5 May 1940, on the seven hundredth anniversary of its consecration, that he reflected on 'Christendom' and its implications. It was not unreal or extravagant to consider the Christian citizen of Great Britain as wrestling against the spiritual hosts of wickedness in the heavenly places. He believed that 'for us and for our Allies this war is *The Good Fight*'.[35] *May God Defend the Right* was also the plea of Nathaniel Micklem, Principal of Mansfield College, Oxford, though as a committed Liberal he might have chosen his title with more care. 'The reign of Christ in the hearts of men can never be furthered by the sword', he conceded, 'in that sense we hesitate to say we fight for Christ, for He needs none to fight for him with earthly weapons; but we believe ourselves to be fighting not merely for the decencies of international life but for Christian civilization on the Continent of Europe.' There was no peace for the world except in Christendom. By that phrase he did not mean a given state of human society pretending to be the Kingdom of God, nor a political order controlled by ecclesiastics, nor one composed of professing or practising Christians, but rather an order 'in which the living God is publicly acknowledged and his righteousness and justice are accepted as the ultimate ground and sanction of human law'.[36] It was because Europe had to so great an extent repudiated its Christian ancestry that civilization had come to disaster. Echoes of these sentiments could be heard from many contemporary pulpits, but there were other opinions.

'The devilry of Hitlerism', proclaimed A. R. Vidler in his editorial in the October 1939 issue of *Theology*, 'does not automatically transfer us into angels of light or prophets of the Lord.' He thought it right to draw attention to what he considered the shortcomings of French policy in the years after the Peace of Versailles. Such a robust utterance provoked rumblings. Following the events of May 1940, his publishers felt that the time was not ripe for such arguments. The journal might have to close. It was not right to publish material which could be interpreted as 'anti-British' propaganda or as 'tending to weaken the national will for victory...'. Vidler stood his ground and the controversy died away.[37] It is interesting to note, in passing, that in July 1937 he had been lamenting that talk of war was preventing reflection on 'a menace that is more certain – namely, depopulation'. In a later editorial

---

[34] E. F. Braley, *Letters of Herbert Hensley Henson* (London, 1950), p. 123.

[35] H. Hensley Henson, *Last Words in Westminster Abbey* (London, 1941), p. 82.

[36] N. Micklem, *May God Defend the Right* (London, 1939), pp. 127 and 139. In his autobiography, Micklem records a conversation at an Oxford High Table around this date where suicide seemed to those present an urgent problem. N. Micklem, *The Box and the Puppets* (London, 1957), p. 115.

[37] A. R. Vidler, *Scenes from a Clerical Life* (London, 1977), pp. 114–15.

he stressed the distinction between fighting for Christian civilization or Christendom and fighting for Christianity. To talk of the former implied that 'Christendom is still a going concern which has to be defended instead of a kind of social order which has in future to be re-created'.[38]

Here was a note which many thought prophetic. It was scarcely conceivable in radical Christian quarters that the Britain of the summer of 1940 was a Christian civilization which merited conservation. The young Martin Wight, for example, declaring himself to be a conscientious objector, expressed the view that the war was 'the convulsion of a civilization that has forsaken its Christian origins'. It was a divine judgment on that civilization. To take part in the war would not solve the 'fundamental problem of spiritual apostasy'. The task, rather, was 'to prepare the foundations of a new civilization that will be less in conflict with the Kingdom of God'.[39] Others had also expended much energy in exposing its shortcomings and inner corruption. The young Donald Mackinnon pointed an accusing finger at the debilitating role played in this respect by *Songs of Praise*. The hymn book was an indication of spiritual sterility and determination to eliminate the message of redemption from the Christian Gospel. A generation had lent credence to the notion that Christ had come to reveal the perfectibility of man. It had neglected the awful truth that the restoration of the *natural* order demanded of God an intervention that was in every sense supernatural. 'In this present hour of judgment', he concluded, 'God is surely recalling us to a comprehension of the utterness of our dependence upon Him. He is revealing to us the bankruptcy of our achievement apart from the impact of His grace...'.[40] Another fluent exponent of this perspective was Langmead Casserley, who did not believe that any Christian could desire the perpetuation of the existing industrialized imperialistic order of society. 'The West', though dear because it contained so many relics of the first Christendom, was not the Kingdom upon earth, nor even a very good basis from which to journey to that Kingdom. Between the West and the Kingdom there was no broad highway, only a wilderness upon whose verge men sat waiting for Moses.[41]

There were some who discerned 'Moses' in the conclusions of the Malvern conference on 'The Life of the Church and the Order of Society' held in January 1941. Anglicans, from Dorothy Sayers to T. S. Eliot, had a good deal to say there about civilization. There were pleas to think 'in terms of a

---

[38] *Theology*, October 1940.
[39] Cited by Hedley Bull in his introduction to Martin Wight, *Systems of States* (Leicester, 1977), p. 4.
[40] D. M. Mackinnon, *God the Living and the True* (London, 1940), pp. 31 and 87.
[41] J. V. Langmead Casserley, *The Fate of Modern Culture* (London, 1940), and *Providence and History: A Tale of Two Cities* (London, 1940).

wider perspective' and 'to see the divine purpose at work, even in the collapse of a civilization which has brought about its own destruction because it has been founded on the profit-motive and the artificial segregation of the human race into separatist national sovereignties, and privileged and non-privileged classes'. The coming civilization, Kenneth Ingram further indicated, would be based on planned production for communal use. The task of the church was to provide the nucleus of those who would 'lead the vanguard in the social–political–religious struggle'.[42] Middleton Murry declared that the church failed to provide leadership because it showed 'no sign of having known despair'.[43] Mackinnon's complex address, for whose obscurity he apologized, could not be criticized on such grounds. He stated that as members of the Established Church Anglicans had particularly allowed themselves to be blinded to the true condition of British society. They found it 'hard to admit the fundamental contradiction between the assumptions of our capitalist–industrialist civilization, and those of the faith to which as Christians we are pledged to bear witness'. The burden of his paper he summarized as being that there was a fundamental opposition between the church and the modern nation state. That was 'a fact underlying the whole conflict of our time'.[44] It was an assertion which did not easily marry with Britain as the ark of Christian civilization.

William Temple concluded that the Malvern conference had 'put the Church on the map'. Mervyn Stockwood, who was telling the inhabitants of a Bristol air-raid shelter that the archbishop was 'running a show to put the world right', was equally pleased. Temple himself was prolific in speech and on paper, expounding the conviction that 'faith and freedom must stand or fall together; for it is only faith in God that can make the world safe for freedom or freedom safe for the world'.[45] He stressed, however, that he did not believe that 'we are fighting for Christianity'. Christianity could only be freely accepted and could not be served by physical force. But, while true of Christianity itself, it did not follow that it was also 'true of a civilization largely influenced by Christianity and threatened by one which has deliberately repudiated the fundamental elements in the Christian conception of life and the way to live'. In short, 'we are fighting to keep open the possibility of a still more truly Christian civilisation in the future'. Christianity would have more to say about the right ordering of life 'than had been heard for some centuries'.[46]

---

[42] *Malvern 1941: The Life of the Church and the Order of Society* (London, 1941), pp. 176–7.
[43] *Ibid.*, p. 197.
[44] *Ibid.*, pp. 107 and 116.
[45] W. Temple, *Thoughts in War-Time* (London, 1940), p. 130.
[46] *Towards a Christian Order* (London, 1942), pp. 8–9.

Attempts to give content to a 'still more truly Christian civilization' were not lacking. Sir Richard Acland launched *Our Struggle*. He urged that if all men could not be persuaded, at once, to accept 'our new morality' then 'at least we shall make sure that the destiny of our nation and of mankind is in the hands of those who do accept it'. To love your neighbour as yourself 'must be made an established fact'.[47] Sydney Dark believed that the church was being presented with a great chance, perhaps the last chance, to influence the evolution of society. 'Without the vision that the Christian religion can provide, the people perish, whether they live in a democracy or under a Totalitarian tyranny.'[48] However, he wanted to crush capitalism with rather more verve than envisaged at Malvern. In the mind of Sir Stafford Cripps, *Towards a Christian Order* was the same as *Towards Christian Democracy*. He argued that the churches had 'condoned conditions which Christ would have stigmatised as intolerable, partly because they could see no way of improving matters, and partly because they had compromised with society as it existed'. It was the function of the church 'to create those moral standards compelling material changes...'.[49] Sir Stafford saw his own career in the light of that injunction.

The simplicity of these visions stood in marked contrast to the intricate discussions associated with J. H. Oldham and the 'Moot', that group of intellectuals and professional people which had first met in April 1938. On the outbreak of war, T. S. Eliot (whose lectures on 'The Idea of a Christian Society' had been delivered six months earlier) wrote to Karl Mannheim suggesting that while many of their friends had been expecting war for some time, its arrival confused them. 'We are involved in an enormous catastrophe which includes a war' was how he put it.[50] The *Christian News-Letter* would attempt to bring enlightenment and would 'enter imaginatively into the ordeal through which the nation is passing'.[51] The *News-Letter*, however, was only a means to a 'greater end' – the growth of a body of people dedicated to the task of creating a new order of society. The choice before mankind, it suggested, lay between Communism, Fascism and something more difficult to define but offering 'for most of us' the only satisfactory alternative. The objective was 'a community of free persons united under the rule of law,

---

[47] Sir R. Acland, *Our Struggle*, Australian edition, 1940, pp. 20–1.
[48] S. Dark, *The Church, Impotent or Triumphant?* (London, 1941), p. 8.
[49] S. Cripps, *Towards Christian Democracy* (London, 1945), p. 33.
[50] For Eliot's own views see R. Kojecký, *T. S. Eliot's Social Criticism* (London, 1971); A. D. Moody, *Thomas Stearns Eliot: Poet* (Cambridge, 1979) – especially Appendix C; A. Cunningham, 'Continuity and Coherence in Eliot's Religious Thought', in G. Martin (ed.), *Eliot in Perspective* (London, 1970); D. L. Edwards contributes a helpful introduction to the 1982 reprint of *The Idea of a Christian Society*.
[51] *Christian News-Letter*, 18 October 1939.

directing its activities increasingly to Christian ends and leavened by Christian insight, values and standards'.[52] Here were the makings, almost, of a Christian conspiracy. In optimistic moments, it seemed to some members of the Moot that it might be the agency for mobilizing 'the intelligent people of good will in this country' who were invariably thought to be waiting for a lead. In gloomy moments, it was thought that the Moot might serve as a nucleus which might enable a Christian minority to survive the coming tyranny. Vidler, in particular, was impressed by the latter role. He was already sending out a confidential letter to friends and colleagues. In April 1940 there was a gathering of the 'St Deiniol's Koinonia' in Essex.[53] Its members were very conscious that they appeared to be witnessing the uprooting of the Christian tradition over large areas of Europe. Alike in the areas occupied by the Russians and the Germans, massacres and removals of population were accompanied by systematic attacks on cultural and religious life. The *Christian News-Letter* had no doubt that what was left of a 'Christian' civilization was now forced to contend against monstrous evils 'all of which, upon close analysis, reveal themselves to be fruits of its own vices, wrong answers to its own unanswered problems and accentuated forms of its own decay'.[54] There was no denying the gravity, complexity and urgency of the task of ensuring Christian survival.

Even so, members of the Moot could not agree on whether analysis or action was the first priority. Noting that Hitler started with six people, Mannheim in April 1940 wanted the Moot to ensure that a 'well-established programme' should be available in three months.[55] Three months, even bearing in mind the circumstances, seemed a decidedly short time to many hard-pressed university professors in which to agree on the nature of the ailments which afflicted civilization and to find a prescription for their remedy. It was already apparent that some deep philosophical chasms between members had to be bridged, not least between Thomas Torrance and H. A. Hodges in the matter of interpreting Dilthey.[56] In general, however, the basis of a Christian civilization was explored with exemplary thoroughness

[52] *Ibid.*, 22 November 1939.
[53] Vidler, *Clerical Life*, p. 109. Paul Tillich commented during his European journey in 1936 'the idea of the religious order is encountered everywhere'. He added that nobody believed any longer 'that the masses can be directly re-educated. This is a retreat, to be sure. But it also makes it possible for the leading intellectual and religious forces to regroup and gather strength.' P. Tillich, *My Travel Diary: 1936* (London, 1970), p. 85.
[54] *Christian News-Letter*, 14 February 1940.
[55] Cited in Kojecký, *Eliot's Social Criticism*, p. 176.
[56] Comments by T. F. Torrance on the paper by H. A. Hodges 'Christian Thinking To-Day' can be found in a set of Moot papers in the John Baillie collection, New College, Edinburgh.

and immodest expertise. Hodges, a Professor of Philosophy, addressed the Malvern conference on what the church should say about the threat of a post-war slump, the revival of the rural community, the recasting of the monetary system and the subordination of mass production to human values. At least he had the good judgment to declare not only that his paper could not be published but that it could not be made suitable for publication.

Roman Catholics stood apart from these learned exchanges on the crisis of the times. In the summer of 1940 a certain delicacy attached to their position. The example of Vichy France was not, perhaps, without attraction in certain Roman Catholic quarters, or at least there were anxieties both within and without the church that this might be so. The *Clergy Review* published in June 1940 an article by Christopher Hollis on 'Catholics and the War'. He had evidently felt a need to convince his co-religionists that 'whatever the pressure against religion may be in England and France, it is as nothing to the pressure against it in Russia and Germany...'. The article had, in fact, been written in April and Hollis added a note that 'It was strange that two months ago any Catholic in any country could doubt that the cause of Catholicism required the defeat of Nazi Germany. It is incredible if any who value Catholicism doubt today.'[57] Christopher Dawson, who took over the editorship of the *Dublin Review* in July, declared that 'The Christian cause at the present time is also the common cause of all who are defending our civilization against the blind assault of mass despotism and the idolatry of power which has resulted in a new paganism that is destructive of all moral and intellectual values.' His own writings, so frequently referred to in contemporary discussion, made it clear that Christianity had long since ceased to dominate society and culture. However, the 'sublimated Christianity' of liberals and humanitarians was not to be despised, at least not in present circumstances. The 'working religion of Western democracy' was significant and could not be regarded with complacency or indifference: 'The cause of God and the cause of man are one.'[58]

John Baillie, the Scottish theologian and member of the Moot, had been in France and witnessed at first hand the collapse of the French army. This experience forced him to ask himself whether the Christian religion held out

---

[57] *Clergy Review*, vol. xviii (June 1940), no. 6. See also Michael J. Walsh, 'Ecumenism in War-Time Britain: The Sword of the Spirit and Religion and Life, 1940–1945', *Heythrop Journal*, vol. xxiii (1982), and G. White, 'The Fall of France', in *Studies in Church History*, vol. xx (Oxford, 1983), pp. 431–41.

[58] *Dublin Review*, vol. ccvii, no. 414 (July 1940). Dawson's best-known writings were *Christianity and the New Age* (London, 1931); *Religion and the Modern State* (London, 1935); *Progress and Religion* (London, 1937).

any hope in the triumph of justice in the present world.[59] Iulia de Beausobre, with the physical resilience which survived a Soviet labour camp and the spiritual patience which proved compatible with marriage to Lewis Namier, brooded on *The Tragedy of France and the Testing of England* in a meditation written in July 1940. 'In a moment of crisis such as this', she wrote, 'the grand abandonment which is the first step towards transfiguration can only be achieved through a sustained readiness to be an instrument of God, and through a sustained effort in sincerity. We are hard pressed for time... And yet it is at once, now, that we must bring about the change in ourselves and in our country.' She claimed that 'The transfiguration of England through the will of every citizen of the British Empire to make of himself an instrument of God is the crying need of the whole world.'[60] No outsider was more prolific and cogent in his comments on Britain's plight than Reinhold Niebuhr. 'In terms of the enemy which civilization is called upon to oppose', he wrote, 'history has never confronted decent men with a more sharply defined "evil".' Yet moral and religious scruples should not be abandoned, even in the present crisis. Commenting on 'Europe's catastrophe', he argued that it was not in the providence of God 'that the destruction of civilisations should be complete, before a new civilisation arises... We have no right to capitulate to anarchy in a period of anarchy. It may be in God's providence that the island of sanity and order which we are able to preserve in a disintegrating civilisation shall become the basis of a new world.'[61] Perhaps the 'miracle of Dunkirk' meant that the reference to 'the island of sanity and order' was to be taken literally?

The *Christian News-Letter* noted that many of those who had taken part in the evacuation experienced it 'as a miraculous intervention of Providence'. Unexpected and inexplicable happenings awakened the minds of men to 'a sense of the mystery of existence'. Nevertheless, it cautioned against too naive an interpretation of the connection 'between our prayers and the deliverance granted to us'.[62] There were others who were less restrained in their acknowledgment of the hand of God – an acknowledgment which at least one foreigner in Britain found ludicrous.[63] Perhaps Stanley Baldwin had the right perspective. With many millions, as he supposed, he had prayed hard at the time of Dunkirk 'and never did prayer seem to be more speedily

[59] J. Baillie, 'Does God Defend the Right?', *Christian News-Letter*, 30 October 1940. Another scholar to wrestle with these issues was Edwyn Bevan, *Christians in a World at War* (London, 1940). Bevan's book was published in May.

[60] I. de Beausobre, *The Tragedy of France and the Testing of England* (London, 1940), pp. 27 and 31.

[61] R. Niebuhr, *Europe's Catastrophe and the Christian Faith* (London, 1940), p. 24.

[62] *Christian News-Letter*, 19 June 1940.

[63] C. Ritchie, *The Siren Years: Undiplomatic Diaries, 1937–1945* (London, 1975), p. 61

answered to the full', but there had also been prayers for France and the next day she surrendered. It was hard to say 'Thy will be done'. It was apparent to him that mere 'mites' could never see God's plan, 'a plan on such a scale that it *must* be incomprehensible'.[64] The *Christian News-Letter* reiterated that it did not follow that, because the British Commonwealth seemed to embody a higher conception of life than the tyrannies it was fighting, God would grant victory. The religious mind knew that life did not offer such clear and simple solutions.[65]

The secular mind found much of the foregoing discussion either absurd or distasteful. The *Freethinker* was forthright. It took the gravest exception to any notion that the war was being 'fought for the preservation of Christianity'.[66] Beatrice Webb, who had latterly been expounding the succulent attractions of a new civilization elsewhere, reacted 'philosophically' to the plight of Britain in 1940, taking it as proof that '"Western Civilisation" is going, going, gone.'[67] The Dean of Canterbury was eager to agree. J. B. Priestley was prepared to admit that 'the decay of religious belief' was a hindrance to democracy, but in existing circumstances he had no desire to see packed churches and chapels, prayers at every hour and loud *Te Deums* and *Hallelujahs*. He himself had no wish to be converted and baptized. There was no need for an explicitly Christian basis for society. He much preferred to be a man of good will, 'determined that all that is best in our civilisation must be preserved'. The churches had all proved as faulty as the societies in which they were set. However, he was certain that 'the fundamental values of the new society must be spiritual and therefore religious values' – a claim whose meaning was apparently self-evident.[68] This advice was indeed matched by long-awaited comments from a newly Episcopalian poet in New York. In order to defend civilization, W. H. Auden told Stephen Spender, it was necessary to kill Germans and destroy German property while minimizing the loss of English lives and property. Further, it was necessary to create things from houses to poems that were worth preserving and to educate people to understand what civilization really meant.[69]

Learned men at Oxford and Cambridge who had spent a lifetime explaining what it really meant took fresh stock of their positions. Gilbert Murray,

---

[64] Middlemas and Barnes, *Baldwin*.

[65] *Christian News-Letter*, 3 July 1940.

[66] Cited in J. Herrick, *Vision and Realism: A Hundred Years of 'The Freethinker'* (London, 1982), p. 84.

[67] N. Mackenzie (ed.), *The Letters of Sidney and Beatrice Webb*, vol. III, *1912–1947* (London, 1978), p. 440.

[68] J. B. Priestley, *Out of the People* (London, 1941), p. 109.

[69] H. Carpenter, *W. H. Auden. A biography* (London, 1981), p. 309.

registering alarm at the waxing domestic power of his cook, still had sufficient liberty to make fundamental assertions. He was coming to the conclusion that he and his contemporaries belonged to a 'martyred' generation, but there was 'no warrant for any wholesale condemnation of modern civilization, no warrant for rejecting our own ideals of progress, humanity and justice'. There was no hint, here, of the good pagan's failure, though some fear that, the war apart, the march of progress was being hindered by the popularity of football pools.[70] The President of Corpus, Sir Richard Livingstone, another guardian of civilization, also felt that the legacy of Greece was being threatened by the insidious activities of Mr Moores of Liverpool. He remembered that Lord Bryce had replied to a questioner who had asked what would be the effect of the disappearance of religious education from schools by saying that the impact could not be judged until three generations had passed. Livingstone had no doubt that he was witnessing 'the weakening or dissolution of the traditions and beliefs which for many centuries have ruled Western civilisation and held it together'. Those who rejected Christian beliefs could not be surprised if Christian morals collapsed. Greek thought and Christianity, he supposed, had created 'the soul of Western Civilisation', formed its mind and were the vitamins of its lifeblood. It was not too late to suggest that 'everyone' should have an idea of them.[71] Murray was less enthusiastic about the Christian contribution to this synthesis. Somewhat obsessed by his own kitchen arrangements at this time he was already moving to the view that the advent of 'real democracy', coinciding with two world wars, was cooking 'the goose of civilisation'.[72] The *Nordic Twilight* of 1940 worried E. M. Forster in Cambridge. Much as he longed for peace, he could not contemplate life under German domination, for 'if you make power and not understanding your god...you atrophy the impulse to create. Creation is disinterested. Creation is passionate understanding. Creation lies at the heart of civilization like fire at the heart of the earth.' He took comfort from the knowledge that 'violence has so far never worked. Even when it conquers, it fails in the long run.' He permitted himself to say that this failure 'may be due to the Divine Will', though it might also be ascribed 'to the strange nature of Man, who refuses to live by bread alone, and alone among the animals has attempted to understand his

[70] G. Murray, *A Conversation with Bryce* (Oxford, 1944), p. 30. In 1940, Murray had collected together lectures given over a quarter century on the theme 'Stoic, Christian and Humanist'. While it might be true that what was being endangered in Europe was 'the Christian spirit', it was a spirit as humanized and liberalized in the nineteenth century.
[71] R. Livingstone, *Education for a World Adrift* (Cambridge, 1943), p. 96.
[72] P. Clarke, *Liberals and Social Democrats* (Cambridge, 1981), pp. 284 and 287.

surroundings'.[73] Elsewhere in Cambridge it was comforting to know that civilization was 'always recognisable'. These words were spoken by G. M. Trevelyan to Harold Nicolson as they surveyed Trinity College silver and port. The new Master was struggling to feel at home in the Lodge 'before the bomb comes'.[74]

G. D. H. Cole did not feel so comfortable in the civilization that surrounded him. He hated Nazism so deeply that there was nothing he wanted more than its overthrow. He desired 'our civilisation' to be saved but he did not trust the government (he was writing in November 1939) 'either to make this a war for democracy or to conduct either war or negotiations for peace by democratic methods'. He claimed that Mr Chamberlain was more shocked by Hitler's methods than by his ideas. Christianity was not, for Cole, a matter for serious consideration. Nevertheless, a little transcendental reference slipped into his language when considering Hitler. No doubt he was 'a much greater sinner than any of our statesmen, if you judge him by his deeds. But he has, and they have not, the excuse of being out of his mind. There can be no lasting peace with Hitler, because he thinks he is God, and above all human morality.' A little later, he added that 'Hitler menaces us to-day, a demon of our own making, the Frankenstein monster of our own incompetence and folly.'[75] It was a little naughty of Cole to be talking about Gods and demons at all, though he clearly found difficulty in distinguishing between them. Clarification on this score might have come from C. S. Lewis. It was on 15 July 1940 that 'Screwtape' entered his mind.[76] His contribution to the Battle of Britain was to illumine the plausible wiles of the Devil – and the personification of Evil seemed not inappropriate to some disbelievers in the existence of God.

Harold Laski thought that for something like a century and a half it had been the 'central purpose of Western civilisation' to find the secret of combining individual freedom with social order. The Nazi system represented a challenge to that central purpose. He had two explanations for the contemptuous attitude of Nazi party leaders towards Christianity. They disliked 'its insistence of the universality of the rights of man' but, no doubt, they also coveted 'the immense property of the Churches as a fund through which to cope with their financial difficulties'. He suggested that 'the philosophies of Greece and Christianity' had discovered the infinite worth of the individual

[73] E. M. Forster, *Nordic Twilight* (London, 1940), pp. 31–2.
[74] N. Nicolson (ed.), *Harold Nicolson: Diaries and Letters, 1939–1945* (London, 1967), p. 140; M. Moorman, *George Macaulay Trevelyan* (London, 1980), p. 231.
[75] G. D. H. Cole, *War Aims* (London, 1939), pp. 28–9 and 58.
[76] Roger Lancelyn Green and Walter Hooper, *C. S. Lewis, a Biography* (London, 1974), p. 191.

being and thus insisted that the justification of social institutions lay in their power to evoke that worth. This 'central tradition of Western civilisation' was one 'which all political parties have shared in common. Conservative and Socialist, Liberals and even Communist, Christian and Jew and Agnostic, may have differed about its realisation in method or in pace; about the validity of the large ends it has in view they have hardly differed at all.' In contrast, the Nazi leaders represented 'that ultimate corruption of the human spirit which pervades and infects every government which denies its responsibility to ordinary men. Like the Satan of Milton's great epic, they have identified good with evil.' It followed, therefore, that it was not Christian civilization as such which Laski wished to defend but he supposed that Christianity had a place in that Western civilization whose purpose it was 'To make the common man the master of his own destiny.'[77] On these grounds perhaps Christianity merited the two cheers that E. M. Forster was prepared to accord to democracy itself.

Invited to comment on certain propositions about the future ordering of society in *The Times* in December 1940 by representative churchmen, William Beveridge permitted himself the assertion that 'The sense of a Divine Vocation must be restored to a man's daily work.' He was finding the language of crusading infectious and it was to be summed up in his remark that 'A war of faith is what the world is waiting for.'[78] That 'faith', however, was apparently not Christian faith. Beveridge explained that he was not brought up in any religious faith and had never been a member of any religious community. He asserted that 'there should be something in the daily life of every man or woman which he or she does for no personal reward or gain, does ever more and more consciously as a mark of the brotherhood and sisterhood of all mankind'. Marking the brotherhood and sisterhood of man, he was willing to add, 'leads to the fatherhood of God'. It could be said that the Beveridge Report would not be undergirded by any elaborate theological foundation.[79]

By the end of 1940, when the immediate pressure on Britain had eased, the intense discussion of 'Christian civilization' declined, though it did not disappear. Later in the war, and immediately after it, theologians continued to

[77] H. Laski, *The Rights of Man* (London, 1940), pp. 15, 29–31.
[78] W. Beveridge, *The Pillars of Security* (London, 1943), p. 32.
[79] *Ibid.*, pp. 38–9. José Harris points out in her biography that it was incorrect of Beveridge to claim that he had a 'wholly non-religious upbringing'. His father professed no religion, but his mother contrived to circumvent his wishes and the Beveridge children said daily prayers and attended Sunday School and divine service in Calcutta cathedral. J. Harris, *William Beveridge* (Oxford, 1977), pp. 15–16.

address the issue, but with less popular resonance.[80] The question Jacques Maritain had asked in 1939 was whether 'in the face of an unprecedented loosing of pagan violence and of all the means which draw strength from the degradation of the human being, we understand the need of going back to the first source of spiritual energies'.[81] The circumstances of Britain in 1940 produced, at least briefly, a widespread willingness to *look* back at that first source; actually to *go* back was a journey which many could or would not make. 'We have got to be children of God' wrote George Orwell in April 1940, 'even though the God of the Prayer Book no longer exists.'[82]

[80] For example, H. G. Wood, *Christianity and Civilisation* (Cambridge, 1942); J. Baillie, *What is Christian Civilization?* (London, 1945); E. Brunner, *Christianity and Civilisation* (London, 1948).

[81] J. Maritain, *The Twilight of Civilization* (London, 1946), pp. 46–7.

[82] S. Orwell and I. Angus (eds.), *The Collected Essays, Journalism and Letters of George Orwell*, vol. II (London, 1968), pp. 17–18.

A bibliography of the writings of Owen Chadwick

EAMON DUFFY

The list contains all the books, articles and essays published by Owen Chadwick to the end of 1983. A (small) number of book reviews have eluded search.

Abbreviations for Journal titles

E.H.R.	*English Historical Review*
H.J.	*Historical Journal*
J.E.H.	*Journal of Ecclesiastical History*
J.T.S.	*Journal of Theological Studies* (references to volumes in the New Series unless otherwise indicated)
T.H.E.S.	*Times Higher Educational Supplement*
T.L.S.	*Times Literary Supplement*

DRAFTED

Report of the Archbishop's Commission on Church and State, 1970.

EDITOR

Bulletin Anglican (nos. 2–8), December 1952–Autumn 1954.
Pelican History of the Church, 1960–70.
Oxford History of the Christian Church, 1976 (with H. Chadwick).

BOOKS AND SEPARATE PUBLICATIONS
(*including works edited by WOC*)

Only the first printing is noticed.
John Cassian: A Study in Primitive Monasticism, Cambridge 1950.
The Founding of Cuddesdon, Cambridge 1954.
From Bossuet to Newman. The Idea of Doctrinal Development (Birkbeck Lectures 1955–6), Cambridge 1957.
Western Asceticism. Selected Translations with Introductions and Notes (Library of Christian Classics, vol. 12), London 1958.
Creighton on Luther: An Inaugural Lecture, Cambridge 1959.
Mackenzie's Grave, London 1959.
The Mind of the Oxford Movement, London 1960.

Victorian Miniature, London 1960.

The History of the Church. A Select Bibliography (Helps for the Student of History, no. 66), Historical Association Pamphlet 1962.

From Uniformity to Unity 1662–1962 (ed. with Geoffrey Nuttall), London 1962.

Westcott and the University (the Bishop Westcott Memorial Lecture 1962), Cambridge 1963.

The Reformation (vol. 4 of *Pelican History of the Church*), Harmondsworth 1964.

The Victorian Church: Vol. I, London 1966.

Christian Unity (the Peter Ainslie Memorial Lecture 1967 (no. 14)), Grahamstown: Rhodes University 1967.

Edward King, Bishop of Lincoln, 1885–1910 (Lincoln Minster Pamphlets, Series 2, no. 4), Lincoln 1968.

Religion and Science in Victorian England: Legend and Reality (the Selwyn Lectures 1967), *Colloquium – The Australian and New Zealand Theological Review, Suppl.*, Auckland 1968.

Freedom and the Historian: An Inaugural Lecture, Cambridge 1969.

The Victorian Church: Vol. II, London 1970.

The English Bishops and the Nazis (a lecture to the Friends of Lambeth Palace Library), London 1973.

Selwyn College, 1882–1973 A Short History, Cambridge 1973.

Acton and Gladstone (the Creighton Lecture in History 1975), London 1976.

The Secularization of the European Mind in the Nineteenth Century (the Gifford Lectures 1973–4), Cambridge 1977.

Catholicism and History: The Opening of the Vatican Archives (the Herbert Hensley Henson Lectures, delivered in the University of Oxford 1976), Cambridge 1978.

The Making of the Benedictine Ideal (the Thomas Verner Moore Memorial Lecture for 1980), Washington D.C. 1981.

The Popes and European Revolution (*Oxford History of the Christian Church*), Oxford 1981.

Hensley Henson, Oxford 1983.

Newman (Past Masters), Oxford 1983.

ARTICLES, INTRODUCTIONS AND CONTRIBUTIONS TO GROUP PUBLICATIONS

Where an item has appeared in more than one edition, or in subsequent translation, only the first appearance has been noticed.

'Training for the Ministry; The Public Schools', 'By a School Chaplain', *Guardian*, 7 July 1944, p. 232.

'Euladius of Arles', *J.T.S.*, vol. 46 (Old Series), 1944, pp. 200–5.

'The Secret of St. Martin' (letter), *Theology*, vol. 50, 1947, pp. 267–8.

'Letters from Delhi', *Cambridge Review*, vol. 69, 1947–8, pp. 94–6.

'Confirmation', in Canon A. R. Wallace *et al.*, *Religion in the Public Schools*, London 1948.

'The Origins of Prime', *J.T.S.*, vol. 49 (Old Series), 1948, pp. 178–82.

'John Sterling', *The Crescent Magazine*, Easter Term, 1949, pp. 113–15.

'The Agape in Sub-Apostolic Time', *Friends of Reunion Bulletin*, August 1949, pp. 5–8.

'Gregory of Tours and Gregory the Great', *J.T.S.*, vol. 50 (Old Series), 1949, pp. 38–49.

'Cassian, John', *Chambers Encyclopaedia*, vol. 3, 1950, pp. 155–6.

'Pachomius', *Chambers Encyclopaedia*, vol. 10, 1950, p. 299.

'Vincent, Saint, of Lérins', *Chambers Encyclopaedia*, vol. 14, 1950, p. 325.

'Tent-makers', *Theology*, vol. 54, 1951, pp. 42–51.

'The Study of the Fathers', *Church Quarterly Review*, vol. 153, 1952, pp. 509–15.

'Richard Bancroft's Submission', *J.E.H.*, vol. 3, 1952, pp. 58–73.

'Great Pastors – I. St. Basil the Great', *Theology*, vol. 56, 1953, pp. 19–23.

'The Case of Philip Nicols, 1731', *Transactions of the Cambridge Bibliographical Society*. vol. 1, 1953, pp. 422–31.

'The Evidence of Dedications in the Early History of the Welsh Church', in N. K Chadwick, *Studies in Early British History*, Cambridge 1954, pp. 173–88.

'Gildas and the Monastic Order', *J.T.S.*, vol. 5, 1954, pp. 78–80.

'Le Père Bouyer et le Protestantisme', *Bulletin Anglican*, no. 11, Summer 1955, pp. 16–21.

'Une délégation anglicane à Moscou', *Bulletin (Oecuménique) Anglican*, no. 15, December 1956, pp. 16–24.

'The English Church and the Continent in the Sixteenth Century', in *The English Church and the Continent*, London 1959, pp. 60–72.

'Arminianism in England', *Religion in Life*, no. 29, 1960, pp. 548–55.

'Direct Impact on Social Habits', *The Times*, Supplement on the Bible in English, 27 March 1961, pp. iv–v.

Benjamin J. Armstrong, *Armstrong's Norfolk Diary* (ed. H. B. J. Armstrong), with an Introduction by Owen Chadwick, London 1963.

'The Limitations of Keble' (nominally a review of G. Battiscombe, *John Keble, a Study in Limitations*, London 1963), *Theology*, vol. 67, 1964, pp. 46–52.

'Vatican', *Observer*, 14 March 1965, p. 11.

'Franks and Administration', *Cambridge Review*, vol. 87, 1965–6, pp. 475–6.

'The Historical Writing of Professor Gordon Rupp', *Drew Gateway*, vol. 36, no. 1–2, 1965–6 (no pagination).

'"Secrets of the Scrolls". A Reply to John Allegro', *Evening News*, 17 December 1965, p. 8.

'The Church of England and the Church of Rome, from the Beginning of the Nineteenth Century to the Present Day', in S. Runciman *et al.*, *Anglican Initiatives in Christian Unity*, London 1967, pp. 73–107.

'Council', *Encyclopaedia Britannica*, vol. 6, 1967, pp. 632–7, 640–2.

'England, Church of', *Encyclopaedia Britannica*, vol. 8, 1967, pp. 432–7.

'Hardouin, Jean', *Encyclopaedia Britannica*, vol. 11, 1967, p. 96.

'Josephus, Flavius', *Encyclopaedia Britannica*, vol. 13, 1967, pp. 89–90.

'Newman, John Henry', *Encyclopaedia Britannica*, vol. 16, 1967, pp. 363–4.

'Oxford Movement', *Encyclopaedia Britannica*, vol. 16, 1967, pp. 1183–5.

'Selwyn, George Augustus', *Encyclopaedia Britannica*, vol. 20, 1967, p. 198.

'Simeon, Charles', *Encyclopaedia Britannica*, vol. 20, 1967, pp. 549–50.

'The Papacy and World War II', *J.E.H.*, vol. 18, 1967, pp. 71–9.

'Monasticism', *International Encyclopaedia of the Social Sciences*, ed. D. L. Sills, vol. 10, New York, London 1968, pp. 415–19.

'The Papacy and World War II: Further Documents', *J.E.H.*, vol. 19, 1968, pp. 227–31.

'The Established Church under Attack', in A. Symondson (ed.), *The Victorian Crisis of Faith*, London 1970, pp. 191–206.

'The Anglican Practice in the Election of Bishops', *Concilium*, vol. 7, 1972, pp. 140–6.

'Should there be Parties in the Church in the Future? An Anglican Answer', *Concilium*, vol. 8, 1973, pp. 101–9.

'The Present Stage of the Kirchenkampf Enquiry', *J.E.H.*, vol. 24, 1973, pp. 33–60.

'Catholicism' (the Charles Gore Lecture, given in Westminster Abbey, 10 October 1972), *Theology*, vol. 76, 1973, pp. 171–80.

'The Idea of a National Church: Gladstone and Henson', in M. Simon (ed.), *Aspects de l'Anglicanisme*, Paris 1974, pp. 183–206.

'Gregory of Tours', *The New Encyclopaedia Britannica*, Macropaedia, vol. 8, 1974, pp. 422–3.

'Protestantism, History of', *The New Encyclopaedia Britannica*, Macropaedia, vol. 15, 1974, pp. 108–20.

'Tait, Archibald Campbell', *New Encyclopaedia Britannica*, Micropaedia, vol. 9, 1974, pp. 776–7.

'Indifference and Morality', in P. N. Brooks (ed.), *Christian Spirituality: Essays Presented to Gordon Rupp*, Cambridge 1975, pp. 203–30.

'Charles Kingsley at Cambridge', a lecture given 23 January 1975 at the centenary of Charles Kingsley under the auspices of Magdalene College, *H.J.*, vol. 18, 1975, pp. 303–25.

'John Knox and Revolution' (the Andrew Lang Memorial Lecture, St Andrews, Scotland, on the Fourth Centenary of the death of Knox), *Andover Newton Quarterly*, vol. 15, 1975, pp. 250–66.

'Kingsley's Chair', *Theology*, vol. 78, 1975, pp. 2–8.

'From 1822 until 1916', in G. E. Aylmer and Reginald Cant, *A History of York Minster*, Oxford 1977, pp. 272–312.

'Gibbon and the Church Historians', in G. W. Baverstock *et al.*, *Edward Gibbon and the Decline and Fall of the Roman Empire*, Harvard 1977, pp. 219–32.

'The Making of a Reformed Prince: Frederick III, Elector Palatine', in R. Buick Knox (ed.), *Reformation and Dissent: Essays in Honour of Geoffrey Nuttall*, London 1977, pp. 44–69.

'The Victorian Diocese of St. Albans', in Robert Runcie (ed.), *Cathedral and City*, London 1977, pp. 71–100.

'Weizsäcker, the Vatican and the Jews of Rome', *J.E.H.*, vol. 28, 1977, pp. 179–99.

'Lord Acton at the First Vatican Council', *J.T.S.*, vol. 28, 1977, pp. 465–97.

'Sir Herbert Butterfield', *Cambridge Review*, vol. 101, 1979, pp. 6–8.

'Young Gladstone and Italy', *J.E.H.*, vol. 30, 1979, pp. 243–59.

'Kirchengeschichte-Weltgeschichte: Europa und die Weltchristenheit', in T. Rendtorff (ed.), *Europäische Theologie*, Gütersloh 1980, pp. 79–87.

'The British Ambassador and the Conclave of 1878', in *Wissen Glaube Politik: Festschrift für Paul Asveld*, Graz 1981, pp. 155–60.

'Christianity and Industrial Society', in G. Barraclough (ed.), *The Christian World*, London 1981, pp. 249–62.

'Introduction: Prince Albert as Chancellor of the University of Cambridge', in John A. S. Phillips, *Prince Albert and the Victorian Age*, Cambridge 1981, pp. 1–16.

'The Italian Enlightenment', in R. Porter and M. Teich, *The Enlightenment in National Context*, Cambridge 1981, pp. 90–105.

'Cassianus, Johannes', *Theologische Realenzyklopädie*, vol. 7, Berlin, New York, 1981, pp. 650–7.

'The Oxford Movement and its Reminiscencers' (a lecture delivered on Wednesday, 27 April 1983, in the Oxford Examination Schools in commemoration of the 150th Anniversary of John Keble's Assize Sermon), *Oriel College Record*, 1983, pp. 14–26.

SERMONS

The Gospel and Worship: a sermon preached before the University of Cambridge in Great St Mary's Church on Sunday, 22 February 1948, *Cambridge Review*, vol. 69, 1947–8, pp. 406–7.

The Commemoration Sermon: St. John's College, Cambridge 1952, *The Eagle*, vol. 55, 1953, pp. 23–6.

Christian Community in History: The Fourth Phase: A Mission to Society: a sermon preached in Great St Mary's Church on Sunday, 7 February 1954, *Cambridge Review*, vol. 75, 1953–4, pp. 309–10.

An Address Given to the Annual Pilgrimage to Little Gidding: Saturday, 13 July 1957, *Annual Report of the Friends of Little Gidding 1956–7*, Sawston, Cambs., n.d.

Christus Victor: in C. H. Smyth, *Good Friday at St Margaret's*, London 1957, pp. 133–47.

The University Sermon: preached in Great St Mary's Church on Sunday, 2 November 1958, at the Commemoration of Benefactors, *Cambridge Review*, vol. 80, 1958–9, pp. 133–5.

The Text of the Sermon Preached at King's Cliffe, Northamptonshire: to mark the bi-centenary of the death of William Law (reprinted *Emmanuel College Magazine*, vol. 43, 1960–1, pp. 29–34), *Anglican World*, no. 6, 1961, pp. 53–5.

Beati Simplices: a sermon preached in St Benet's Church, Cambridge, 11 May 1963, *The Franciscan*, vol. 5, 1963, pp. 134–7.

I Will Make All My Goodness Pass Before Thee: a sermon preached to the Members of the British Association for the Advancement of Science in St Mary's Church, Southampton, on 30 August 1964, *The Advancement of Science*, vol. 21, 1964, pp. 413–15.

A Strange Land: the sermon preached at Cuddesdon College Festival 1966, Oxford, privately printed 1967.

Tennyson and Virgil: an address to the Tennyson Society in Bag Enderby Church, on Sunday, 4 August 1968, Tennyson Soc., Tennyson Memorial Sermon, Lincoln 1968.

Links in the Historic Chain: preached at the consecration of Simon, Bishop of Buckingham, and Philip, Bishop of Crediton, in Westminster Abbey on 18 October 1974, *Oxford Diocesan Magazine*, vol. 7, December 1974, pp. 5–6.

Arthur Gamble: Old Denstonian Chronicle, vol. 12, 1975, p. 585.

Armistice Day: Theology, vol. 79, 1976, pp. 322–9.

What Cannot Be, Love Counts it Done: a sermon preached on the centenary of the dedication of the Chapel of Keble College, Oxford, 25 April 1976, *Christian*, vol. 3, 1976, pp. 313–16, 321.

Is Religion an Escape?: a sermon preached in Boston Cathedral, Boston, Mass. 1976.

Afterwards, No One Remembered: a sermon preached at the Feast Service of St Paul's School, in St Paul's Cathedral, 1 February 1977, *The Pauline*, vol. 95, 1977, pp. 132–4.

The Thirteenth Century of Gloucester Cathedral: Annual Report of the Friends of Gloucester Cathedral, 1981, pp. 17–19.

Selwyn and Lichfield: a sermon preached on the occasion of the Thanksgiving Service in Lichfield Cathedral, 21 May 1983, *Selwyn College Calendar*, Michaelmas 1983, pp. 44–5.

REVIEWS

W. J. Sparrow Simpson, *The Monastic Ideal. Theology*, vol. 46, 1943, p. 240.

S. L. Greenslade, *Schism in the Early Church. History*, vol. 39, 1944, p. 294.

A Manual of Eastern Orthodox Prayers and Gilbert Shaw, *A Pilgrim's Book of Prayers. Theology*, vol. 48, 1945, pp. 259–60.

G. D. Carleton, *The English Psalter. Theology*, vol. 49, 1946, pp. 181–2.

H. Munro Chadwick, *The Nationalities of Europe and the Growth of National Ideologies. History*, vol. 33, 1948, pp. 137–8.

J. Lebreton and J. Zeiller, *The History of the Primitive Church*, vol. 4. *Theology*, vol. 51, 1948, pp. 76–7.

Francis Dvornik, *The Photian Schism: History and Legend. Cambridge Review*, vol. 70, 1948–9, pp. 140–2.

E. A. Thompson, *A History of Attila and the Huns. Cambridge Review*, vol. 70, 1948–9, pp. 170–1.

Horton Davies, *The Worship of the English Puritans. Cambridge Review*, vol. 70, 1948–9, p. 236.

A. M. Ramsey, *The Glory of God and the Transfiguration of Christ. Cambridge Review*, vol. 70, 1948–9, p. 629.

C. Delisle Burns, *The First Europe: A Study of the Establishment of Medieval Christendom, A.D. 400–800. History*, vol. 34, 1949, pp. 263–4.

T. A. Goggin, *The Times of St Gregory of Nyssa as Reflected in the Letters and the 'Contra Eunonium'. History*, vol. 34, 1949, pp. 282–3.

Walter Shewring, *Rich and Poor in Christian Tradition. Theology*, vol. 52, 1949, p. 199.

Hugh Watt, *John Knox in Controversy. Church of England Newspaper*, 15 September 1950, p. 8.

Mary Tarcisia Ball, *Nature and the Vocabulary of Nature in the Works of St Cyprian. History*, vol. 35, 1950, p. 150.

T. M. Parker, *The English Reformation to 1558. J.E.H.*, vol. 1, 1950, pp. 243–4.

H. de Lubac, *Corpus Mysticum: l'Eucharistie et l'Eglise au moyen âge. J.T.S.*, vol. 1, 1950, pp. 217–19.

T. G. Jalland, *The Origin and Evolution of the Christian Church. Theology*, vol. 53, 1950, pp. 356–7.

L. Bouyer, *La Vie de S. Antoine. Theology*, vol. 53, 1950, pp. 437–8.

A. H. M. Jones, *Constantine and the Conversion of Europe. History*, vol. 36, 1951, p. 111.

Robert Sencourt, *St Paul, Envoy of Grace*, and L. E. Elliott-Binns, *The Beginnings of Western Christendom*. History, vol. 36, 1951, p. 143.

Jean-Michel Hanssens, SJ, *Amalarii episcopi opera liturgica omnia*. J.T.S., vol. 2, 1951, pp. 211–13.

Gordon Rupp, *Luther's Progress to the Diet of Worms*. Theology, vol. 54, 1951, pp. 314–15.

Howard Marshall and J. P. Jordan, *Oxford v. Cambridge: The Story of the University Rugby Match*. Cambridge Review, vol. 73, 1951–2, p. 492.

A. E. Welsford, *Life in the Early Church to AD 313*, and Hans Lietzmann, *A History of the Early Church*, vol. 4, and J. R. Palanque and P. de Labriolle, *The Church in the Christian Roman Empire*, vol. 2. Cambridge Review, vol. 74, 1952–3, p. 18.

Cyril Garbett, *In An Age of Revolution*. Economist, vol. 163, April–June 1952, p. 316.

A. Penna, *Principi e Carattere dell'Esegesi di S. Gerolamo*. J.T.S., vol. 3, 1952, p. 125.

M. L. W. Laistner, *Christianity and Pagan Culture in the Later Roman Empire*. J.T.S., vol. 3, 1952, pp. 272–4.

W. H. C. Frend, *The Donatist Church: A Movement of Protest in Roman North Africa*. Cambridge Review, vol. 74, 1952–3, p. 332.

J. T. McNeill, *A History of the Cure of Souls*. J.E.H., vol. 4, 1953, pp. 115–16.

R. P. C. Hanson, *Origen's Doctrine of Tradition*. Cambridge Review, vol. 75, 1953–4, p. 552.

E. G. Jay, *Origen's Treatise on Prayer*. Cambridge Review, vol. 76, 1954–5, p. 65.

R. V. Sellers, *The Council of Chalcedon*. Church of England Newspaper, 29 January 1954, p. 7.

E. L. Mascall, *Corpus Christi*. Church Times, 27 January 1954, p. 68.

E. E. Y. Hales, *Pio Nono*. Church Times, 9 April 1954, p. 276.

J. G. Davies, *The Spirit, the Church and the Sacraments*. Church Times, 19 November 1954, p. 880.

S. C. Carpenter, *The Church in England 597–1688*. Economist, vol. 171, April–June 1954, p. 968.

A. J. Toynbee, *A Study of History*. Economist, supplement to vol. 173, 6 November 1954, p. 1.

Albert Peel (ed.), *Tracts ascribed to Richard Bancroft*. J.E.H., vol. 5, 1954, pp. 113–14.

G. W. Bromiley, *Zwingli and Bullinger*. J.T.S., vol. 5, 1954, pp. 102–4.

Hubert Vanderhoven and François Masai, *Aux Sources du Monachisme Bénédictin, I: Regula Magistri*. J.T.S., vol. 5, 1954, pp. 275–9.

Ruth Rouse and Stephen Neill, *A History of the Ecumenical Movement 1517–1948*. J.T.S., vol. 5, 1954, pp. 294–6.

Gordon Rupp, *The Righteousness of God*. Theology, vol. 57, 1954, pp. 135–8.

Philip Magnus, *Gladstone*. Bulletin Anglican, no. 10, Spring 1955, pp. 22–7.

J. J. O'Meara, *The Young Augustine*. Church of England Newspaper, 28 January 1955, p. 8.

H. F. Woodhouse, *The Doctrine of the Church in Anglican Theology 1537–1663*. Church Times, 7 January 1955, p. 4.

P. Broutin, *L'Evêque dans la tradition pastorale du XVIe siècle*. J.T.S., vol. 6, 1955, p. 160.

F. Pelster, *Zur Enzyklika 'Aeterni Patris': Text und Kommentar*. J.T.S., vol. 6, 1955, p. 351.

Max Thurian, *La Confession. Theology*, vol. 58, 1955, p. 80.

N. Sykes, *Old Priest, New Presbyter. Church Times*, 13 April 1956, p. 5.

Arnold Toynbee, *An Historian's Approach to Religion. Economist*, vol. 180, July–September 1956, p. 789.

Kenneth Muir, *John Milton. J.E.H.*, vol. 7, 1956, p. 127.

Margaret Cropper, *Sparks among the Stubble. J.E.H.*, vol. 7, 1956, p. 128.

J. R. Geiselmann, *Die Theologische Anthropologie Johann Adam Möhlers: ihr geschichtlicher Wandel. J.T.S.*, vol. 7, 1956, pp. 328–9.

F. Bullock, *A History of Training for the Ministry. Theology*, vol. 59, 1956, p. 127.

B. Steidle, *Antonius Magnus Eremita: Studia ad antiquum monachismum spectantia. J.T.S.*, vol. 8, 1957, pp. 170–1.

Irénée Hausherr, *Direction spirituelle en Orient autrefois. J.T.S.*, vol. 8, 1957, p. 172.

Georges Bavaud, *La Dispute de Lausanne (1536): un étage de l'evolution doctrinale des Réformateurs romands. J.T.S.*, vol. 8, 1957, pp. 362–3.

Christopher Hill, *Economic Problems of the Church: From Archbishop Whitgift to the Long Parliament. J.T.S.*, vol. 8, 1957, p. 363.

E. W. Hunt, *Dean Colet and His Theology. J.T.S.*, vol. 8, 1957, p. 412.

T. F. Torrance, *Kingdom and Church: A Study in the Theology of the Reformation. J.T.S.*, vol. 8, 1957, p. 412.

Paul van Buren, *Christ in our Place: The Substitutionary Character of Calvin's Doctrine of Reconciliation. J.T.S.*, vol. 8, 1957, p. 413.

W. R. Matthews and W. M. Atkins, *A History of St Paul's Cathedral. J.E.H.*, vol. 9, 1958, pp. 104–5.

E. I. Watkin, *Roman Catholicism in England from the Reformation to 1950. J.E.H.*, vol. 9, 1958, p. 276.

James A. O'Donohue, *Tridentine Seminary Legislation: Its Sources and its Formation. J.T.S.*, vol. 9, 1958, p. 221.

Einar Molland, *Church Life in Norway 1800–1950. J.T.S.*, vol. 9, 1958, pp. 221–3.

Luchesius Smits, *Saint Augustin dans l'oeuvre de Jean Calvin*, vol. 1, *Etude de critique littéraire. J.T.S.*, vol. 9, 1958, p. 420.

George L. Mosse, *The Holy Pretence. J.T.S.*, vol. 9, 1958, pp. 420–1.

Millar Maclure, *The Paul's Cross Sermons 1534–1642. J.E.H.*, vol. 10, 1959, pp. 248–50.

J. Höfer and K. Rahner, *Lexikon für Theologie und Kirche*, vol. 1, *A-Baronius. J.T.S.*, vol. 10, 1959, pp. 173–5.

E. Pichery, *Jean Cassien, Conférences VIII–XVII. J.T.S.*, vol. 10, 1959, p. 226.

Richard H. Trame, *Rodrigo Sanchez de Arévalo 1404–1470. J.T.S.*, vol. 10, 1959, pp. 226–7.

Douglas Horton, *John Norton: The Answer to the Whole Set of Questions of the Celebrated Mr William Apollonius, Pastor of the Church of Middleburg. J.T.S.*, vol. 10, 1959, p. 227.

Wolfgang Renz, *Newman's Idee einer Universität. J.T.S.*, vol. 10, 1959, p. 227.

M. Adreiaen, *Magni Aurelii Cassiodori Expositio Psalmorum. J.T.S.*, vol. 10, 1959, pp. 409–10.

P. B. Corbett, *The Latin of the Regula Magistri. J.T.S.*, vol. 10, 1959, p. 410.

Luchesius Smits, *Saint Augustin dans l'oeuvre de Jean Calvin*, vol. 2. *J.T.S.*, vol. 10, 1959, pp. 462–3.

Publications of Owen Chadwick

J. Höfer and K. Rahner, *Lexikon für Theologie und Kirche*, vol. 2. *J.T.S.*, vol. 10, 1959, p. 463.

Il Monachesimo Orientale (Orientalia Christiana Analecta, vol. 153). *J.T.S.*, vol. 10, 1959, p. 463.

H. C. Porter, *Reformation and Reaction in Tudor Cambridge*. *Theology*, vol. 62, 1959, pp. 69–70.

A. M. Allchin, *The Silent Rebellion*. *Theology*, vol. 62, 1959, pp. 207–8.

H. Richard Niebuhr and D. D. Williams, *The Ministry in Historical Perspective*. *Theology*, vol. 62, 1959, p. 371.

Jasper Rootham, *Demi-Paradise*. *Cambridge Review*, vol. 81, 1959–60, p. 359.

I. Schapera (ed.), *Livingstone's Private Journals*, and Tony Lanman, *From the Hands of the Wicked*. *Economist*, vol. 197, October–December 1960, pp. 246–7.

Mark H. Curtis, *Oxford and Cambridge in Transition*. *J.E.H.*, vol. 11, 1960, pp. 247–8.

Olive Brose, *Church and Parliament: The Reshaping of the Church of England, 1828–1860*. *J.E.H.*, vol. 11, 1960, pp. 255–6.

W. K. Jordan, *Philanthropy in England 1480–1660*. *J.T.S.*, vol. 11, 1960, pp. 213–16.

Alvar Ellegård, *Darwin and the General Reader: The Reception of Darwin's Theory of Evolution in the British Periodical Press, 1859–1872*. *J.T.S.*, vol. 11, 1960, pp. 216–17.

John L. Murphy, *The Notion of Tradition in John Driedo*. *J.T.S.*, vol. 11, 1960, p. 248.

Gerhard Müller, *Franz Lambert von Avignon und die Reformation in Hessen*. *J.T.S.*, vol. 11, 1960, pp. 428–9.

W. A. M. Beek, *John Keeble's Literary and Religious Contribution to the Oxford Movement*. *J.T.S.*, vol. 11, 1960, pp. 429–30.

Nigel Abercrombie, *The Life and Work of Edmund Bishop*. *J.T.S.*, vol. 11, 1960, pp. 430–2.

J. Höfer and K. Rahner, *Lexikon für Theologie und Kirche*, vol. 3. *J.T.S.*, vol. 11, 1960, pp. 432–3.

E. Pichery, *Jean Cassien, Conférences XVIII–XXIV*. *J.T.S.*, vol. 11, 1960, p. 452.

R. J. Lovy, *Les Origines de la Réforme Française: Meaux 1518–46*. *Theology*, vol. 63, 1960, pp. 340–1.

T. S. Bokenkötter, *Cardinal Newman as an Historian*. *E.H.R.*, vol. 76, 1961, pp. 172–3.

Ronald Jasper, *Arthur Cayley Headlam*. *J.E.H.*, vol. 12, 1961, pp. 255–6.

G. Donaldson, *The Scottish Reformation*. *J.T.S.*, vol. 12, 1961, pp. 146–7.

Newport B. White, '*Registrum Diocesis Dublensis*': *A Sixteenth-Century Dublin Precedent Book*. *J.T.S.*, vol. 12, 1961, p. 181.

Ronald Chapman, *Father Faber*. *J.T.S.*, vol. 12, 1961, pp. 391–3.

J. B. Morrall, *Gerson and the Great Schism*. *J.T.S.*, vol. 12, 1961, p. 420.

Carl S. Meyer, *Elizabeth I and the Religious Settlement of 1559*. *Theology*, vol. 64, 1961, pp. 340–1.

G. W. Lampe (ed.), *A Patristic Greek Lexicon*, part 1. *Classical Review*, vol. 12, 1962, pp. 222–4.

Charles Smyth, *The Church and the Nation*. *Economist*, vol. 203, April–June 1962, pp. 1095–6.

Meriol Trevor, *Newman: Light in Winter*. *Economist*, vol. 205, October–December 1962, p. 486.

Father Hugh, S. S. F., *Nineteenth Century Pamphlets at Pusey House: An Introduction for the Prospective User*. *J.E.H.*, vol. 13, 1962, pp. 131–2.

Hans-Oskar Weber, *Die Stellung des Johannes Cassianus zur ausserpachomianischen Mönchstradition: eine Quellensuntersuchung. J.E.H.*, vol. 13, 1962, p. 223.

I. Hausherr, *Les Leçons d'un Contemplatif: le Traité de l'Oraison d'Evagre le Pontique. J.T.S.*, vol. 13, 1962, p. 177.

H. M. Rochais, *Defensor de Ligugé: Livre d'Etincelles I. J.T.S.*, vol. 13, 1962, p. 178.

K. Aland, *Kirchengeschichtliche Entwürfe. J.T.S.*, vol. 13, 1962, p. 178.

Peter Fraenkel, *Testimonia Patrum: The Function of the Patristic Argument in the Theology of Philip Melancthon. J.T.S.*, vol. 13, 1962, pp. 209–10.

Erich Klostermann and Heinz Berthold, *Neue Homilien des Makarios/Symeon I. J.T.S.*, vol. 13, 1962, pp. 438–9.

Théologie de la vie monastique: études sur la tradition patristique. J.T.S., vol. 13, 1962, pp. 439–40.

John McManners, *French Ecclesiastical Society under the Ancien Regime. J.T.S.*, vol. 13, 1962, pp. 478–81.

J. Höfer and K. Rahner, *Lexikon für Theologie und Kirche*, vols. 5 and 6. *J.T.S.*, vol. 13 1962, p. 506.

Waldo H. Dunn, *James Anthony Froude: A Biography*, vol. 1 (1818–1851). *E.H.R.*. vol. 78, 1963, pp. 195–6.

Charles Stephen Dessain, *The Letters and Diaries of John Henry Newman*, vol. 11, *E.H.R.*, vol. 78, 1963, pp. 745–6.

Horton Davies, *Worship and Theology in England: From Watts and Wesley to Maurice 1690–1850*, vol. 3, and *From Newman to Martineau*, vol. 4. *E.H.R.*, vol. 78, 1963, pp. 790–1.

Brian Fothergill, *Nicholas Wiseman. History*, vol. 48, 1963, p. 386.

Hubert Jedin, *A History of the Council of Trent*, vols. 1 and 2. *J.E.H.*, vol. 14, 1963, pp. 103–5.

J. S. Cummins (ed.), *The Travels and Controversies of Friar Domingo Navarrete 1618–1686. J.T.S.*, vol. 14, 1963, pp. 544–6.

Ross Border, *Church and State in Australia 1788–1872. J.T.S.*, vol. 14, 1963, p. 546.

C. S. Dessain, *The Letters and Diaries of John Henry Newman*, vols. 12 and 13. *E.H.R.*, vol. 79, 1964, p. 627.

François Gaquère, *Vers l'Unité Chrétienne: James Drummond et Bossuet: leur correspondance (1685–1704). J.E.H.*, vol. 15, 1964, pp. 273–4.

Antoine Guillaumont, *Les 'Kephalaia Gnostica' d'Evagre le Pontique et l'histoire de l'Origénisme chez les Grecs et chez les Syriens. J.T.S.*, vol. 15, 1964, pp. 173–6.

Jean E. Mortimer, *The Library Catalogue of Anthony Higgin, Dean of Ripon (1608–1624). J.T.S.*, vol. 15, 1964, pp. 210–21.

J. Höfer and K. Rahner, *Lexikon für Theologie und Kirche*, vols. 7 and 8. *J.T.S.*, vol. 15, 1964, p. 458.

J. A. T. Robinson, *The New Reformation? Economist*, vol. 214, January–March 1965, pp. 1391–3.

E. E. Y. Hales, *Pope John and His Revolution. Economist*, vol. 216, July–September 1965, pp. 43–4.

M. Bourdeaux, *Opium of the People: The Christian Religion in the USSR. Economist*, vol. 216, July–September 1965, pp. 702, 707.

Hans Küng, *Structures of the Church. Economist*, vol. 216, July–September 1965, p. 1000.

Publications of Owen Chadwick

Waldo H. Dunn, *James Anthony Froude; a Biography*, vol. 2, *1857–1894*. E.H.R., vol. 80, 1965, p. 626.

P. B. Hinchcliff, *The Anglican Church in South Africa*. E.H.R., vol. 80, 1965, p. 631.

Ignaz von Döllinger (ed. V. Conzemius), *Briefwechsel, I: mit Lord Acton 1850–1869*. J.E.H., vol. 16, 1965, pp. 114–15.

L'Homme devant Dieu: Mélanges offerts au Père Henri de Lubac, Paris 1964. J.T.S., vol. 16, 1965, pp. 207–10.

H. Dörries, E. Klostermann and M. Kroeker, *Die 50 geistlichen Homilien des Makarios*. J.T.S., vol. 16, 1965, pp. 210–11.

Josef Gülden, *Johan Leisentrits Bautzener Messritus und Messgesänge*. J.T.S., vol. 16, 1965, pp. 541–2.

G. F. A. Best, *Temporal Pillars: Queen Anne's Bounty, the Ecclesiastical Commissioners and the Church of England*. J.T.S., vol. 16, 1965, pp. 544–8.

Leslie Weatherhead, *The Christian Agnostic*. Sunday Times, 26 October 1965, p. 46.

Doreen Slatter (ed.), *The Diary of Thomas Nash*. Archives, vol. 7, 1966, p. 179.

Leslie S. Hunter (ed.), *The English Church: A New Look*. Economist, vol. 219, April–June 1966, pp. 151–2.

Damian McElrath, *The Syllabus of Pius IX*. E.H.R., vol. 81, 1966, p. 418.

J. C. Guy, *Jean Cassien: Institutions Cénobitiques*. J.T.S., vol. 17, 1966, pp. 187–8.

Alf Härdelin, *The Tractarian Understanding of the Eucharist*. J.T.S., vol. 17, 1966, pp. 241–3.

F. J. Casta, *Evêques et curés corses dans la tradition pastorale du Concile de Trente (1570–1620)*. J.T.S., vol. 17, 1966, pp. 509–11.

J. Höfer and K. Rahner, *Lexikon für Theologie und Kirche*, vols. 9 and 10. J.T.S., vol. 17, 1966, pp. 520–2.

R. Borius, *Constance de Lyon, Vie de Saint Germain d'Auxerre*. J.T.S., vol. 17, 1966, pp. 559–60.

Hugh Trevor-Roper, *The Rise of Christian Europe*. Sunday Times, 30 January 1966, p. 48.

The Jerusalem Bible. Sunday Times, 23 October 1966, p. 48.

Peter Brown, *Augustine of Hippo*. Catholic Herald, 22 September 1967, p. 6.

George Scott, *The R Cs*. Economist, vol. 222, January–March 1967, p. 832.

Meriol Trevor, *Pope John*. Economist, vol. 224, April–June 1967, p. 1245.

R. C. D. Jasper, *George Bell, Bishop of Chichester*. Economist, vol. 225, October–December 1967, pp. 293–4.

Charles Davis, *A Question of Conscience*. Economist, vol. 225, October–December 1967, p. 861.

W. W. Manross, *The Fulham Papers in the Lambeth Palace Library: American Colonial Section*. E.H.R., vol. 82, 1967, p. 172.

Robert I. Rotberg, *Christian Missionaries and the Creation of Northern Rhodesia, 1880–1924*. E.H.R., vol. 82, 1967, pp. 433–4.

A. R. Vidler, *F. D. Maurice and Company*. Guardian, 8 February 1967, p. 5.

G. V. Bennett and J. D. Walsh, *Essays in Modern Church History in Memory of Norman Sykes*. History, vol. 52, 1967, p. 128.

Ignaz von Döllinger (ed. V. Conzemius), *Briefwechsel, II: mit Lord Acton 1869–1870*. J.E.H., vol. 18, 1967, pp. 124–5.

Publications of Owen Chadwick

Hubert Jedin, *Kirche des Glaubens, Kirche der Geschichte*. *J.T.S.*, vol. 18, 1967, pp. 279–84.

H. Vorgrimler *et al.*, *Das Zweite Vatikanische Konzil: Dokumente und Kommentare Teil I* (first supplement to *Lexikon für Theologie und Kirche*). *J.T.S.*, vol. 18, 1967, pp. 284–5.

W. R. Rinne, *The Kingdom of God in the Thought of William Temple*. *J.T.S.*, vol. 18, 1967, pp. 286–8.

Derwas J. Chitty, *The Desert a City*. *J.T.S.*, vol. 18, 1967, pp. 494–6.

James Mitchell (ed.), *The God I Want*. Sunday Times, 26 March 1967, p. 27.

Marcello Craveri, *The Life of Jesus*. Sunday Times, 12 November 1967, p. 55.

Journal of Contemporary History, vol. 2, no. 4, October 1967, 'Church and Politics'. *Cambridge Review*, vol. 89A, 1967–8, pp. 390–1.

Hewlett Johnson, *Searching for Light*. Economist, vol. 226, January–March 1968, p. 51.

J. S. Conway, *The Nazi Persecution of the Church 1935–45*, Economist, vol. 227, April–June 1968, pp. 51–2.

Robert Currie, *Methodism Divided*. Economist, vol. 228, July–September 1968, p. 50.

David Mathew, *Lord Acton and His Times*. Economist, vol. 229, October–December 1968, Supplement XXII, 9 November.

T. L. Suttor, *Hierarchy and Democracy in Australia 1788–1870*. E.H.R., vol. 83, 1968, p. 194.

John Sparrow, *Mark Pattison and the Idea of a University*. E.H.R., vol. 83, 1968, p. 630.

Philip McNair, *Peter Martyr in Italy: An Anatomy of Apostasy*. *J.T.S.*, vol. 19, 1968, pp. 372–4.

Salvator Martinez, *Ecclesiologia Felicis Antonii Guarnieri O.F.M. Conv*. *J.T.S.*, vol. 19, 1968, pp. 378–9.

C. S. Dessain, *John Henry Newman*. *J.T.S.*, vol. 19, 1968, p. 380.

Bruno Bellone, *I Vescovi dello Stato Pontificio al Concilio Vaticano I*. *J.T.S.*, vol. 19, 1968, pp. 380–2.

Lexikon für Theologie und Kirche: Register. *J.T.S.*, vol. 19, 1968, pp. 443–4.

Karl-Wilhelm Dahm, *Pfarrer und Politik: Soziale Position und politische Mentalität des Deutschen Evangelischen Pfarrerstandes zwischen 1918 und 1933*. *J.T.S.*, vol. 19, 1968, pp. 689–90.

A. Toynbee (ed.), *The Crucible of Christianity*. Economist, vol. 233, October–December 1969, Supplement XIV, 8 November.

C. S. Dessain, *The Letters and Diaries of J. H. Newman*, vol. 17. E.H.R., vol. 84, 1969, p. 424.

Desmond Bowen, *The Idea of the Victorian Church*, and P. T. Marsh, *The Victorian Church in Decline*. H.J., vol. 12, 1969, pp. 718–20.

Horst Weigelt, *Erweckungsbewegung und konfessionelles Luthertum im 19. Jahrhundert: untersucht an Karl V. Raumer*. J.E.H., vol. 20, 1969, p. 185.

F. R. Salter, *Dissenters and Public Affairs in Mid-Victorian England*. J.E.H., vol. 20, 1969, p. 378.

E. G. W. Bill, *Catalogue of the Papers of Roundell Palmer (1812–1895) First Earl of Selborne*. J.E.H., vol. 20, 1969, p. 379.

John Coulson and A. M. Allchin, *The Rediscovery of Newman*. *J.T.S.*, vol. 20, 1969, pp. 357–60.

The New English Bible. Economist, vol. 234, January–March 1970, p. 63.

Publications of Owen Chadwick

Victor Conzemius, *Eglises chrétiennes et totalitarisme national-socialiste: un bilan historiographique. J.E.H.*, vol. 21, 1970, pp. 92–3.

J. Lloyd Mecham, *Church and State in Latin America. J.E.H.*, vol. 21, 1970, p. 93.

Pierre Blet *et al.*, *Le Saint Siège et la guerre mondiale, Juillet 1941–Octobre 1942. J.E.H.*, vol. 21, 1970, pp. 279–80.

R. I. Burns, *The Crusader Kingdom of Valencia. J.T.S.*, vol. 21, 1970, pp. 226–7.

K. Aland (ed.), *Quellen zur Geschichte des Papsttums...von Carl Mirbt. J.T.S.*, vol. 21, 1970, pp. 227–8.

Lexikon für Theologie und Kirche: Das zweite Vatikanische Konzil: Teil III. J.T.S., vol. 21, 1970, pp. 257–9.

Bibliographie de Cartographie Ecclésiastique. Premier Fascicule, Allemagne-Autriche. J.T.S., vol. 21, 1970, p. 285.

R. A. Butler, *The Art of the Possible. Cambridge Evening News*, 12 July 1971, p. 8.

Edward Carpenter, *Cantuar. Economist*, vol. 241, October–December 1971, pp. 67–8.

A. R. Vidler, *A Variety of Catholic Modernists. J.E.H.*, vol. 22, 1971, pp. 163–4.

Hubert Jedin, *Geschichte des Konzils von Trient*, vol. 3. *J.T.S.*, vol. 22, 1971, pp. 651–4.

E. G. W. Bill and J. F. A. Mason, *Christ Church and Reform 1850–1867. E.H.R.*, vol. 87, 1972, pp. 645–6.

C. Nicolaisen and G. Kretschmar, *Dokumente zur Kirchenpolitik: zur Kirchenpolitik des Dritten Reiches*, vol. 1, *Das Jahr 1933. J.T.S.*, vol. 23, 1972, pp. 527–8.

M. A. Crowther, *Church Embattled. E.H.R.*, vol. 88, 1973, p. 205.

W. R. Ward, *Religion and Society in England 1790–1850*, and G. Kitson Clark, *Churchmen and the Condition of England 1832–1885. H.J.*, vol. 16, 1973, pp. 870–4.

Peter Matheson, *Cardinal Contarini at Regensburg. J.E.H.*, vol. 24, 1973, pp. 79–81.

J. H. Walgrave, *Unfolding Revelation: The Nature of Doctrinal Development. J.E.H.*, vol. 24, 1973, pp. 323–4.

R. M. Bigler, *The Politics of German Protestantism: The Rise of the Protestant Church Elite in Prussia, 1815–1848. J.E.H.*, vol. 24, 1973, pp. 425–6.

Peter Brock, *Pacificism in Europe to 1914. J.E.H.*, vol. 24, 1973, pp. 427–9.

Werner Schütz, *Geschichte der Christlichen Predigt. J.T.S.*, vol. 24, 1973, pp. 620–1.

J. A. T. Robinson, *The Human Face of God. Sunday Times*, 18 March, 1973, p. 31.

W. W. Manross, *S.P.G. Papers in the Lambeth Palace Library. Calendar and Indexes. H.J.*, vol. 17, 1974, p. 662.

Derek Baker (ed.), *Sanctity and Secularity: The Church and the World* (Studies in Church History, vol. 10). *J.E.H.*, vol. 25, 1974, pp. 199–200.

P. Blet *et al.*, *Actes et Documents du Saint Siège relatifs à la Seconde Guerre Mondiale*, vols. 6 and 7. *J.E.H.*, vol. 25, 1974, pp. 332–4.

A. G. Dickens, *The German Nation and Martin Luther. J.E.H.*, vol. 25, 1974, pp. 415–16.

Ernst Bammel, *Die Reichsgründung und der deutsche Protestantismus. J.E.H.*, vol. 25, 1974, pp. 441–2.

D. F. Wright, *Common Places of Martin Bucer. J.T.S.*, vol. 25, 1974, p. 255.

H. J. Schonfield, *The Pentecost Revolution. Sunday Times*, 30 June 1974, p. 39.

Jurgen Moltmann, *The Crucified God. Sunday Times*, 8 September 1974, p. 40.

Lord Longford, *The Life of Jesus Christ. Sunday Times*, 6 October 1974, p. 36.

F. L. Cross and E. A. Livingstone, *The Oxford Dictionary of the Christian Church*, 2nd edn. *T.L.S.*, 22 November 1974, pp. 1319–20.

Albert Marrin, *The Last Crusade. American Historical Review*, vol. 80, 1975, p. 648.

F. W. Dillistone, *Charles Raven. Conference*, vol. 12, 1975, pp. 35–6.

E. G. W. Bill, *University Reform in Nineteenth Century Oxford*. E.H.R., vol. 90, 1975, p. 214.

Clive Binfield, *George Williams and the YMCA*. E.H.R., vol. 90, 1975, p. 227.

C. S. Dessain and T. Gornall, *The Letters and Diaries of John Henry Newman*, vols. 23–5. E.H.R., vol. 90, 1975, pp. 390–3.

C. S. Dessain and T. Gornall, *Letters and Diaries of John Henry Newman*, vol. 26. E.H.R., vol. 90, 1975, p. 931.

Regis Ladous, *L'Abbé Portal et la Compagne anglo-romaine 1890–1911*. E.H.R., vol. 90, 1975, p. 934.

P. Blet *et al.*, *Actes et Documents du Saint Siège relatifs à la Seconde Guerre Mondiale*, vol. 8. J.E.H., vol. 26, 1975, pp. 193–7.

Klaus Erich Pollmann, *Landesherrliches Kirchenregiment und soziale Frage: der even-gelische Oberkirchenrat der altpreussischen Landeskirche und die sozialpolitische Bewegung der Geistlichen nach 1890*. J.E.H., vol. 26, 1975, pp. 425–6.

R. Kottje and Bernd Moeller, *Ökumenische Kirchengeschichte*, vol. 3, *Neuzeit*. J.E.H., vol. 26, 1975, pp. 426–7.

J. Staedtke, U. Gäbler and E. Zsindely (eds.), *Heinrich Bullinger, Werke*, vols. 1 and 2. J.T.S., vol. 26, 1975, pp. 216–18.

O. Labarthe and B. Lescare, *Registre de la Compagnie des Pasteurs de Genève*, vol. 4, *1575–1582*. J.T.S., vol. 26, 1975, pp. 218–20.

C. Brooke, *The Monastic World*. J.T.S., vol. 26, 1975, p. 475.

Actes du Colloque: L'Amiral de Coligny et son temps. J.T.S., vol. 26, 1975, p. 533.

Rudolf Lill, *Die Wende im Kulturkampf: Leo XIII, Bismarck und die Zentrumspartie 1878–80*. E.H.R., vol. 91, 1976, pp. 222–3.

Uriel Tal, *Christians and Jews in Germany: Religious Politics and Ideology in the Second Reich 1870–1914*. H.J., vol. 19, 1976, pp. 558–9.

Derek Baker, ed., *The Materials and Methods of Ecclesiastical History* (Studies in Church History, vol. 11); *Church, Society and Politics* (Studies in Church History, vol. 12). J.E.H., vol. 27, 1976, pp. 303–7.

Ulrich Gäbler, *Hüldrych Zwingli im 20 Jahrhundert*. J.T.S., vol. 27, 1976, pp. 248–9.

D. Baker, *The Bibliography of the Reform 1450–1648 Relating to the United Kingdom and Ireland for the Years 1955–78*. J.T.S., vol. 27, 1976, p. 278.

Horton Harris, *The Tübingen School*. J.T.S., vol. 27, 1976, pp. 509–10.

Benedicta Ward, *The Sayings of the Desert Fathers; The Wisdom of the Desert Fathers*. *Medium Aevum*, vol. 45, 1976, pp. 296–8.

Michael Grant, *Saint Paul*. Sunday Times, 25 April 1976, p. 41.

S. Prickett, *Romanticism and Religion*. Sunday Times, 6 June 1976, p. 41.

John Henry Newman, *The Idea of a University* (ed. I. T. Ker). T.H.E.S., 9 July 1976, p. 13.

Louis Allen, *John Henry Newman and the Abbé Jager*. E.H.R., vol. 92, 1977, p. 452.

Charles Morazé, *The History of Mankind: Cultural and Scientific Development*, vol. 5, *The Nineteenth Century 1779–1905*. E.H.R., vol. 92, 1977, pp. 622–3.

Cahiers du Mouvement Social. E.H.R., vol. 92, 1977, p. 923.

C. S. Dessain and T. Gornall, *The Letters and Diaries of John Henry Newman*, vols. 24–30. E.H.R., vol. 92, 1977, p. 923.

R. B. McDowell, *The Church of Ireland 1869–1969*. History, vol. 62, 1977, p. 145.

George Kreuzer, *Die Honoriusfrage im Mittelalter und in der Neuzeit. J.E.H.*, vol. 28, 1977, pp. 98–9.

Klaus Schatz, *Kirchenbild und päpstliche Unfehlbarkeit bei den deutschsprachigen Minoritätsbischöfen auf dem I Vatikanum. J.E.H.*, vol. 28, 1977, pp. 108–9.

John Brooke and Julia Gandy, *The Prime Minister's Papers: Wellington, Political Correspondence*, vol. 1, *1833–November 1834. J.E.H.*, vol. 28, 1977, pp. 324–5.

Stefan Lösch and R. Reinhardt, *Verzeichnis der gedruckten Arbeiten Johann Adam Möhlers (1796–1838). J.T.S.*, vol. 28, 1977, pp. 248–9.

George Denzler, *Das Papsttum und der Amtszölibat. J.T.S.*, vol. 28, 1977, pp. 249–53.

Wolfgang Huber and Johannes Schwedtfeger (eds.), *Kirche Zwischen Krieg und Frieden. T.L.S.*, 4 November 1977, p. 1293.

C. S. Dessain and Thomas Gornall, *The Letters and Diaries of John Henry Newman*, vol. 31, *E.H.R.*, vol. 93, 1978, pp. 683–4.

John Newton, *Search for a Saint: Edward King. Epworth Review*, 5 January 1978, pp. 132–3.

Brian Heeney, *A Different Kind of Gentleman: Parish Clergy as Professional Men in Early and Mid-Victorian England. History*, vol. 63, 1978, p. 318.

Theologische Realenzyklopädie, vol. 1, parts 1–4, and *Dizionario degli istituti di perfezione*, parts 1–3. *J.E.H.*, vol. 29, 1978, pp. 113–16.

Christof Windhorst, *Täuferisches Taufverständnis: Balthasar Hubmaiers Lehre zwischen traditioneller und reformatorischer Theologie. J.T.S.*, vol. 29, 1978, pp. 269–70.

G. R. Potter, *Zwingli. J.T.S.*, vol. 29, 1978, pp. 270–1.

F. R. Bridge, *Austro-Hungarian Documents Relating to the Macedonian Struggle 1896–1912. J.T.S.*, vol. 29, 1978, pp. 283–4.

J. C. Wright, *'Über den Parteien': die politische Haltung der evangelischen Kirchenführer 1918–1933. J.T.S.*, vol. 29, 1978, p. 285.

Anthony Quinton, *The Politics of Imperfection: The Religious and Secular Traditions of Conservative Thought in England from Hooker to Oakeshott. T.H.E.S.*, 27 October 1978, p. 19.

Klaus Scholder, *Die Kirchen und das Dritte Reich*, vol. 1, *1918–1934. T.L.S.*, 20 October 1978, pp. 1205–6.

Paul Misner, *Papacy and Development. Newman and the Primacy of the Pope. Zeitschrift für Kirchengeschichte*, vol 27, 1978, pp. 440–1.

A. B. Hasler, *Piux IX (1846–1878), Päpstliche Unfehlbarkeit und I Vatikanisches Konzil. E.H.R.*, vol. 94, 1979, pp. 28–9.

James Bentley, *Ritualism and Politics in Victorian Britain. History*, vol. 64, 1979, p. 114.

Philip Rousseau, *Ascetics, Authority and the Church in the Age of Jerome and Cassian. J.E.H.*, vol. 30, 1979, p. 297.

R. Aubert (ed.), *Concilium Vaticanum I: Concordance, index listes de fréquence, tables comparatives*, and Philippe Dehaye (ed.), *Concilium Vaticanum II: Concordance, index, listes de fréquence, tables comparatives. J.E.H.*, vol. 30, 1979, pp. 403–4.

Klaus Schatz, SJ (ed.), *Ignatius von Senestrey... Tagebuch vom I Vatikanischen Konzil. J.E.H.*, vol. 30, 1979, pp. 503–4.

Vincent F. Blehl, *John Henry Newman, A Bibliographical Catalogue of His Writings. J.T.S.*, vol. 30, 1979, p. 406.

Christopher Weber, *Kardinäle und Prälaten in den letzten Jahrzehnten des Kirchenstaates. J.T.S.*, vol. 30, 1979, pp. 589–92.

Ian Ker and Thomas Gornall, *The Letters and Diaries of John Henry Newman*, vol. 1. *E.H.R.*, vol. 95, 1980, p. 228.

Ian Ker and Thomas Gornall, *The Letters and Diaries of John Henry Newman*, vols. 2, 3 and 4. *E.H.R.*, vol. 95, 1980, pp. 858–60.

John F. Morley, *Vatican Diplomacy and the Jews during the Holocaust 1939–1945*, and Yehuda Bauer, *The Holocaust in Historical Perspective*, and Yehuda Bauer, *The Jewish Emergence from Powerlessness*. *H.J.*, vol. 24, 1980, pp. 1023–4.

S. S. Acquaviva, *The Decline of the Sacred in Industrial Society*. *History*, vol. 65, 1980, p. 82.

Theologische Realenzyklopädie, vols. 2 and 3. *J.E.H.*, vol. 31, 1980, pp. 251–3.

J. D. Holmes, *The Theological Papers of John Henry Newman on Biblical Inspiration and on Infallibility*. *J.E.H.*, vol. 31, 1980, p. 393.

Sophie Olszamowska-Skowvouska, *Les Accords de Vienne et de Rome entre le Saint-Siège et la Russie 1880–1882*. *J.E.H.*, vol. 31, 1980, pp. 396–7.

Theologische Realenzyklopädie, vol. 4. *J.E.H.*, vol. 31, 1980, pp. 399–400.

Manfred Clauss, *Die Beziehungen des Vatikans zu Polen während des 2 Weltkrieges* *J.E.H.*, vol. 31, 1980, pp. 512–13.

R. Aubert, *The Christian Centuries: The Church in a Secularised Society*. *J.T.S.*, vol. 31, 1980, pp. 265–7.

Jean Delumeau, *Catholicism between Luther and Voltaire: A New View of the Counter-Reformation*. *J.T.S.*, vol. 31, 1980, pp. 299–300.

D. H. Farmer, *The Oxford Dictionary of the Saints*. *Medium Aevum*, vol. 49, 1980, pp. 90–1.

Michael Despland, *La Religion en Occident: évolution des idées et du reçu*. *History*, vol. 66, 1981, p. 78.

Nicholas Temperley, *The Music of the English Parish Church*. *J.T.S.*, vol. 32, 1981, pp. 300–4.

W. D. J. Cargill Thompson, *Studies in the Reformation: Luther to Hooker*. *J.T.S.*, vol. 32, 1981, p. 332.

Jean Rott, *Correspondance de Martin Bucer*, vol. 1, *Jusqu'en 1524*. *J.E.H.*, vol. 32, 1981, pp. 96–8.

Walter Adolph, *Geheime Aufzeichnungen aus dem nationalsozialistischen Kirchenkampf: 1935–1943* (ed. Ulrich von Hehl). *J.E.H.*, vol. 32, 1981, pp. 110–12.

P. Blet *et al.*, *Le Saint Siège et Les Victimes de la Guerre. Janvier 1944–Juillet 1945*. *J.E.H.*, vol. 32, 1981, pp. 252–4.

Theologische Realenzyklopädie, vol. 5, parts 1–4. *J.E.H.*, vol. 32, 1981, p. 255.

Gustav A. Kreig, *Der Mystische Kreis: Wesen und Werden der Theologie Pierre Poirets*. *J.E.H.*, vol. 32, 1981, p. 384.

Salvatore Bordonali, *Riflessi Diplomatici e Politici della Crisi del Potere Temporale negli anni formativi dell'Unità Italiana 1859–1861*. *E.H.R.*, vol. 97, 1982, pp. 447–8.

Anton van de Sande, *La Curie Romaine au début de la Restauration: le problème de la continuité dans la politique de Restauration du Saint-Siège 1814–1817*. *E.H.R.*, vol. 97, 1982, p. 652.

Giuseppe Battelli (ed.), *Giacomo Lercaro, Lettere dal Concilio*. *J.E.H.*, vol. 33, 1982, p. 156.

Theologische Realenzyklopädie, vol. 5, part 5, vol. 6, parts 1–5. *J.E.H.*, vol. 33, 1982, pp. 117–18.

Dizionario degli istituti di perfezione, parts 5 and 6. *J.E.H.*, vol. 33, 1982, pp. 485–6.

Theologische Realenzyklopädie, vol. 7, parts 1–3. *J.E.H.*, vol. 33, 1982, p. 341.

R. Aubert *et al.*, *The Church between Revolution and Restoration. J.E.H.*, vol. 33, 1982, pp. 507–8.

M. Buschkühl, *Die Irische, Schottische und Römische Frage: Disraeli's Schlüsselroman 'Lothair' (1870). J.E.H.*, vol. 33, 1982, p. 510.

Theologische Realenzyklopädie, vol. 7, parts 4–5, vol. 8, parts 1–2. *J.E.H.*, vol. 33, 1982, pp. 512–13.

P. Blet *et al.*, *Le Saint Siège et La Guerre Mondiale. Janvier 1944–Mai 1945. J.E.H.*, vol. 33, 1982, pp. 664–5.

Theologische Realenzyklopädie, vol. 8, parts 4–5, vol. 9, parts 1–2. *J.E.H.*, vol. 33, 1982, pp. 666–7.

D. Mack Smith, *Mussolini. Spectator*, 27 February 1982, pp. 19–20.

Christopher Weber, *Der 'Fall Spahn' (1901). E.H.R.*, vol. 98, 1983, pp. 451–2.

T. Gornall, *The Letters and Diaries of John Henry Newman*, vol. 5. *E.H.R.*, vol. 98, 1983, p. 669.

John E. Groh, *Nineteenth Century German Protestantism: The Church as Social Model. J.E.H.*, vol. 34, 1983, p. 155.

A. de Vogüé, ed., *Les Règles des Saints Pères, Trois Règles de Lérins au Ve Siècle* (Sources chrétiennes, no. 297), *J.T.S.*, vol. 34, 1983, pp. 700–1.

Index

Index

Auden, W. H., 295
Augustine of Hippo, St, 8, 9–27, 81, 82, 163
  rule of, 58
Augustinian canons (*see also* Cambridge: religious houses (Barnwell Priory, Holy Sepulchre)), 45–6, 59
Austin friars, 60, 73
Austria, 174–94
  religious houses, 61, 185, 189, 192
Austrian Enlightenment, 169–94
Auvergne (France), 148, 155
Auxerre (France), 157

Baalbek (Heliopolis) (Lebanon), 16
Babington, Thomas, 219
Bagration, Gen., 213
Bailén (Spain), battle of (1808), 208
Baillie, John, 293, 299 n80
Baldwin, Stanley, 1st Earl, 282, 294–5
Bankes, Henry, 218
banks, rural, in Calabria, 266, 270
Baptists, 78, 142, 143
Barebones Parliament, *see under* parliaments
Bari (Italy), 204
Baring, Thomas, 218
Barnes, E. W., Bishop of Birmingham, 287 n33
Barnwell Priory, *see under* Cambridge: religious houses
Barrington-Ward, Robert, 285–6
Basil, St, 45, 81
Basle (Switzerland), bishop of, 197
Bastwicke, John, 115, 116
Bavaria, 210
Baxter, Richard, 85
Bayle, Pierre, 170, 173
Beale, Dr William, 115
Beales, Derek, 169–94
Beard, Thomas, 128
Beaufort, Lady Margaret, 59, 67 n60, 75
Beaverbrook, 1st Baron (Max Aitken), 280
Bec (France), 155
Belgium, 189, 195, 200, 206
Benedict, St (*see also* Benedictine order), 5
  rule of, 32, 36, 40, 44, 58
Benedict XIV, Pope, 193
Benedictine order (*see also* Cambridge: religious houses (St Radegund)), 40, 47, 57 n25, 152, 154

Bentham, J., 193
Bergisel (Austria), battle of (1809), 210
Bernard of Clairvaux, St, 34, 36, 40, 41, 42–3, 47
Bernard of Tiron, 35
Bernold of Constance, 35
Berry (France), 147
Best, Geoffrey, 1–8
Bethlehemite friars, 60 n36, 74
Bevan, Edwyn, 294 n59
Beveridge, William, 1st Baron, 298
Bevilacqua, Piero, 263, 264
Bevin, Ernest, 280
Bible (*see also* Old Testament)
  important to Müntzer, 80, 82–3, 85, 86
  in Italian, 238
Biddle, Martin, 51
bishops, *see* episcopacy
Bismarck, Prince Otto von, 275
Black Death, 68
Blackfriars, *see* Dominican friars
Blairy (France), 156
Blake, Robert, 135, 140
Blanning, T. C. W., 195–214
Blois (France), diocese of, 165
Boccaccio, Giovanni: *Decameron*, 46–7, 280
Bogiero, Don Basilio, 206
Bohemia, 80, 82, 83
Böhmer, Heinrich, 79
Bois, Paul, 195–6
Boismurie (France), 163
boisselage, 148
Bologna (Italy), 237
Bonaparte, Joseph, 204
Bonaparte, Napoleon, 201, 202, 211, 212, 226
Book of the Poor in Spirit, 81
Borbón, Luis de, Cardinal, Archbishop of Toledo, 204
Bordeaux (France), 168 n105
  Parlement of, 155, 159
Borodino (U.S.S.R.), battle of (1812), 212–13
Bossuet, J. B., 179 n32, 182, 192
Boys' Brigade, 286
Bradford, William, 143
Bradley, Ian, 219, 221
Briouze (France), 156
Briscoe, John, 221
British Academy, 3, 4
British and Foreign Bible Society, 286

320

Index

Campania (Italy), 204
canons
  regular (*see also* Augustinian,
    Gilbertine, Premonstratensian
    canons), 34, 36, 37, 41, 47, 57–8
  secular, 34, 56, 72
Canterbury (Kent), 52
  archbishops of, *see* Lang, Laud, Parker,
    Sumner, Temple (William)
Capecelatro, Giuseppe, Archbishop of
  Taranto, 204
Capella, Martianus, 30 n5
capitalism, in Europe, 95, 97, 99–100, 102
Capuchin order, 183, 190, 210
Cardona, Don Carlos de, 257–8, 265–72,
  273–8
Cardona, Nicola de, 274, 277
Carey, William: *Missionary Sermons*, 280
Carmelite friars, 60, 73
Carnuntum, 177
Cartesianism (*see also* Descartes), 172, 175
Carthage (Tunisia), 11–12, 16, 24
Carthusian order, 36, 45, 160
Casazza, Ercole, 267
Cassa Rurale di Cosenza, 266
Casserley, J. V. Langmead, 289
Cassian, St John, 5
Cassiciacum, 18
Cassiodorus, 30
Castelfidardo (Italy), battle of (1860),
  238–9, 242
Castres (France), diocese of, 147
Catanzaro (Italy), province of, 259–60,
  262, 264
Catherine II (the Great), Empress of
  Russia, 187
Catholic Apostolic Church, 225
Catholic Church (*see also* anticlericalism,
  papacy, religious orders)
  in England: 19th cent., 221, 222,
    226–7, 235–56; 20th cent., 293
  and Europe, concept of, 91, 94, 98–9
  and European counter-revolution
    (1789–1815), 195–210 *passim*
  in Ireland (19th cent.), 238–9, 240,
    243, 252
  in Italy (19th–20th cent.), 265–71
  in N. Africa (4th–5th cent.), 9–27
  revival since *c.* 1870, 102
Cato the Younger, 172
Cavour, Camillo, Count, 238, 249
Cecil, James, *see* Salisbury, 4th Marquis of

Cecil, Nelly, 280
Cellarius, Martin, 84
Celsus, 10, 16
Chadwick, Henry, 4, 9–27
Chadwick, Ruth, 4
Chadwick, William Owen, life and
  work, 1–8, 169, 235, 243, 301–17
Chalcedon, council of, 30 n6
Chalcedonians, 27
Chalmers, Thomas, 215, 220, 223, 225,
  227, 228
  and Irish potato famine, 229–32
Châlons-sur-Marne (France), diocese
  of, 150
Chamberlain, Neville, 280, 297
Champagne (France), 147, 159
chantries, 62–4
Charlemagne, Holy Roman Emperor,
  163
Charles I, King of England, 105, 110,
  117, 120, 130
Charles IV, King of Spain, 204
Charlesworth, M. P., 2, 5
Charron, Pierre, 173
Chartreux, order of the, *see* Carthusian
  order
Chaucer, Geoffrey, 58
Chesterton (Cambs.), 73
chouannerie, 198, 199
'Christian Civilization', debate on
  (1940), 279–99
Christian News-Letter, 291–2, 294, 295
Christian Observer, 218, 221, 222, 224
Christian Scientists, 283
Christian Stoicism, 172–3, 177, 179, 185,
  190–1
Christianity
  and Enlightenment, 169–94
  in Roman empire (4th–5th cent.),
    9–27
Chrysostom, St John, 18
Church of England (*see also* evangelical
  social thought)
  and Long Parliament, 105–24
  and Second World War, 280, 286,
    287–93
churches, medieval (*see also under*
  Cambridge, London), 51–2
Churchill, Sir Winston, 279, 281, 282
Cicero, 21, 22, 30 n5, 175, 190
Cingari, Gaetano, 197, 203
Circumcellions, 11, 12–15

Index

Index

Hague, The (Netherlands), International Court at, 93
hair-styles, clerical, 31, 34
Halberstadt (E. Germany), 79
Haldane, James, 221
Halifax, 1st Viscount (Edward Wood), 281, 282
Halle (E. Germany), 181
Haller, Albrecht von, 178, 179, 186
Hart, J., 115
Harz mountains (Germany), 78
Haspinger, Father Joachim, 210
Hauser, Arnold, 214
Hautvilliers (France), 155
Hay, Denys, 90
Helfaut (France), 156
Heliopolis, see Baalbek
Helvétius, C.-A., 182, 187
Henry VI, King of England, 69, 71
Henry VIII, King of England, 63-4
Henson, H. Hensley, 287-8
Herder, J. G., 190
Herefordshire, 112
hermits, 35, 36, 38, 39
Heuilley (France), 156
High Commission, Court of, 106, 109, 116, 121
Hilary of Orléans, Master, 41
Hilary of Poitiers, St, 30 n6
Hildegard of Bingen, St, 81
Hill, Christopher, 103
Hilton, Boyd, 215-33
Hippo Regius (Algeria), 10, 11, 17, 19, 20, 23
Hippolytus, 17
Hispaniola expedition (1655), 135-40
history, attitudes to, 96, 97-8, 99
Hitler, Adolf, 215, 286, 292, 297
Hoare, Sir Samuel (later 1st Viscount Templewood), 282
Hodges, H. A., 292-3
Hofer, Andreas, 210
Holbach, Baron d', 187
Holl, Karl, 79
Hollis, Christopher, 293
Home, Charles Douglas-, 13th Earl of, 286
Home and Foreign Review, see *Rambler*
Honorius, Roman Emperor, 11
hospitals, medieval (*see also under* Cambridge), 59, 74
Huddersfield (Yorks.), 3
Hugh of Rouen, 41

Hugh of St Victor, 42
humanism, and education, 99, 103-4
Hume, David, 182, 278
Hume, Joseph, 218
Hundred Roll (1279), 69
Hungary (*see also* Austria), 190, 191
Huskisson, William, 218
Hussite movement, 81
Hyde, Sir Edward (later 1st Earl of Clarendon), 112

iconoclasm, attitudes to, in Long Parliament, 109-10
Idungus of Regensburg, 40
Ignatius Loyola, St, 99
India, 94
Infallibility, Papal, 240
Information, Ministry of, Religious Division, 279 n4
Ingram, Kenneth, 290
international law, 93
Ireland
   17th cent., 126, 132, 133
   19th cent.: Catholic Church in, 238-9, 240, 243, 252; Home Rule Question, 235, 243, 247, 255, 256; poor relief, 217, 221, 229-31, 232; potato famine (1845-7), 229-31, 232, 233
Ireton, Henry, 129, 130, 132, 133
Irish Brigade of St Patrick, 238-9
Irving, Edward, 225, 226
Isabella of Parma, 176-7, 183
Isidore of Seville, St, 31
Isola di Capo Rizzuto (Italy), 263, 265
Issy (France), 157
Italy (*see also* papacy, papal states, Rome)
   4th-5th cent., 18, 23, 26
   medieval, 34, 35, 51-2, 65-6
   18th cent., 189, 193, 195, 200, 202-4, 206, 209
   19th cent., 202, 209, 235-56, 261-8, 269-71
   20th cent., 257-78
Ivo of Chartres, St, 39

Jacobins, 197, 204
Jamaica (W.I.), 136
James, St, cult of, 209
James I, King of England, 106
James of Vitry, 45
Jansenism, 175, 182, 184, 190, 192-3, 202

Index

Jemolo, A. C., 271
Jerome, St, 81
Jesuits, 172, 175, 190, 209
Jews
  in medieval towns, 59–60, 73
  and paganism, 9, 12
Joachim of Fiore, 83, 84, 260, 277
Jocelyn, Robert, see Roden
John Cassian, St, see Cassian
John Chrysostom, St, see Chrysostom
John Fisher, St, see Fisher
John of Wisbech, Abbot of Crowland, 75
Johnson, Hewlett, Dean of Canterbury, 295
Johnson, Samuel, 77
Joseph II, Holy Roman Emperor, 178, 179, 183, 185–90, 192
  education and youth, 175–6
  religious reforms, 185, 189, 192, 202, 209–10
  visits France, 177, 178, 185–6, 188
Joshua, Book of, 137–40, 145
Julian, Roman Emperor, 11, 16, 173
Jumièges (France), 155
Justin, 9

Kant, Immanuel, 190
Karfachevsky, Andrei, 211
Karlstadt, Andrew, 79, 80, 81, 85
Kaunitz, Count (later Prince), 180–1, 182, 183, 185
Keene, Derek, 51
Keir, Gillian, 51
Kent, 111, 112
Kerr, Philip, see Lothian
Klingenstein, G., 181
Knights Templar, 34–5
Knowles, David, 29
Knox, John, 5, 78, 87
Kochetkov, A. N., 207, 213
Kutuzov, Gen., 212

Labeo, Cornelius, 21
La Bretonne, Restif de, 157
Labriola, Arturo, 272
La Charité, 42
La Ferté-sur-Grosne (France), 157
La Harpe, 186
land-holding, Italy (20th cent.), 258–9, 262–4, 276
Lang, Cosmo, Archbishop of Canterbury, 280

language, as a unifying factor, 91, 92, 100
Lanjuinais, J., 186–7
La Rochefoucauld, duc de, 172 n11
Laski, Harold, 297–8
Latimer, Hugh, 103
Latin language, 91, 100
Lau, Franz, 78
Laud, William, Archbishop of Canterbury, 107–8, 115, 116–17, 138
Laval (France), 162
Lavaur (France), diocese of, 147
Lavoisier, A. L., 186
Law, William, 80
law, importance of, in European nation states, 92–3, 100, 103
laymen, in religious life (12th cent.), 34, 35–6
Le Bret, 186
Lecce (Italy), 209
Lectoure (France), bishop of, 166
Le Fèvre, 81
Lega del Lavoro Calabrese, 257, 267, 270, 273, 275–7
Leibniz, G. W. von, 175
Leighton, Alexander, 115, 116
Leipzig (E. Germany), 79
Lemberg (Lvov) (U.S.S.R.), university, 190
Leo IX, Pope, 31
Leo XIII, Pope, 256, 270
Leopold II, Holy Roman Emperor (Grand Duke of Tuscany), 178, 191–2, 202
leprosy, 59, 74
Lessay (France), 154
Levellers, 131, 142 n75
Lever, Thomas, 103
Levi, C.: Christ Stopped at Eboli, 277
Lewis, C. S., 297
Libellus de diversis ordinibus et professionibus qui sunt in aecclesia (12th cent.), 35–6, 37–8, 39–40, 57
Liber trium virorum et spiritualium virginum (1513), 81
Liège (Belgium), diocese of, 36
Ligne, prince de, 174, 183–5
Lilburne, John, 112, 115, 116, 142 n75
Lincoln, 51, 55 n18
Lincolnshire, 111, 121
Liniata (N. Africa), 10–11
Lipsius, Justus, 172, 173, 191